Y0-BCR-637

KAMOME
SHIRAHAMA

Witch Hat Atelier

VOLUME

4

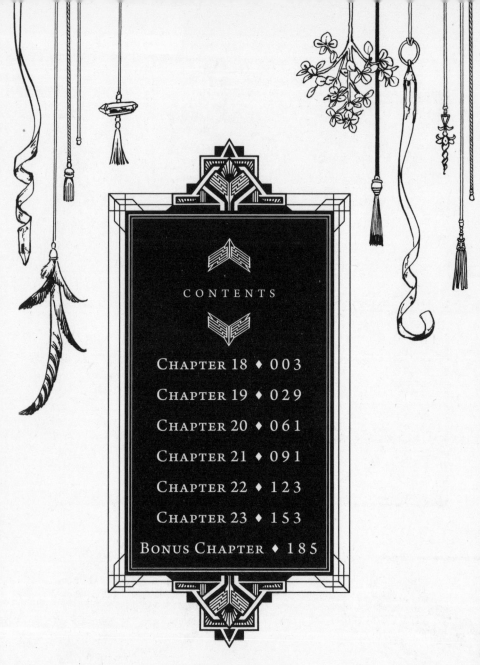

CONTENTS

WITCH HAT ATELIER

♦

KAMOME
SHIRAHAMA

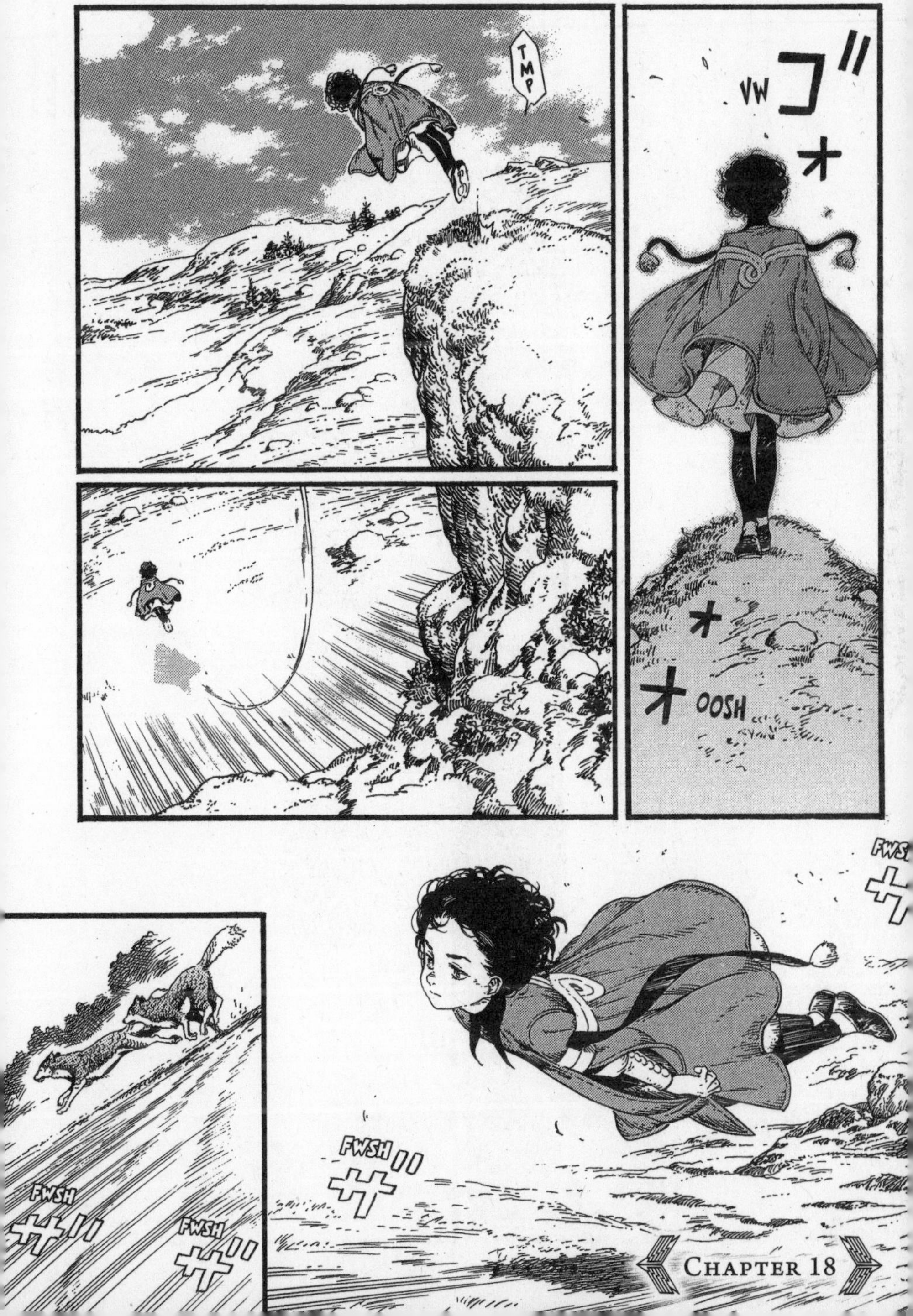
VW
OOSH
TMP
FWS
FWSH
FWSH
FWSH

Chapter 18

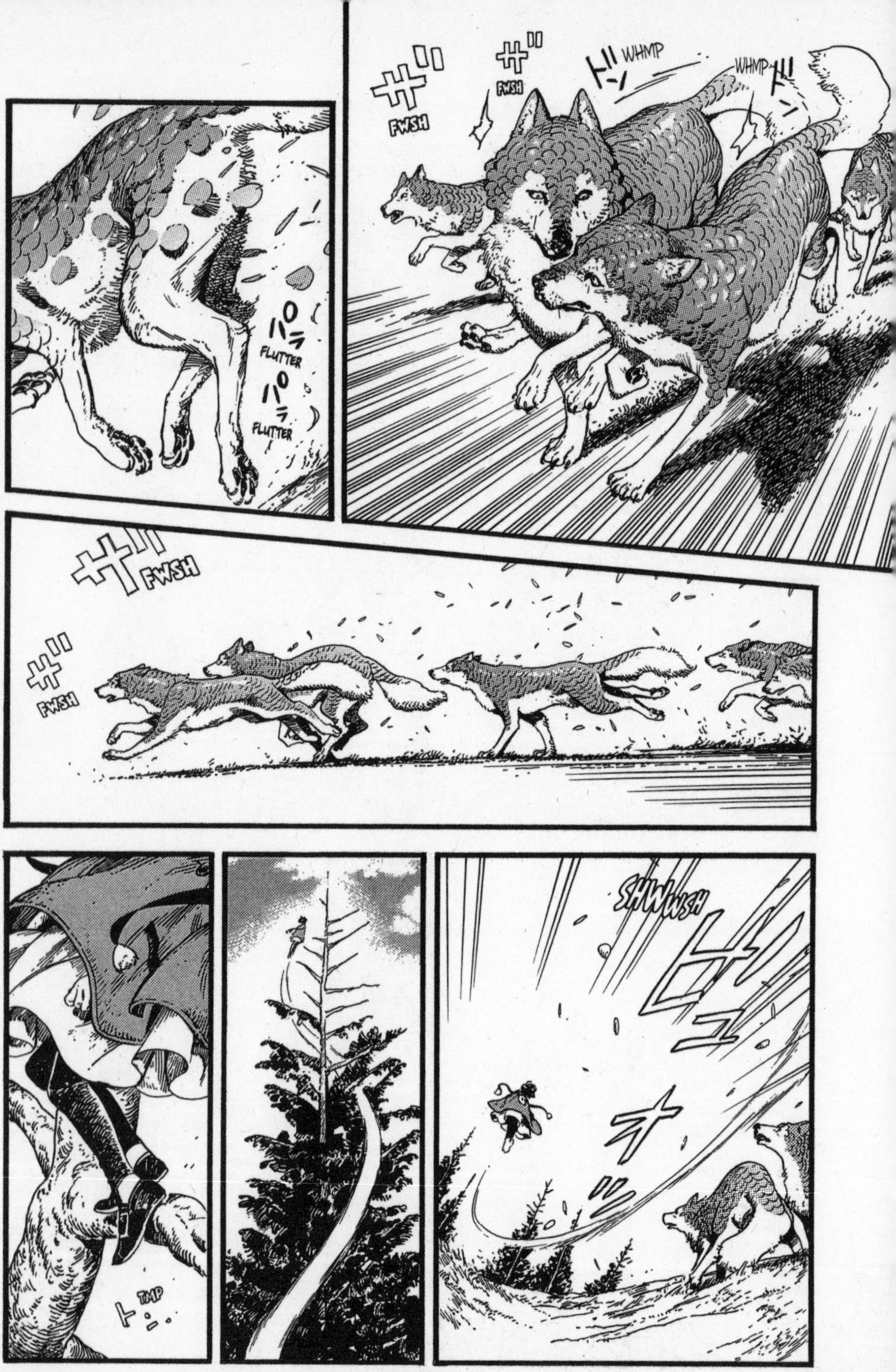

WHMP
WHMP
FWSH
FWSH
FLUTTER
FLUTTER
FWSH
FWSH
SHWUSH
TMP

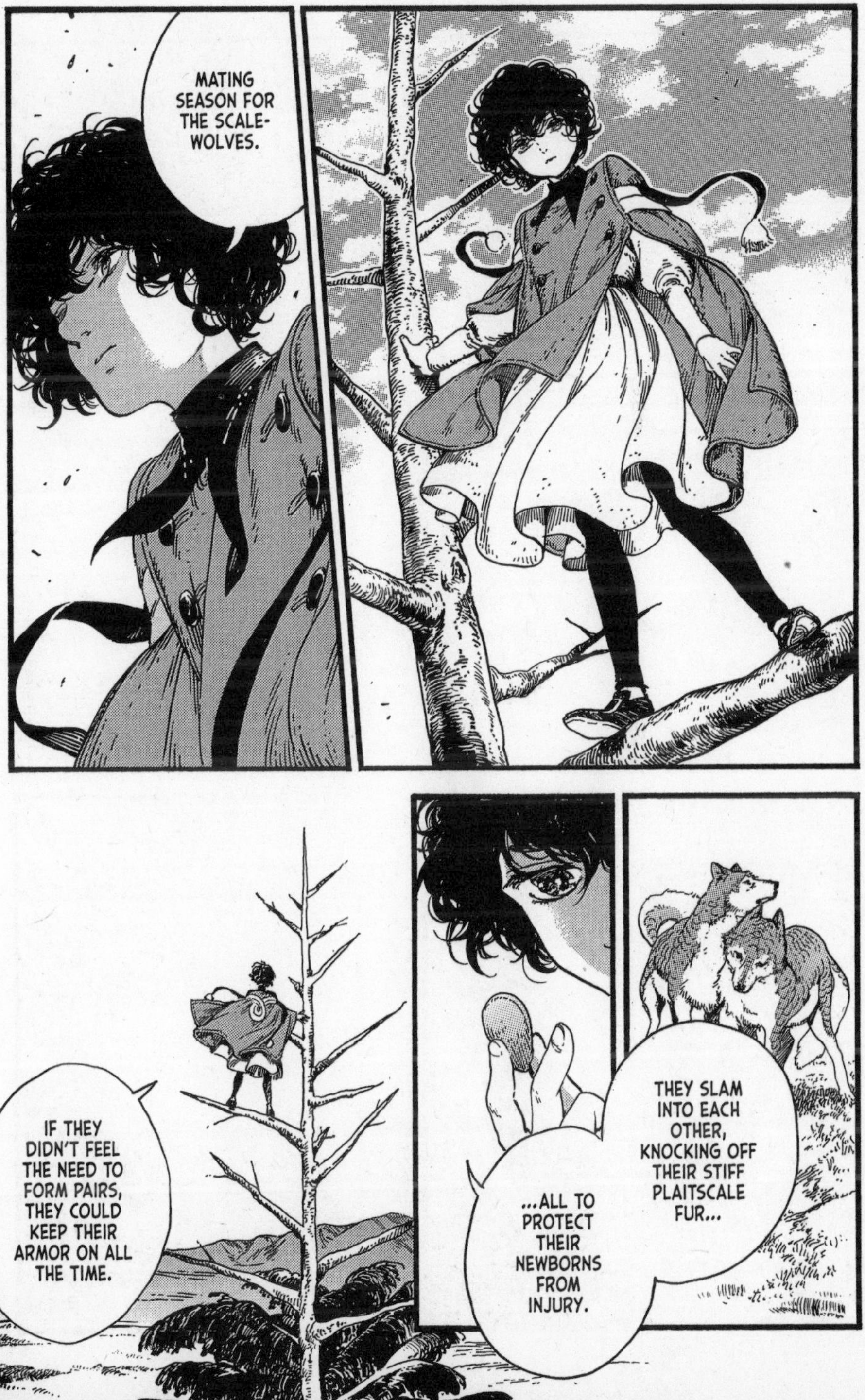
MATING SEASON FOR THE SCALE-WOLVES.
THEY SLAM INTO EACH OTHER, KNOCKING OFF THEIR STIFF PLAITSCALE FUR...
...ALL TO PROTECT THEIR NEWBORNS FROM INJURY.
IF THEY DIDN'T FEEL THE NEED TO FORM PAIRS, THEY COULD KEEP THEIR ARMOR ON ALL THE TIME.

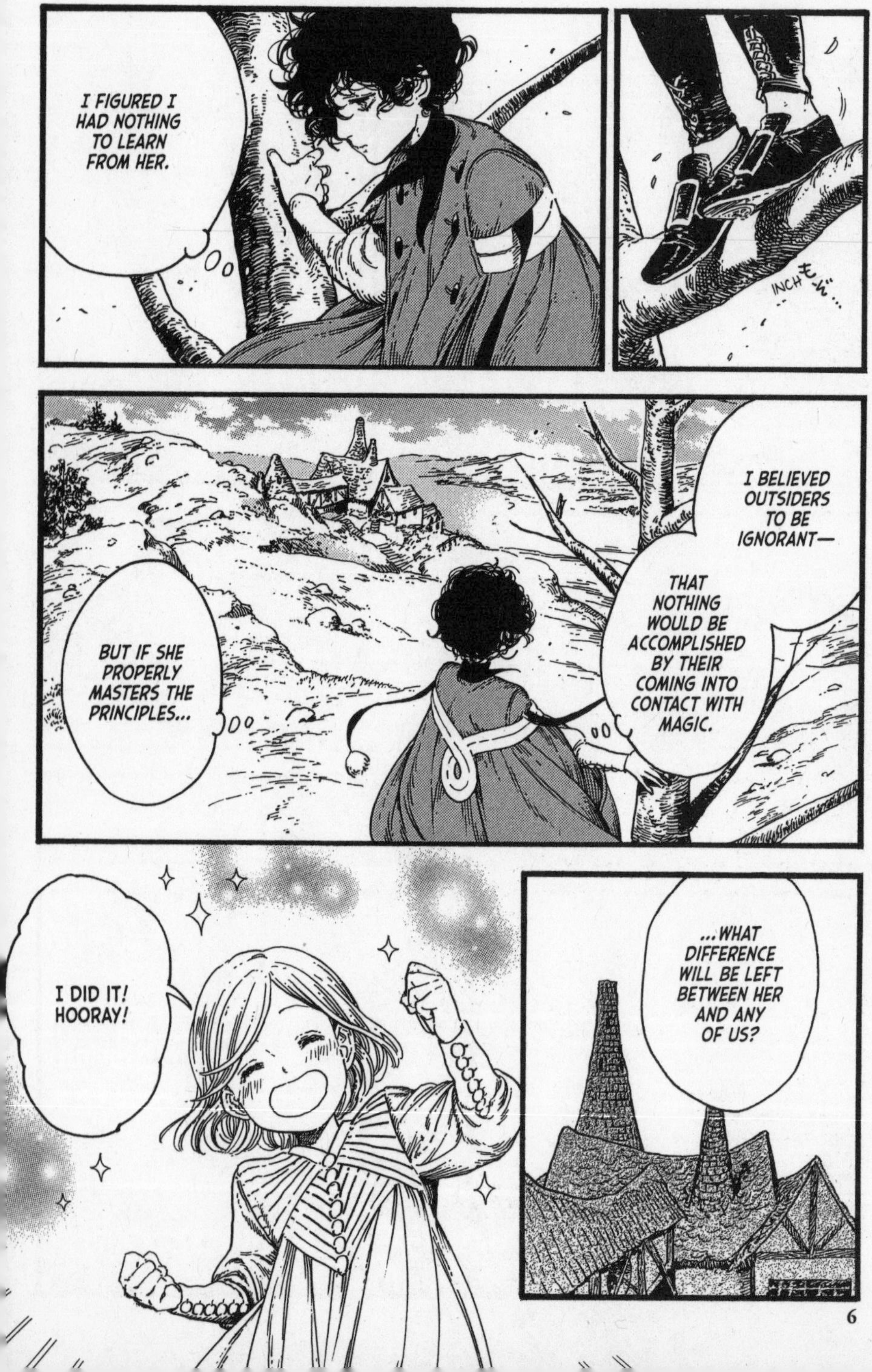
INCH
もぞ…
I FIGURED I HAD NOTHING TO LEARN FROM HER.
I BELIEVED OUTSIDERS TO BE IGNORANT—
THAT NOTHING WOULD BE ACCOMPLISHED BY THEIR COMING INTO CONTACT WITH MAGIC.
BUT IF SHE PROPERLY MASTERS THE PRINCIPLES...
...WHAT DIFFERENCE WILL BE LEFT BETWEEN HER AND ANY OF US?
I DID IT! HOORAY!

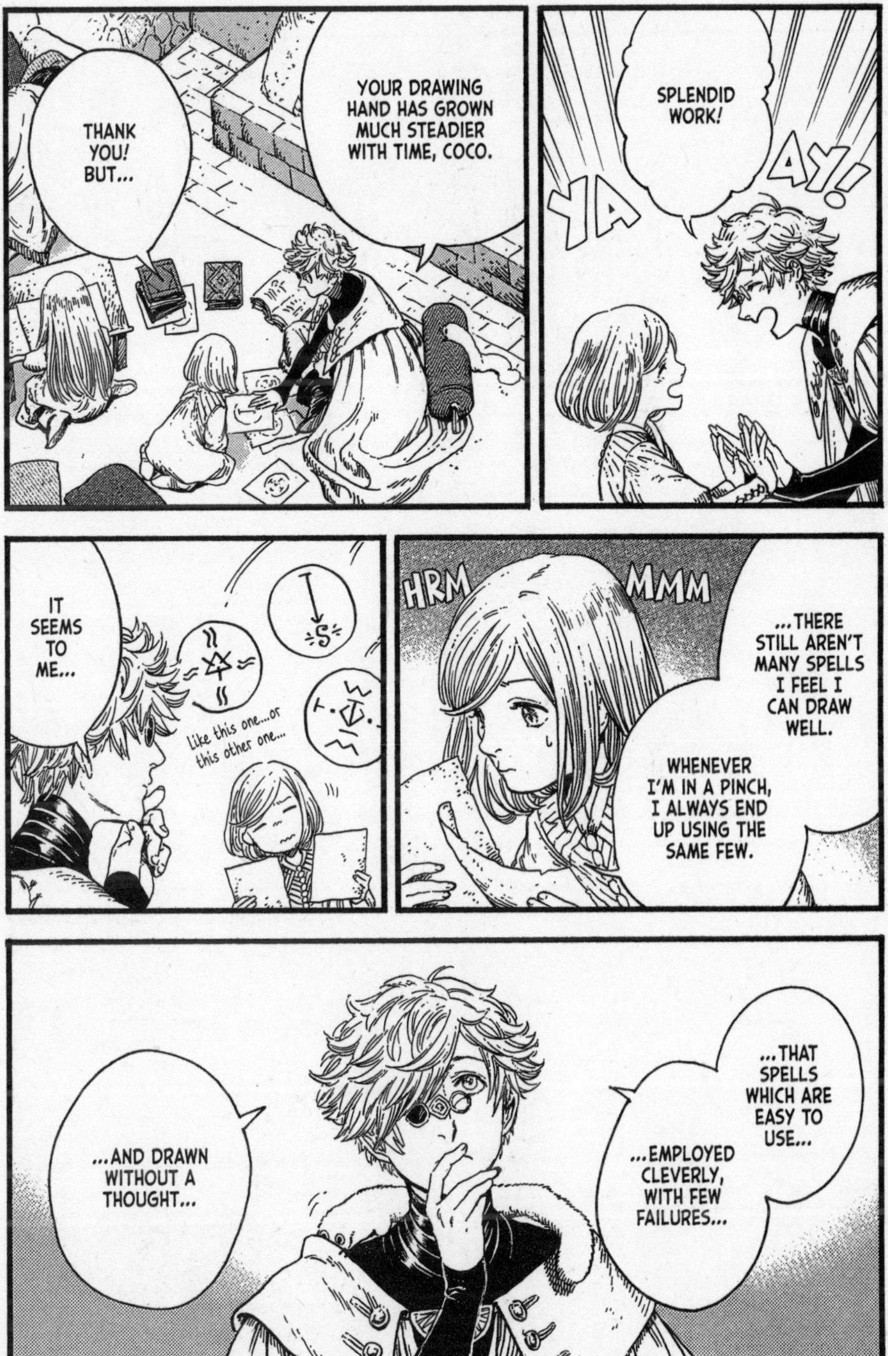
SPLENDID WORK!
YA AY!
YOUR DRAWING HAND HAS GROWN MUCH STEADIER WITH TIME, COCO.
THANK YOU! BUT...
HRM MMM
...THERE STILL AREN'T MANY SPELLS I FEEL I CAN DRAW WELL.
WHENEVER I'M IN A PINCH, I ALWAYS END UP USING THE SAME FEW.
Like this one...or this other one...
IT SEEMS TO ME...
...THAT SPELLS WHICH ARE EASY TO USE...
...EMPLOYED CLEVERLY, WITH FEW FAILURES...
...AND DRAWN WITHOUT A THOUGHT...

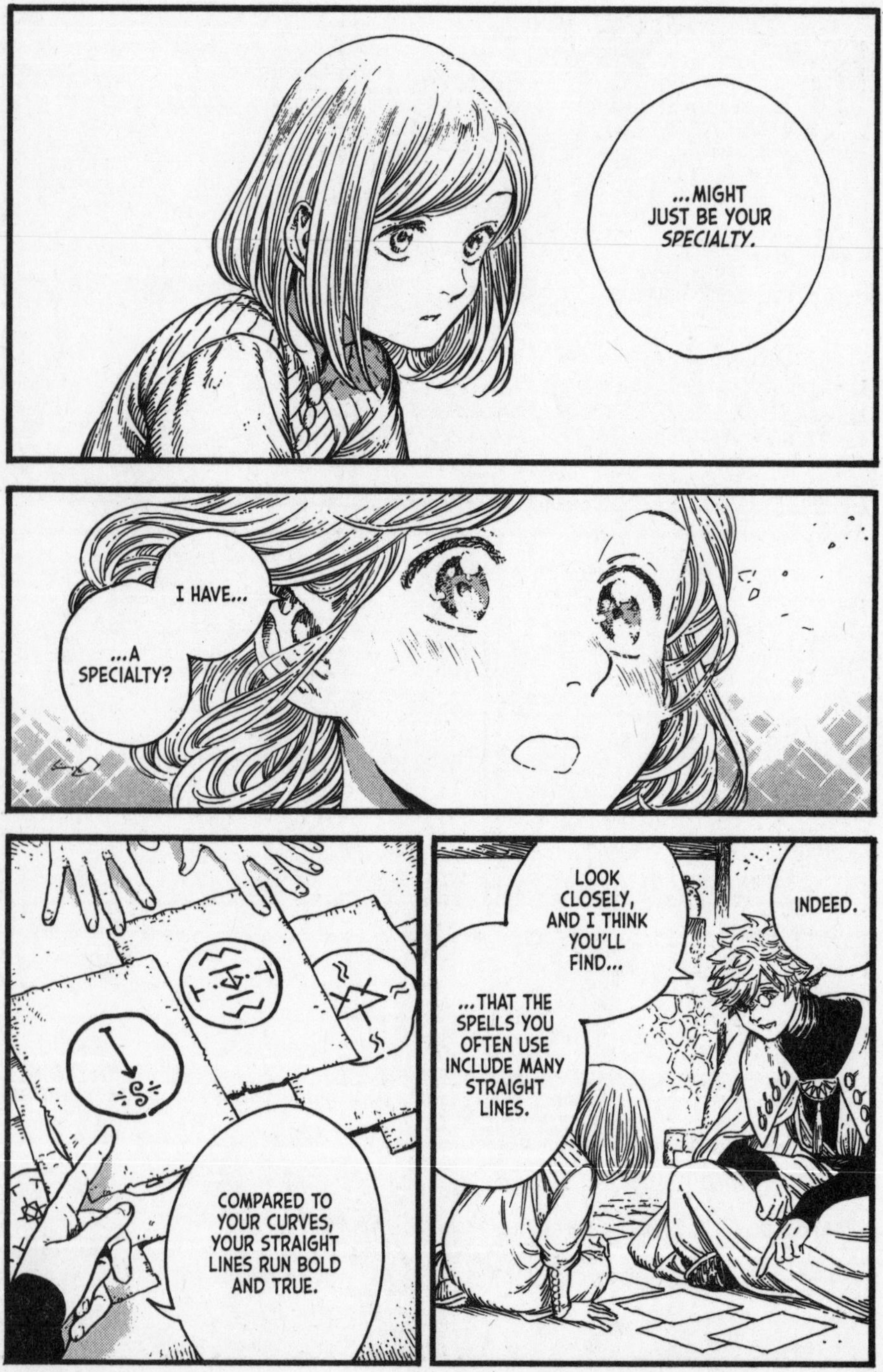
...MIGHT JUST BE YOUR *SPECIALTY.*
I HAVE...
...A SPECIALTY?
INDEED.
LOOK CLOSELY, AND I THINK YOU'LL FIND...
...THAT THE SPELLS YOU OFTEN USE INCLUDE MANY STRAIGHT LINES.
COMPARED TO YOUR CURVES, YOUR STRAIGHT LINES RUN BOLD AND TRUE.

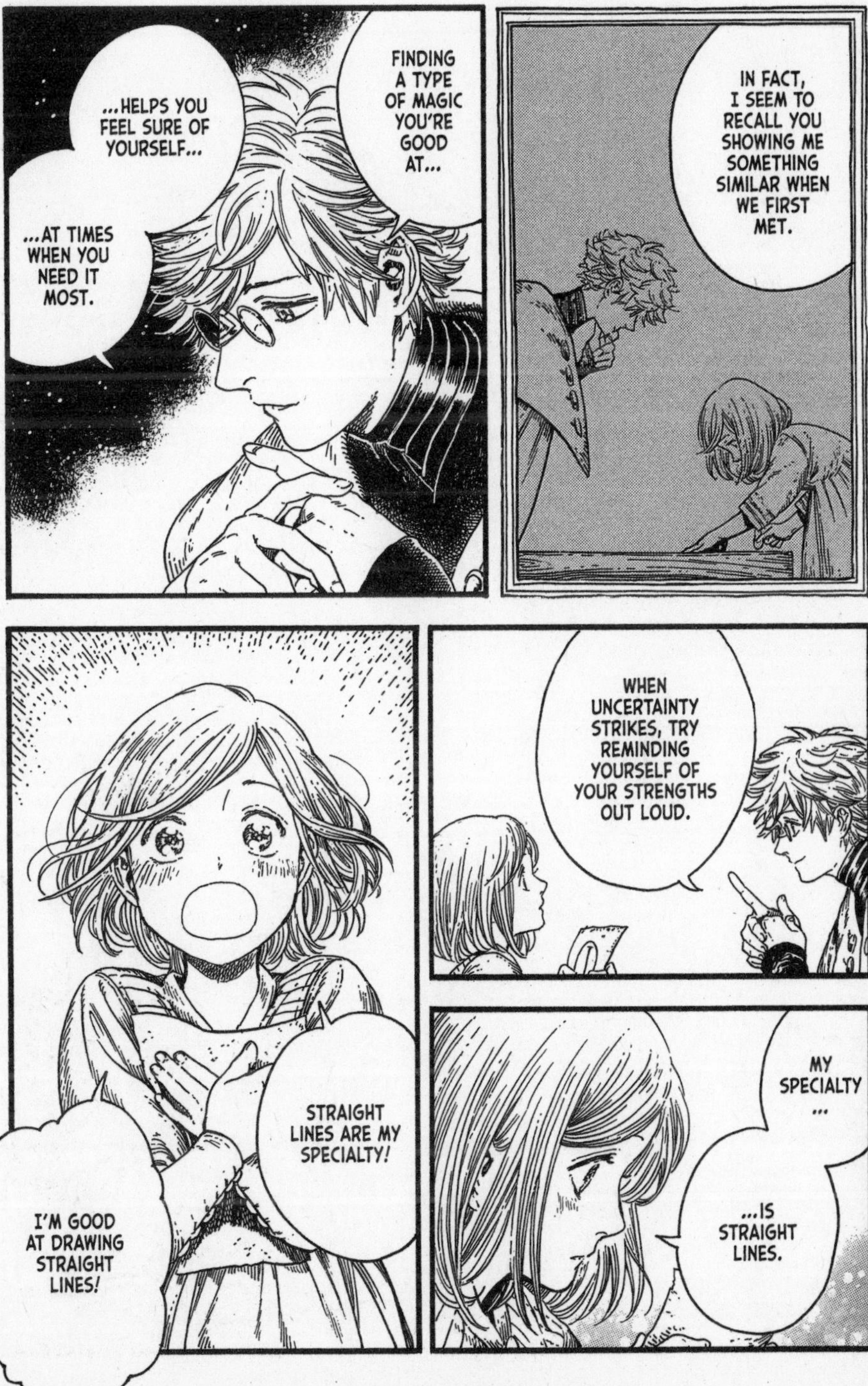
IN FACT, I SEEM TO RECALL YOU SHOWING ME SOMETHING SIMILAR WHEN WE FIRST MET.
FINDING A TYPE OF MAGIC YOU'RE GOOD AT...
...HELPS YOU FEEL SURE OF YOURSELF...
...AT TIMES WHEN YOU NEED IT MOST.
WHEN UNCERTAINTY STRIKES, TRY REMINDING YOURSELF OF YOUR STRENGTHS OUT LOUD.
MY SPECIALTY...
...IS STRAIGHT LINES.
STRAIGHT LINES ARE MY SPECIALTY!
I'M GOOD AT DRAWING STRAIGHT LINES!

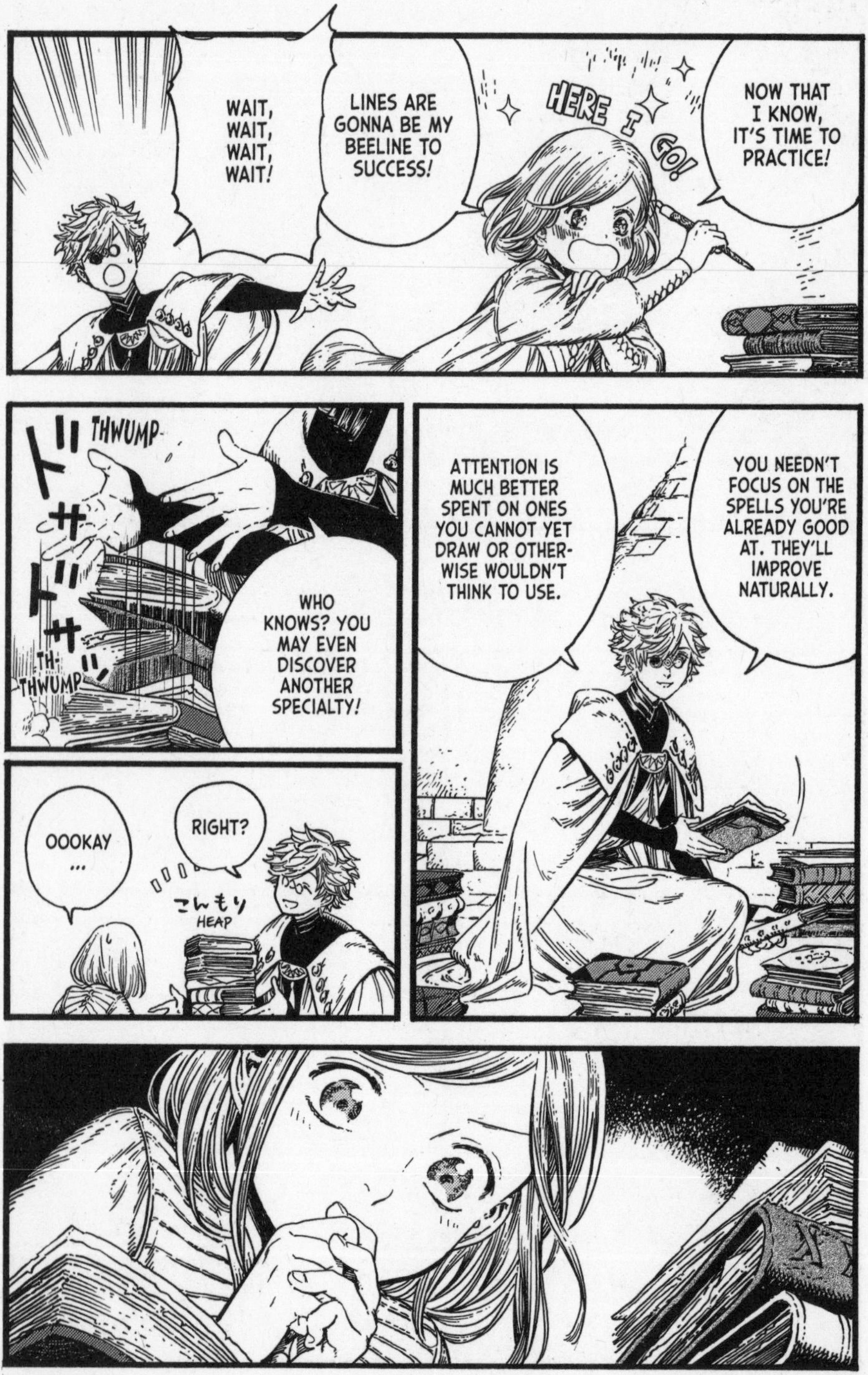
NOW THAT I KNOW, IT'S TIME TO PRACTICE!
HERE I GO!
LINES ARE GONNA BE MY BEELINE TO SUCCESS!
WAIT, WAIT, WAIT, WAIT!
YOU NEEDN'T FOCUS ON THE SPELLS YOU'RE ALREADY GOOD AT. THEY'LL IMPROVE NATURALLY.
ATTENTION IS MUCH BETTER SPENT ON ONES YOU CANNOT YET DRAW OR OTHER-WISE WOULDN'T THINK TO USE.
THWUMP
WHO KNOWS? YOU MAY EVEN DISCOVER ANOTHER SPECIALTY!
TH-THWUMP
RIGHT?
こんもり
HEAP
OOOKAY ...

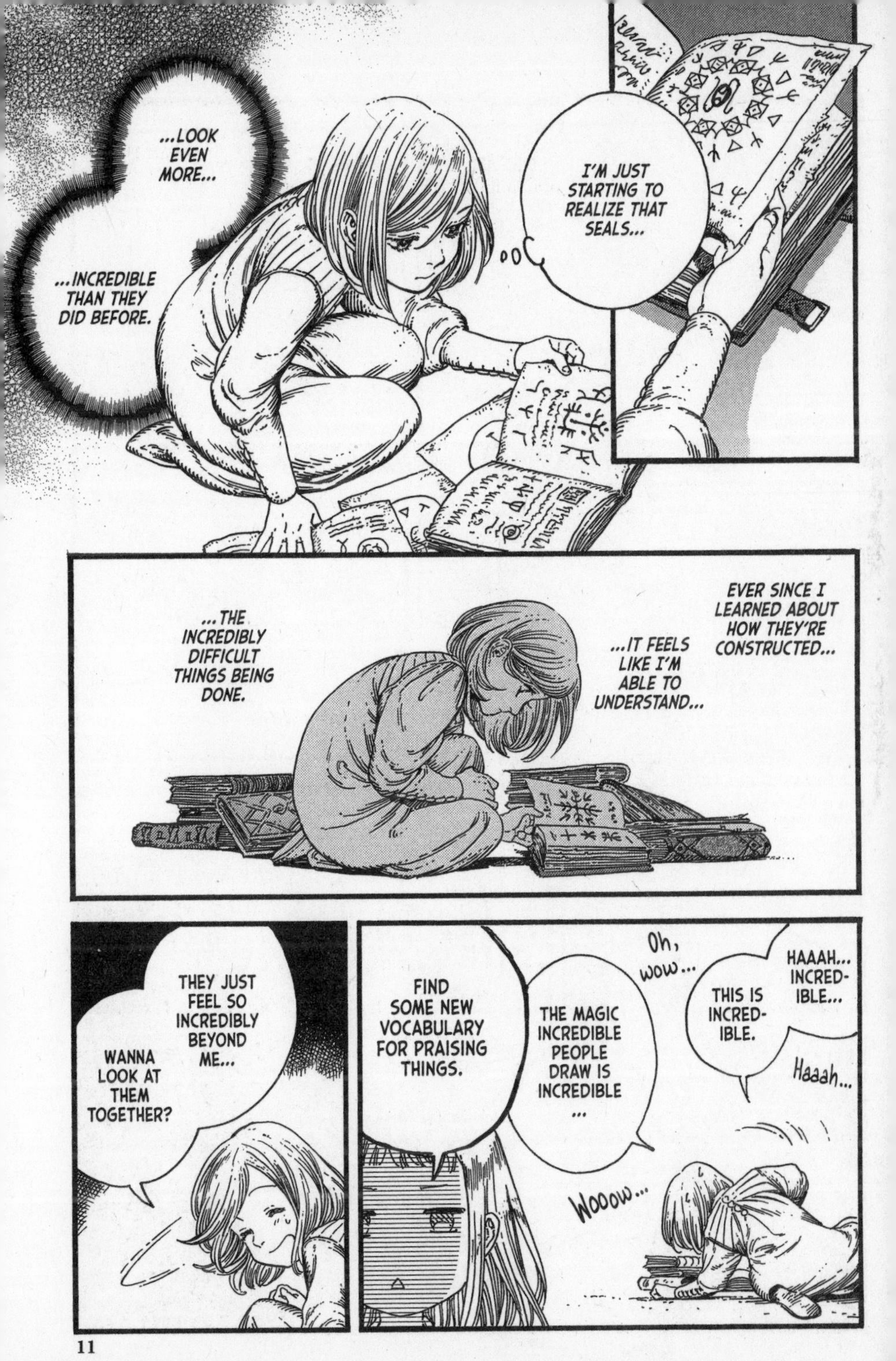
I'M JUST STARTING TO REALIZE THAT SEALS...
...LOOK EVEN MORE...
...INCREDIBLE THAN THEY DID BEFORE.
EVER SINCE I LEARNED ABOUT HOW THEY'RE CONSTRUCTED...
...IT FEELS LIKE I'M ABLE TO UNDERSTAND...
...THE INCREDIBLY DIFFICULT THINGS BEING DONE.
HAAAH... INCRED-IBLE...
THIS IS INCRED-IBLE.
Haaah...
Oh, wow...
THE MAGIC INCREDIBLE PEOPLE DRAW IS INCREDIBLE ...
Wooow...
FIND SOME NEW VOCABULARY FOR PRAISING THINGS.
THEY JUST FEEL SO INCREDIBLY BEYOND ME...
WANNA LOOK AT THEM TOGETHER?

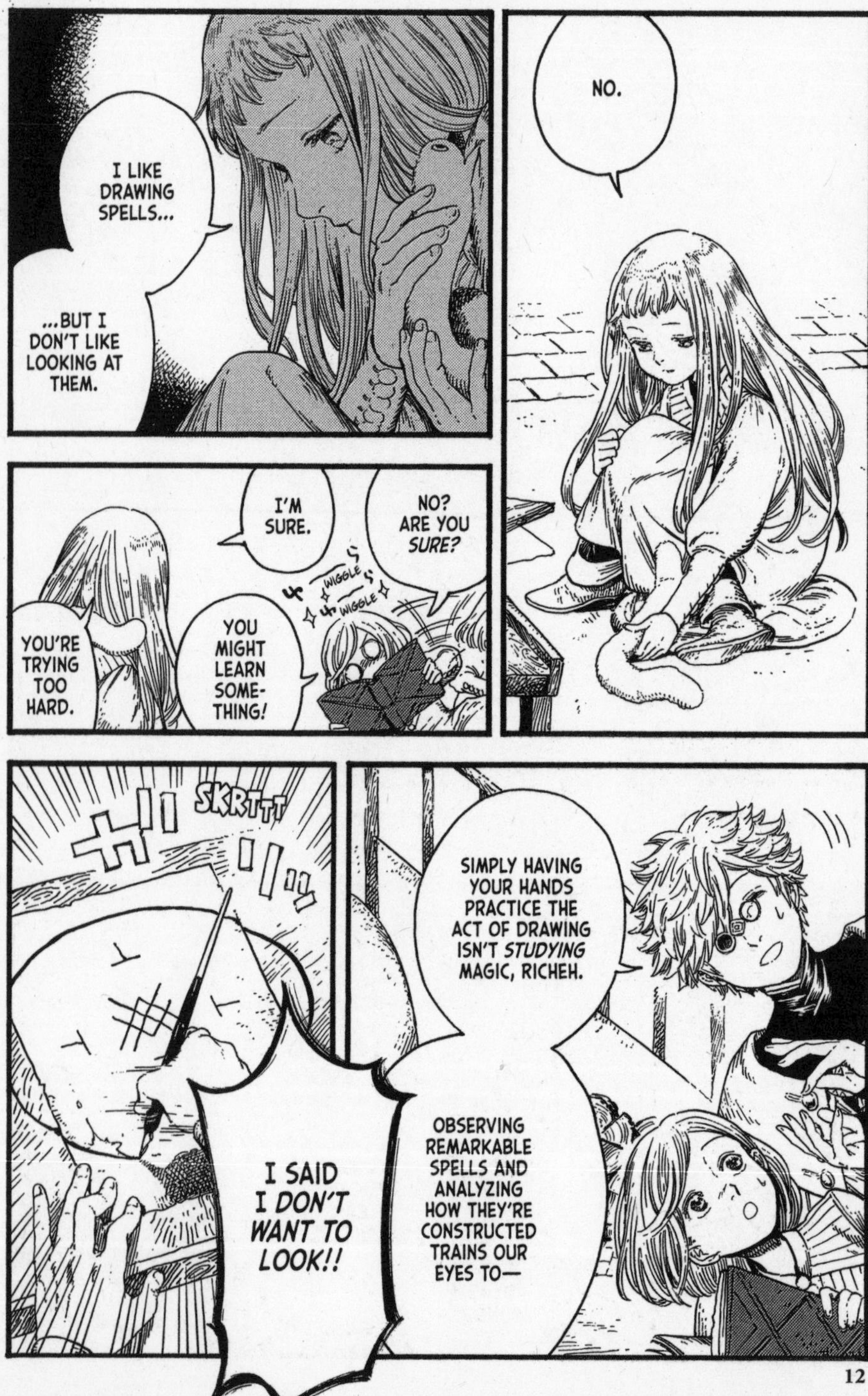
NO.
I LIKE DRAWING SPELLS...
...BUT I DON'T LIKE LOOKING AT THEM.
NO? ARE YOU *SURE?*
I'M SURE.
WIGGLE
WIGGLE
YOU MIGHT LEARN SOME-THING!
YOU'RE TRYING TOO HARD.
SIMPLY HAVING YOUR HANDS PRACTICE THE ACT OF DRAWING ISN'T *STUDYING* MAGIC, RICHEH.
OBSERVING REMARKABLE SPELLS AND ANALYZING HOW THEY'RE CONSTRUCTED TRAINS OUR EYES TO—
SKRTTT
I SAID I *DON'T WANT TO LOOK!!*

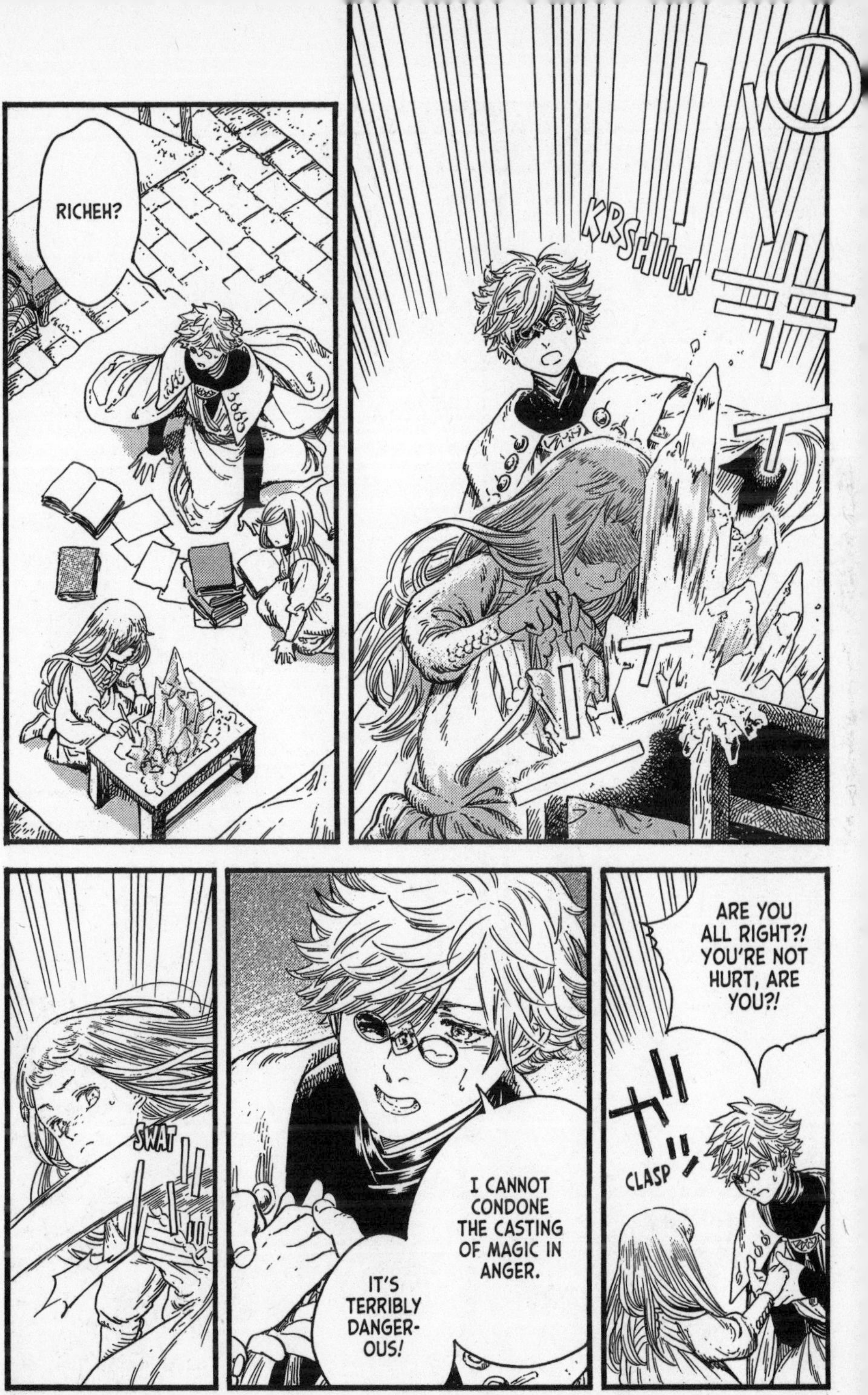
KRSHIIIN
RICHEH?
ARE YOU ALL RIGHT?! YOU'RE NOT HURT, ARE YOU?!
CLASP
I CANNOT CONDONE THE CASTING OF MAGIC IN ANGER.
IT'S TERRIBLY DANGER-OUS!
SWAT

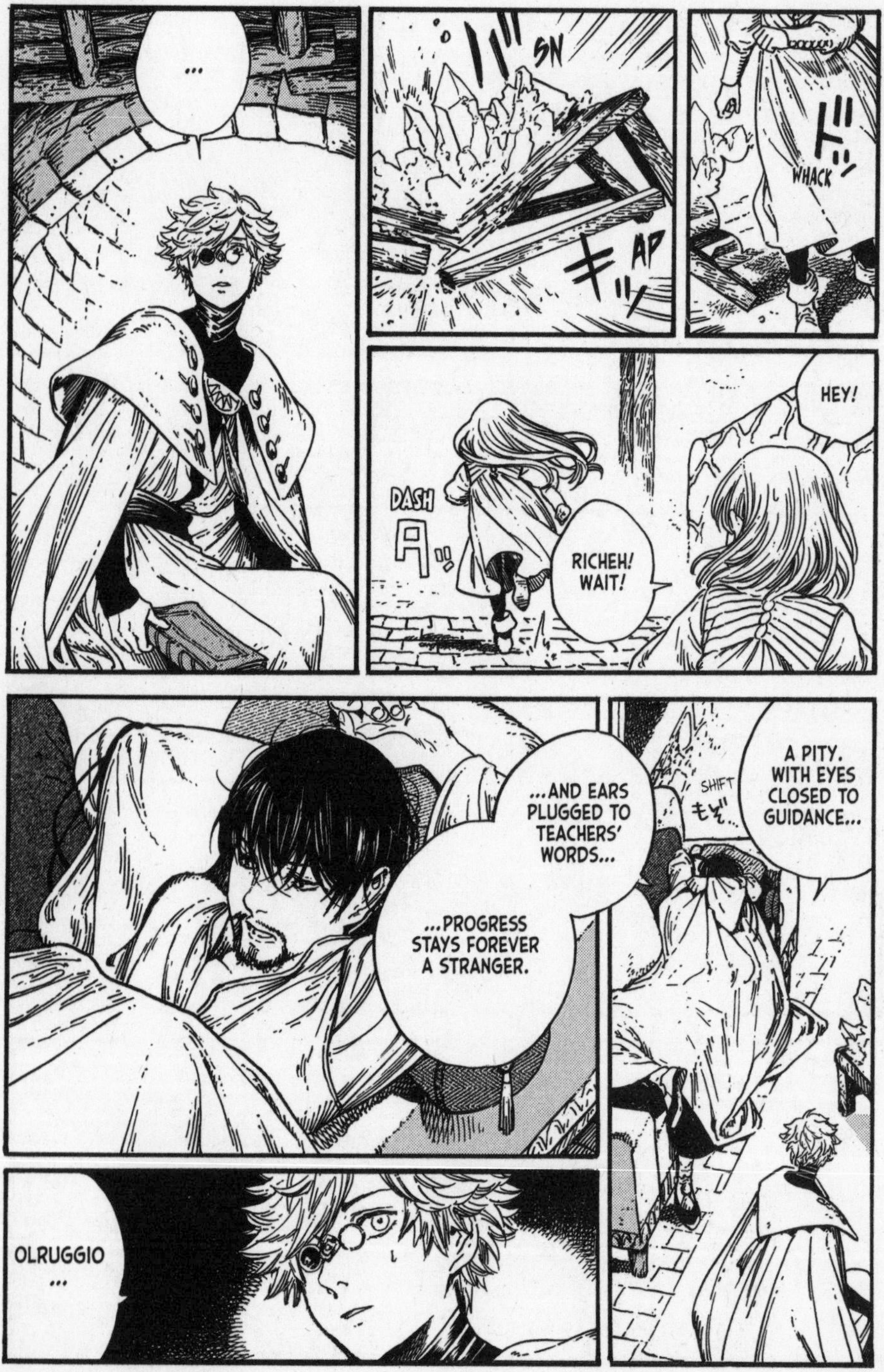
WHACK
SNAP
HEY!
RICHEH! WAIT!
DASH
...
A PITY. WITH EYES CLOSED TO GUIDANCE...
SHIFT
...AND EARS PLUGGED TO TEACHERS' WORDS...
...PROGRESS STAYS FOREVER A STRANGER.
OLRUGGIO ...

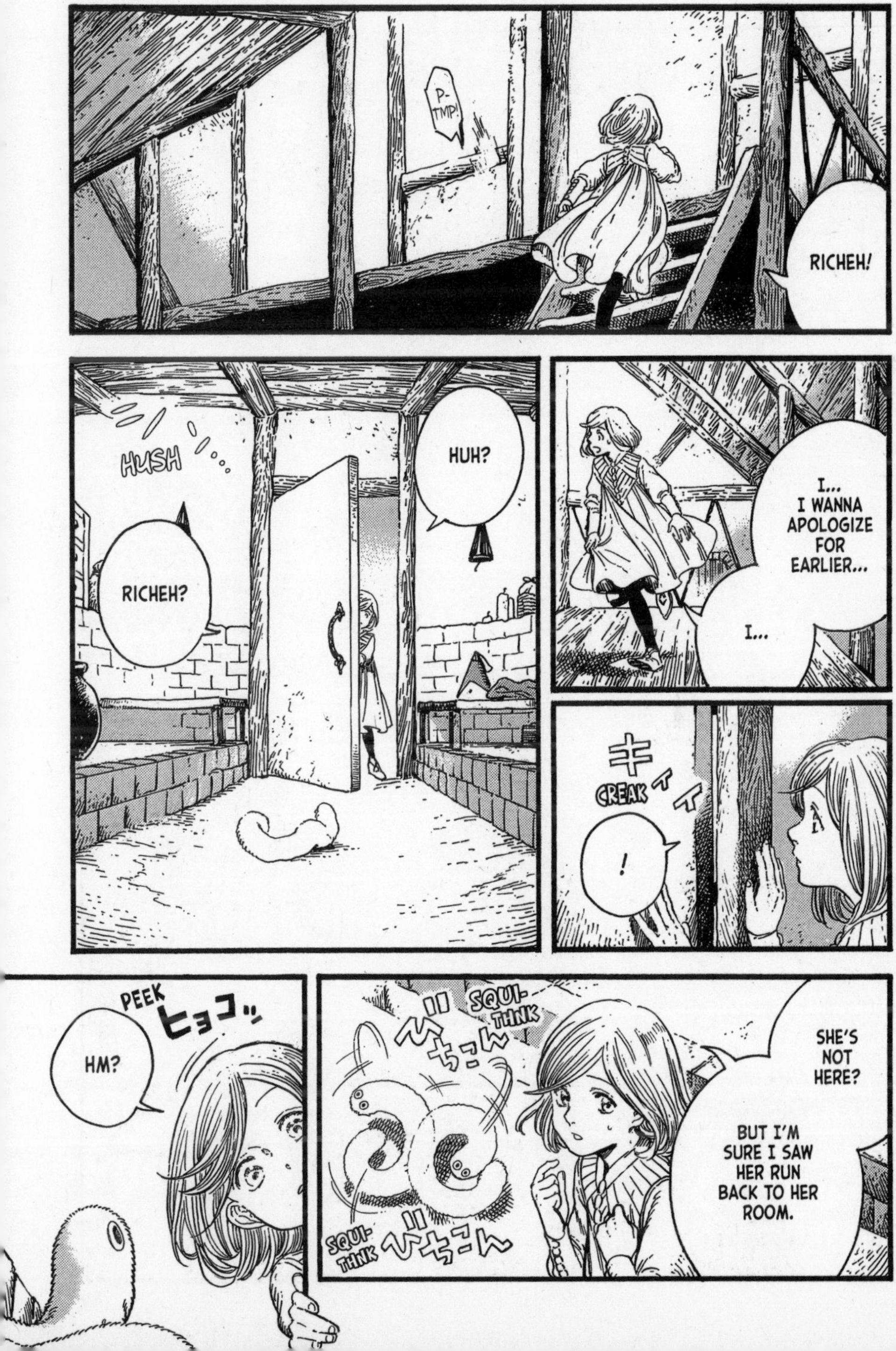
P-TMP!
RICHEH!
I... I WANNA APOLOGIZE FOR EARLIER...
I...
キィィ
CREAK
!
HUH?
HUSH
RICHEH?
SHE'S NOT HERE?
BUT I'M SURE I SAW HER RUN BACK TO HER ROOM.
SQUI-THNK
SQUI-THNK
PEEK
ヒョコッ
HM?

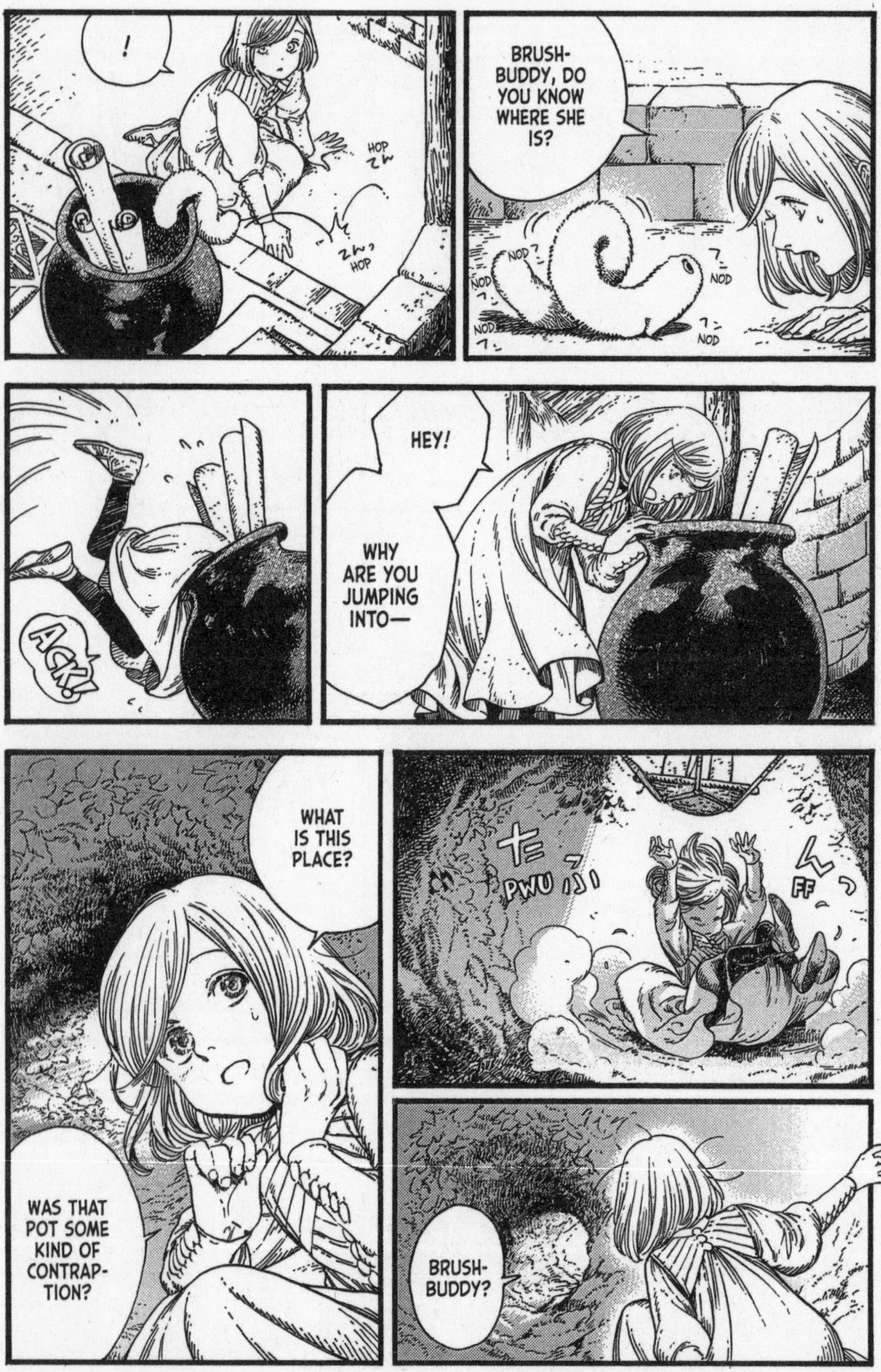
BRUSH-BUDDY, DO YOU KNOW WHERE SHE IS?
NOD
NOD
NOD
NOD
NOD
!
HOP
HOP
HEY!
WHY ARE YOU JUMPING INTO—
ACK!
PWU
FF
BRUSH-BUDDY?
WHAT IS THIS PLACE?
WAS THAT POT SOME KIND OF CONTRAPTION?

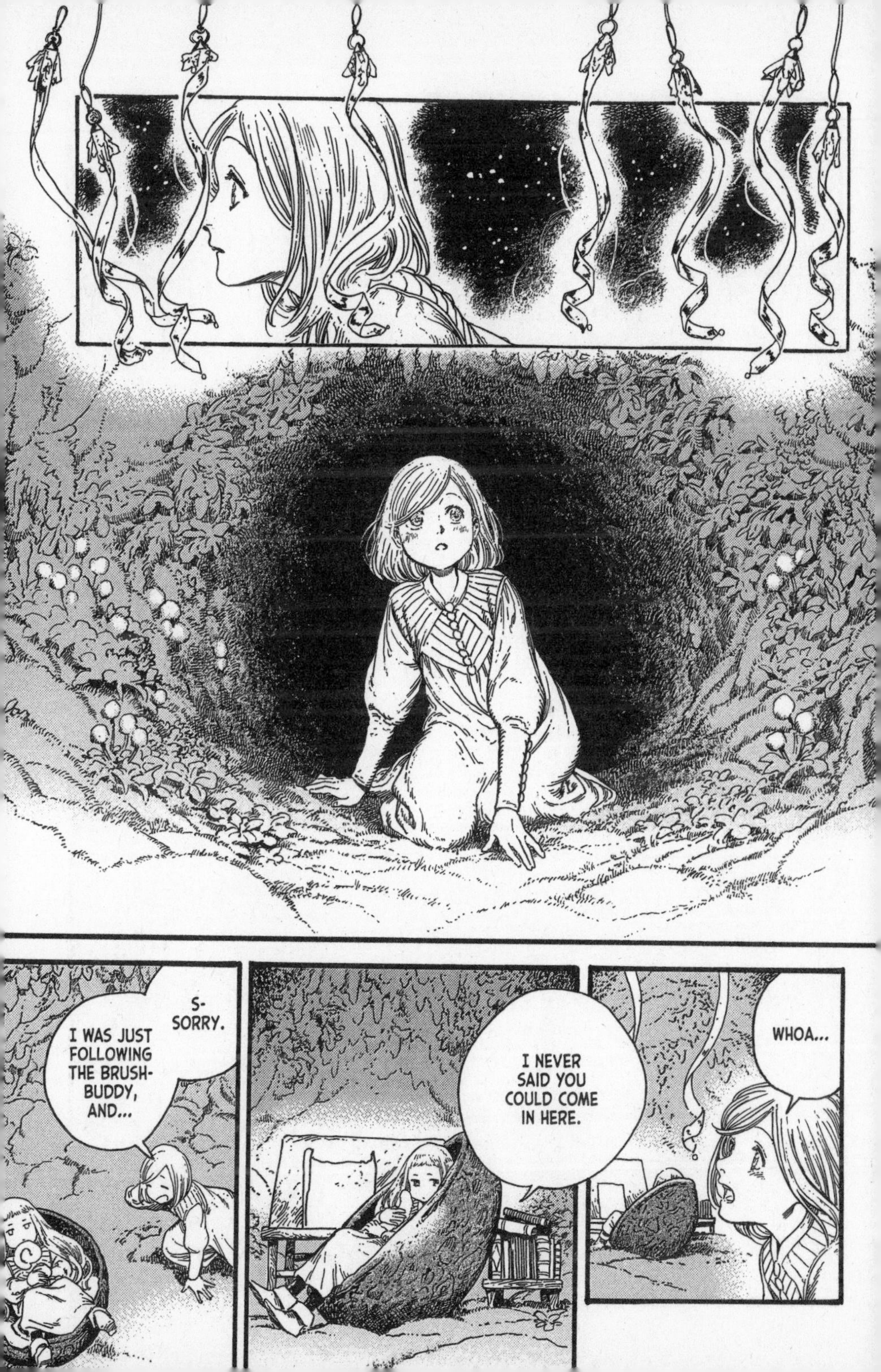
WHOA...
I NEVER SAID YOU COULD COME IN HERE.
S- SORRY.
I WAS JUST FOLLOWING THE BRUSH-BUDDY, AND...

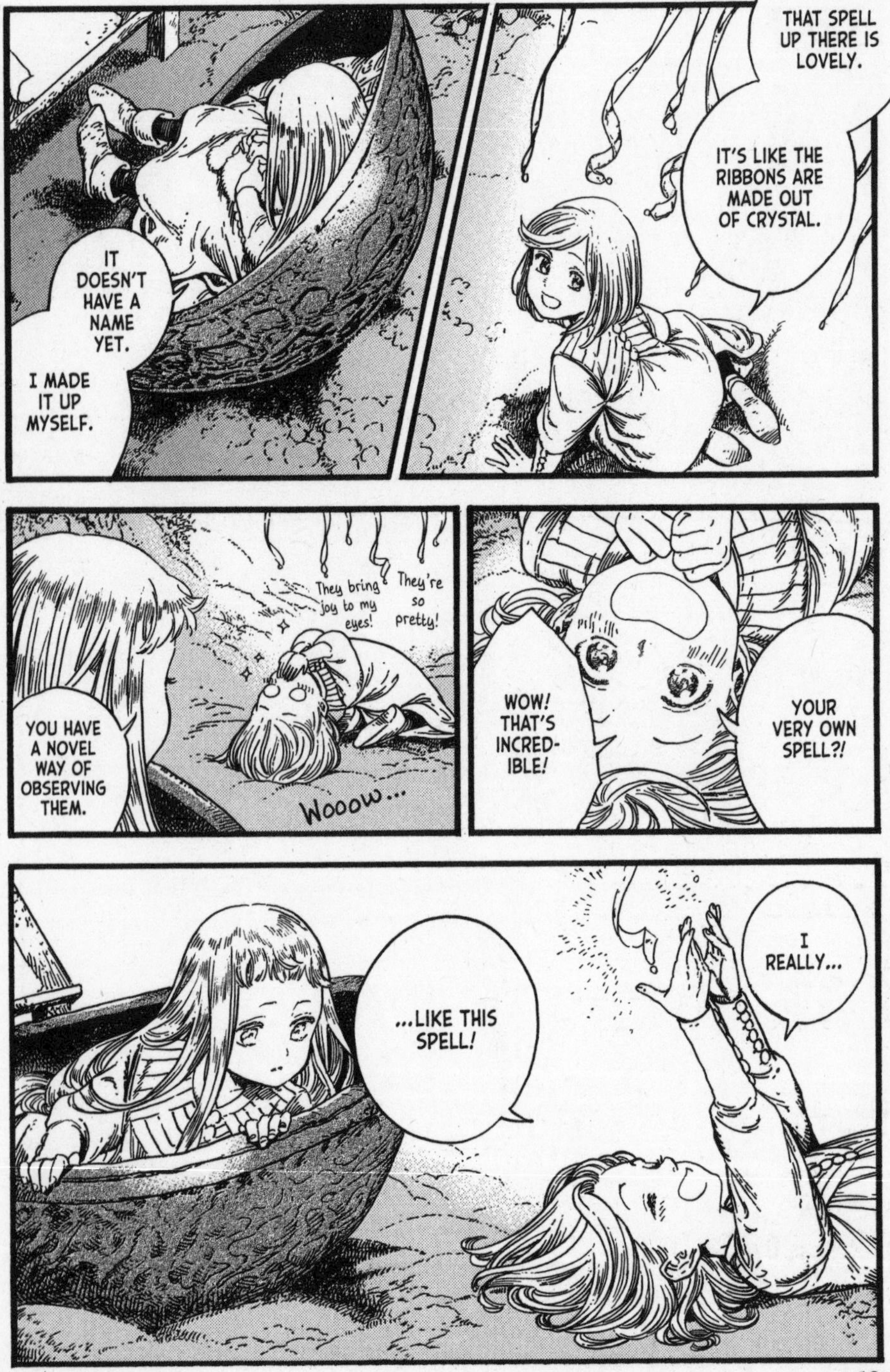
THAT SPELL UP THERE IS LOVELY.
IT'S LIKE THE RIBBONS ARE MADE OUT OF CRYSTAL.
IT DOESN'T HAVE A NAME YET.
I MADE IT UP MYSELF.
YOUR VERY OWN SPELL?!
WOW! THAT'S INCRED-IBLE!
They're so pretty!
They bring joy to my eyes!
YOU HAVE A NOVEL WAY OF OBSERVING THEM.
Wooow...
I REALLY...
...LIKE THIS SPELL!

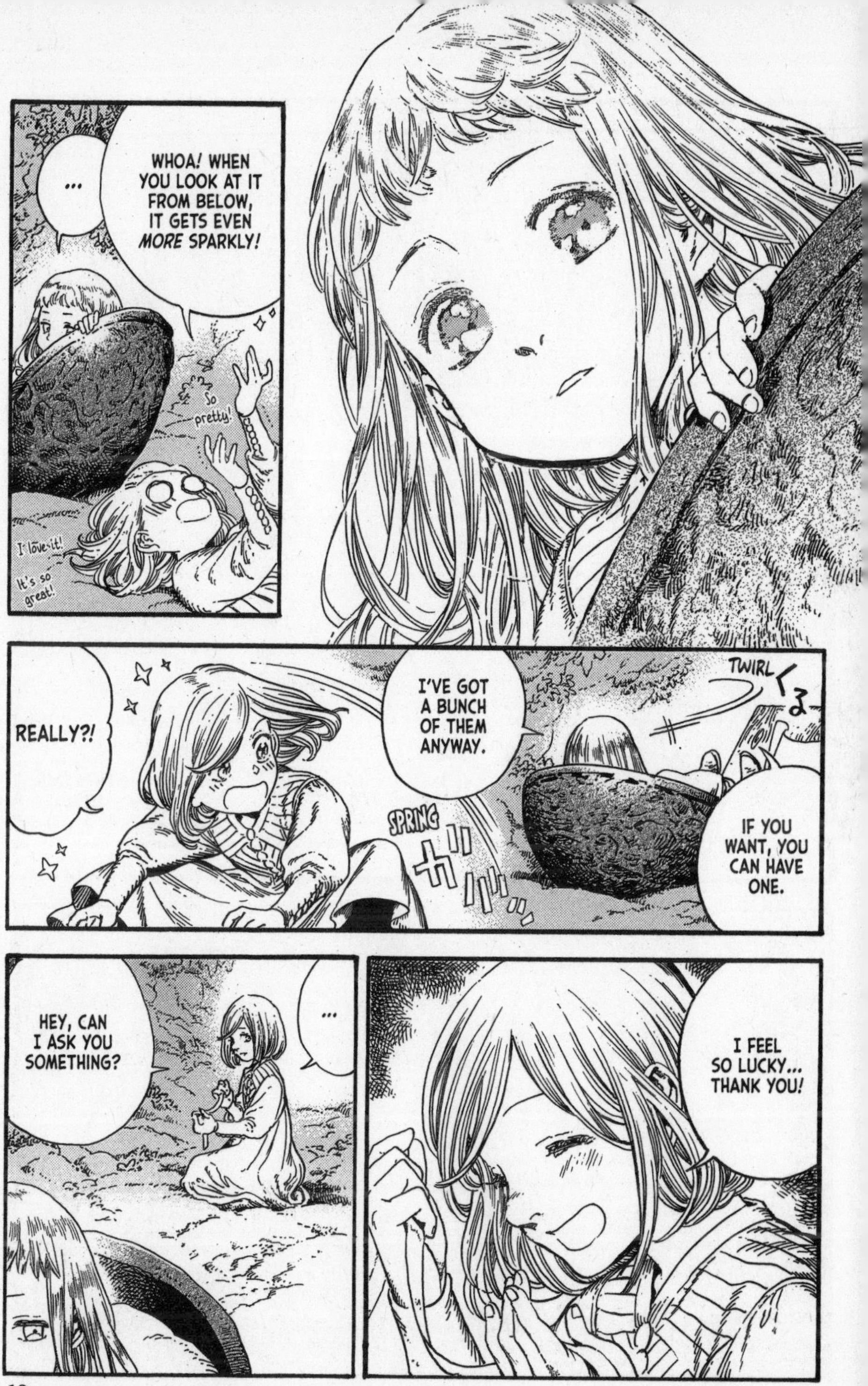
WHOA! WHEN YOU LOOK AT IT FROM BELOW, IT GETS EVEN *MORE* SPARKLY!
...
So pretty!
I love it!
It's so great!
TWIRL
IF YOU WANT, YOU CAN HAVE ONE.
I'VE GOT A BUNCH OF THEM ANYWAY.
SPRING
REALLY?!
I FEEL SO LUCKY... THANK YOU!
...
HEY, CAN I ASK YOU SOMETHING?

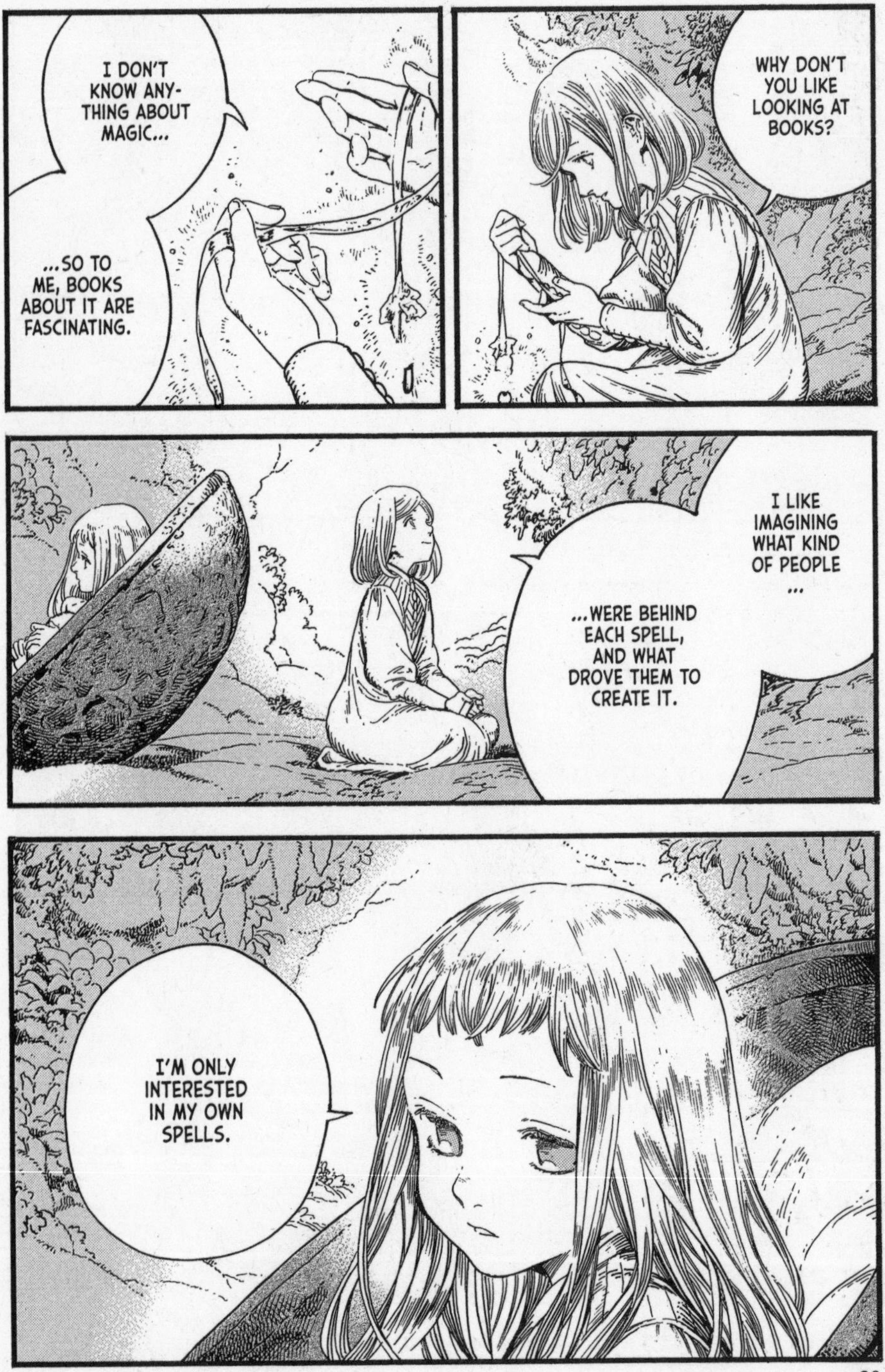
WHY DON'T YOU LIKE LOOKING AT BOOKS?
I DON'T KNOW ANY-THING ABOUT MAGIC...
...SO TO ME, BOOKS ABOUT IT ARE FASCINATING.
I LIKE IMAGINING WHAT KIND OF PEOPLE ...
...WERE BEHIND EACH SPELL, AND WHAT DROVE THEM TO CREATE IT.
I'M ONLY INTERESTED IN MY OWN SPELLS.

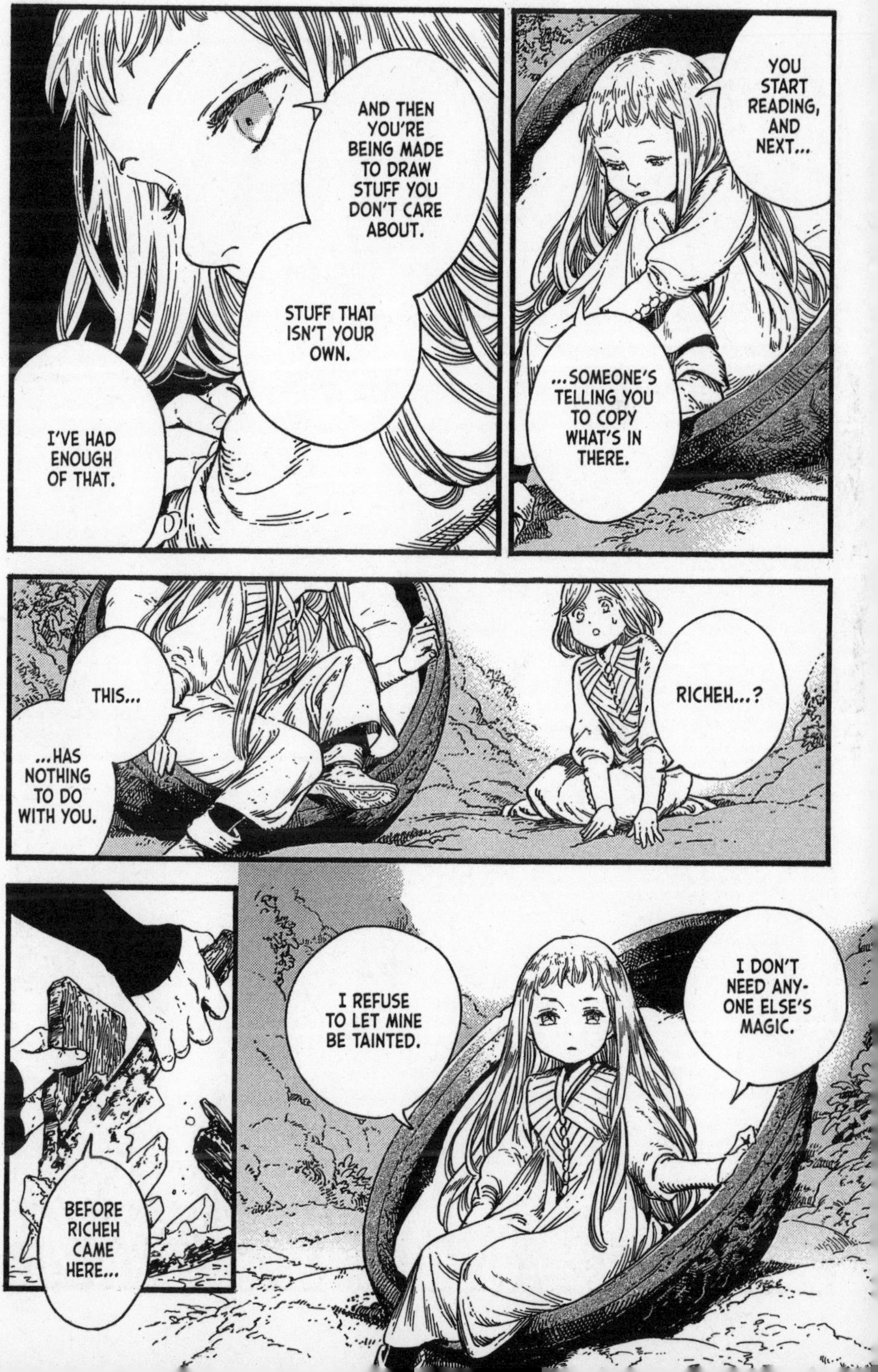
YOU START READING, AND NEXT...
...SOMEONE'S TELLING YOU TO COPY WHAT'S IN THERE.
AND THEN YOU'RE BEING MADE TO DRAW STUFF YOU DON'T CARE ABOUT.
STUFF THAT ISN'T YOUR OWN.
I'VE HAD ENOUGH OF THAT.
RICHEH...?
THIS...
...HAS NOTHING TO DO WITH YOU.
I DON'T NEED ANY-ONE ELSE'S MAGIC.
I REFUSE TO LET MINE BE TAINTED.
BEFORE RICHEH CAME HERE...

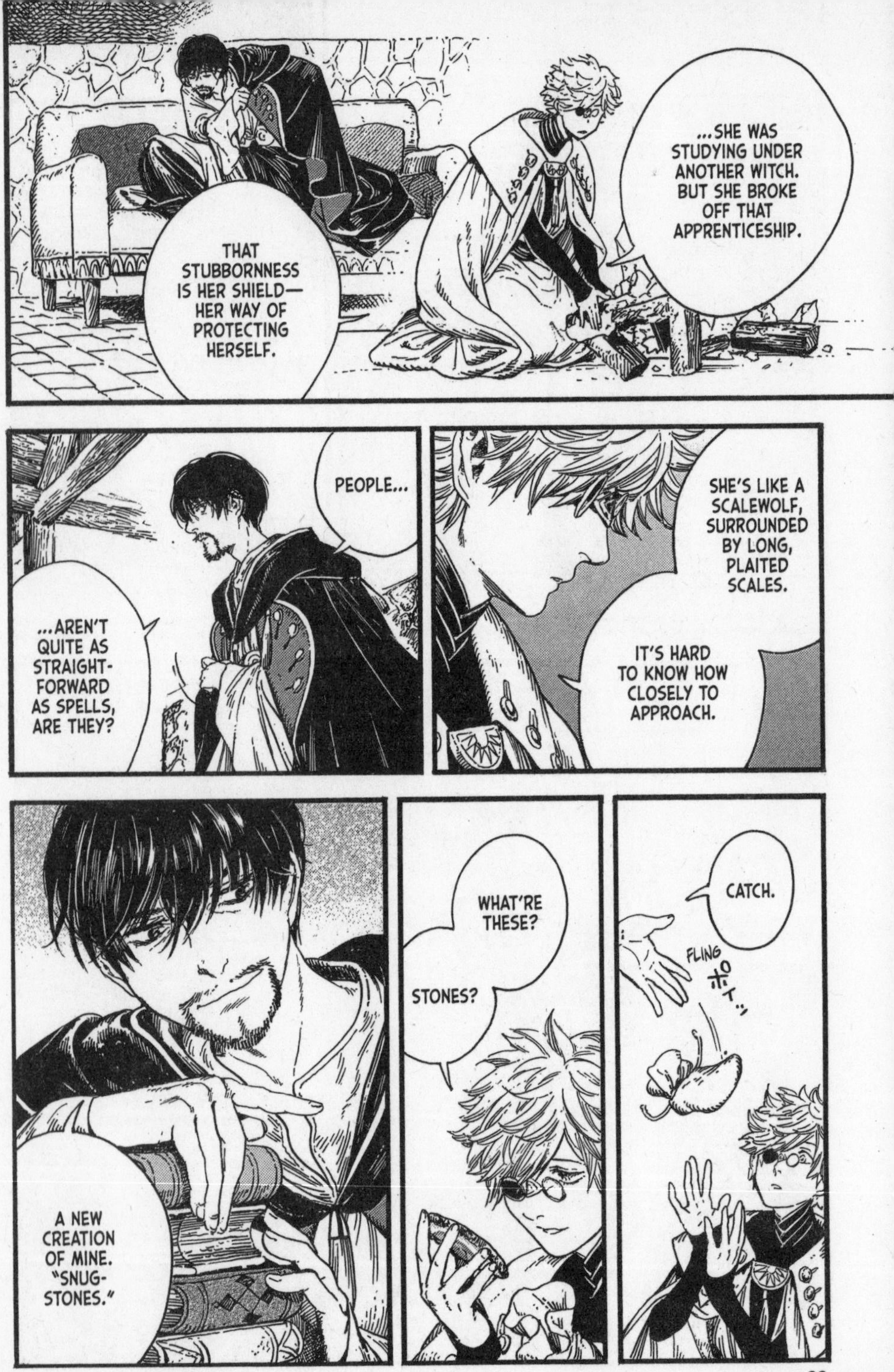
...SHE WAS STUDYING UNDER ANOTHER WITCH. BUT SHE BROKE OFF THAT APPRENTICESHIP.
THAT STUBBORNNESS IS HER SHIELD—HER WAY OF PROTECTING HERSELF.
SHE'S LIKE A SCALEWOLF, SURROUNDED BY LONG, PLAITED SCALES.
IT'S HARD TO KNOW HOW CLOSELY TO APPROACH.
PEOPLE...
...AREN'T QUITE AS STRAIGHT-FORWARD AS SPELLS, ARE THEY?
CATCH.
FLING
WHAT'RE THESE?
STONES?
A NEW CREATION OF MINE. "SNUG-STONES."

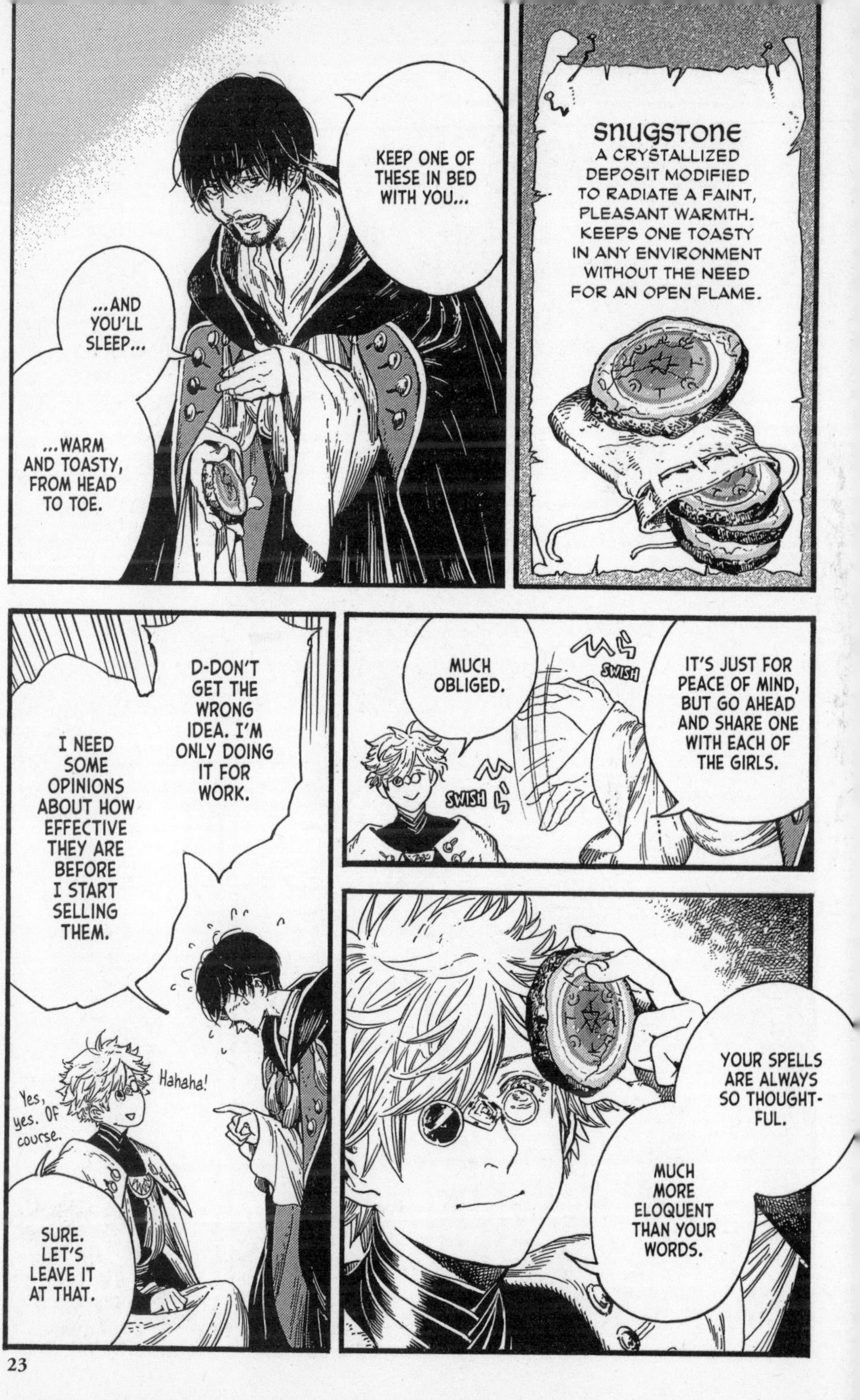
SNUGSTONE
A CRYSTALLIZED DEPOSIT MODIFIED TO RADIATE A FAINT, PLEASANT WARMTH. KEEPS ONE TOASTY IN ANY ENVIRONMENT WITHOUT THE NEED FOR AN OPEN FLAME.
KEEP ONE OF THESE IN BED WITH YOU...
...AND YOU'LL SLEEP...
...WARM AND TOASTY, FROM HEAD TO TOE.
IT'S JUST FOR PEACE OF MIND, BUT GO AHEAD AND SHARE ONE WITH EACH OF THE GIRLS.
SWISH
MUCH OBLIGED.
SWISH
YOUR SPELLS ARE ALWAYS SO THOUGHT-FUL.
MUCH MORE ELOQUENT THAN YOUR WORDS.
D-DON'T GET THE WRONG IDEA. I'M ONLY DOING IT FOR WORK.
I NEED SOME OPINIONS ABOUT HOW EFFECTIVE THEY ARE BEFORE I START SELLING THEM.
Hahaha!
Yes, yes. Of course.
SURE. LET'S LEAVE IT AT THAT.

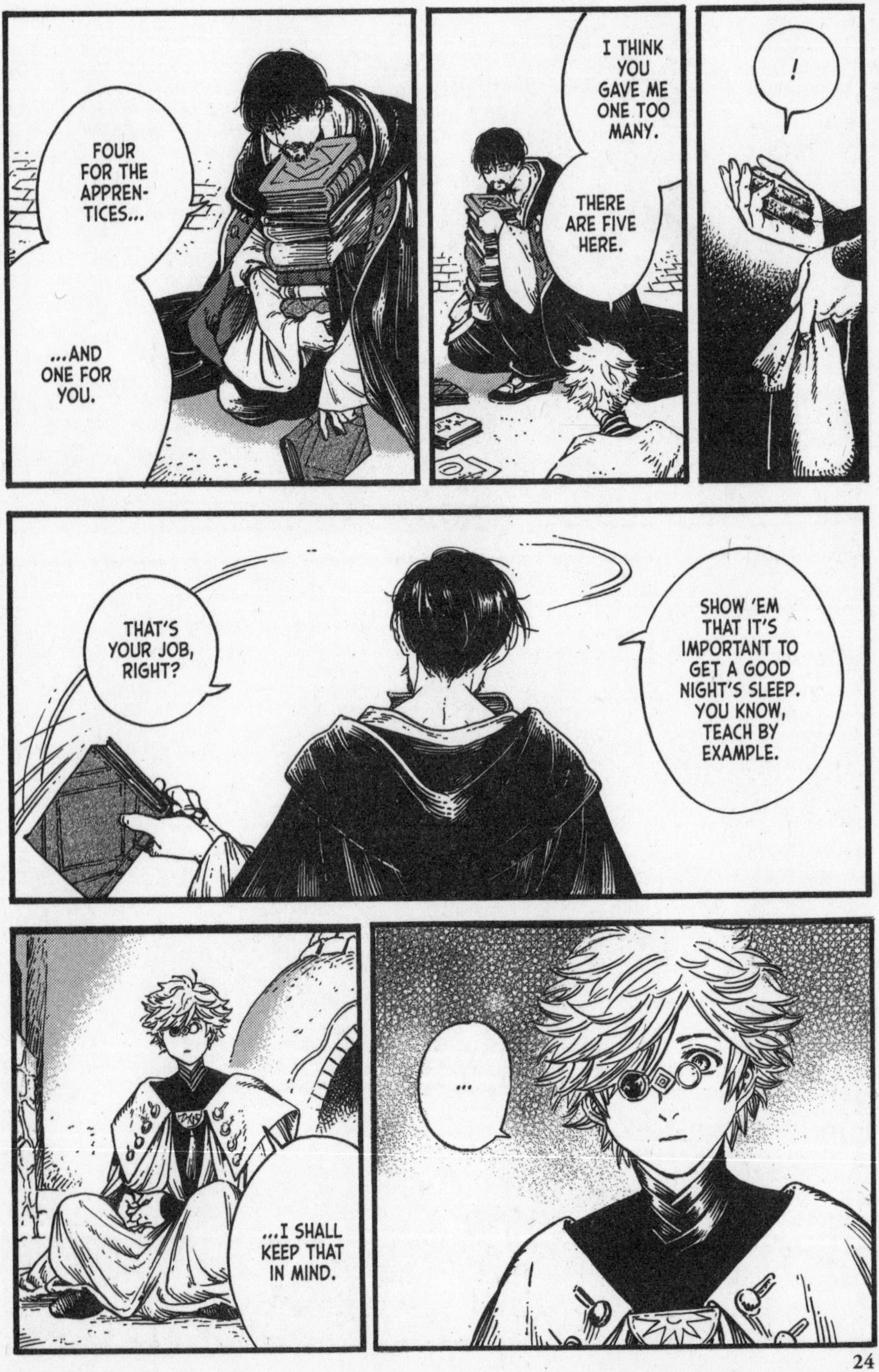
!
I THINK YOU GAVE ME ONE TOO MANY.
THERE ARE FIVE HERE.
FOUR FOR THE APPREN-TICES...
...AND ONE FOR YOU.
SHOW 'EM THAT IT'S IMPORTANT TO GET A GOOD NIGHT'S SLEEP. YOU KNOW, TEACH BY EXAMPLE.
THAT'S YOUR JOB, RIGHT?
...
...I SHALL KEEP THAT IN MIND.

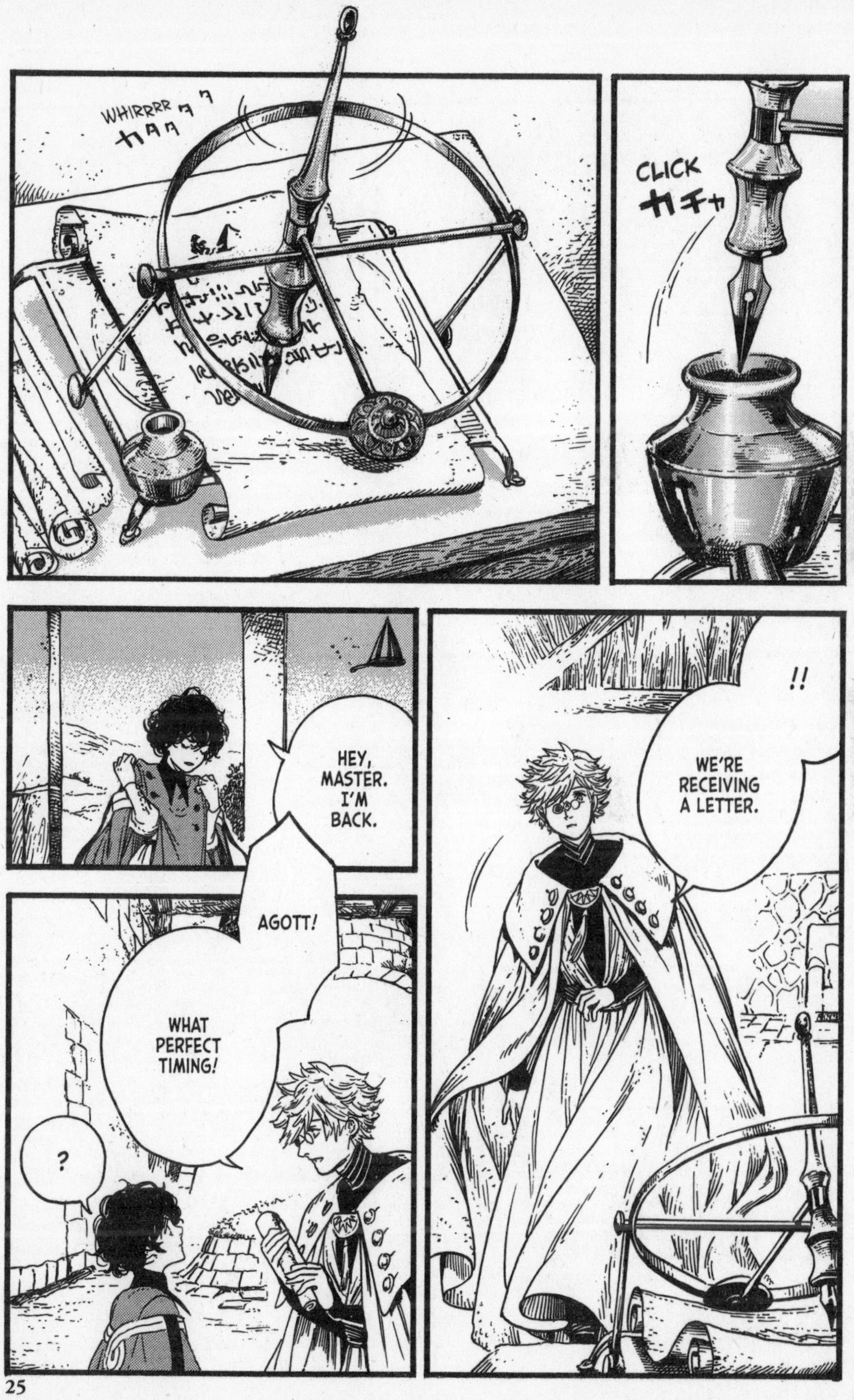
CLICK
カチャ
WHIRRRR
カタタ
!!
WE'RE RECEIVING A LETTER.
HEY, MASTER. I'M BACK.
AGOTT!
WHAT PERFECT TIMING!
?

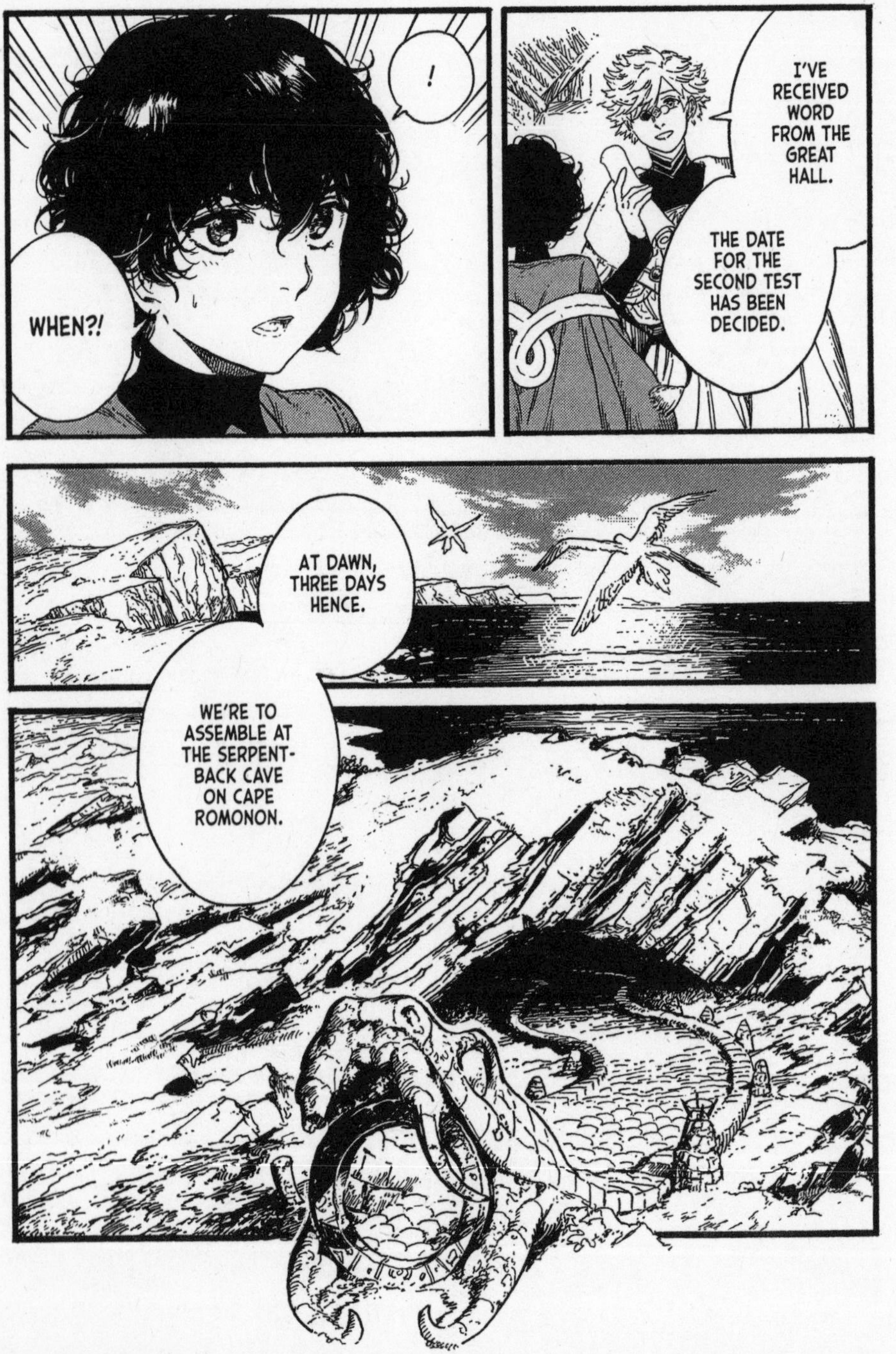
I'VE RECEIVED WORD FROM THE GREAT HALL.
THE DATE FOR THE SECOND TEST HAS BEEN DECIDED.
!
WHEN?!
AT DAWN, THREE DAYS HENCE.
WE'RE TO ASSEMBLE AT THE SERPENT-BACK CAVE ON CAPE ROMONON.

Chapter 18 ♦ End

Witch Hat Atelier

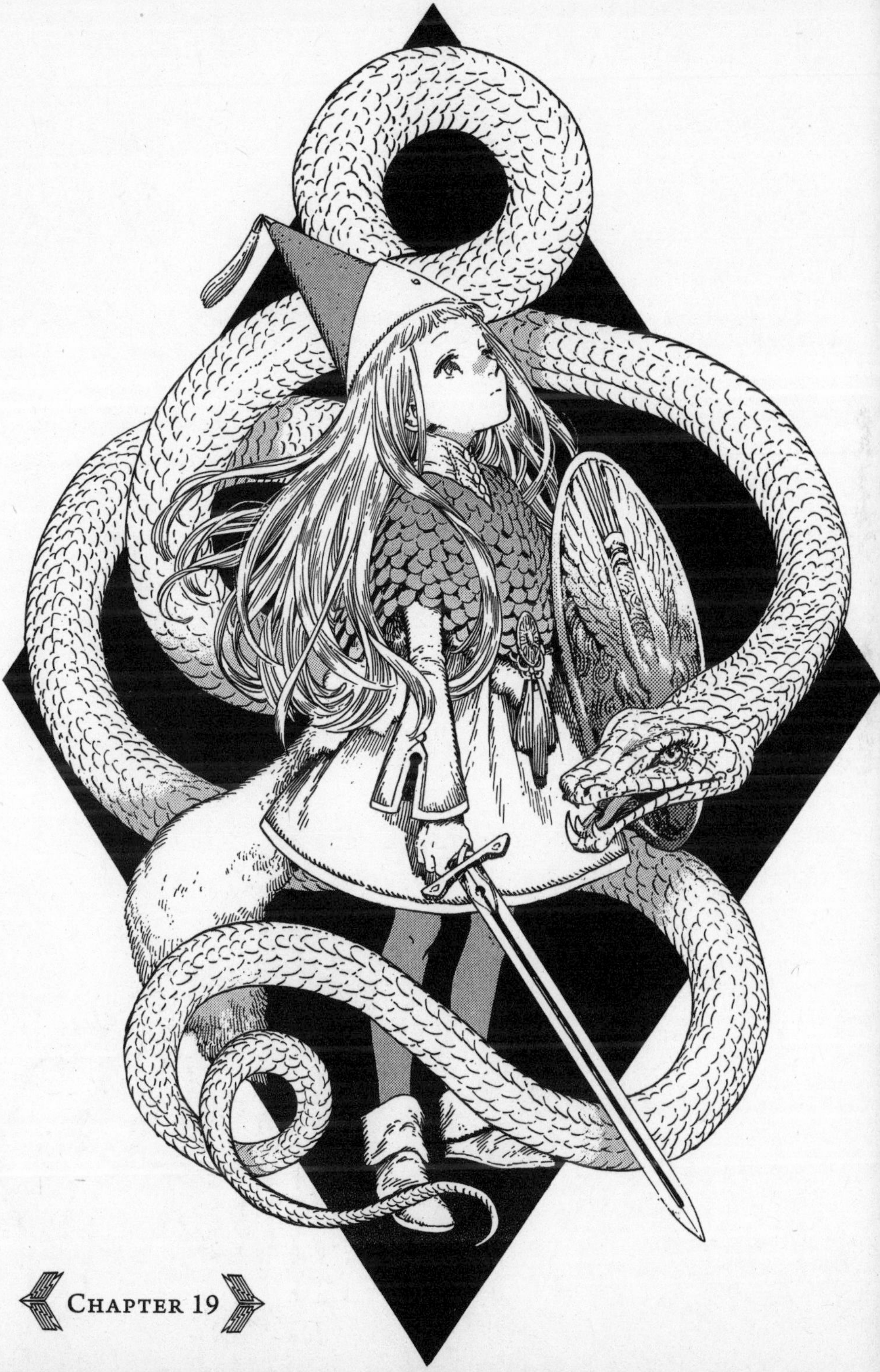

Chapter 19

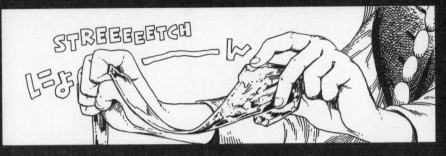

STREEEEETCH

ARE YOU TRYING TO MAKE A RIBBON OUT OF CRYSTAL?

PUULL

CRUMPLE

HMPH!

THAT'S AN ADORABLE SPELL, RICHEH-LETTE.

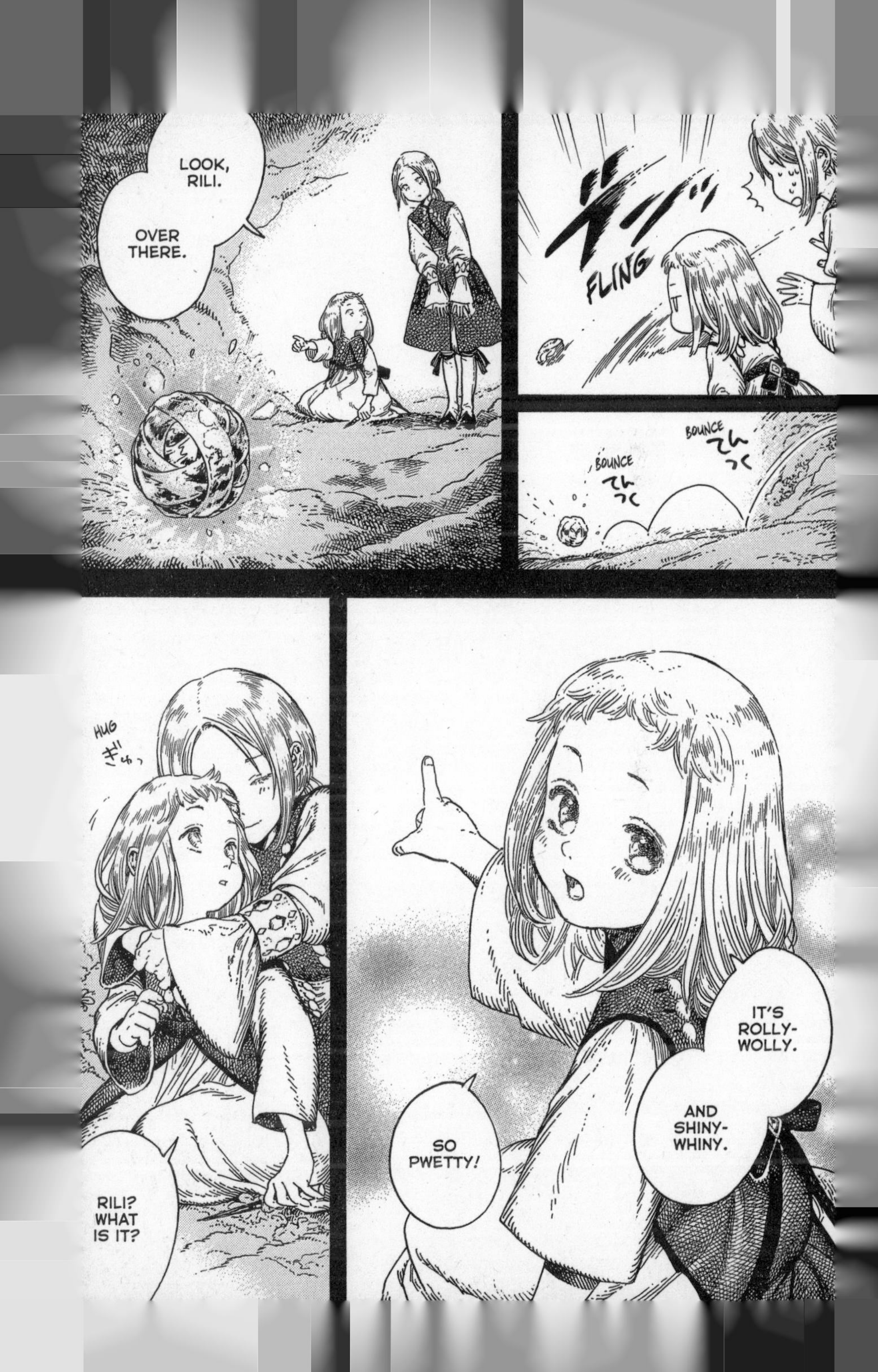
FLING
BOUNCE
BOUNCE
LOOK, RILI.
OVER THERE.
IT'S ROLLY-WOLLY.
AND SHINY-WHINY.
SO PWETTY!
HUG
RILI? WHAT IS IT?

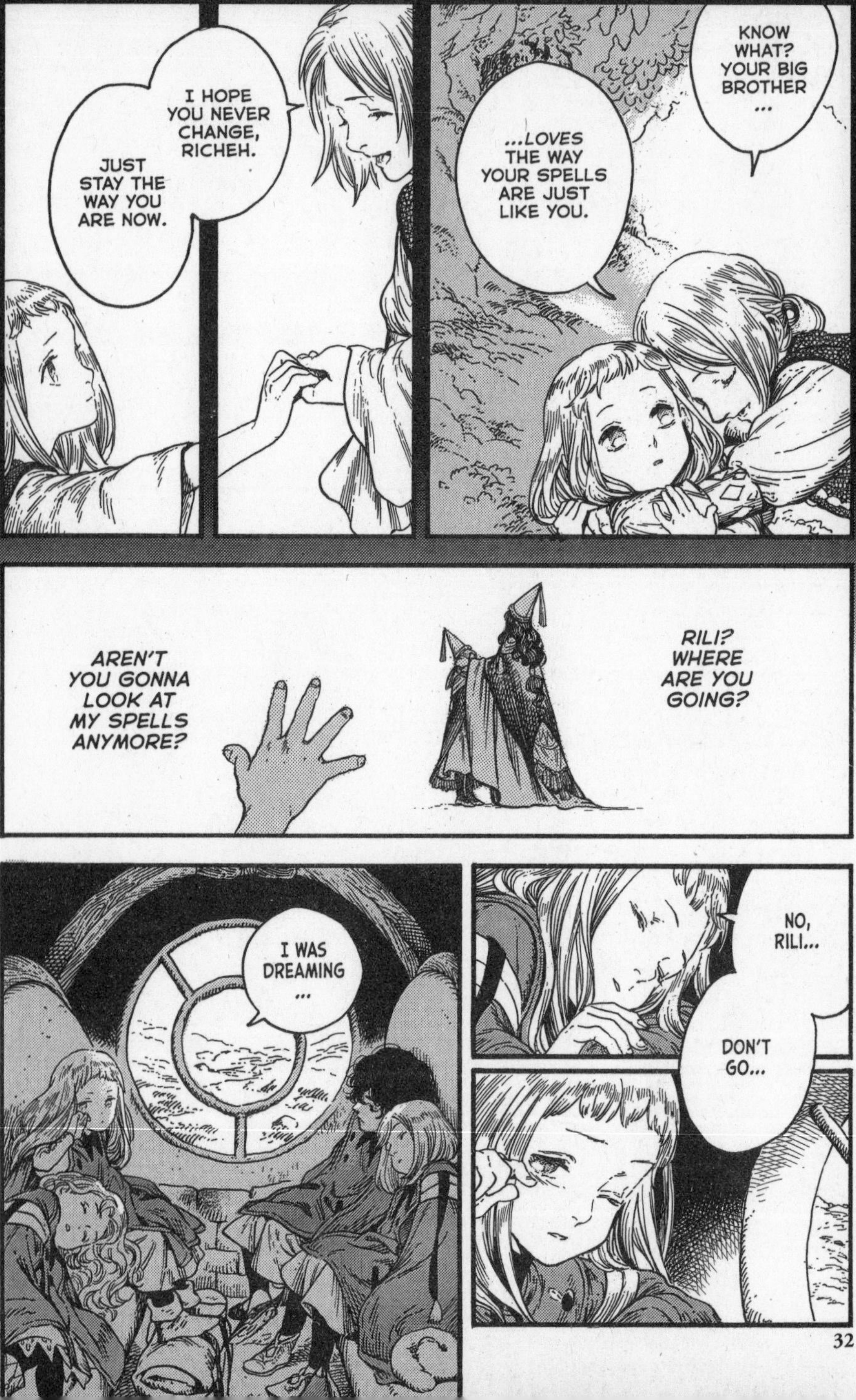
KNOW WHAT? YOUR BIG BROTHER ...
...LOVES THE WAY YOUR SPELLS ARE JUST LIKE YOU.
I HOPE YOU NEVER CHANGE, RICHEH.
JUST STAY THE WAY YOU ARE NOW.
RILI? WHERE ARE YOU GOING?
AREN'T YOU GONNA LOOK AT MY SPELLS ANYMORE?
NO, RILI...
DON'T GO...
I WAS DREAMING ...

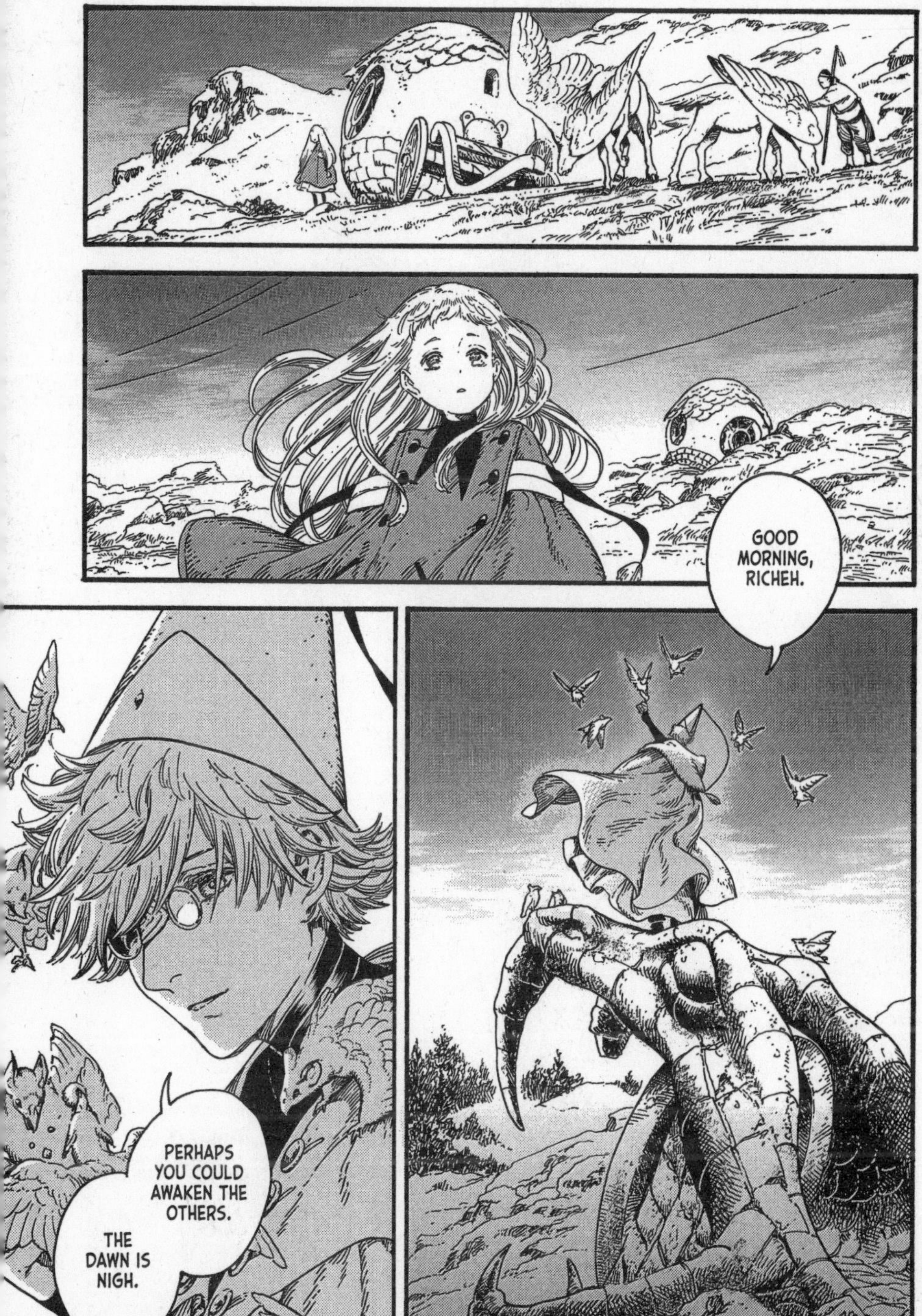
GOOD MORNING, RICHEH.
PERHAPS YOU COULD AWAKEN THE OTHERS.
THE DAWN IS NIGH.

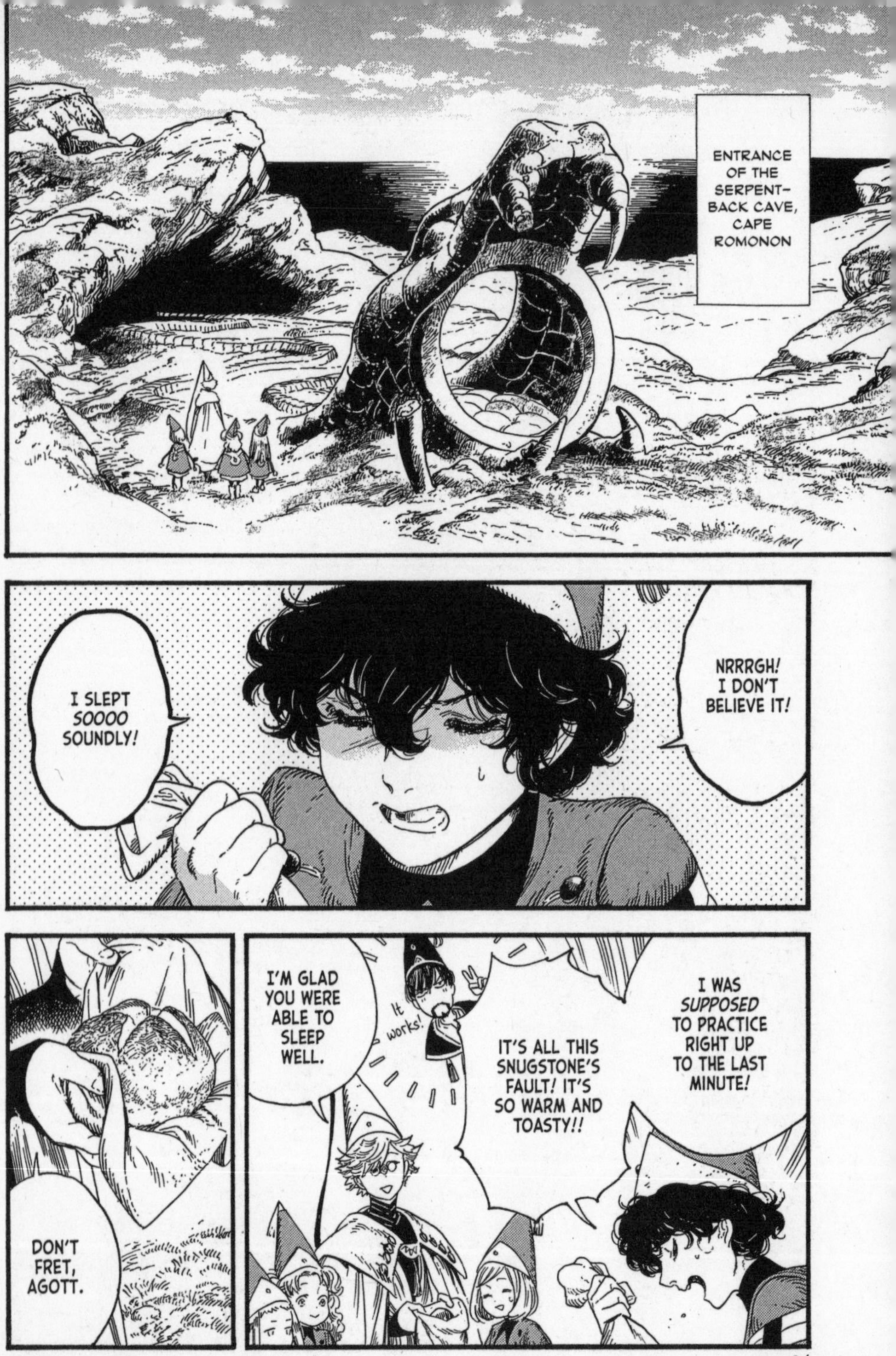
ENTRANCE OF THE SERPENT-BACK CAVE, CAPE ROMONON
NRRRGH! I DON'T BELIEVE IT!
I SLEPT *SOOOO* SOUNDLY!
I WAS *SUPPOSED* TO PRACTICE RIGHT UP TO THE LAST MINUTE!
IT'S ALL THIS SNUGSTONE'S FAULT! IT'S SO WARM AND TOASTY!!
It works!
I'M GLAD YOU WERE ABLE TO SLEEP WELL.
DON'T FRET, AGOTT.

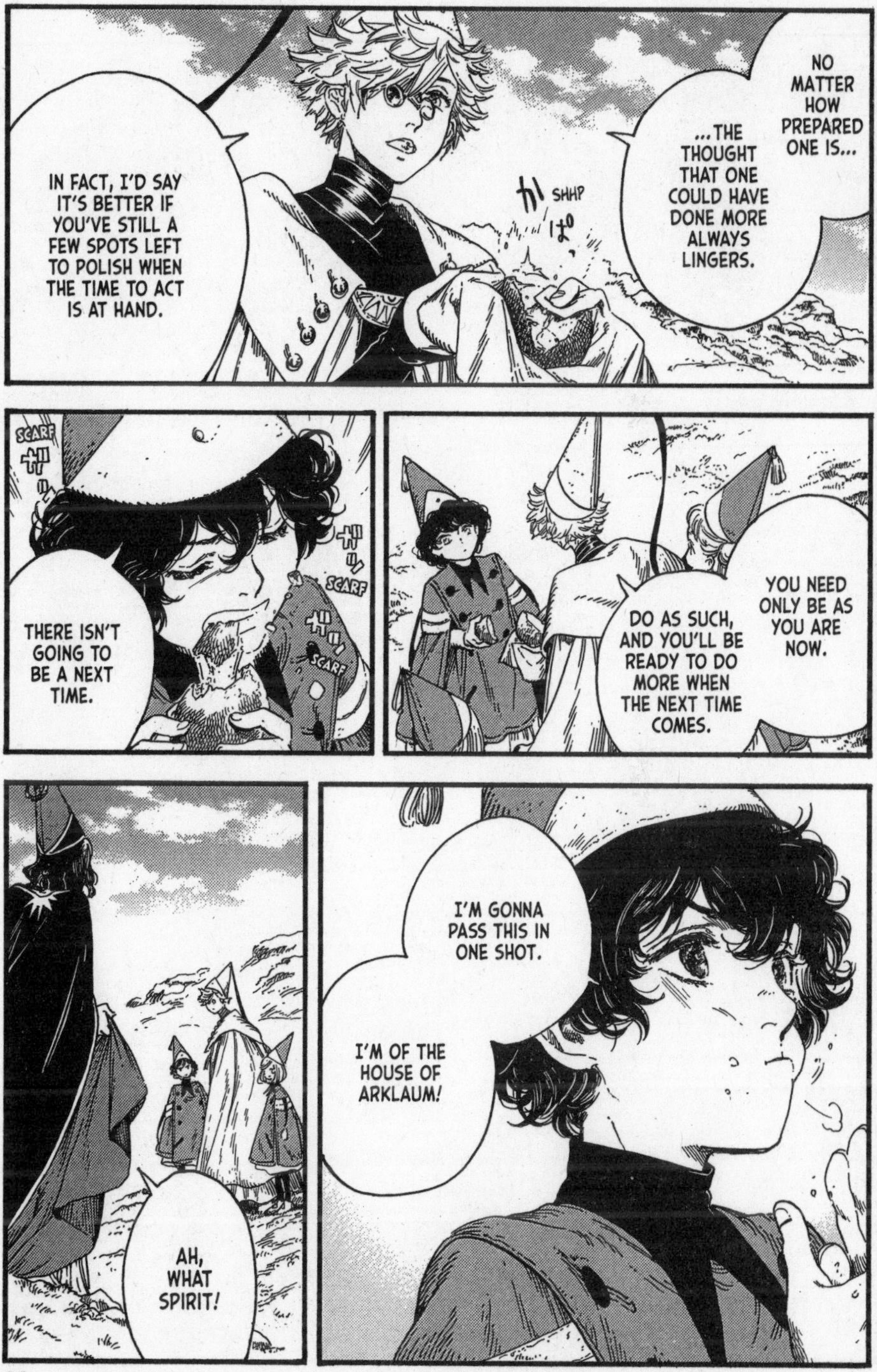
NO MATTER HOW PREPARED ONE IS...
...THE THOUGHT THAT ONE COULD HAVE DONE MORE ALWAYS LINGERS.
SHHP
IN FACT, I'D SAY IT'S BETTER IF YOU'VE STILL A FEW SPOTS LEFT TO POLISH WHEN THE TIME TO ACT IS AT HAND.
YOU NEED ONLY BE AS YOU ARE NOW.
DO AS SUCH, AND YOU'LL BE READY TO DO MORE WHEN THE NEXT TIME COMES.
SCARF
SCARF
SCARF
THERE ISN'T GOING TO BE A NEXT TIME.
I'M GONNA PASS THIS IN ONE SHOT.
I'M OF THE HOUSE OF ARKLAUM!
AH, WHAT SPIRIT!

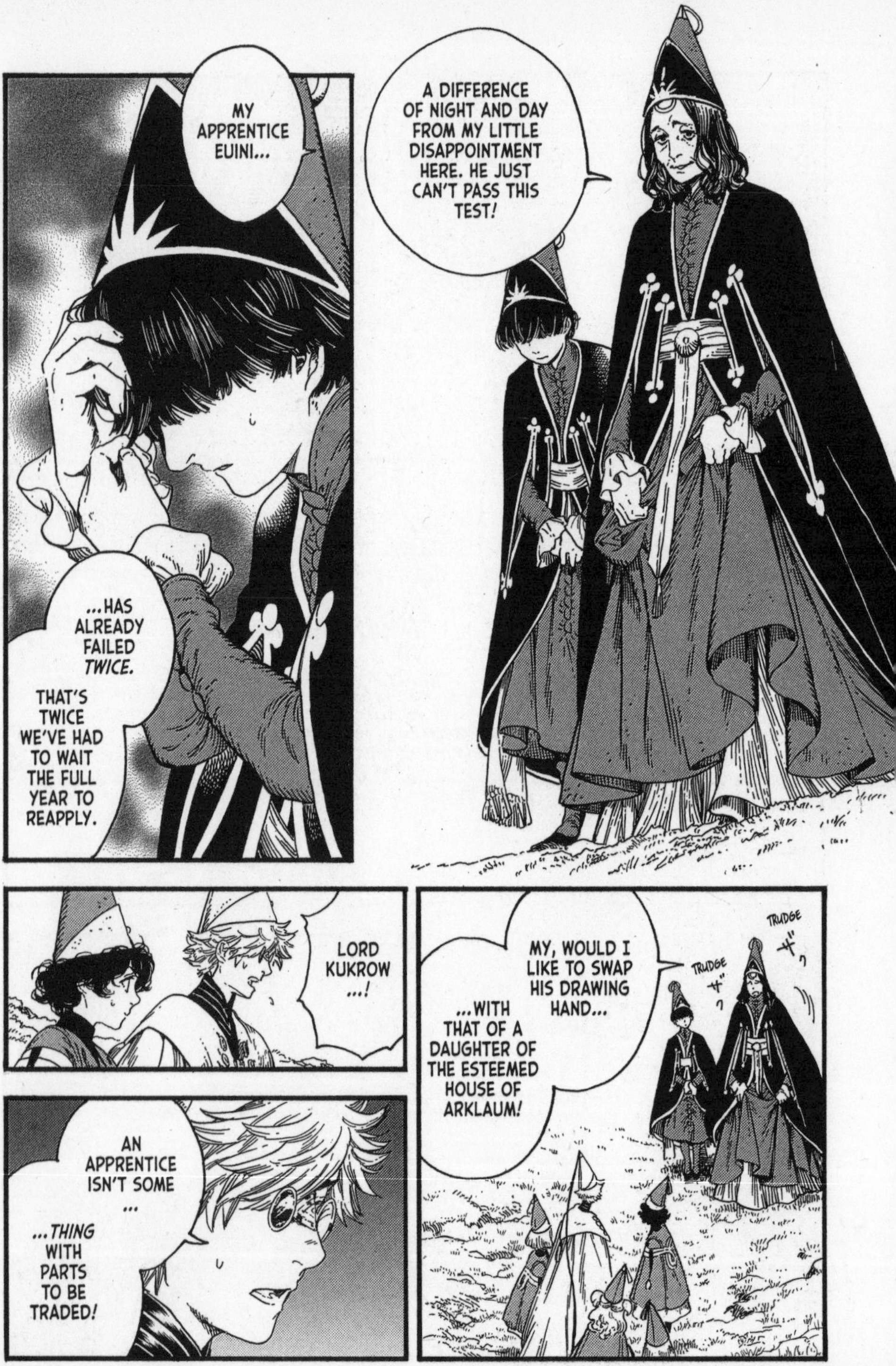
A DIFFERENCE OF NIGHT AND DAY FROM MY LITTLE DISAPPOINTMENT HERE. HE JUST CAN'T PASS THIS TEST!
MY APPRENTICE EUINI...
...HAS ALREADY FAILED *TWICE.*
THAT'S TWICE WE'VE HAD TO WAIT THE FULL YEAR TO REAPPLY.
TRUDGE
TRUDGE
MY, WOULD I LIKE TO SWAP HIS DRAWING HAND...
...WITH THAT OF A DAUGHTER OF THE ESTEEMED HOUSE OF ARKLAUM!
LORD KUKROW ...!
AN APPRENTICE ISN'T SOME ...
...*THING* WITH PARTS TO BE TRADED!

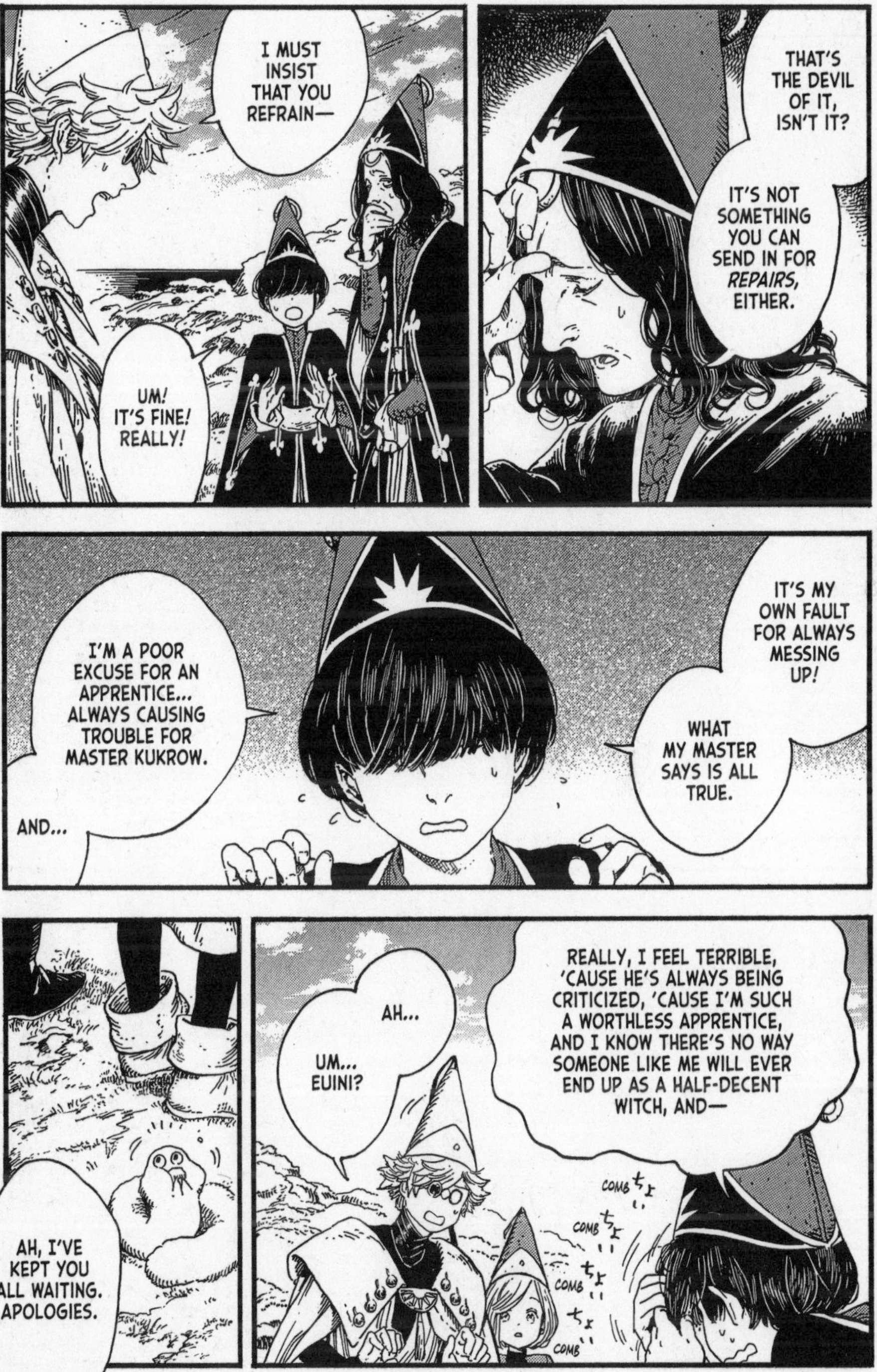
THAT'S THE DEVIL OF IT, ISN'T IT?
IT'S NOT SOMETHING YOU CAN SEND IN FOR *REPAIRS*, EITHER.
I MUST INSIST THAT YOU REFRAIN—
UM! IT'S FINE! REALLY!
IT'S MY OWN FAULT FOR ALWAYS MESSING UP!
WHAT MY MASTER SAYS IS ALL TRUE.
I'M A POOR EXCUSE FOR AN APPRENTICE... ALWAYS CAUSING TROUBLE FOR MASTER KUKROW.
AND...
REALLY, I FEEL TERRIBLE, 'CAUSE HE'S ALWAYS BEING CRITICIZED, 'CAUSE I'M SUCH A WORTHLESS APPRENTICE, AND I KNOW THERE'S NO WAY SOMEONE LIKE ME WILL EVER END UP AS A HALF-DECENT WITCH, AND—
AH...
UM... EUINI?
COMB
COMB
COMB
COMB
AH, I'VE KEPT YOU ALL WAITING. APOLOGIES.

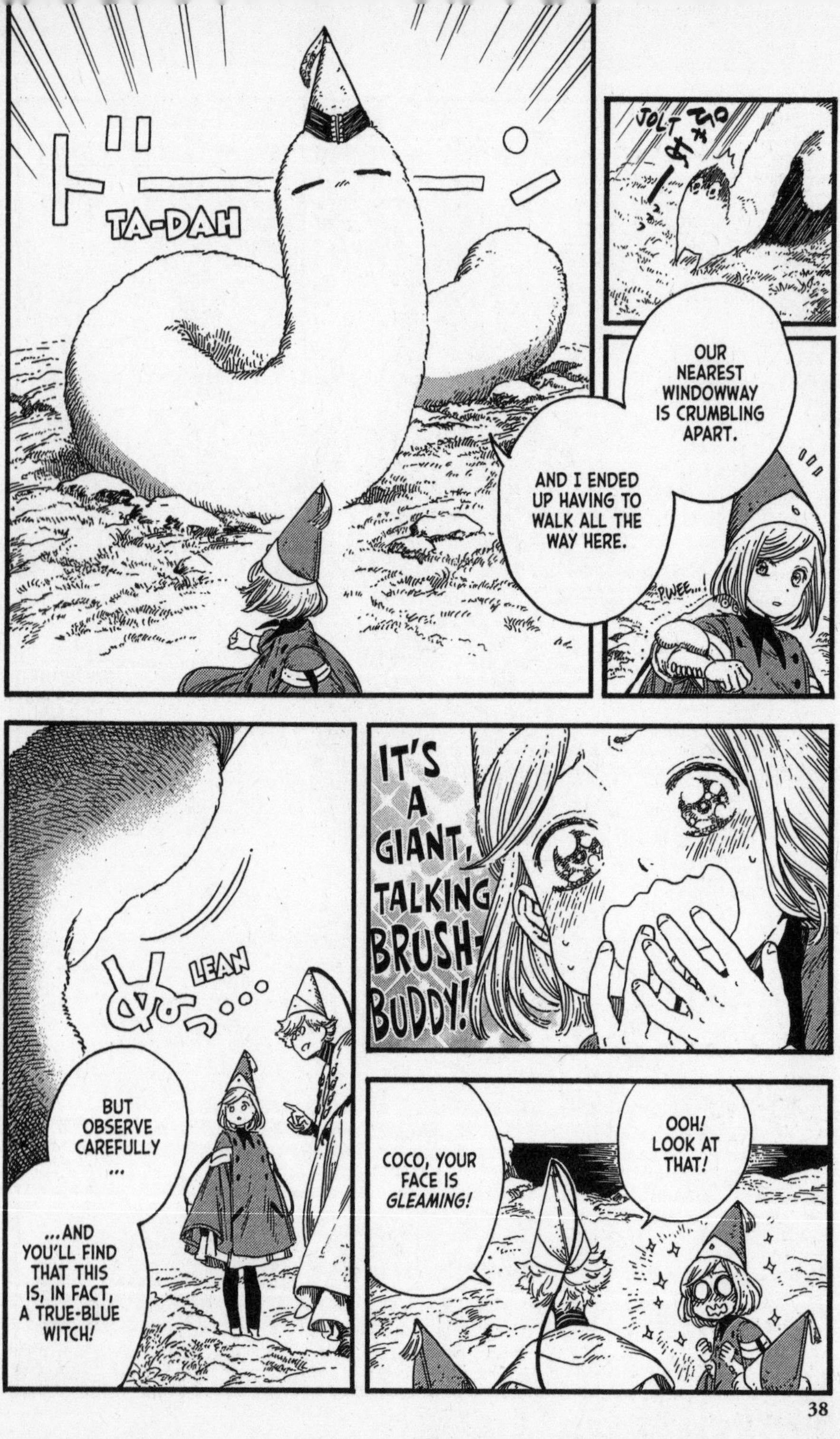
JOLT
OUR NEAREST WINDOWWAY IS CRUMBLING APART.
AND I ENDED UP HAVING TO WALK ALL THE WAY HERE.
PWEE...!
TA-DAH
IT'S A GIANT, TALKING BRUSH-BUDDY!
OOH! LOOK AT THAT!
COCO, YOUR FACE IS *GLEAMING!*
LEAN
BUT OBSERVE CAREFULLY ...
...AND YOU'LL FIND THAT THIS IS, IN FACT, A TRUE-BLUE WITCH!

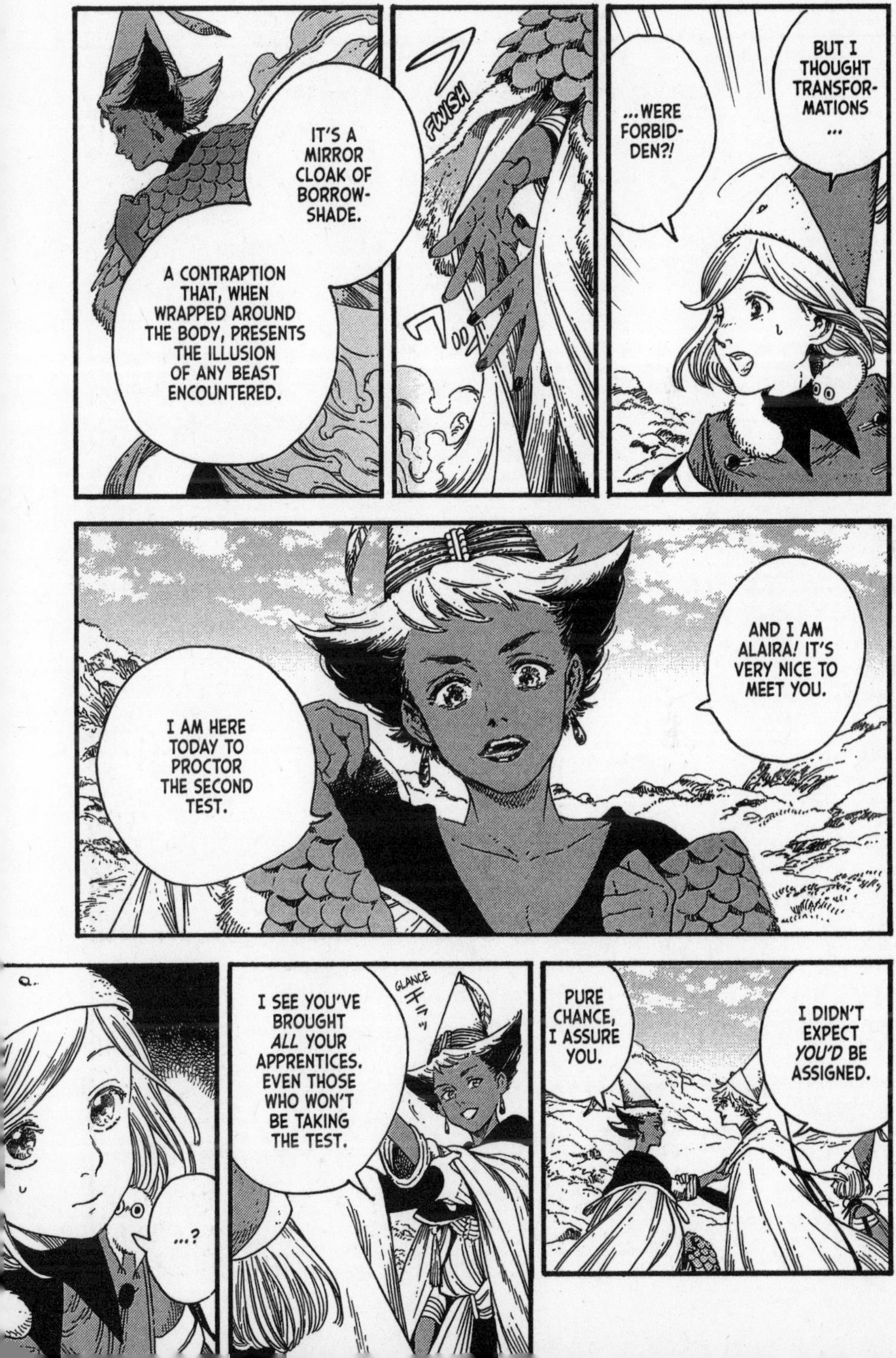
BUT I THOUGHT TRANSFORMATIONS...
...WERE FORBIDDEN?!
FWISH
IT'S A MIRROR CLOAK OF BORROWSHADE.
A CONTRAPTION THAT, WHEN WRAPPED AROUND THE BODY, PRESENTS THE ILLUSION OF ANY BEAST ENCOUNTERED.
AND I AM ALAIRA! IT'S VERY NICE TO MEET YOU.
I AM HERE TODAY TO PROCTOR THE SECOND TEST.
I DIDN'T EXPECT *YOU'D* BE ASSIGNED.
PURE CHANCE, I ASSURE YOU.
GLANCE
I SEE YOU'VE BROUGHT *ALL* YOUR APPRENTICES. EVEN THOSE WHO WON'T BE TAKING THE TEST.
...?

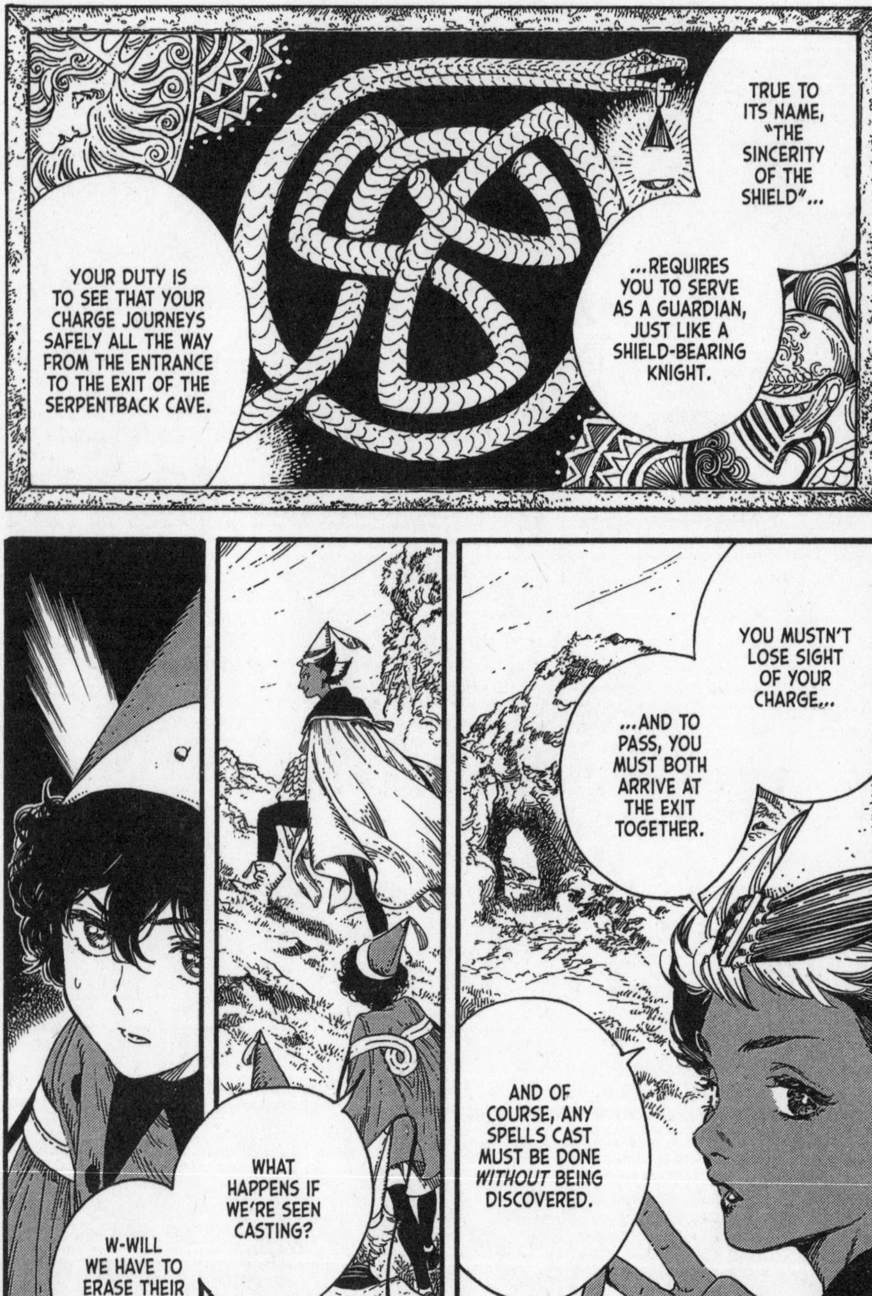
TRUE TO ITS NAME, "THE SINCERITY OF THE SHIELD"...
...REQUIRES YOU TO SERVE AS A GUARDIAN, JUST LIKE A SHIELD-BEARING KNIGHT.
YOUR DUTY IS TO SEE THAT YOUR CHARGE JOURNEYS SAFELY ALL THE WAY FROM THE ENTRANCE TO THE EXIT OF THE SERPENTBACK CAVE.
YOU MUSTN'T LOSE SIGHT OF YOUR CHARGE...
...AND TO PASS, YOU MUST BOTH ARRIVE AT THE EXIT TOGETHER.
AND OF COURSE, ANY SPELLS CAST MUST BE DONE *WITHOUT* BEING DISCOVERED.
WHAT HAPPENS IF WE'RE SEEN CASTING?
W-WILL WE HAVE TO ERASE THEIR MEMORIES ...?

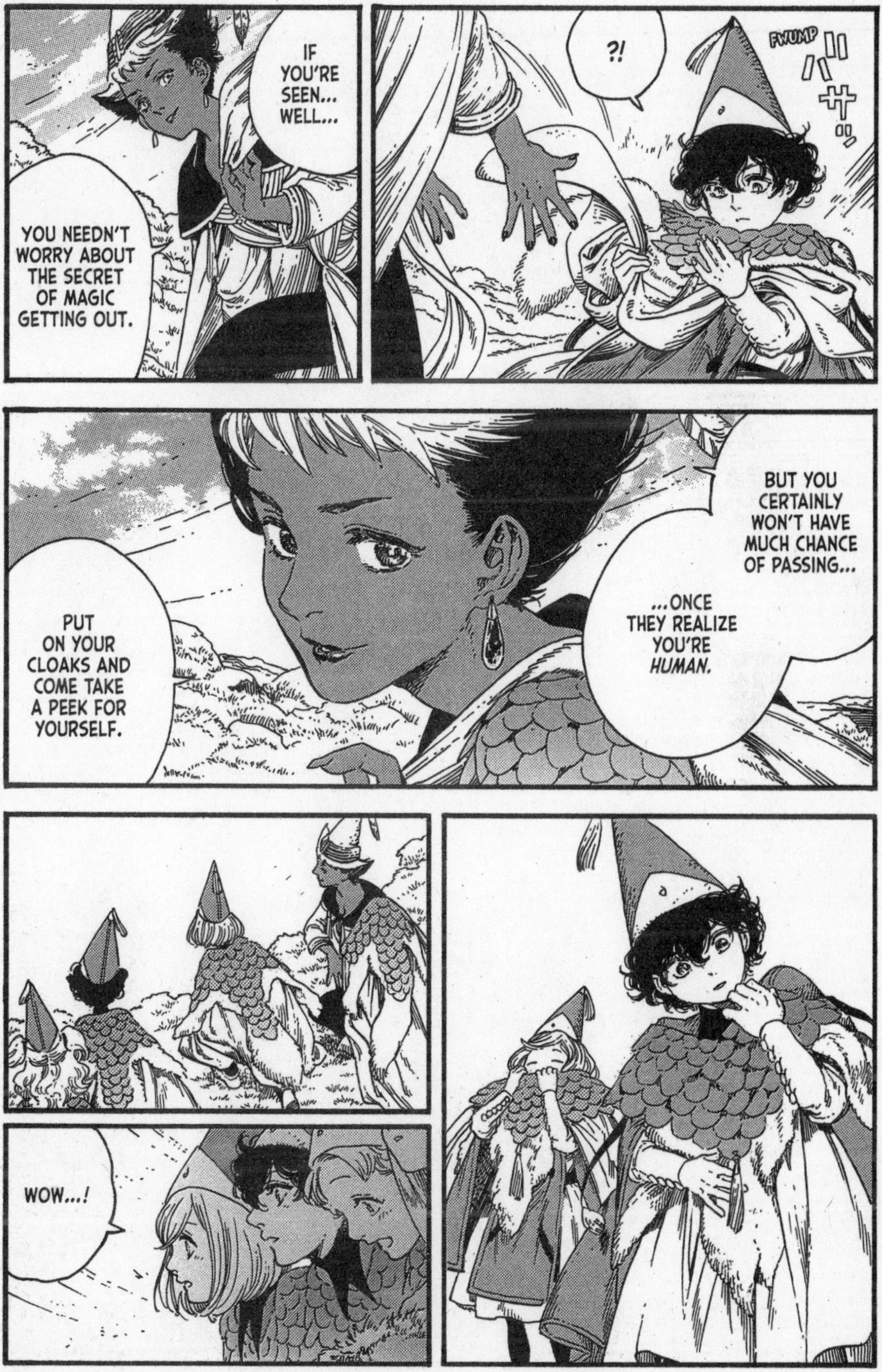
?!
FWUMP
IF YOU'RE SEEN... WELL...
YOU NEEDN'T WORRY ABOUT THE SECRET OF MAGIC GETTING OUT.
BUT YOU CERTAINLY WON'T HAVE MUCH CHANCE OF PASSING...
...ONCE THEY REALIZE YOU'RE *HUMAN.*
PUT ON YOUR CLOAKS AND COME TAKE A PEEK FOR YOURSELF.
WOW...!

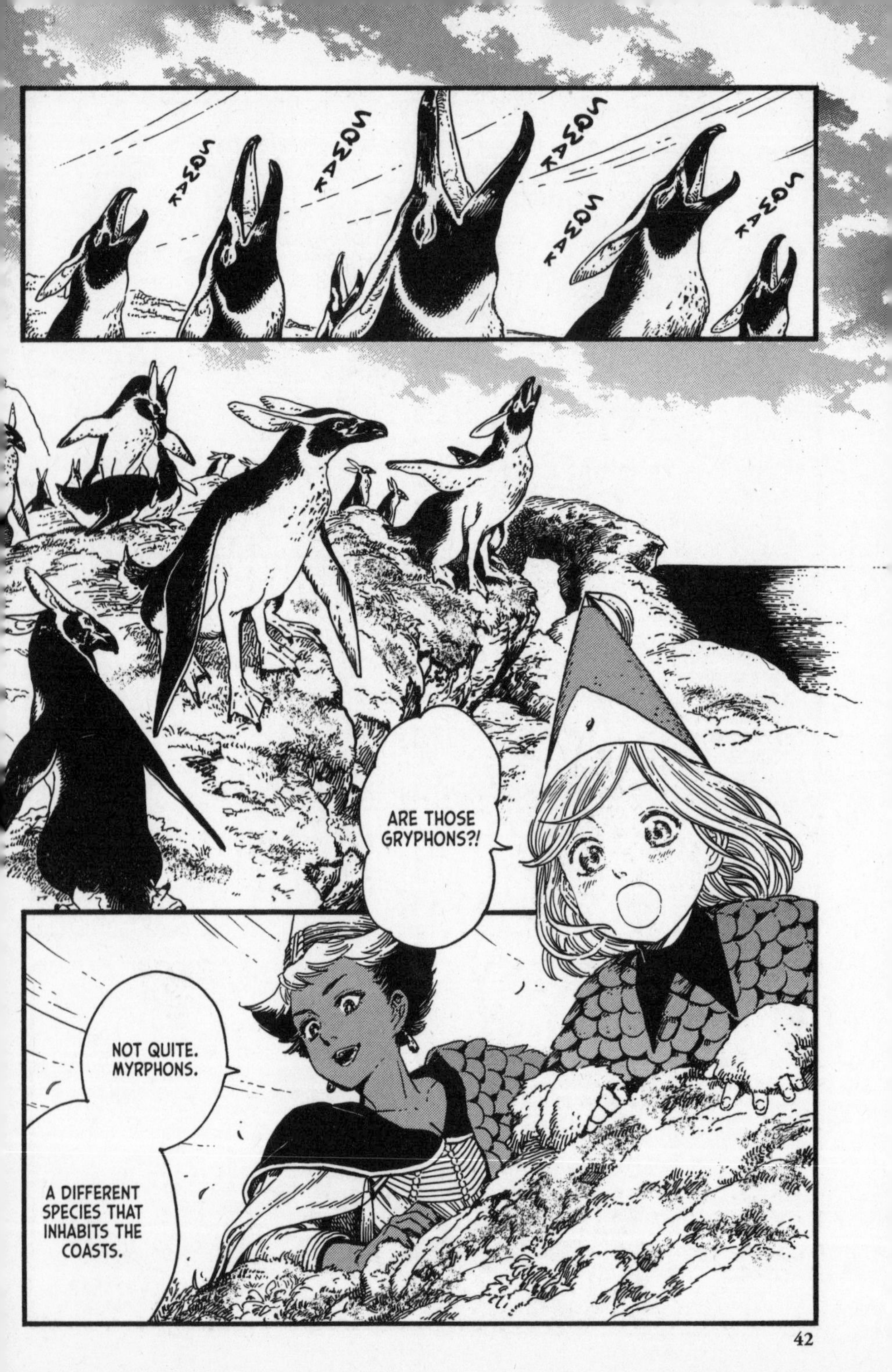
SQWAK
SQWAK
SQWAK
SQWAK
SQWAK
ARE THOSE GRYPHONS?!
NOT QUITE. MYRPHONS.
A DIFFERENT SPECIES THAT INHABITS THE COASTS.

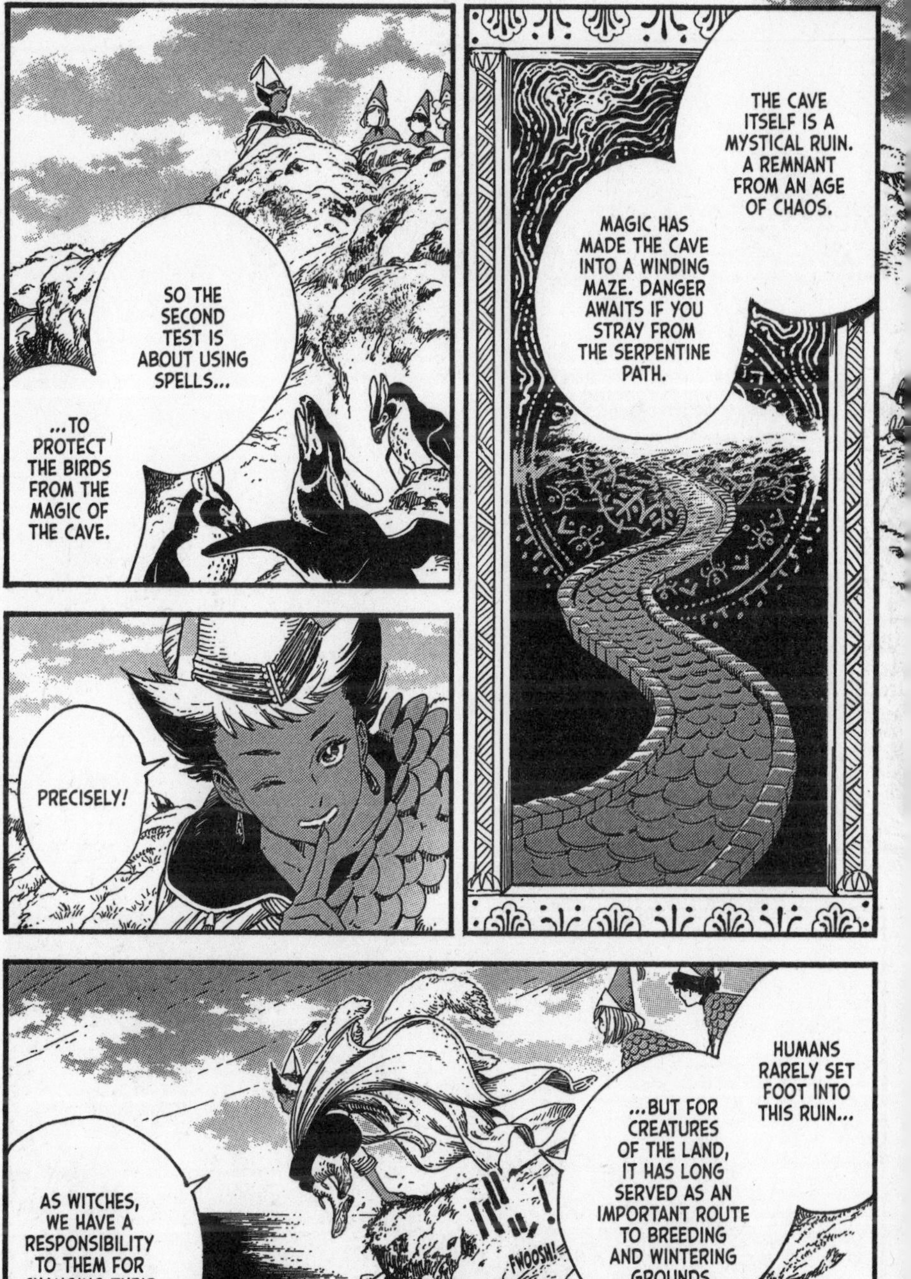
THE CAVE ITSELF IS A MYSTICAL RUIN. A REMNANT FROM AN AGE OF CHAOS.
MAGIC HAS MADE THE CAVE INTO A WINDING MAZE. DANGER AWAITS IF YOU STRAY FROM THE SERPENTINE PATH.
SO THE SECOND TEST IS ABOUT USING SPELLS...
...TO PROTECT THE BIRDS FROM THE MAGIC OF THE CAVE.
PRECISELY!
HUMANS RARELY SET FOOT INTO THIS RUIN...
...BUT FOR CREATURES OF THE LAND, IT HAS LONG SERVED AS AN IMPORTANT ROUTE TO BREEDING AND WINTERING GROUNDS.
FWOOSH!
AS WITCHES, WE HAVE A RESPONSIBILITY TO THEM FOR CHANGING THEIR WORLD.

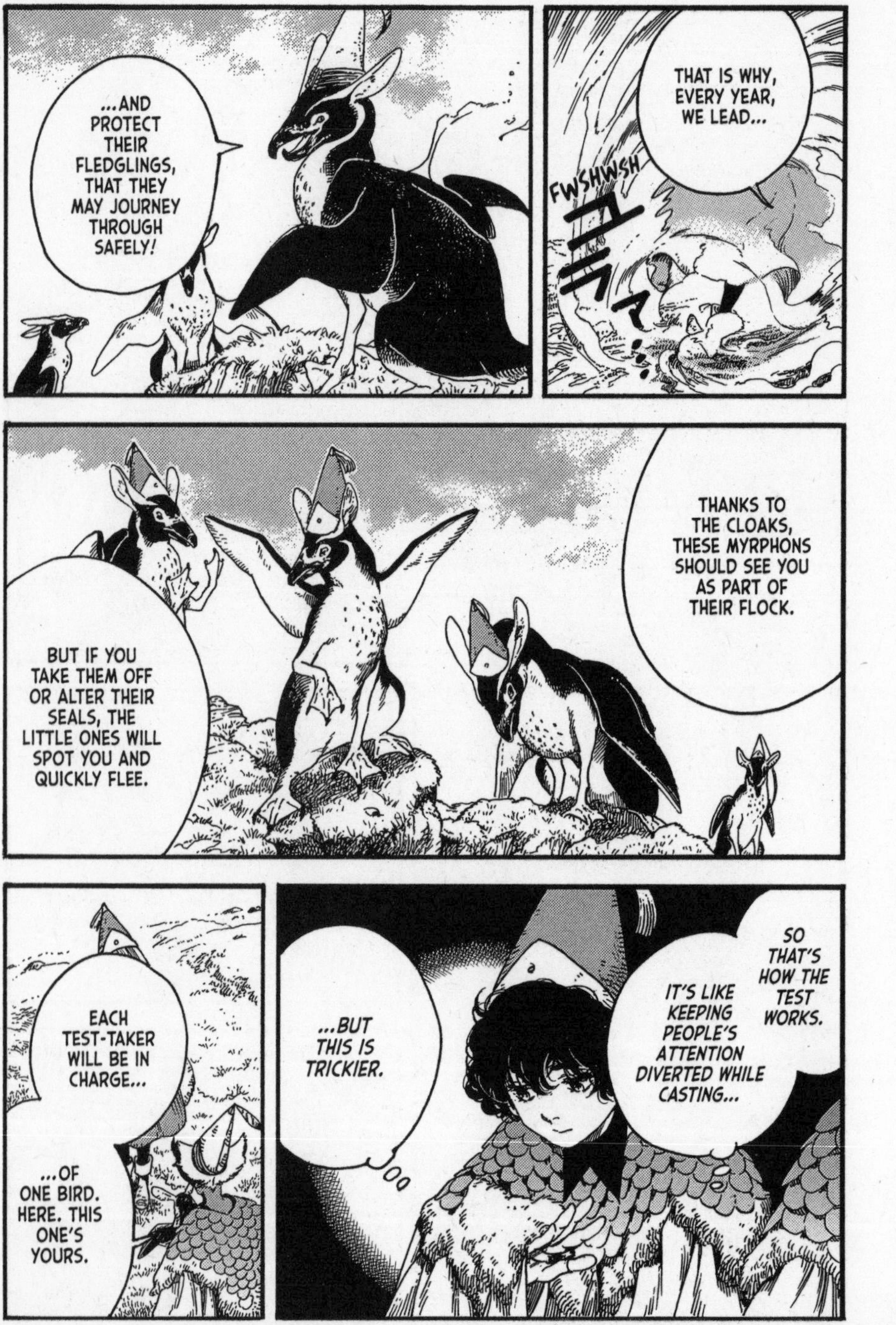
THAT IS WHY, EVERY YEAR, WE LEAD...
FWSHWSH
...AND PROTECT THEIR FLEDGLINGS, THAT THEY MAY JOURNEY THROUGH SAFELY!
THANKS TO THE CLOAKS, THESE MYRPHONS SHOULD SEE YOU AS PART OF THEIR FLOCK.
BUT IF YOU TAKE THEM OFF OR ALTER THEIR SEALS, THE LITTLE ONES WILL SPOT YOU AND QUICKLY FLEE.
SO THAT'S HOW THE TEST WORKS.
IT'S LIKE KEEPING PEOPLE'S ATTENTION DIVERTED WHILE CASTING...
...BUT THIS IS TRICKIER.
EACH TEST-TAKER WILL BE IN CHARGE...
...OF ONE BIRD. HERE. THIS ONE'S YOURS.

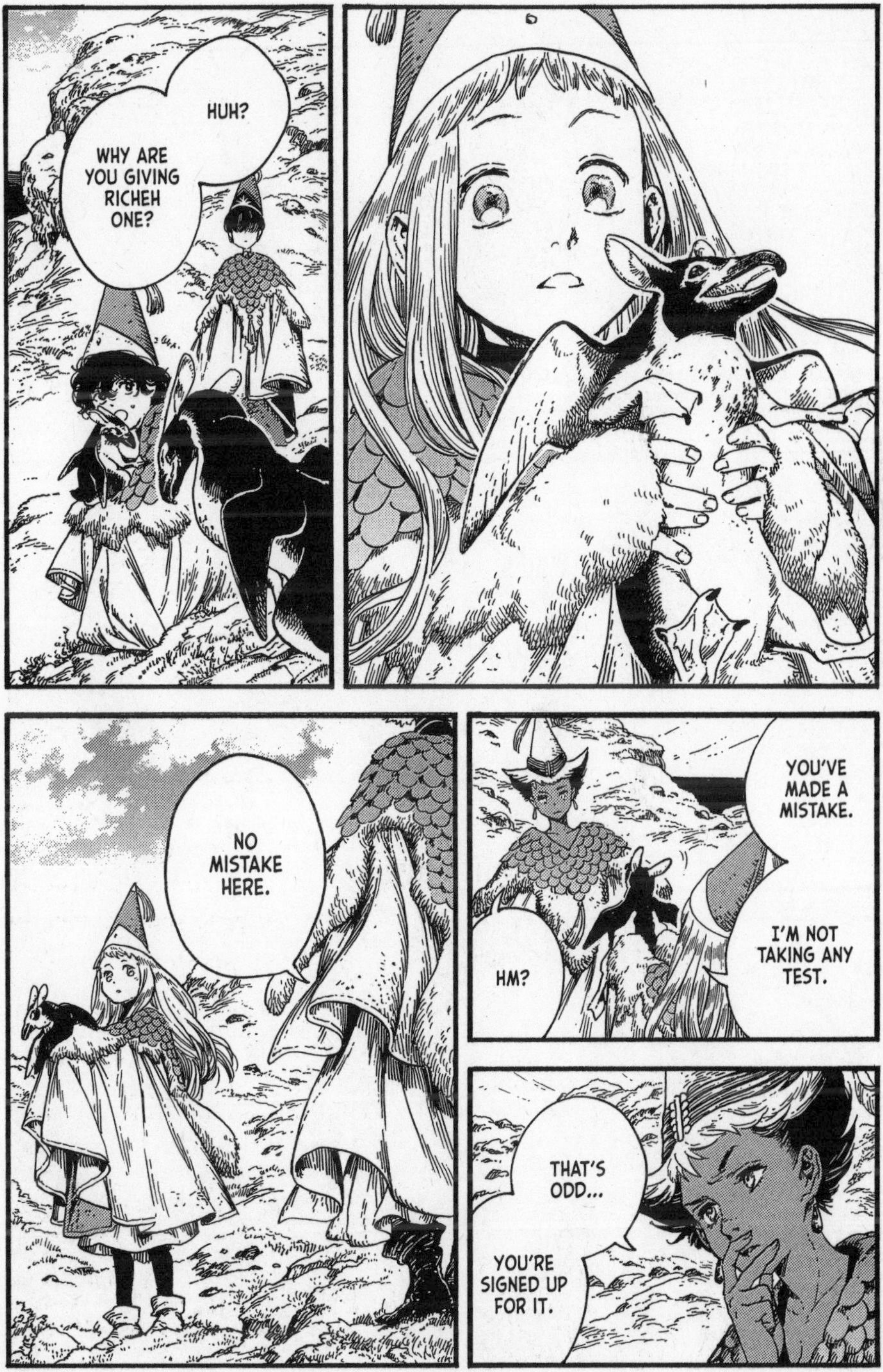
HUH?
WHY ARE YOU GIVING RICHEH ONE?
YOU'VE MADE A MISTAKE.
I'M NOT TAKING ANY TEST.
HM?
THAT'S ODD...
YOU'RE SIGNED UP FOR IT.
NO MISTAKE HERE.

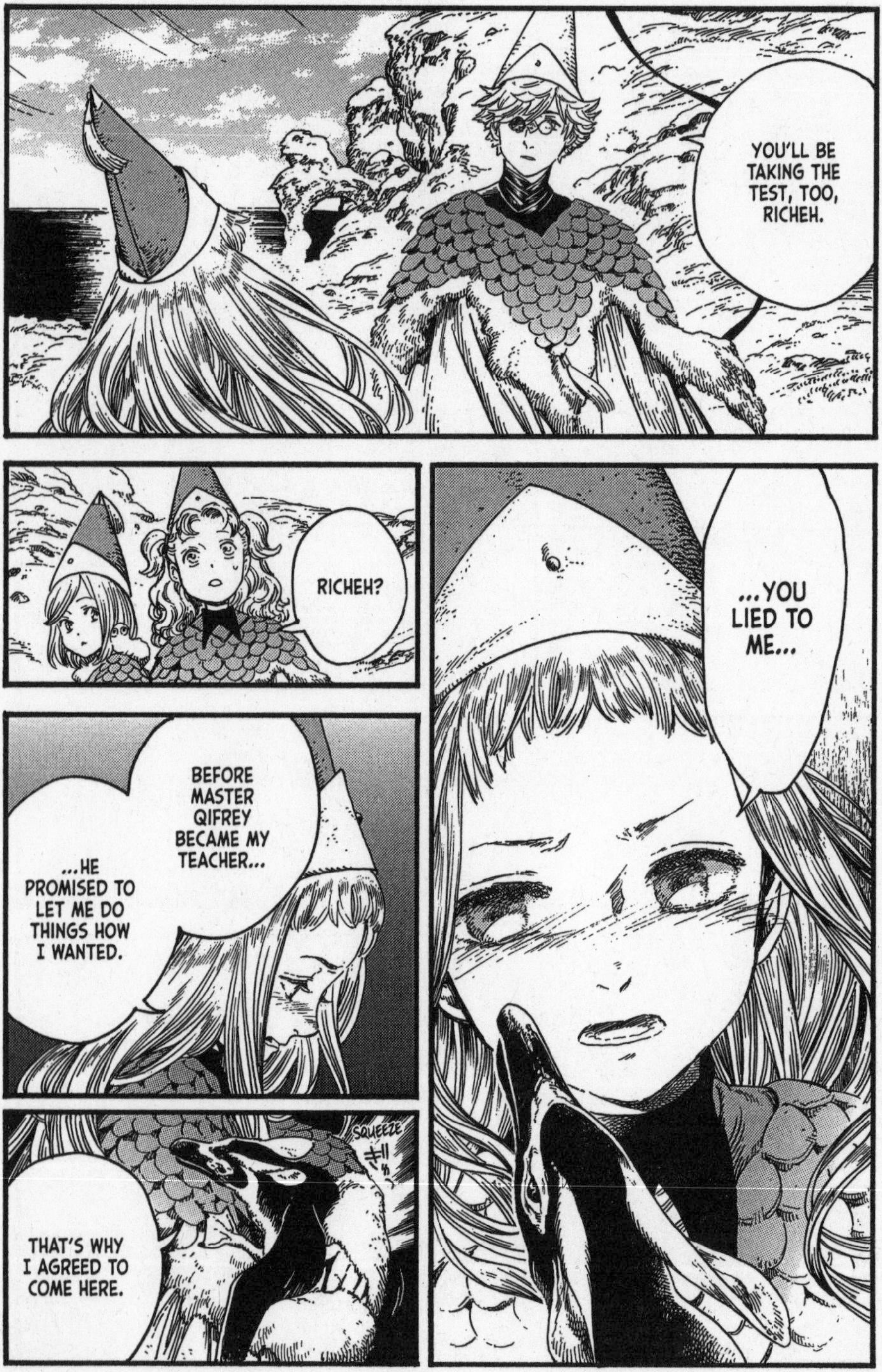
YOU'LL BE TAKING THE TEST, TOO, RICHEH.
...YOU LIED TO ME...
RICHEH?
BEFORE MASTER QIFREY BECAME MY TEACHER...
...HE PROMISED TO LET ME DO THINGS HOW I WANTED.
SQUEEZE
THAT'S WHY I AGREED TO COME HERE.

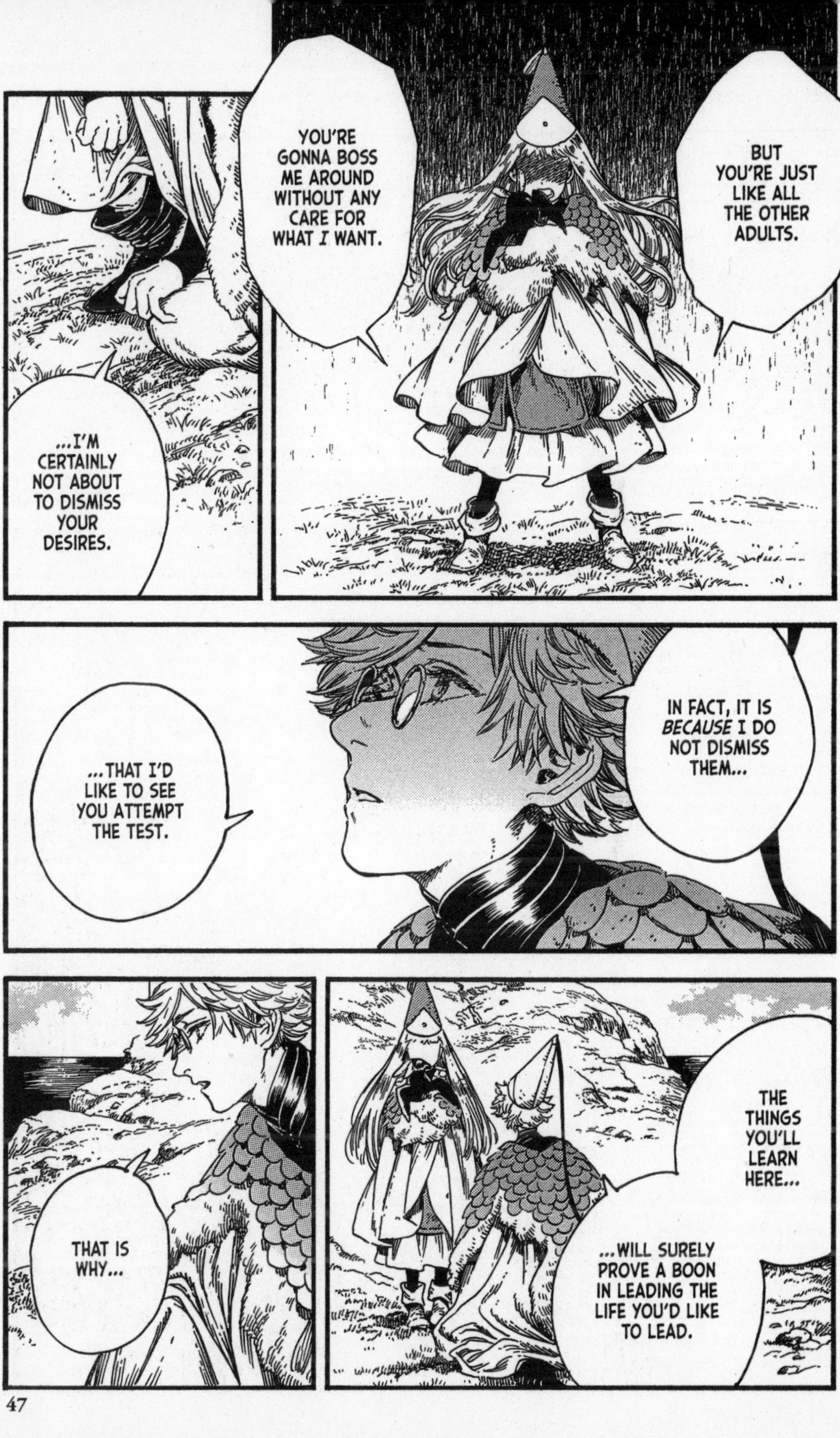
BUT YOU'RE JUST LIKE ALL THE OTHER ADULTS.
YOU'RE GONNA BOSS ME AROUND WITHOUT ANY CARE FOR WHAT *I* WANT.
...I'M CERTAINLY NOT ABOUT TO DISMISS YOUR DESIRES.
IN FACT, IT IS *BECAUSE* I DO NOT DISMISS THEM...
...THAT I'D LIKE TO SEE YOU ATTEMPT THE TEST.
THE THINGS YOU'LL LEARN HERE...
...WILL SURELY PROVE A BOON IN LEADING THE LIFE YOU'D LIKE TO LEAD.
THAT IS WHY...

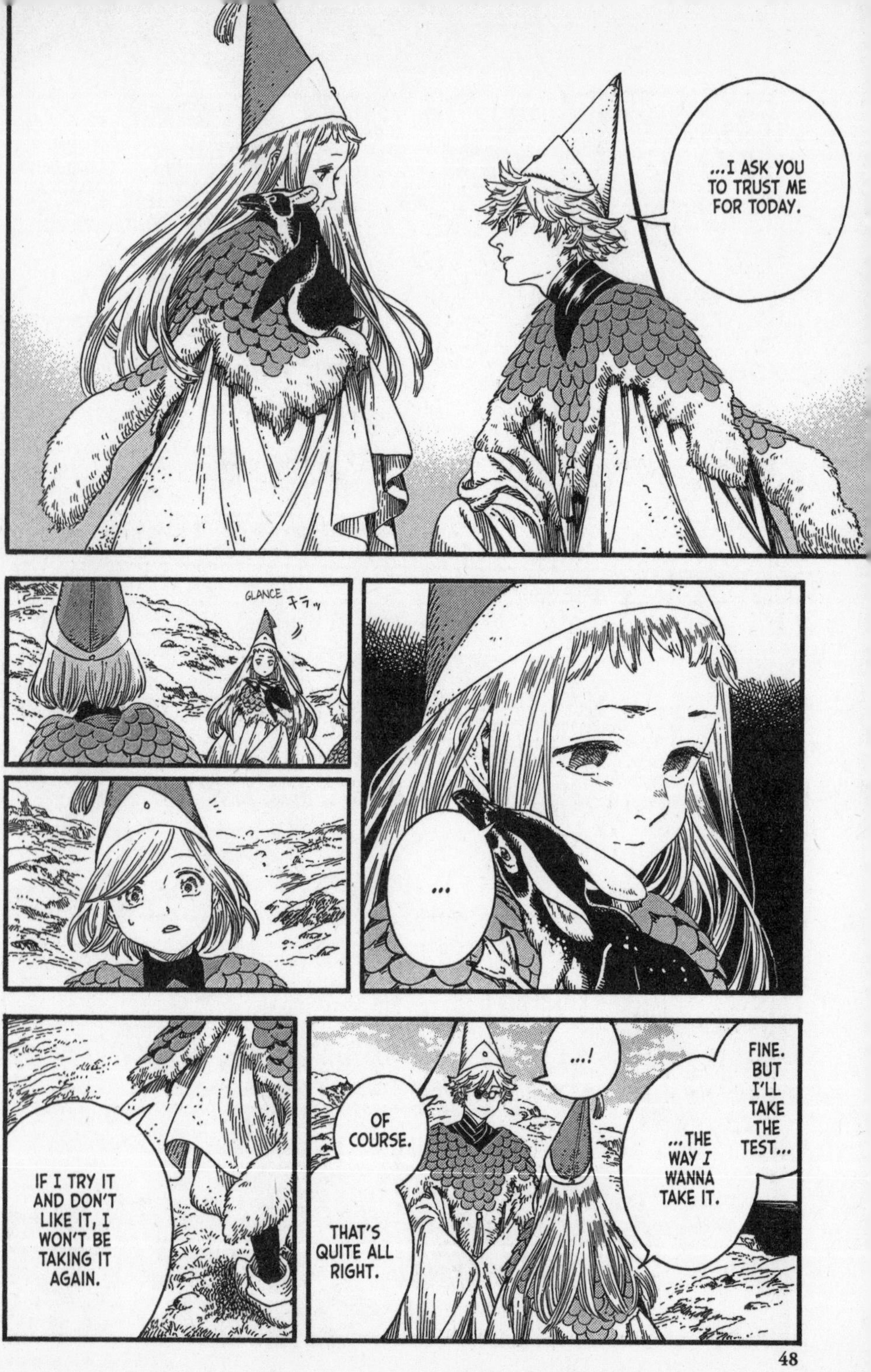
...I ASK YOU TO TRUST ME FOR TODAY.
...
GLANCE
キラッ
FINE. BUT I'LL TAKE THE TEST... ...THE WAY *I* WANNA TAKE IT.
...!
OF COURSE.
THAT'S QUITE ALL RIGHT.
IF I TRY IT AND DON'T LIKE IT, I WON'T BE TAKING IT AGAIN.

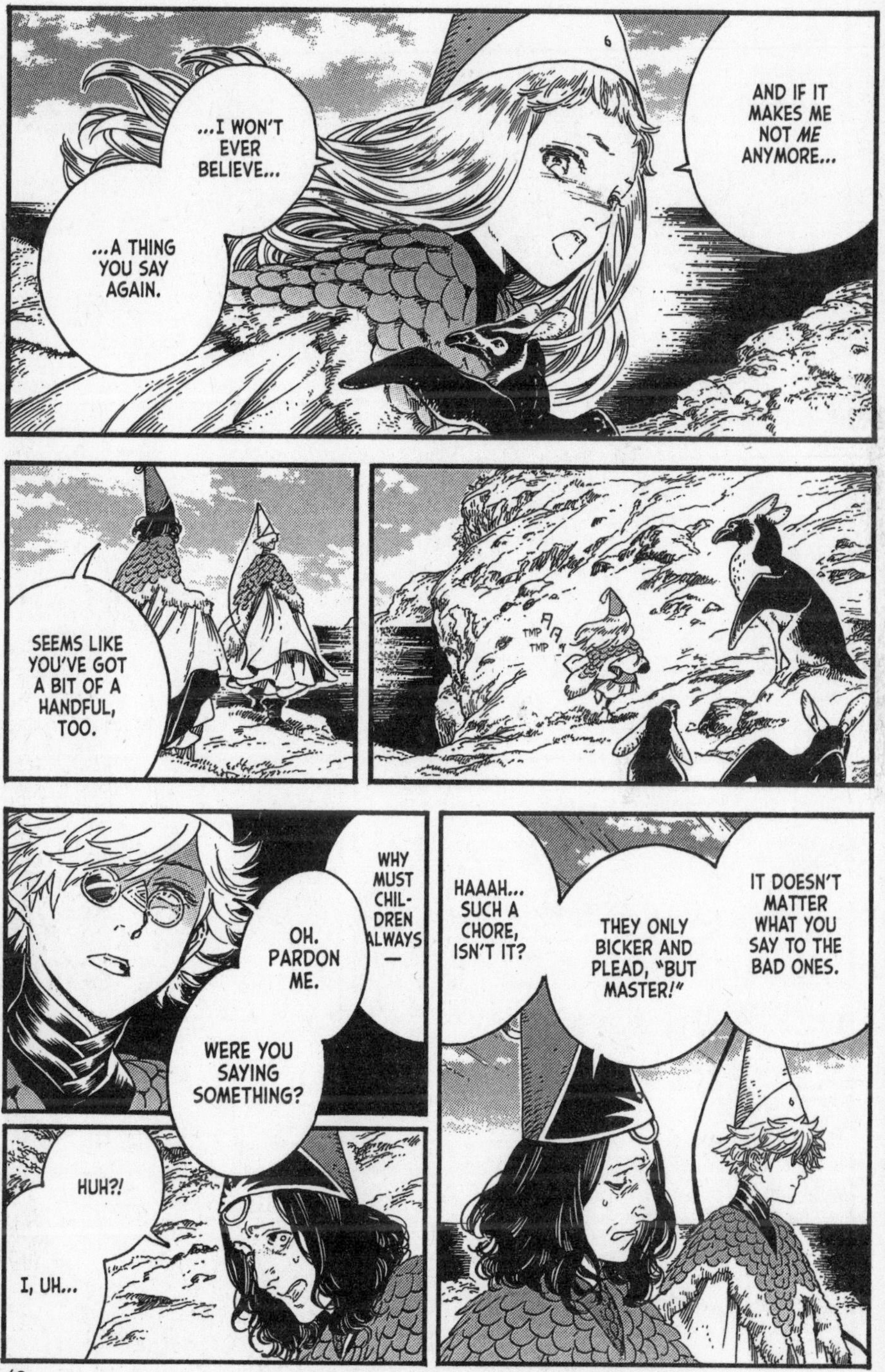
AND IF IT MAKES ME NOT *ME* ANYMORE...
...I WON'T EVER BELIEVE...
...A THING YOU SAY AGAIN.
TMP TMP
SEEMS LIKE YOU'VE GOT A BIT OF A HANDFUL, TOO.
IT DOESN'T MATTER WHAT YOU SAY TO THE BAD ONES.
THEY ONLY BICKER AND PLEAD, "BUT MASTER!"
HAAAH... SUCH A CHORE, ISN'T IT?
WHY MUST CHIL-DREN ALWAYS—
OH. PARDON ME.
WERE YOU SAYING SOMETHING?
HUH?!
I, UH...

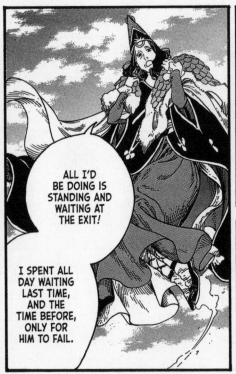

OH, GOODNESS. IT'S THIS LATE ALREADY?
わた FLUSTER
FLUSTER わたた
I NEED TO GET BACK TO THE GREAT HALL!
SURELY YOU JEST?
YOU'LL NOT STAY FOR YOUR OWN APPRENTICE'S TEST?
ALL I'D BE DOING IS STANDING AND WAITING AT THE EXIT!
I SPENT ALL DAY WAITING LAST TIME, AND THE TIME BEFORE, ONLY FOR HIM TO FAIL.
I HAVE WORK TO ATTEND TO. SURELY YOU TWO CAN MANAGE TO LOOK AFTER HIM.
NOW THEN, I'LL LEAVE YOU ALL TO IT.
ぱっ TOSS
FLUMP

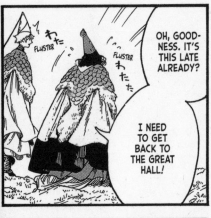

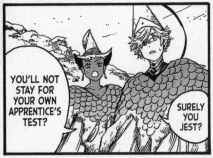

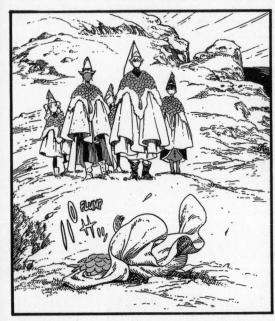

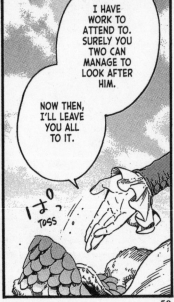

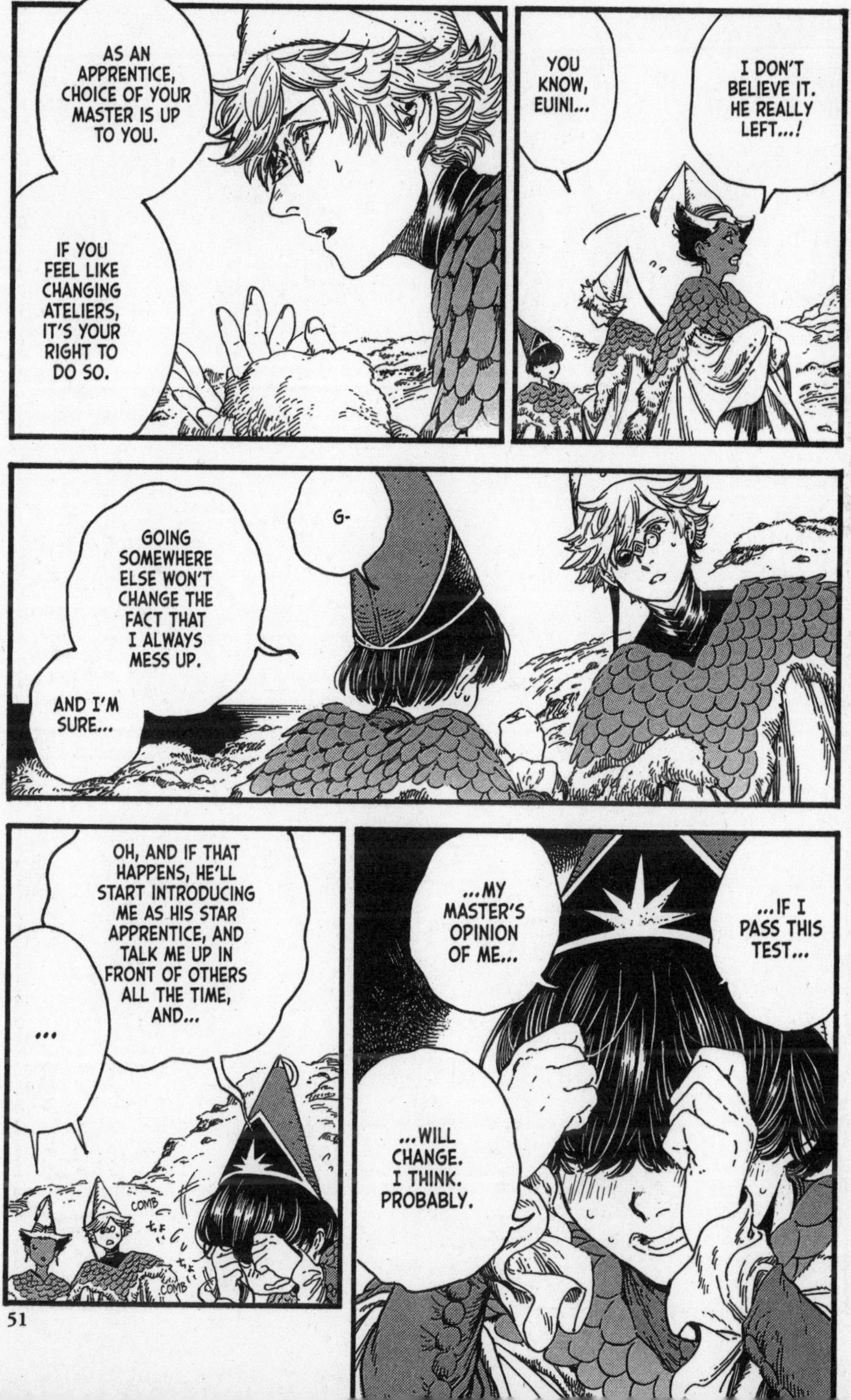
I DON'T BELIEVE IT. HE REALLY LEFT...!
YOU KNOW, EUINI...
AS AN APPRENTICE, CHOICE OF YOUR MASTER IS UP TO YOU.
IF YOU FEEL LIKE CHANGING ATELIERS, IT'S YOUR RIGHT TO DO SO.
G-
GOING SOMEWHERE ELSE WON'T CHANGE THE FACT THAT I ALWAYS MESS UP.
AND I'M SURE...
...IF I PASS THIS TEST...
...MY MASTER'S OPINION OF ME...
...WILL CHANGE. I THINK. PROBABLY.
OH, AND IF THAT HAPPENS, HE'LL START INTRODUCING ME AS HIS STAR APPRENTICE, AND TALK ME UP IN FRONT OF OTHERS ALL THE TIME, AND...
...
COMB
COMB

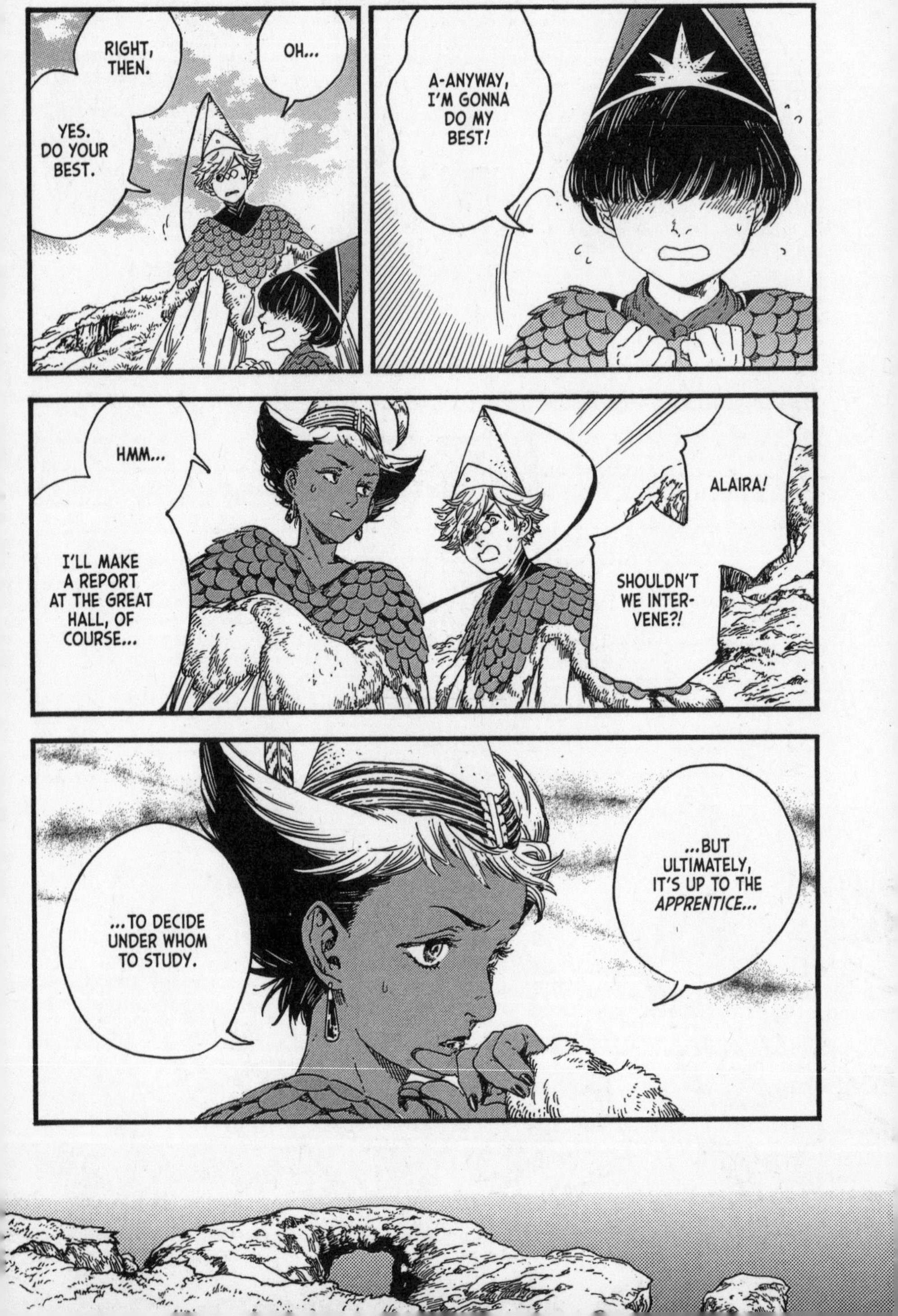
A-ANYWAY, I'M GONNA DO MY BEST!
OH...
RIGHT, THEN.
YES. DO YOUR BEST.
ALAIRA!
SHOULDN'T WE INTER-VENE?!
HMM...
I'LL MAKE A REPORT AT THE GREAT HALL, OF COURSE...
...BUT ULTIMATELY, IT'S UP TO THE *APPRENTICE*...
...TO DECIDE UNDER WHOM TO STUDY.

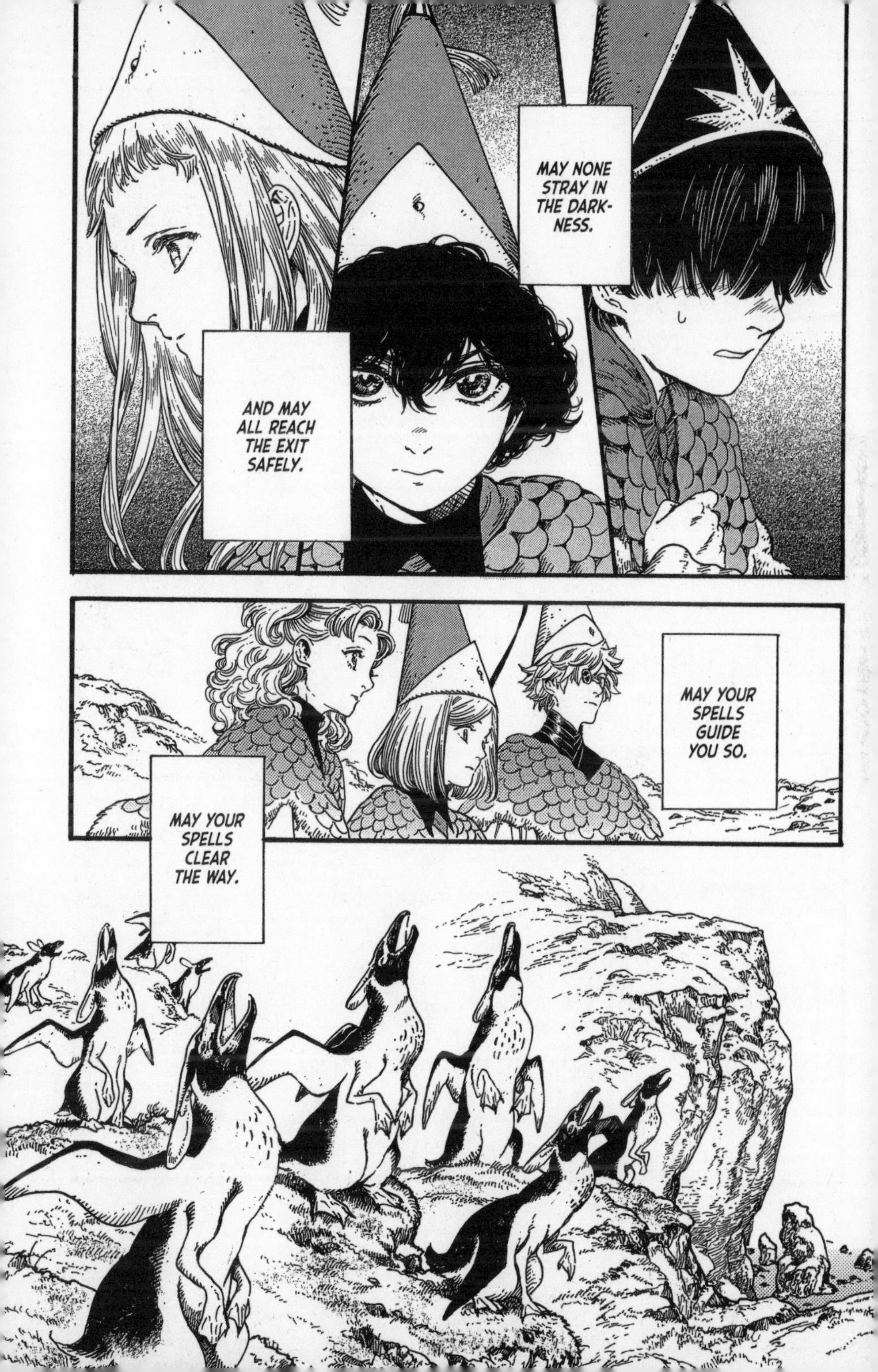
MAY NONE STRAY IN THE DARKNESS.
AND MAY ALL REACH THE EXIT SAFELY.
MAY YOUR SPELLS GUIDE YOU SO.
MAY YOUR SPELLS CLEAR THE WAY.

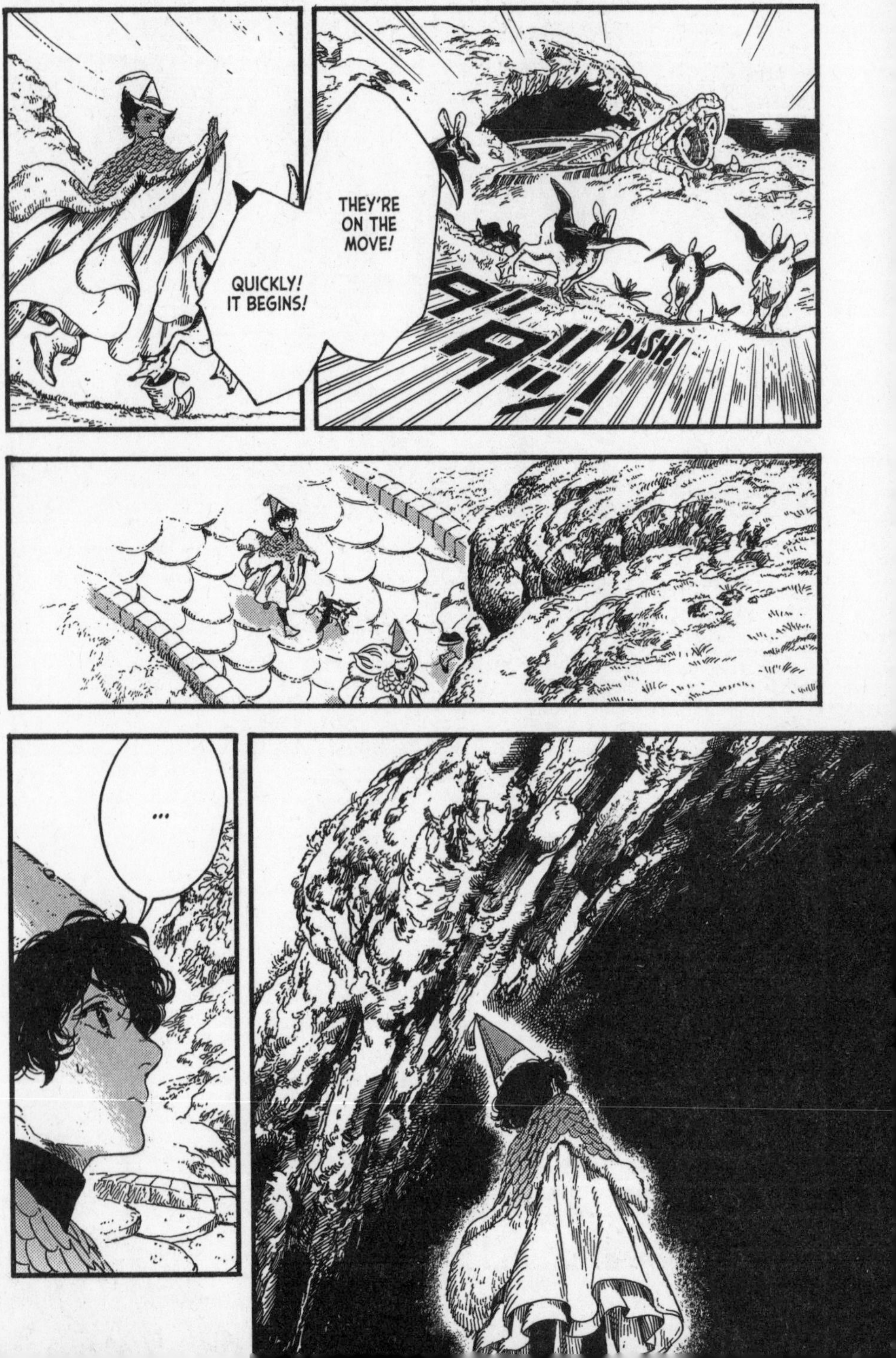
THEY'RE ON THE MOVE!
QUICKLY! IT BEGINS!
DASH!
...

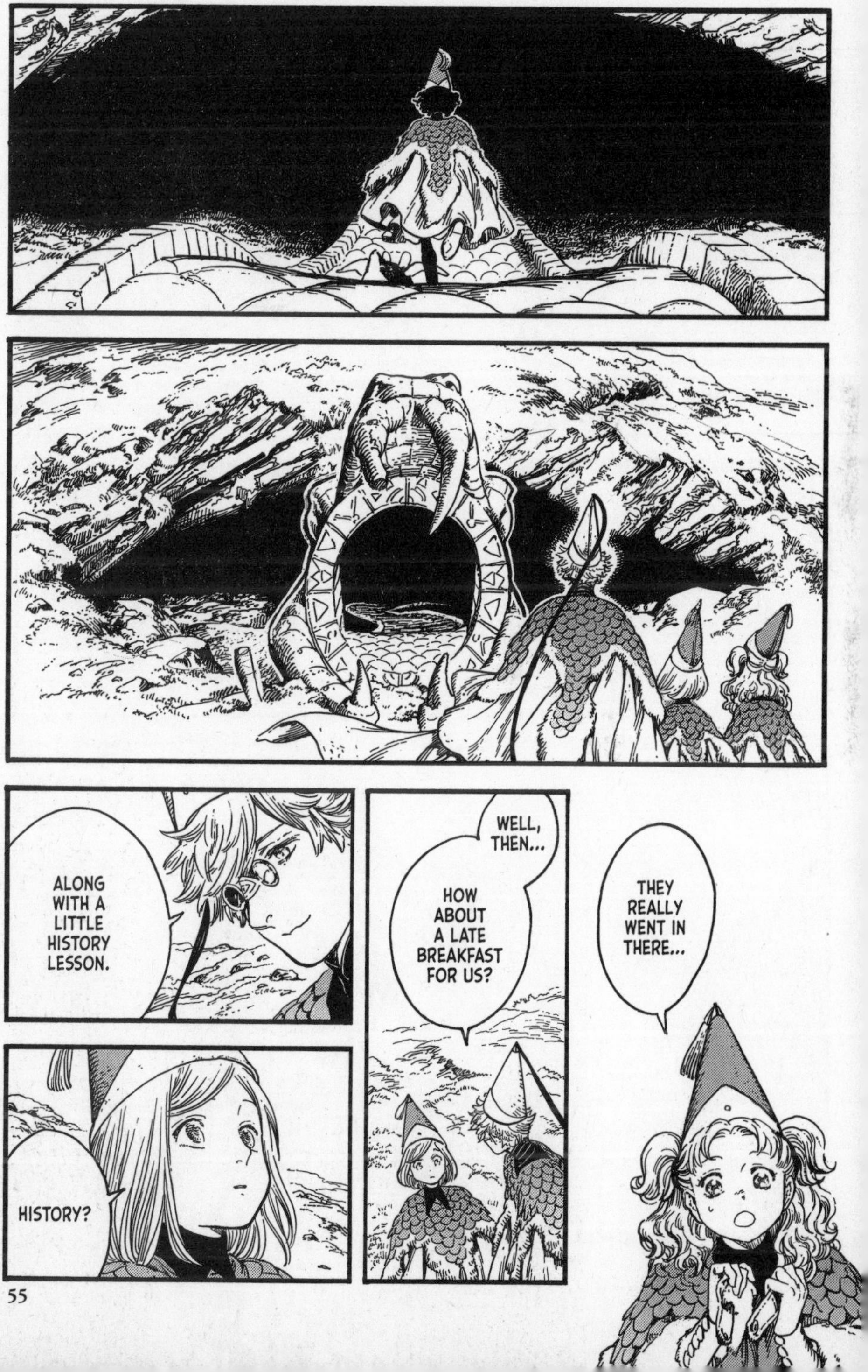
THEY REALLY WENT IN THERE...
WELL, THEN...
HOW ABOUT A LATE BREAKFAST FOR US?
ALONG WITH A LITTLE HISTORY LESSON.
HISTORY?

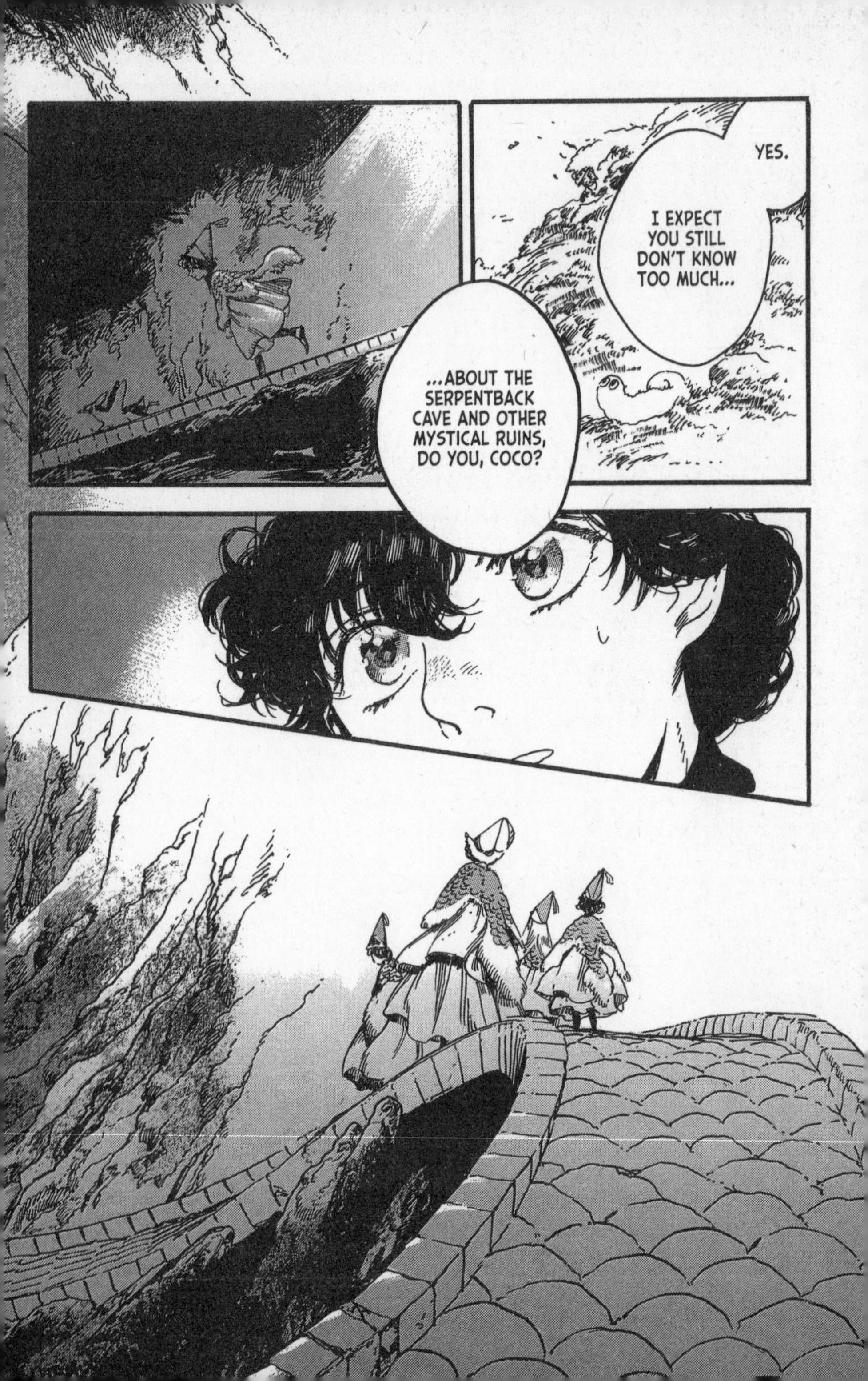
YES.
I EXPECT YOU STILL DON'T KNOW TOO MUCH...
...ABOUT THE SERPENTBACK CAVE AND OTHER MYSTICAL RUINS, DO YOU, COCO?

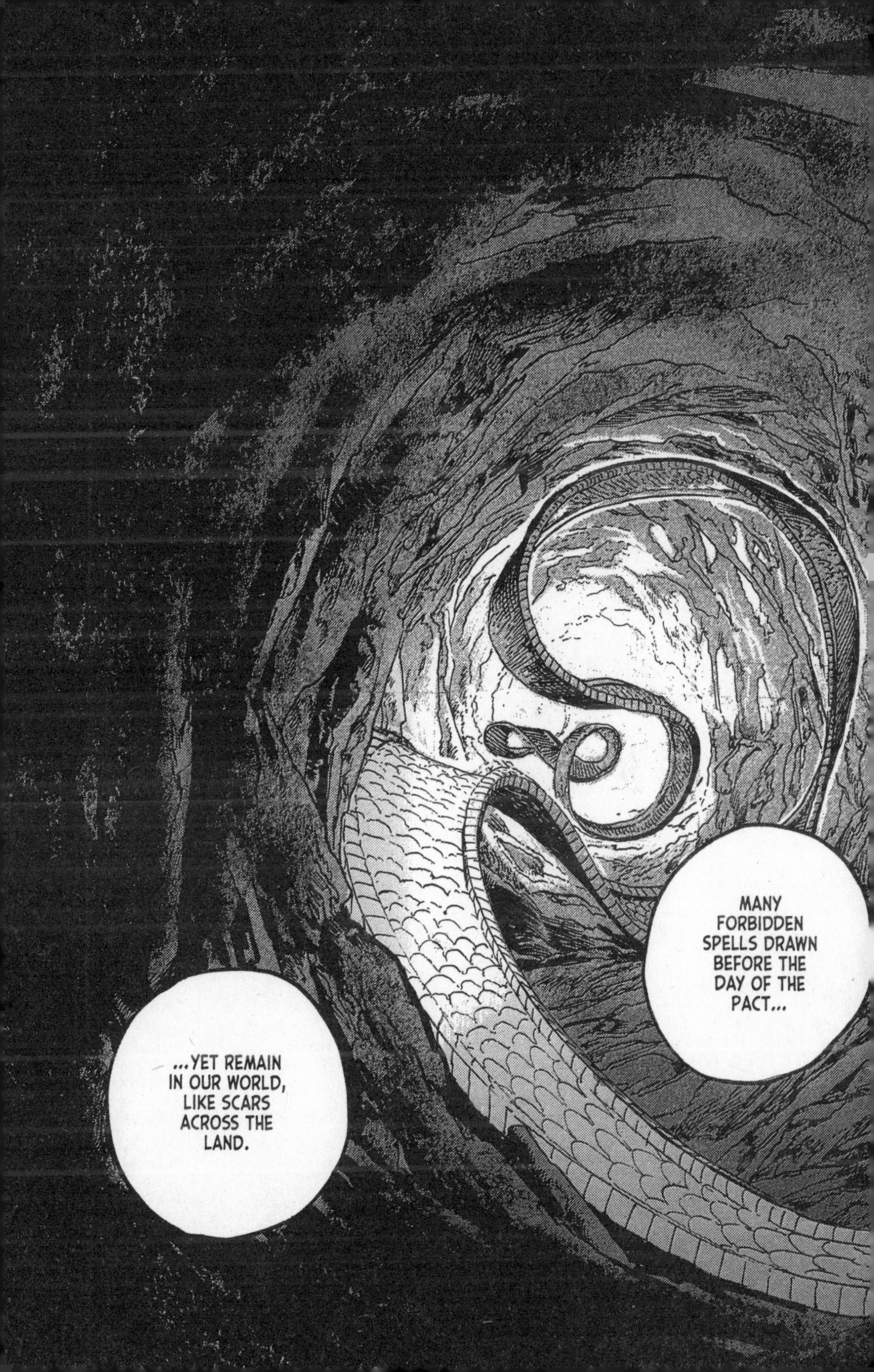
MANY FORBIDDEN SPELLS DRAWN BEFORE THE DAY OF THE PACT...
...YET REMAIN IN OUR WORLD, LIKE SCARS ACROSS THE LAND.

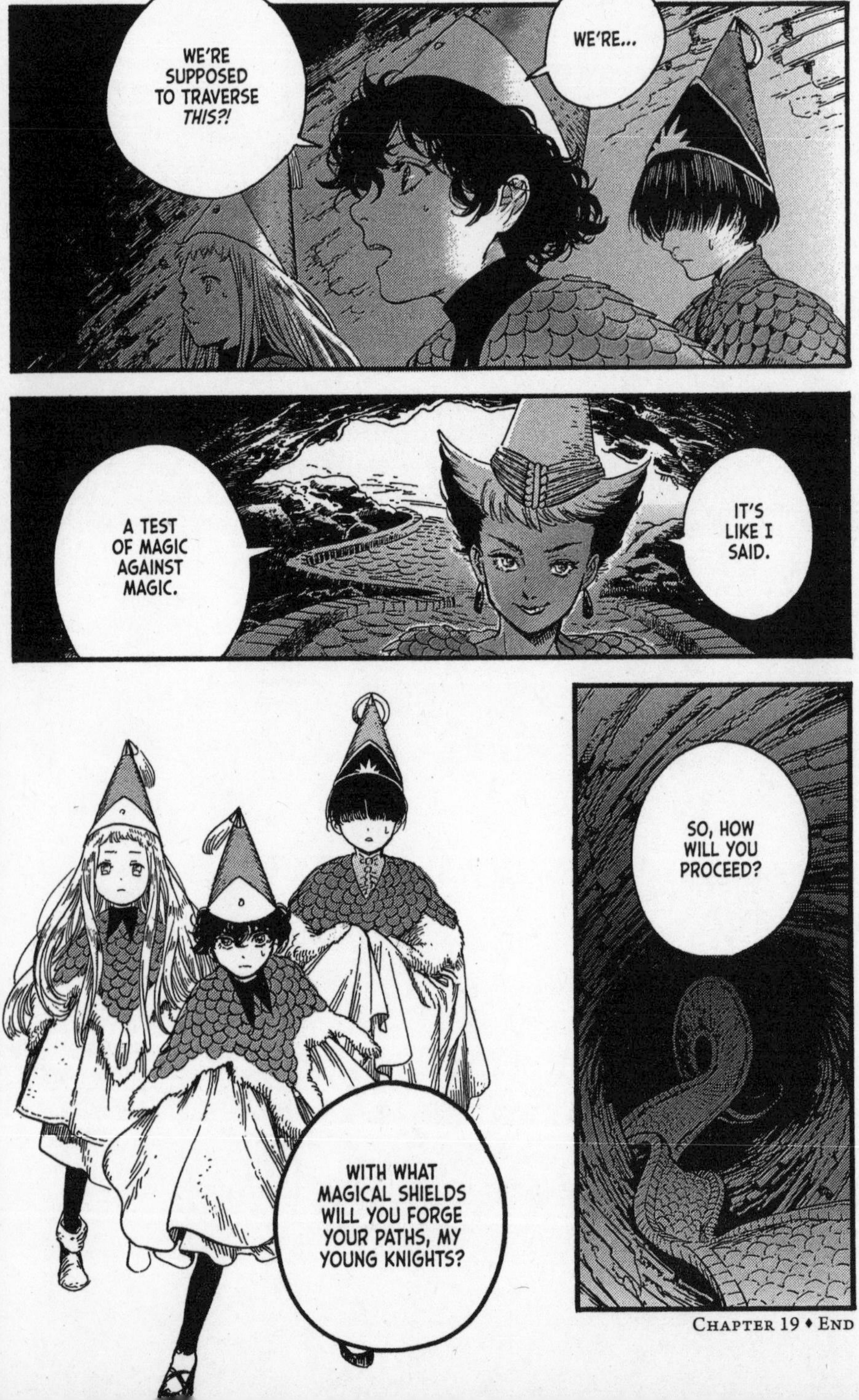
WE'RE...
WE'RE SUPPOSED TO TRAVERSE *THIS?!*
IT'S LIKE I SAID.
A TEST OF MAGIC AGAINST MAGIC.
SO, HOW WILL YOU PROCEED?
WITH WHAT MAGICAL SHIELDS WILL YOU FORGE YOUR PATHS, MY YOUNG KNIGHTS?

CHAPTER 19 ♦ END

Witch Hat Atelier

Chapter 20

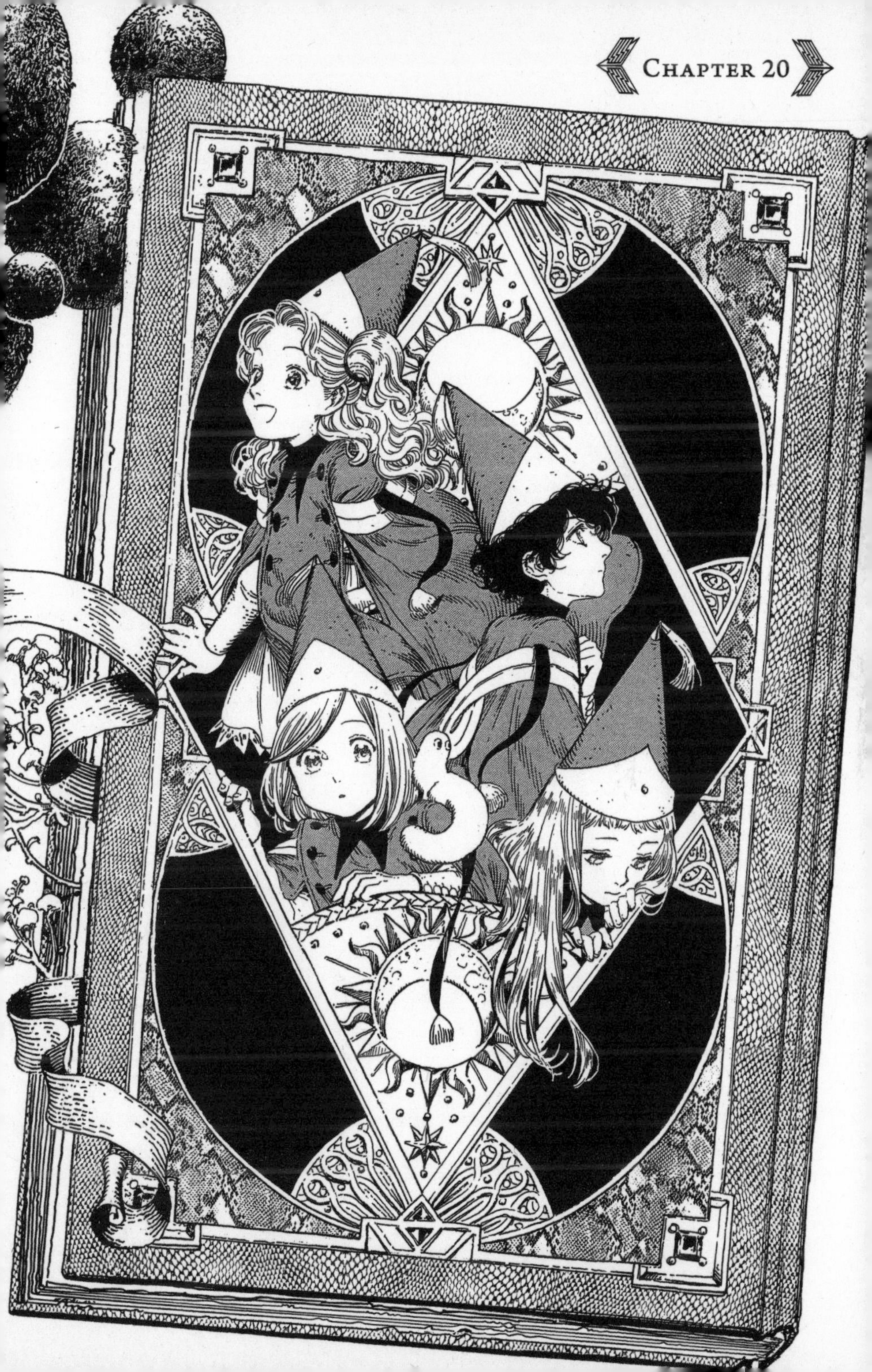

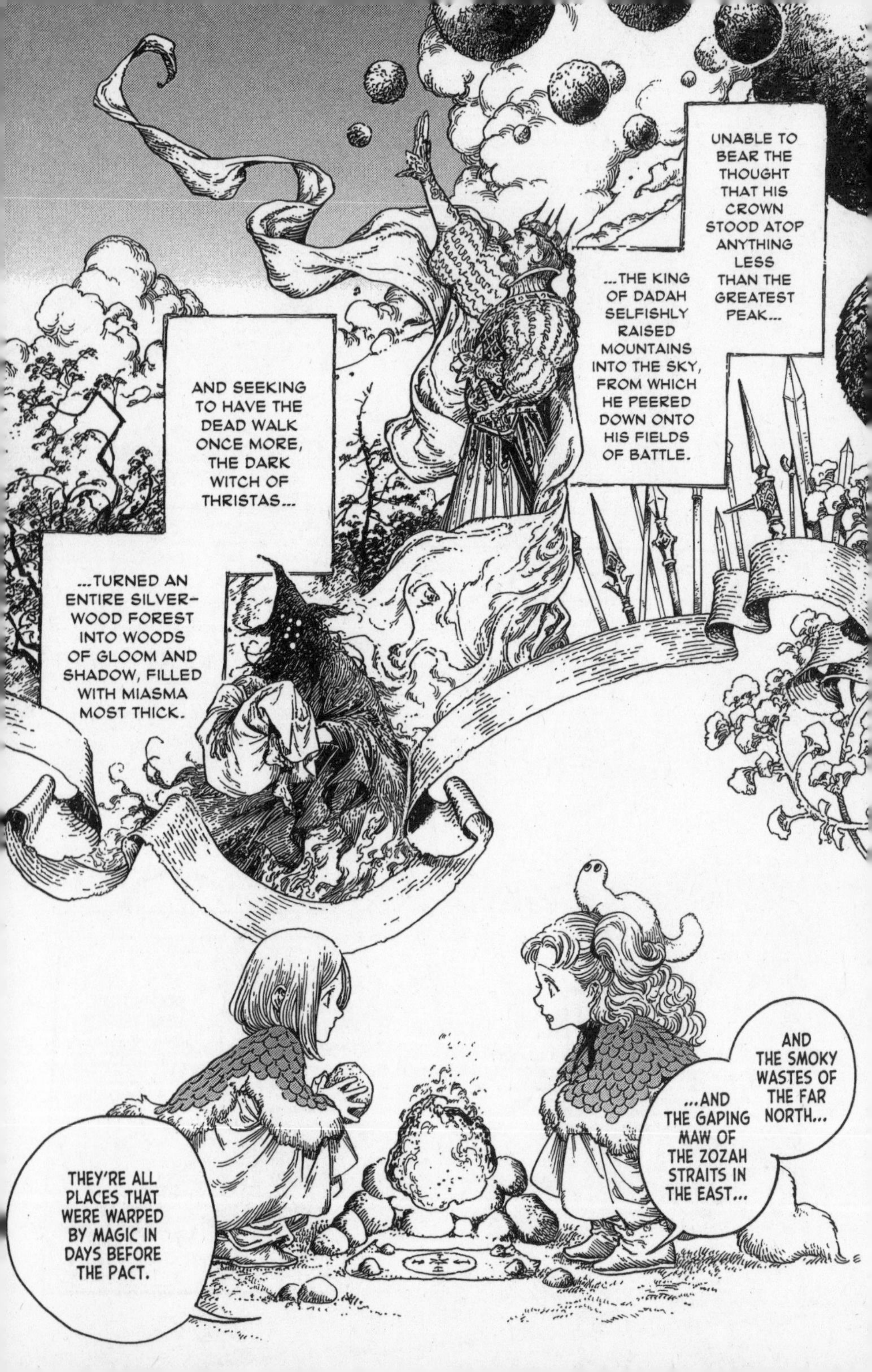
UNABLE TO BEAR THE THOUGHT THAT HIS CROWN STOOD ATOP ANYTHING LESS THAN THE GREATEST PEAK...
...THE KING OF DADAH SELFISHLY RAISED MOUNTAINS INTO THE SKY, FROM WHICH HE PEERED DOWN ONTO HIS FIELDS OF BATTLE.
AND SEEKING TO HAVE THE DEAD WALK ONCE MORE, THE DARK WITCH OF THRISTAS...
...TURNED AN ENTIRE SILVER-WOOD FOREST INTO WOODS OF GLOOM AND SHADOW, FILLED WITH MIASMA MOST THICK.
AND THE SMOKY WASTES OF THE FAR NORTH...
...AND THE GAPING MAW OF THE ZOZAH STRAITS IN THE EAST...
THEY'RE ALL PLACES THAT WERE WARPED BY MAGIC IN DAYS BEFORE THE PACT.

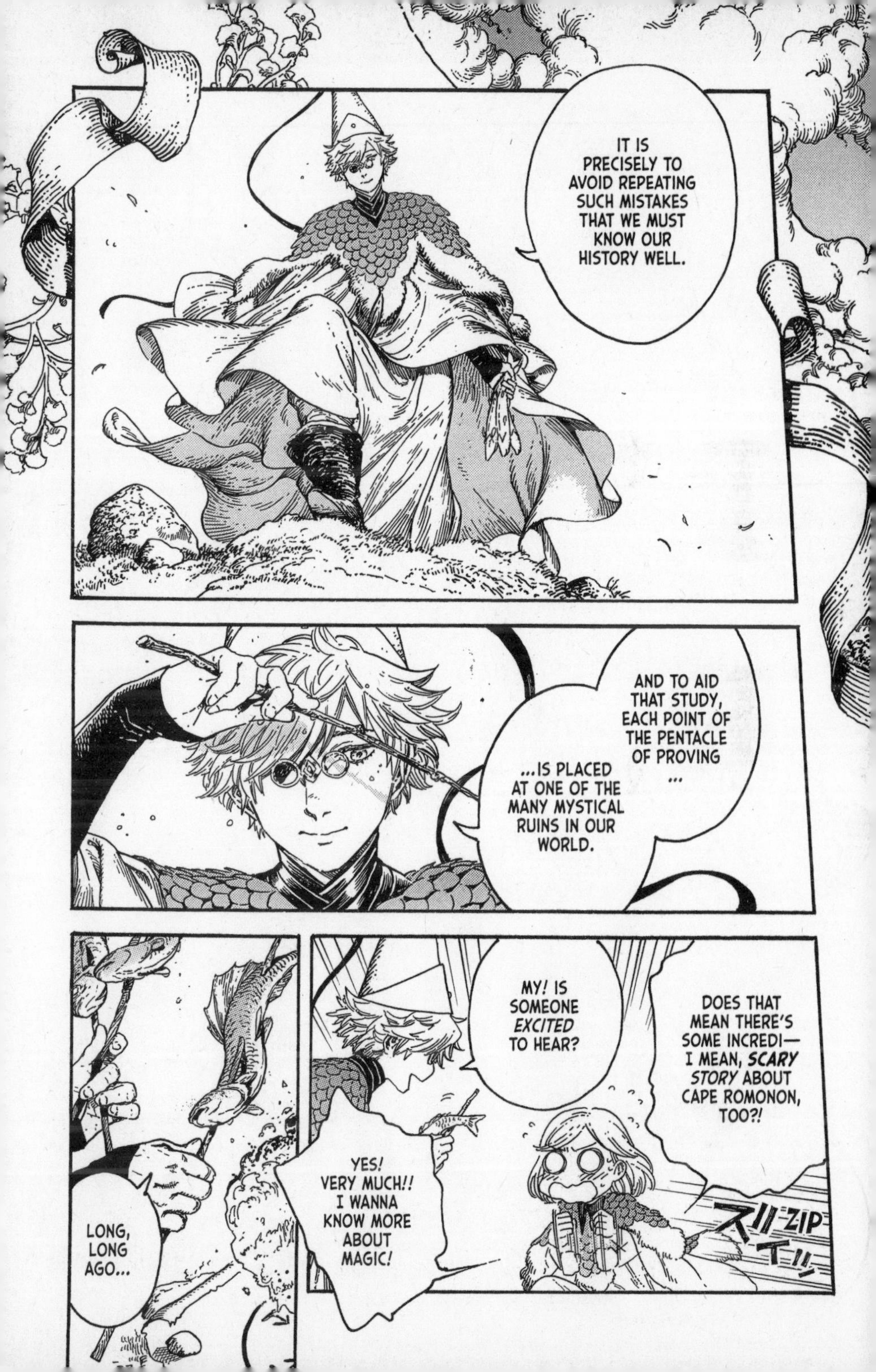
IT IS PRECISELY TO AVOID REPEATING SUCH MISTAKES THAT WE MUST KNOW OUR HISTORY WELL.
AND TO AID THAT STUDY, EACH POINT OF THE PENTACLE OF PROVING ...
...IS PLACED AT ONE OF THE MANY MYSTICAL RUINS IN OUR WORLD.
DOES THAT MEAN THERE'S SOME INCREDI— I MEAN, *SCARY STORY* ABOUT CAPE ROMONON, TOO?!
スーイッ ZIP
MY! IS SOMEONE *EXCITED* TO HEAR?
YES! VERY MUCH!! I WANNA KNOW MORE ABOUT MAGIC!
LONG, LONG AGO...

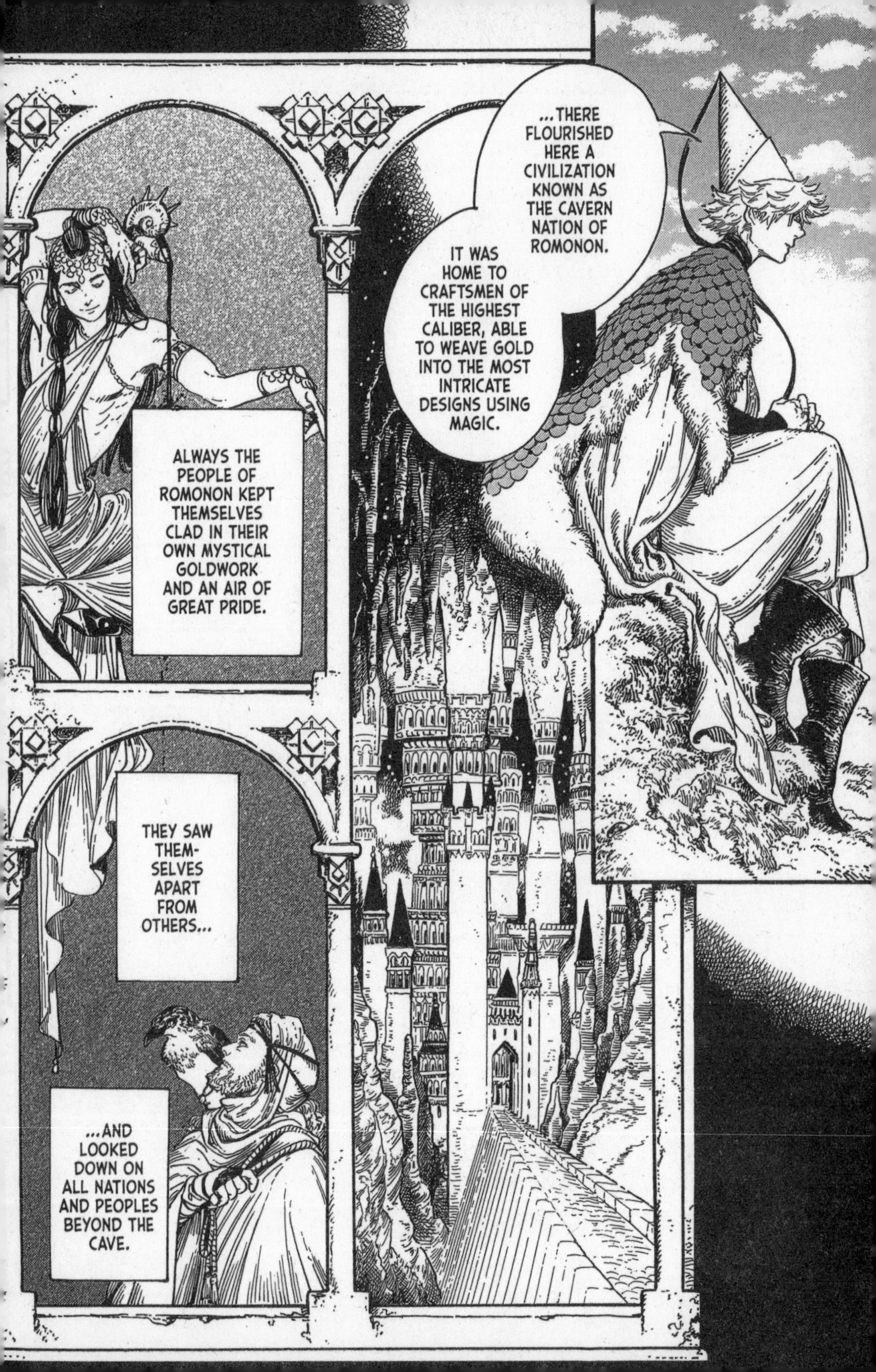
...THERE FLOURISHED HERE A CIVILIZATION KNOWN AS THE CAVERN NATION OF ROMONON.
IT WAS HOME TO CRAFTSMEN OF THE HIGHEST CALIBER, ABLE TO WEAVE GOLD INTO THE MOST INTRICATE DESIGNS USING MAGIC.
ALWAYS THE PEOPLE OF ROMONON KEPT THEMSELVES CLAD IN THEIR OWN MYSTICAL GOLDWORK AND AN AIR OF GREAT PRIDE.
THEY SAW THEM-SELVES APART FROM OTHERS...
...AND LOOKED DOWN ON ALL NATIONS AND PEOPLES BEYOND THE CAVE.

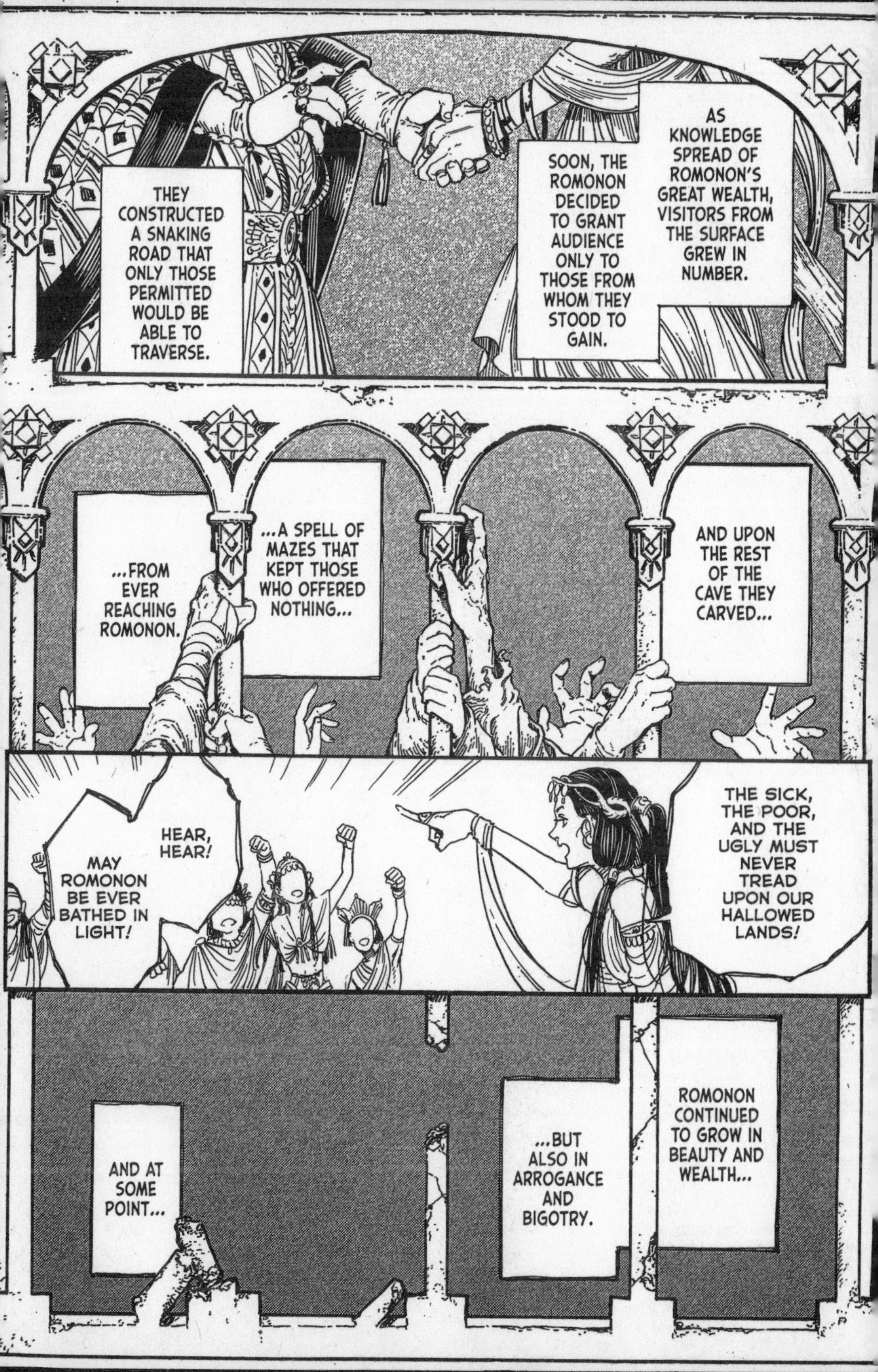
AS KNOWLEDGE SPREAD OF ROMONON'S GREAT WEALTH, VISITORS FROM THE SURFACE GREW IN NUMBER.
SOON, THE ROMONON DECIDED TO GRANT AUDIENCE ONLY TO THOSE FROM WHOM THEY STOOD TO GAIN.
THEY CONSTRUCTED A SNAKING ROAD THAT ONLY THOSE PERMITTED WOULD BE ABLE TO TRAVERSE.
AND UPON THE REST OF THE CAVE THEY CARVED...
...A SPELL OF MAZES THAT KEPT THOSE WHO OFFERED NOTHING...
...FROM EVER REACHING ROMONON.
THE SICK, THE POOR, AND THE UGLY MUST NEVER TREAD UPON OUR HALLOWED LANDS!
HEAR, HEAR!
MAY ROMONON BE EVER BATHED IN LIGHT!
ROMONON CONTINUED TO GROW IN BEAUTY AND WEALTH...
...BUT ALSO IN ARROGANCE AND BIGOTRY.
AND AT SOME POINT...

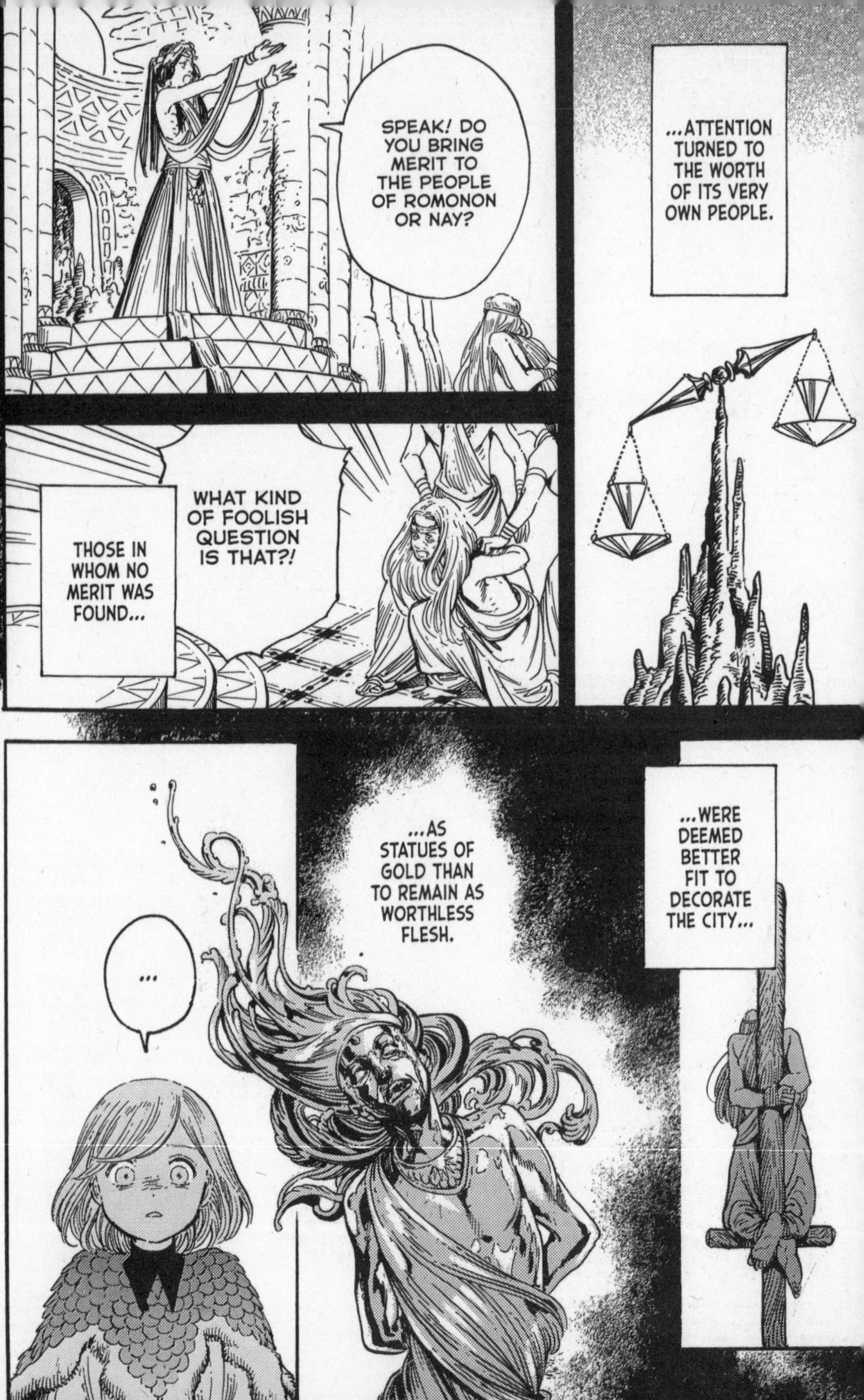
...ATTENTION TURNED TO THE WORTH OF ITS VERY OWN PEOPLE.
SPEAK! DO YOU BRING MERIT TO THE PEOPLE OF ROMONON OR NAY?
WHAT KIND OF FOOLISH QUESTION IS THAT?!
THOSE IN WHOM NO MERIT WAS FOUND...
...WERE DEEMED BETTER FIT TO DECORATE THE CITY...
...AS STATUES OF GOLD THAN TO REMAIN AS WORTHLESS FLESH.
...

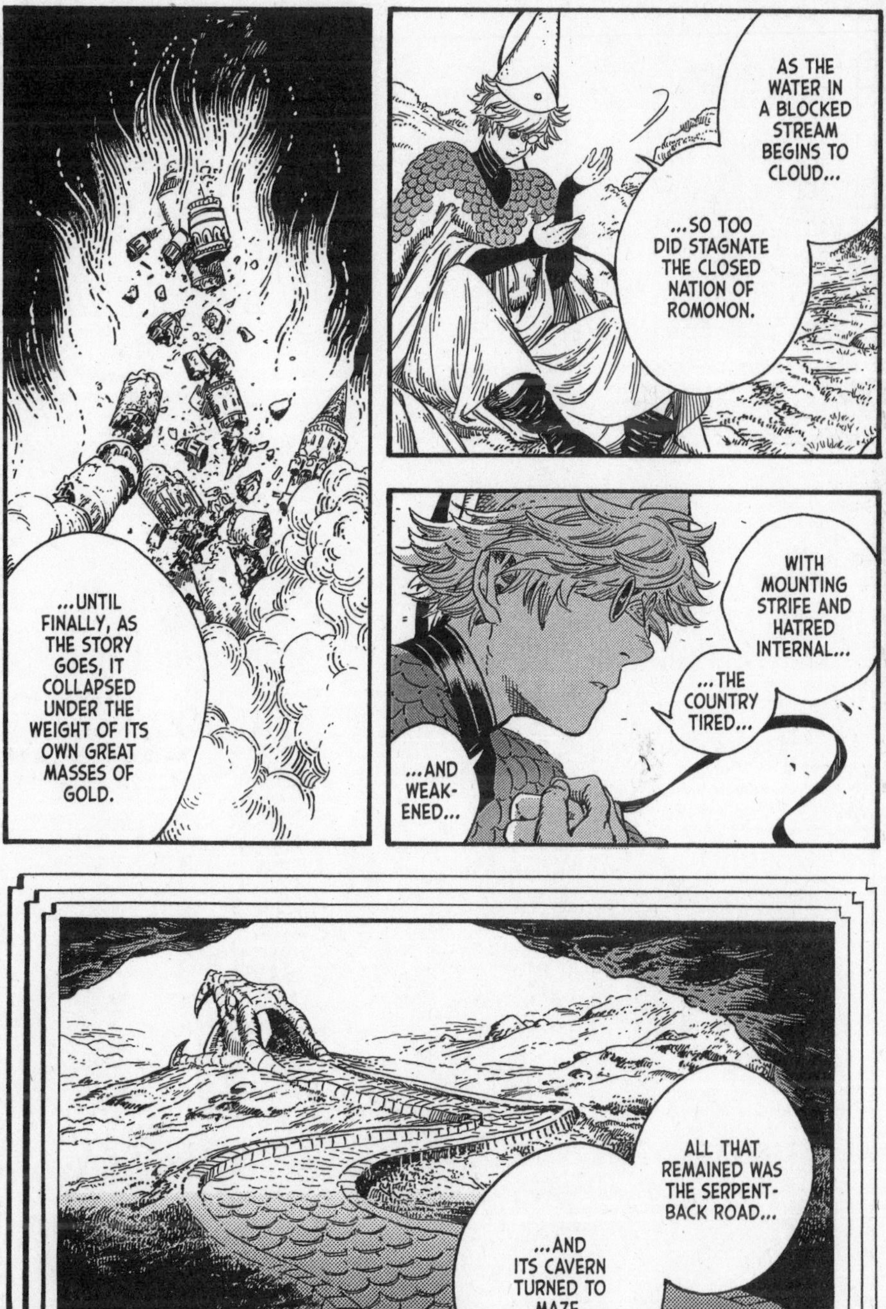
AS THE WATER IN A BLOCKED STREAM BEGINS TO CLOUD...
...SO TOO DID STAGNATE THE CLOSED NATION OF ROMONON.
WITH MOUNTING STRIFE AND HATRED INTERNAL...
...THE COUNTRY TIRED...
...AND WEAK-ENED...
...UNTIL FINALLY, AS THE STORY GOES, IT COLLAPSED UNDER THE WEIGHT OF ITS OWN GREAT MASSES OF GOLD.
ALL THAT REMAINED WAS THE SERPENT-BACK ROAD...
...AND ITS CAVERN TURNED TO MAZE.

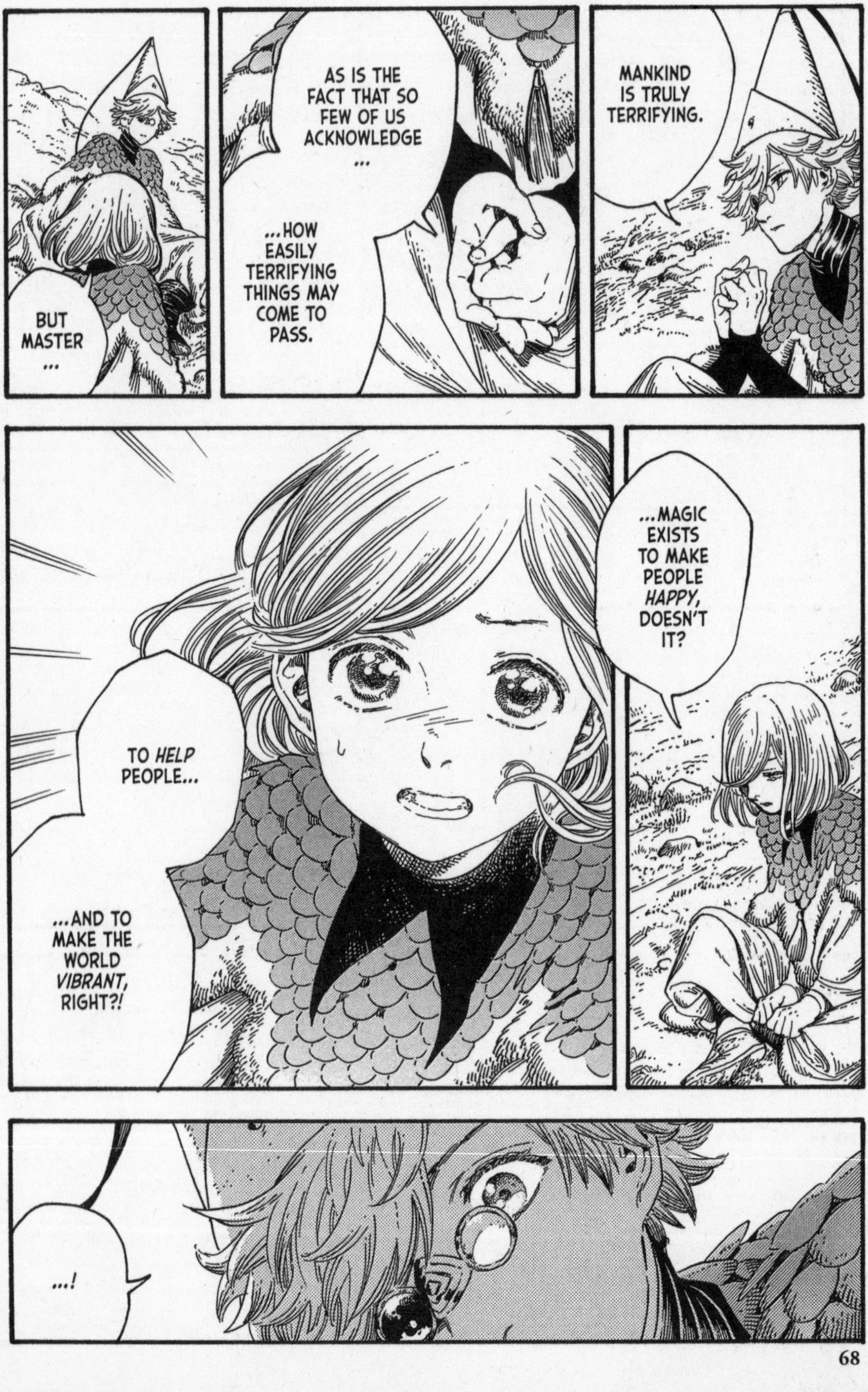
MANKIND IS TRULY TERRIFYING.
AS IS THE FACT THAT SO FEW OF US ACKNOWLEDGE ...
...HOW EASILY TERRIFYING THINGS MAY COME TO PASS.
BUT MASTER ...
...MAGIC EXISTS TO MAKE PEOPLE *HAPPY*, DOESN'T IT?
TO *HELP* PEOPLE...
...AND TO MAKE THE WORLD *VIBRANT*, RIGHT?!
...!

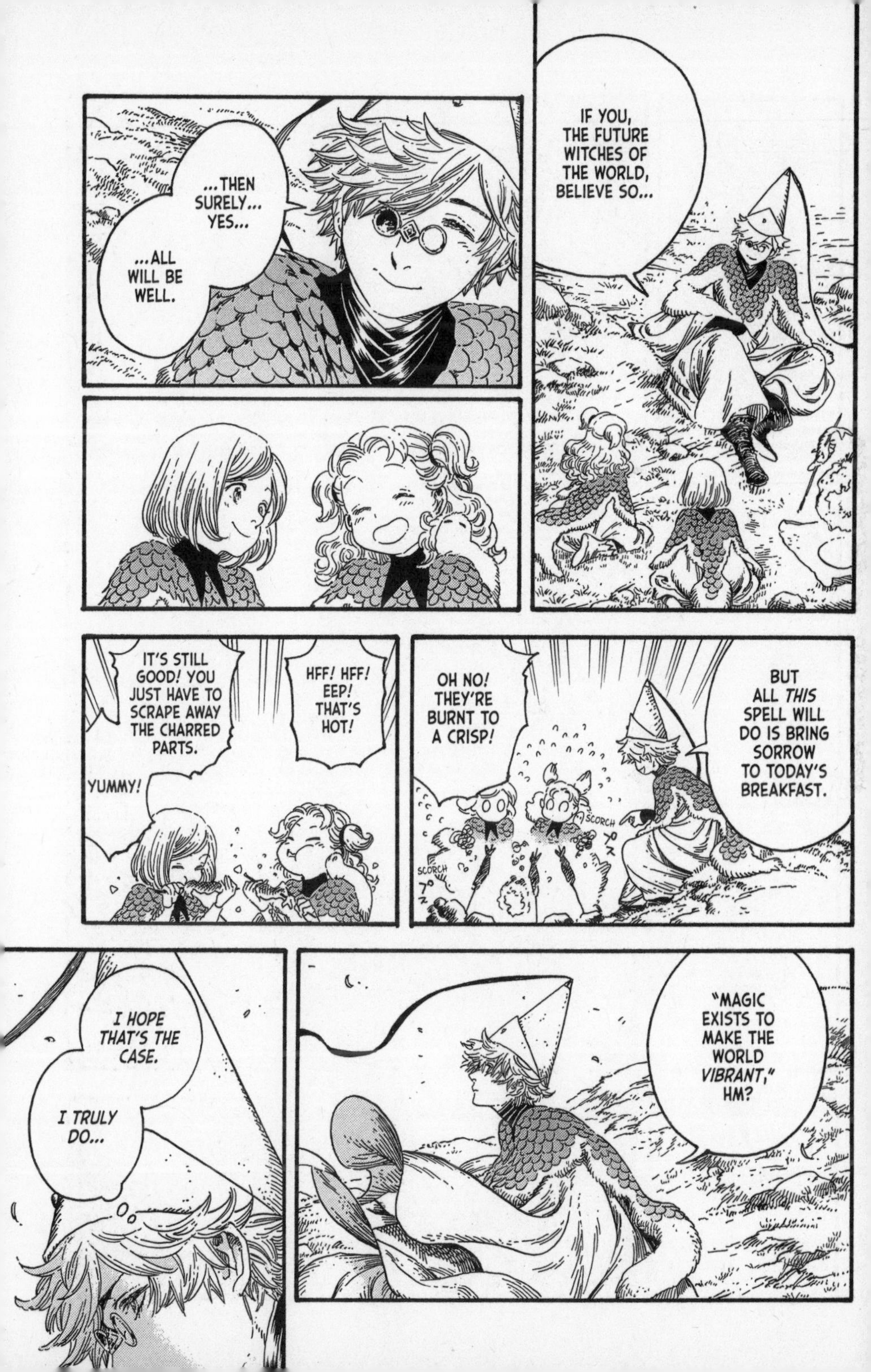
IF YOU, THE FUTURE WITCHES OF THE WORLD, BELIEVE SO...
...THEN SURELY... YES...
...ALL WILL BE WELL.
BUT ALL *THIS* SPELL WILL DO IS BRING SORROW TO TODAY'S BREAKFAST.
OH NO! THEY'RE BURNT TO A CRISP!
SCORCH
SCORCH
HFF! HFF! EEP! THAT'S HOT!
IT'S STILL GOOD! YOU JUST HAVE TO SCRAPE AWAY THE CHARRED PARTS.
YUMMY!
"MAGIC EXISTS TO MAKE THE WORLD *VIBRANT*," HM?
I HOPE THAT'S THE CASE.
I TRULY DO...

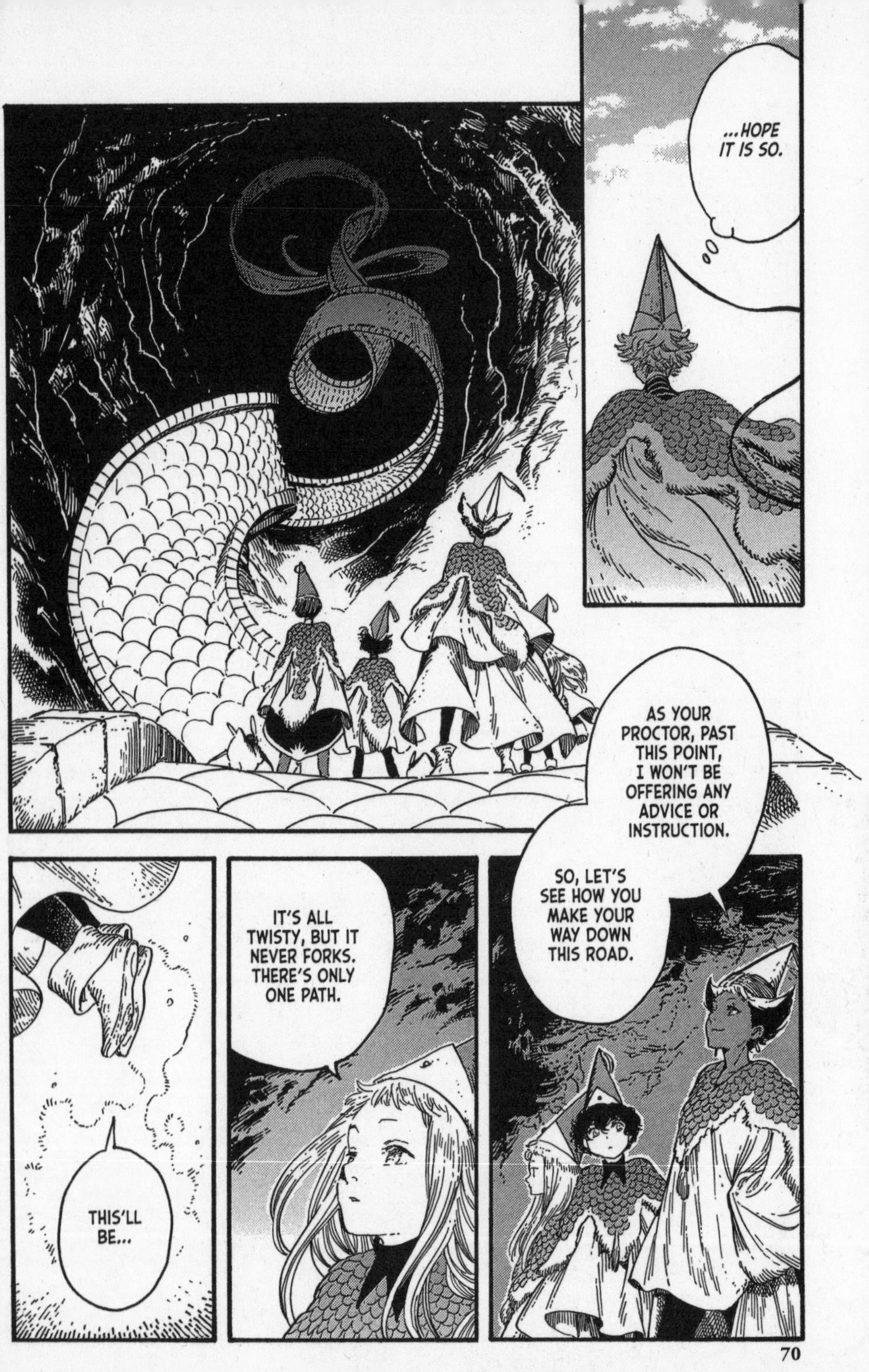
...HOPE IT IS SO.
AS YOUR PROCTOR, PAST THIS POINT, I WON'T BE OFFERING ANY ADVICE OR INSTRUCTION.
SO, LET'S SEE HOW YOU MAKE YOUR WAY DOWN THIS ROAD.
IT'S ALL TWISTY, BUT IT NEVER FORKS. THERE'S ONLY ONE PATH.
THIS'LL BE...

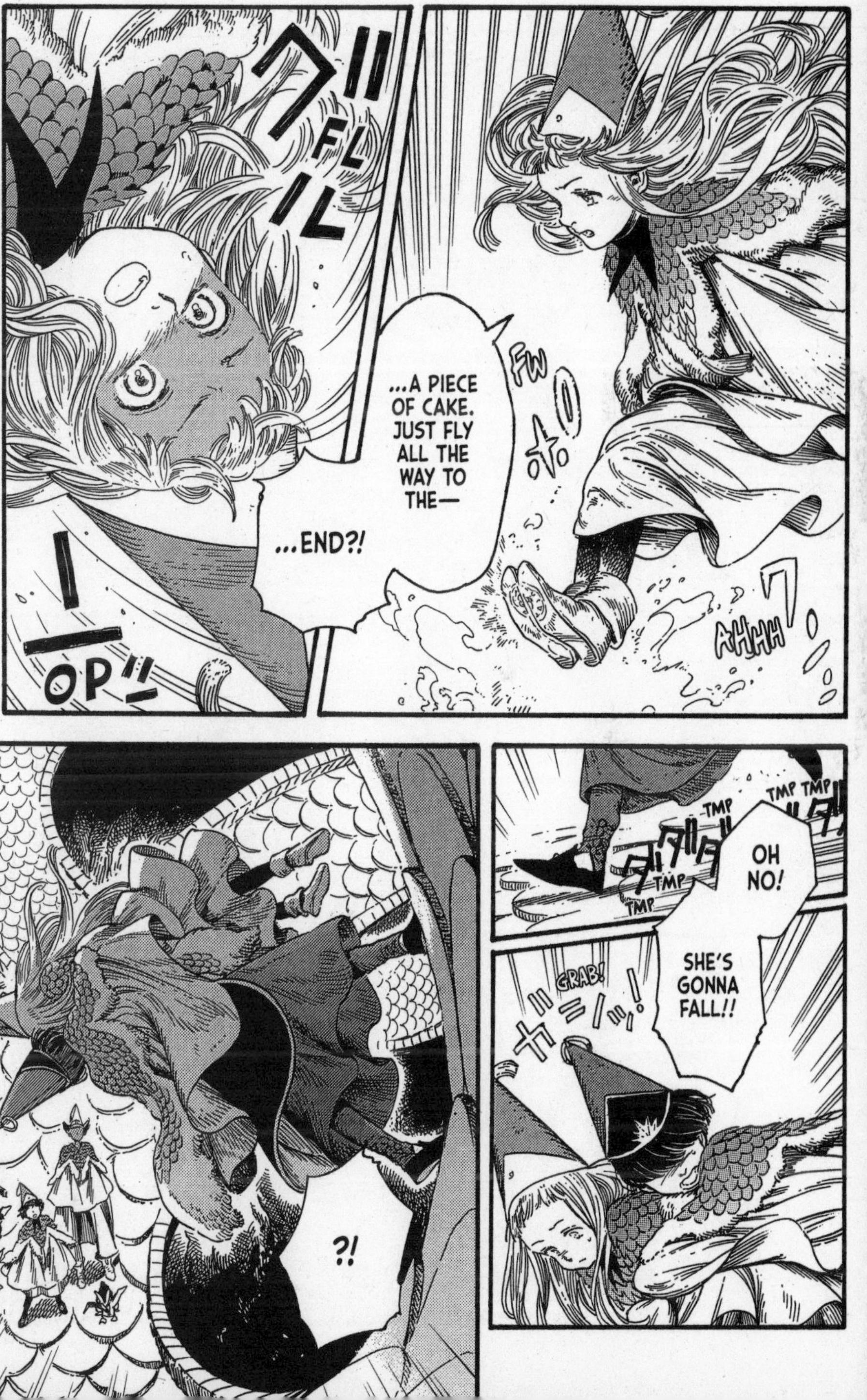

FW
...A PIECE OF CAKE. JUST FLY ALL THE WAY TO THE—
AHHH
FL
...END?!
OP
TMP TMP
TMP
TMP
TMP
OH NO!
SHE'S GONNA FALL!!
GRAB!
?!

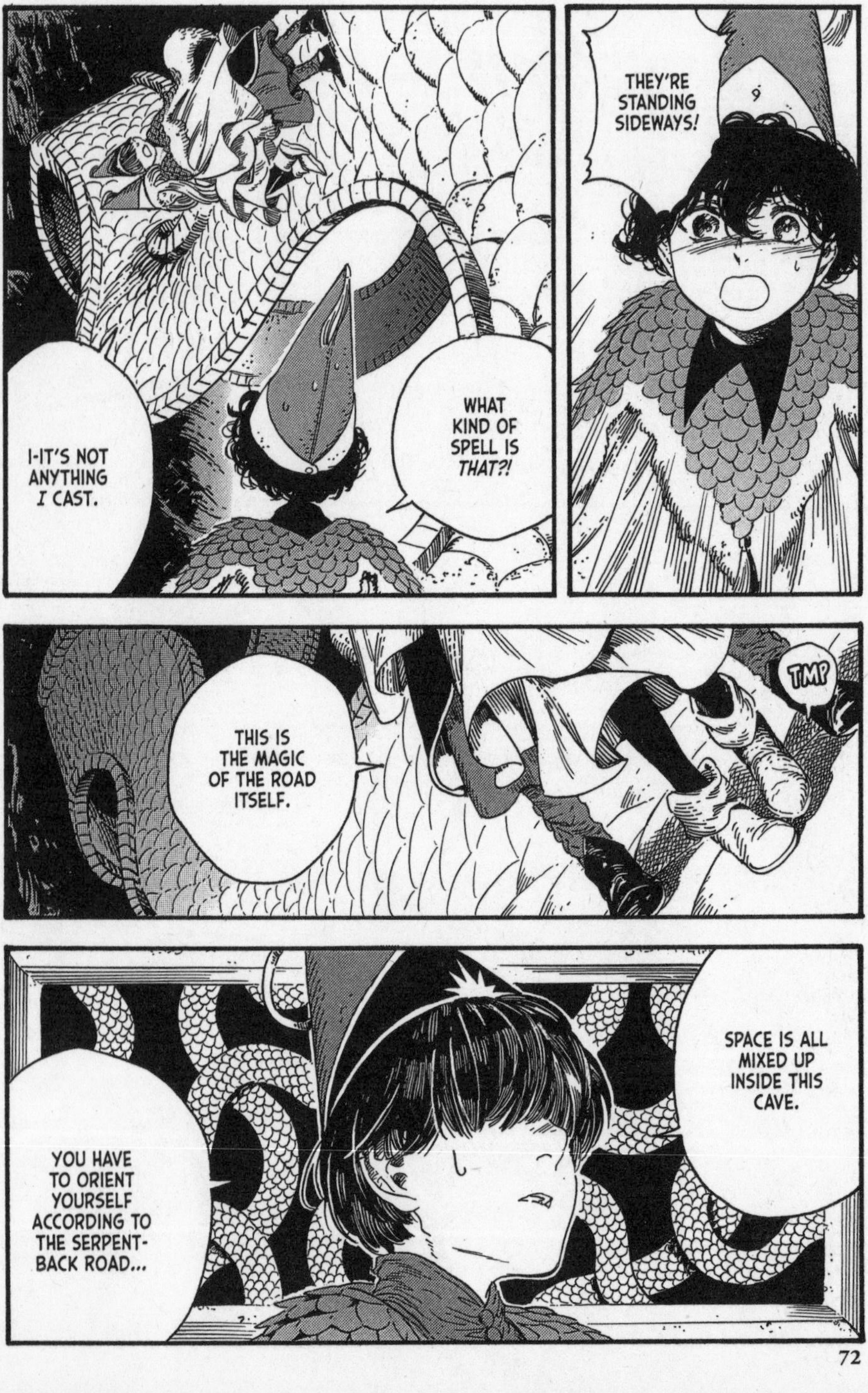
THEY'RE STANDING SIDEWAYS!
WHAT KIND OF SPELL IS *THAT?!*
I-IT'S NOT ANYTHING *I* CAST.
TMP
THIS IS THE MAGIC OF THE ROAD ITSELF.
SPACE IS ALL MIXED UP INSIDE THIS CAVE.
YOU HAVE TO ORIENT YOURSELF ACCORDING TO THE SERPENT-BACK ROAD...

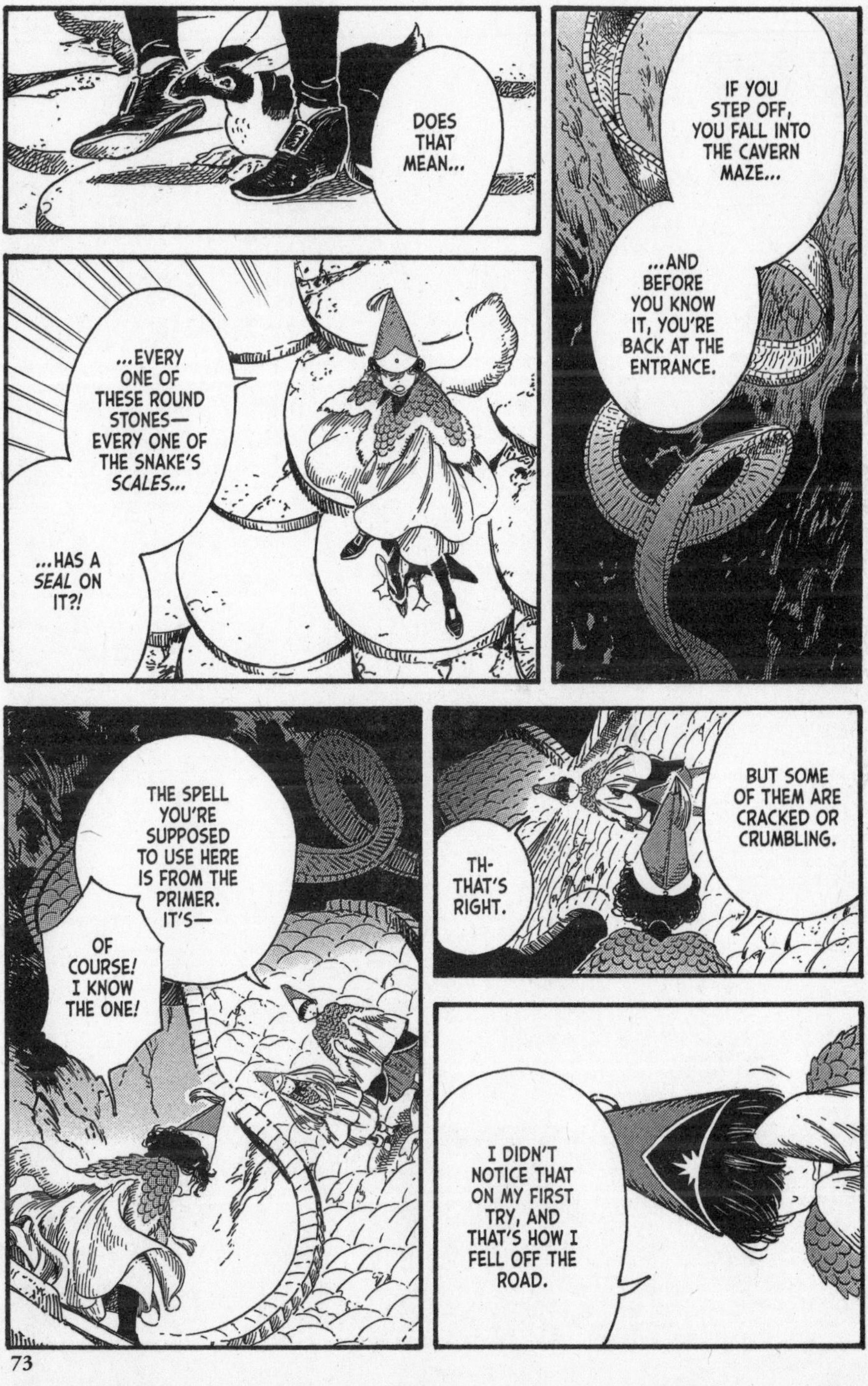
IF YOU STEP OFF, YOU FALL INTO THE CAVERN MAZE...
...AND BEFORE YOU KNOW IT, YOU'RE BACK AT THE ENTRANCE.
DOES THAT MEAN...
...EVERY ONE OF THESE ROUND STONES— EVERY ONE OF THE SNAKE'S *SCALES*...
...HAS A *SEAL* ON IT?!
BUT SOME OF THEM ARE CRACKED OR CRUMBLING.
TH-THAT'S RIGHT.
I DIDN'T NOTICE THAT ON MY FIRST TRY, AND THAT'S HOW I FELL OFF THE ROAD.
THE SPELL YOU'RE SUPPOSED TO USE HERE IS FROM THE PRIMER. IT'S—
OF COURSE! I KNOW THE ONE!

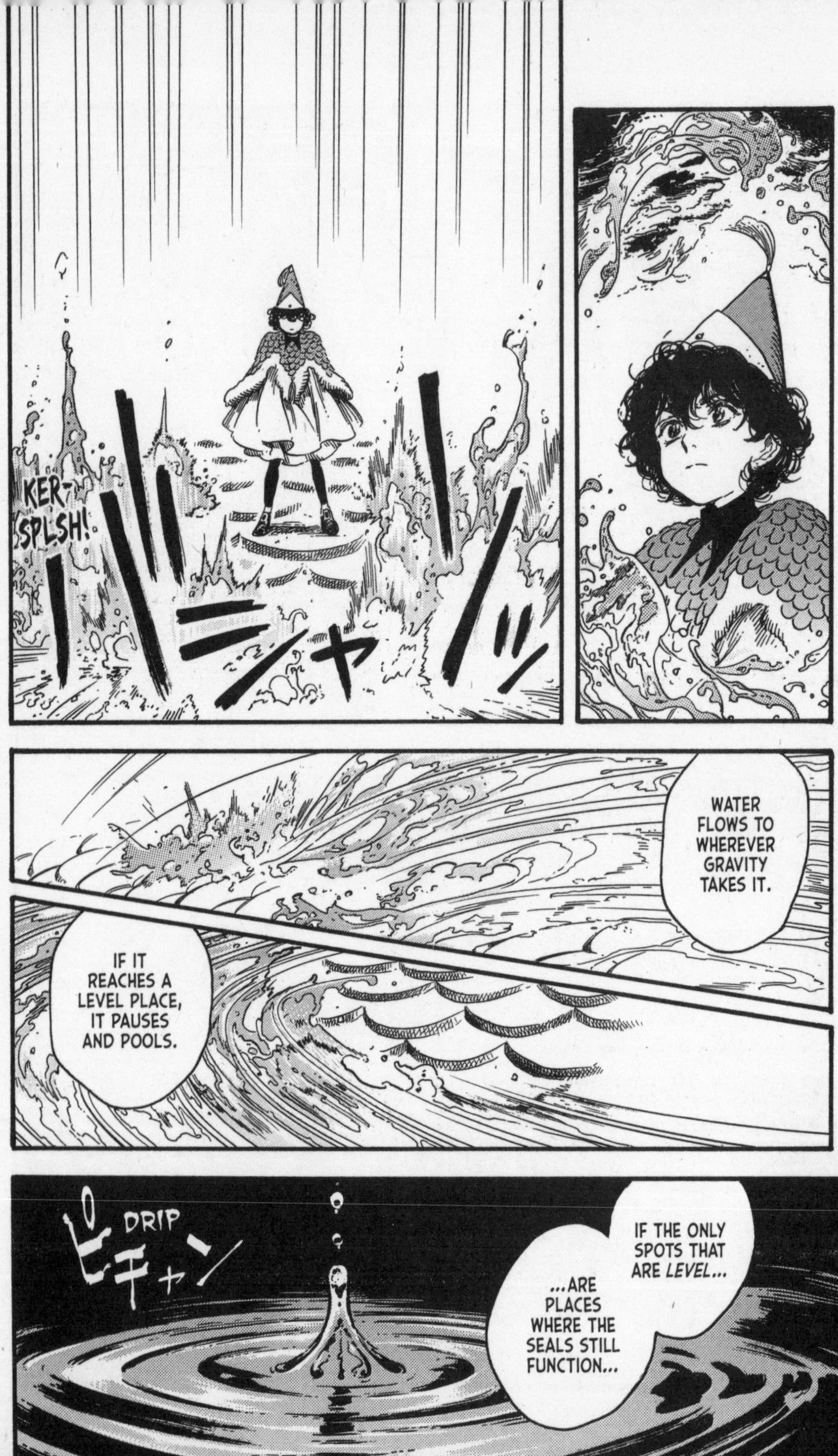
KER-SPLSH!
バシャッ
WATER FLOWS TO WHEREVER GRAVITY TAKES IT.
IF IT REACHES A LEVEL PLACE, IT PAUSES AND POOLS.
DRIP
ピチャン
IF THE ONLY SPOTS THAT ARE *LEVEL*...
...ARE PLACES WHERE THE SEALS STILL FUNCTION...

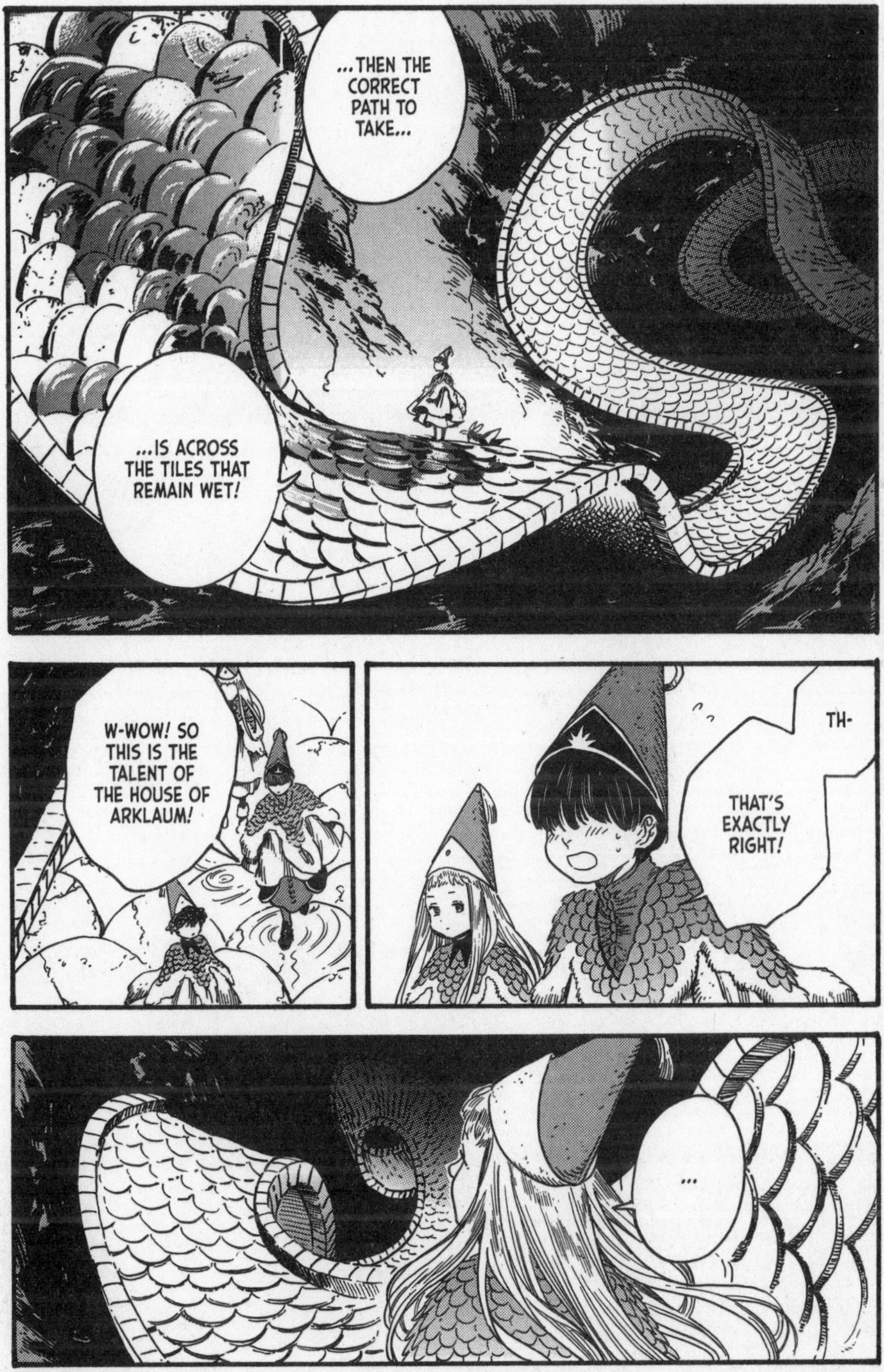
...THEN THE CORRECT PATH TO TAKE...
...IS ACROSS THE TILES THAT REMAIN WET!
TH-
THAT'S EXACTLY RIGHT!
W-WOW! SO THIS IS THE TALENT OF THE HOUSE OF ARKLAUM!
...

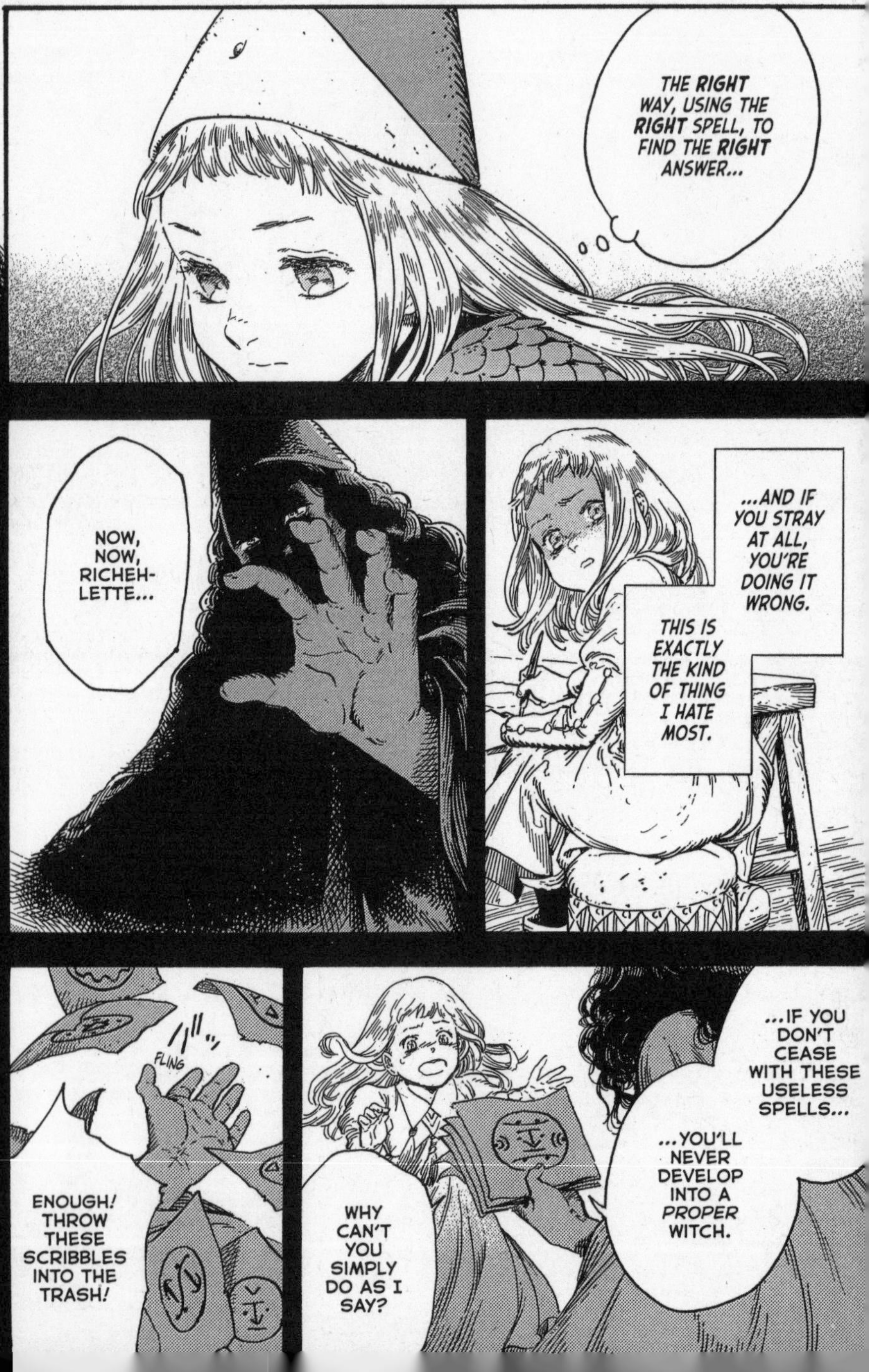
THE RIGHT WAY, USING THE RIGHT SPELL, TO FIND THE RIGHT ANSWER...
...AND IF YOU STRAY AT ALL, YOU'RE DOING IT WRONG.
THIS IS EXACTLY THE KIND OF THING I HATE MOST.
NOW, NOW, RICHEH-LETTE...
...IF YOU DON'T CEASE WITH THESE USELESS SPELLS...
...YOU'LL NEVER DEVELOP INTO A PROPER WITCH.
WHY CAN'T YOU SIMPLY DO AS I SAY?
FLING
ENOUGH! THROW THESE SCRIBBLES INTO THE TRASH!

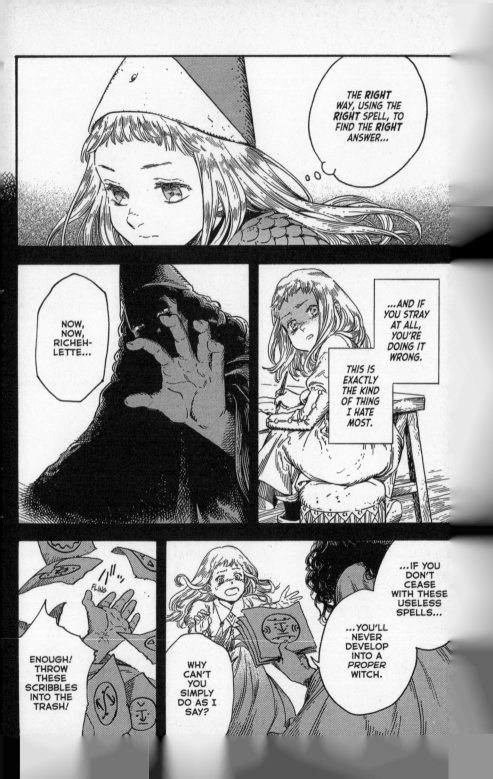

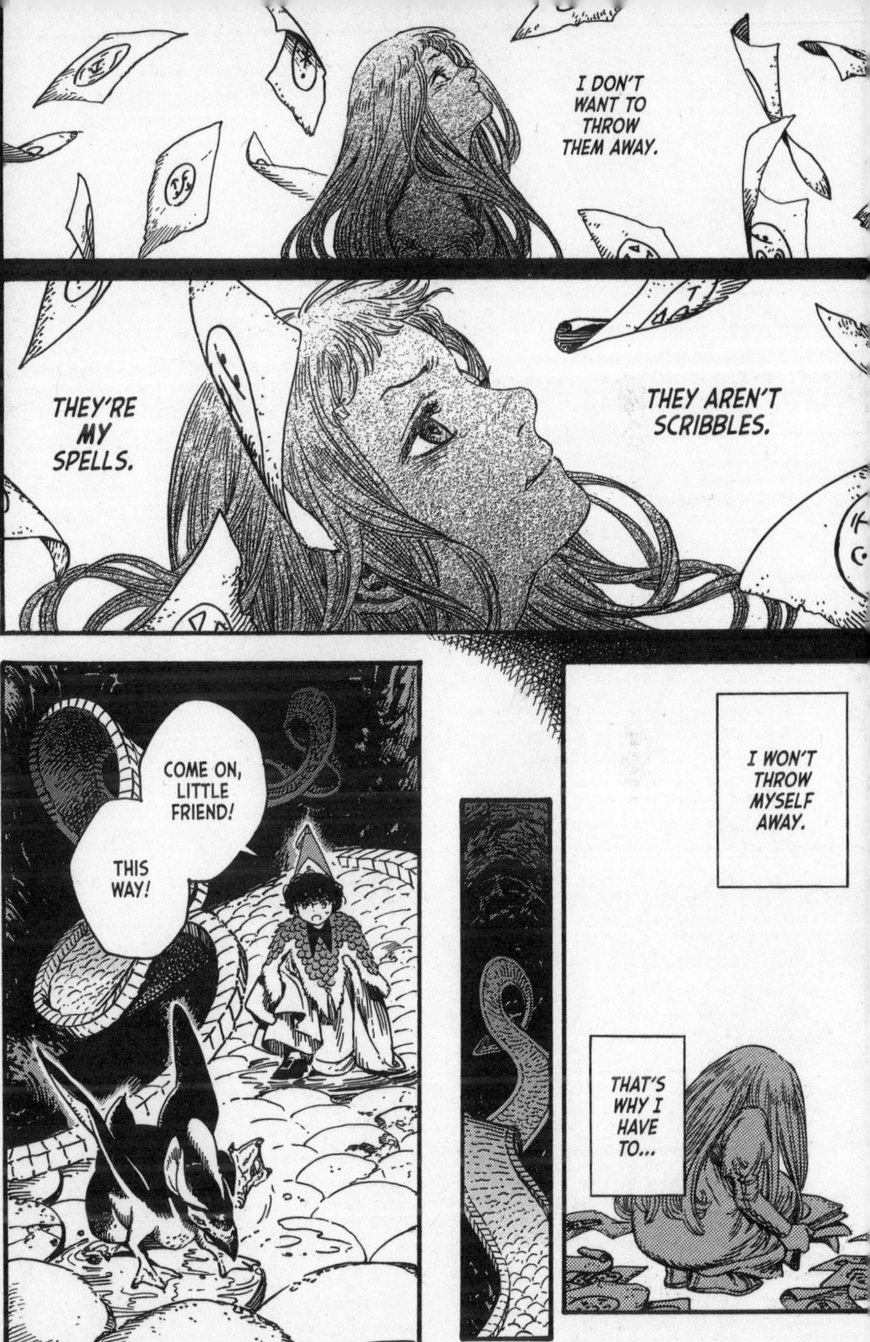
I DON'T WANT TO THROW THEM AWAY.
THEY AREN'T SCRIBBLES.
THEY'RE MY SPELLS.
I WON'T THROW MYSELF AWAY.
THAT'S WHY I HAVE TO...
COME ON, LITTLE FRIEND!
THIS WAY!

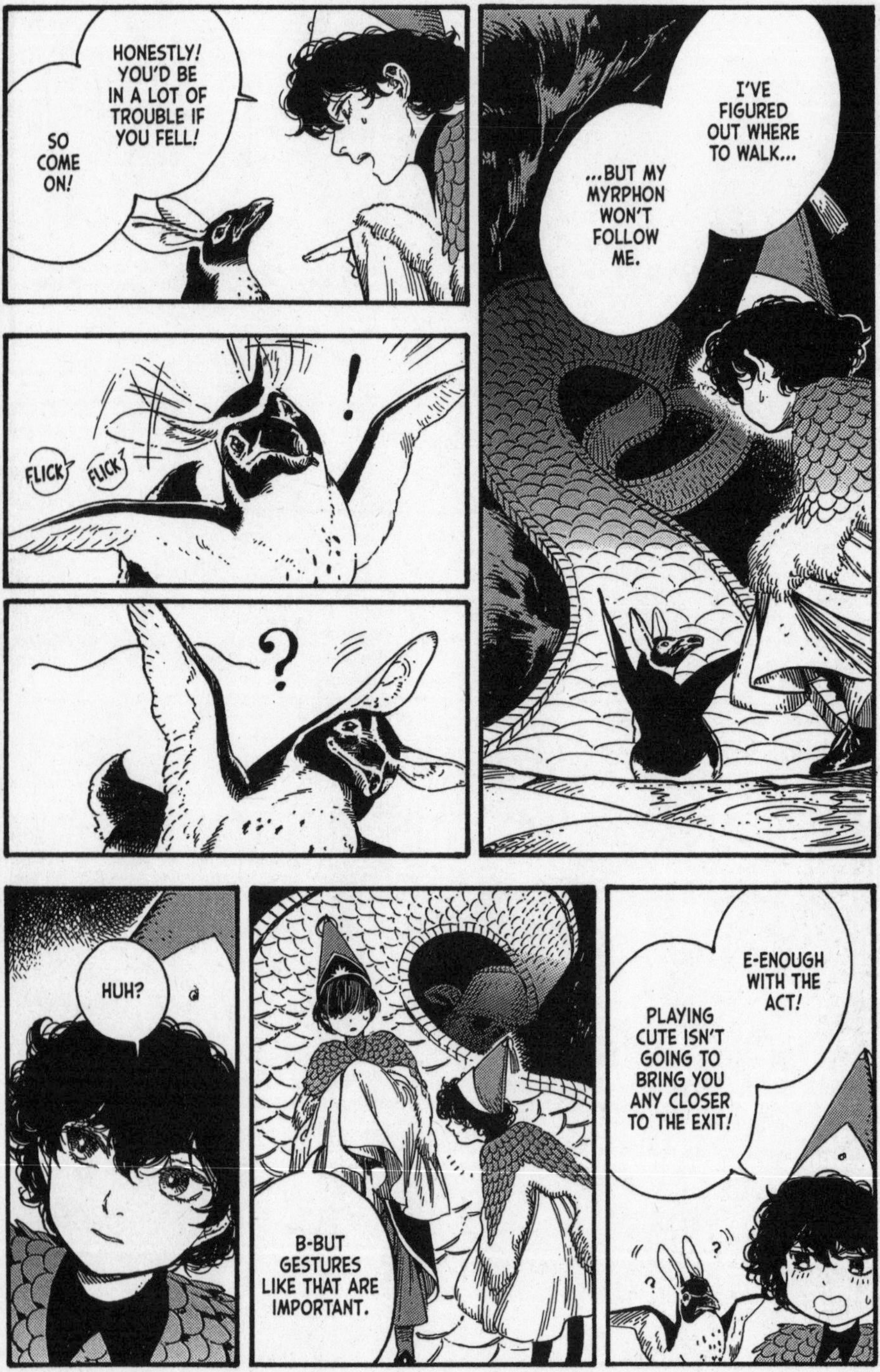
I'VE FIGURED OUT WHERE TO WALK...
...BUT MY MYRPHON WON'T FOLLOW ME.
HONESTLY! YOU'D BE IN A LOT OF TROUBLE IF YOU FELL!
SO COME ON!
!
FLICK
FLICK
?
E-ENOUGH WITH THE ACT!
PLAYING CUTE ISN'T GOING TO BRING YOU ANY CLOSER TO THE EXIT!
B-BUT GESTURES LIKE THAT ARE IMPORTANT.
HUH?

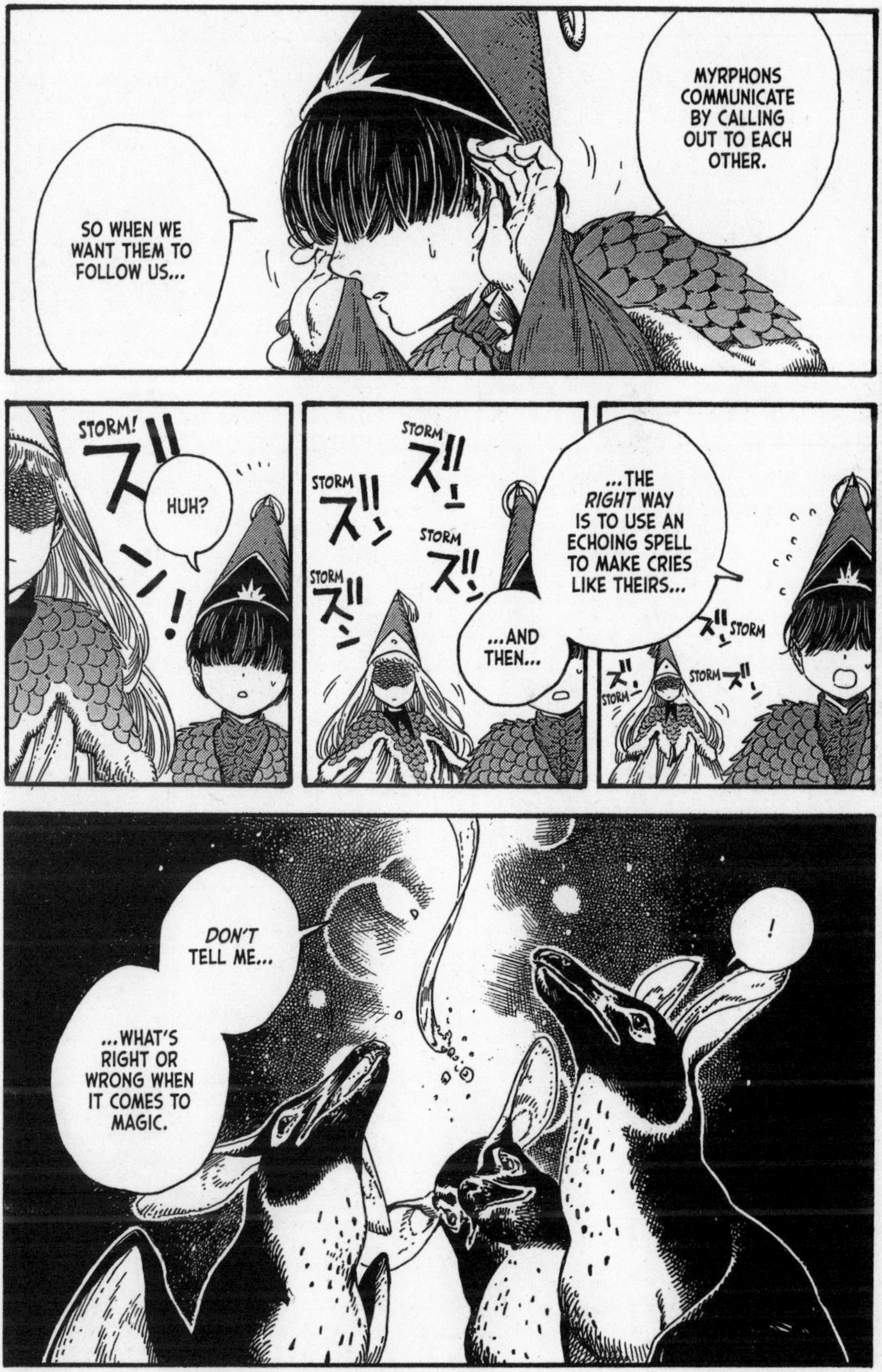
MYRPHONS COMMUNICATE BY CALLING OUT TO EACH OTHER.
SO WHEN WE WANT THEM TO FOLLOW US...
...THE *RIGHT* WAY IS TO USE AN ECHOING SPELL TO MAKE CRIES LIKE THEIRS...
STORM
STORM
STORM
...AND THEN...
STORM
STORM
STORM
STORM
STORM!
HUH?
!
DON'T TELL ME...
...WHAT'S RIGHT OR WRONG WHEN IT COMES TO MAGIC.

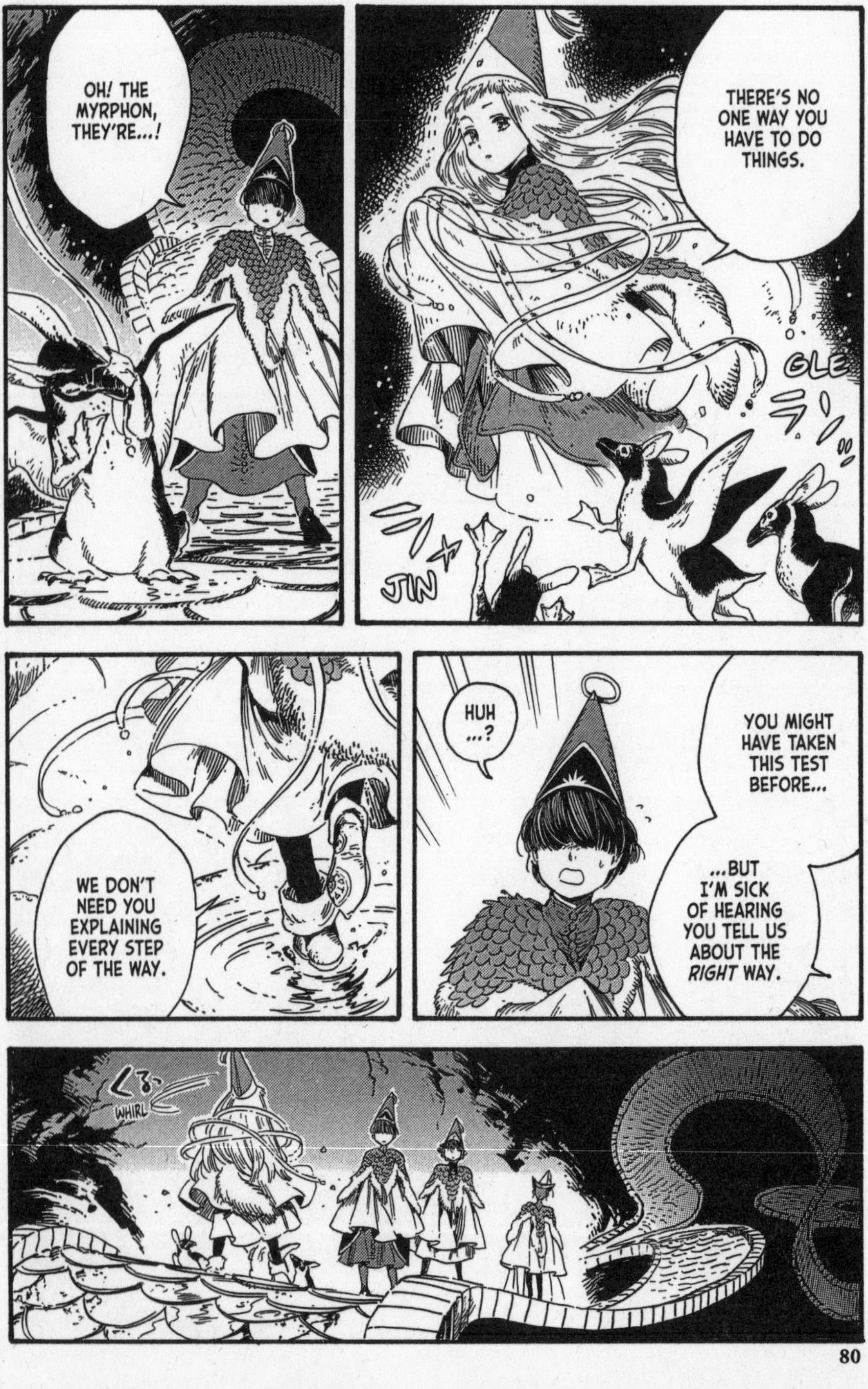
THERE'S NO ONE WAY YOU HAVE TO DO THINGS.
GLE
JIN
OH! THE MYRPHON, THEY'RE...!
YOU MIGHT HAVE TAKEN THIS TEST BEFORE...
HUH ...?
...BUT I'M SICK OF HEARING YOU TELL US ABOUT THE *RIGHT* WAY.
WE DON'T NEED YOU EXPLAINING EVERY STEP OF THE WAY.
WHIRL

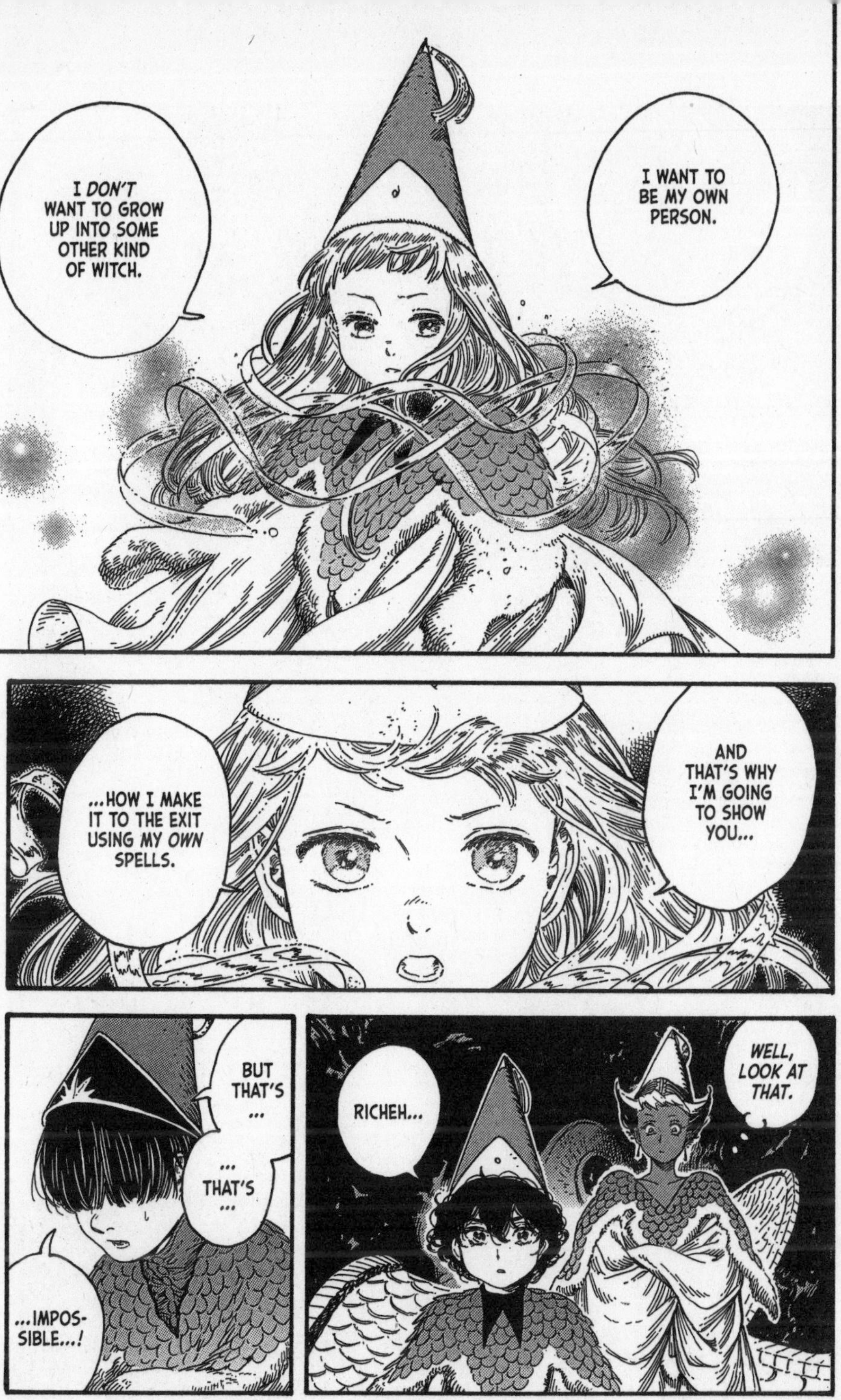
I WANT TO BE MY OWN PERSON.
I *DON'T* WANT TO GROW UP INTO SOME OTHER KIND OF WITCH.
AND THAT'S WHY I'M GOING TO SHOW YOU...
...HOW I MAKE IT TO THE EXIT USING MY *OWN* SPELLS.
WELL, LOOK AT THAT.
RICHEH...
BUT THAT'S ...
... THAT'S ...
...IMPOSSIBLE...!

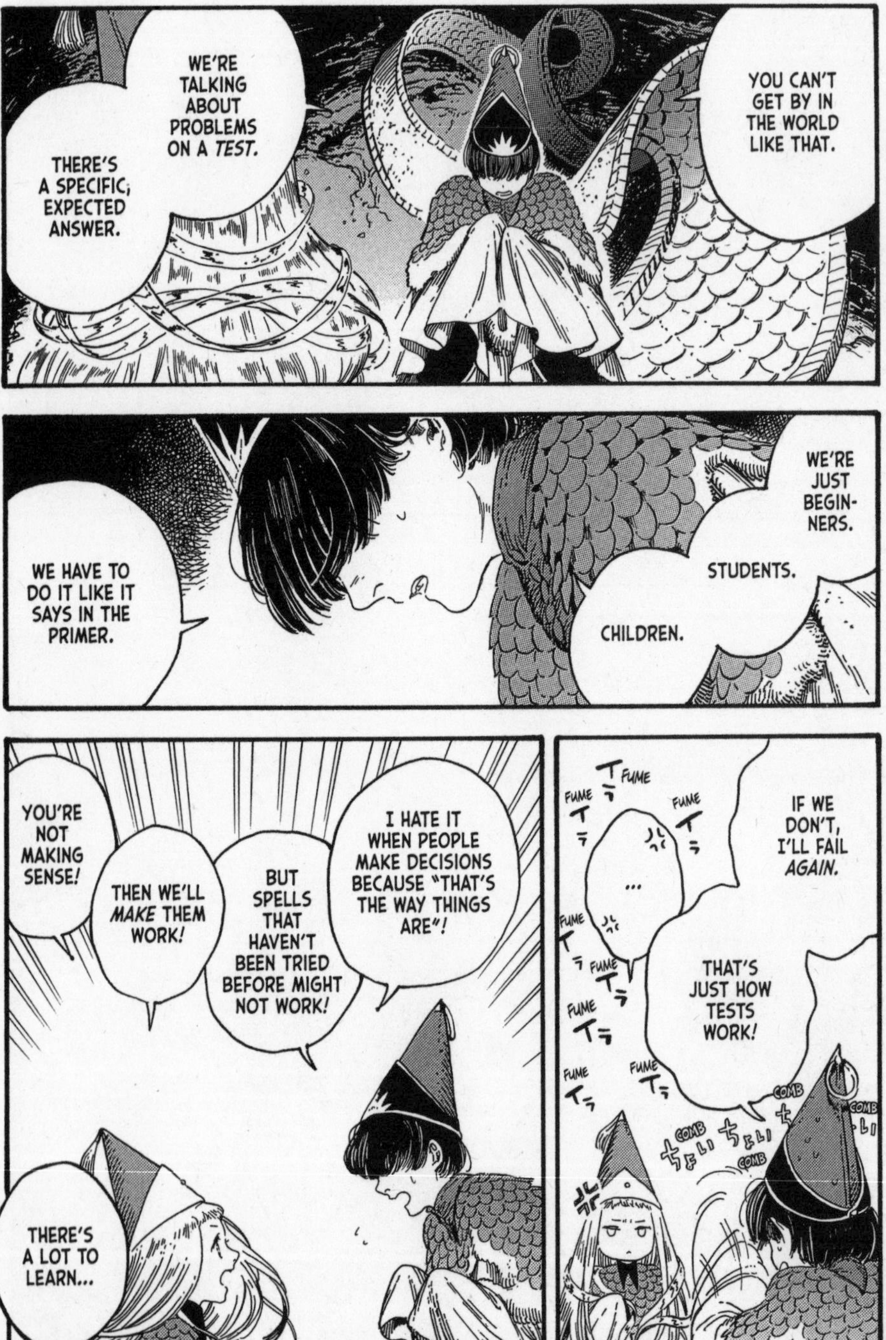
YOU CAN'T GET BY IN THE WORLD LIKE THAT.
WE'RE TALKING ABOUT PROBLEMS ON A *TEST.*
THERE'S A SPECIFIC, EXPECTED ANSWER.
WE'RE JUST BEGIN-NERS.
STUDENTS.
CHILDREN.
WE HAVE TO DO IT LIKE IT SAYS IN THE PRIMER.
IF WE DON'T, I'LL FAIL *AGAIN.*
FUME
FUME
FUME
...
FUME
FUME
FUME
FUME
FUME
THAT'S JUST HOW TESTS WORK!
COMB
COMB
COMB
COMB
I HATE IT WHEN PEOPLE MAKE DECISIONS BECAUSE "THAT'S THE WAY THINGS ARE"!
BUT SPELLS THAT HAVEN'T BEEN TRIED BEFORE MIGHT NOT WORK!
THEN WE'LL *MAKE* THEM WORK!
YOU'RE NOT MAKING SENSE!
THERE'S A LOT TO LEARN...

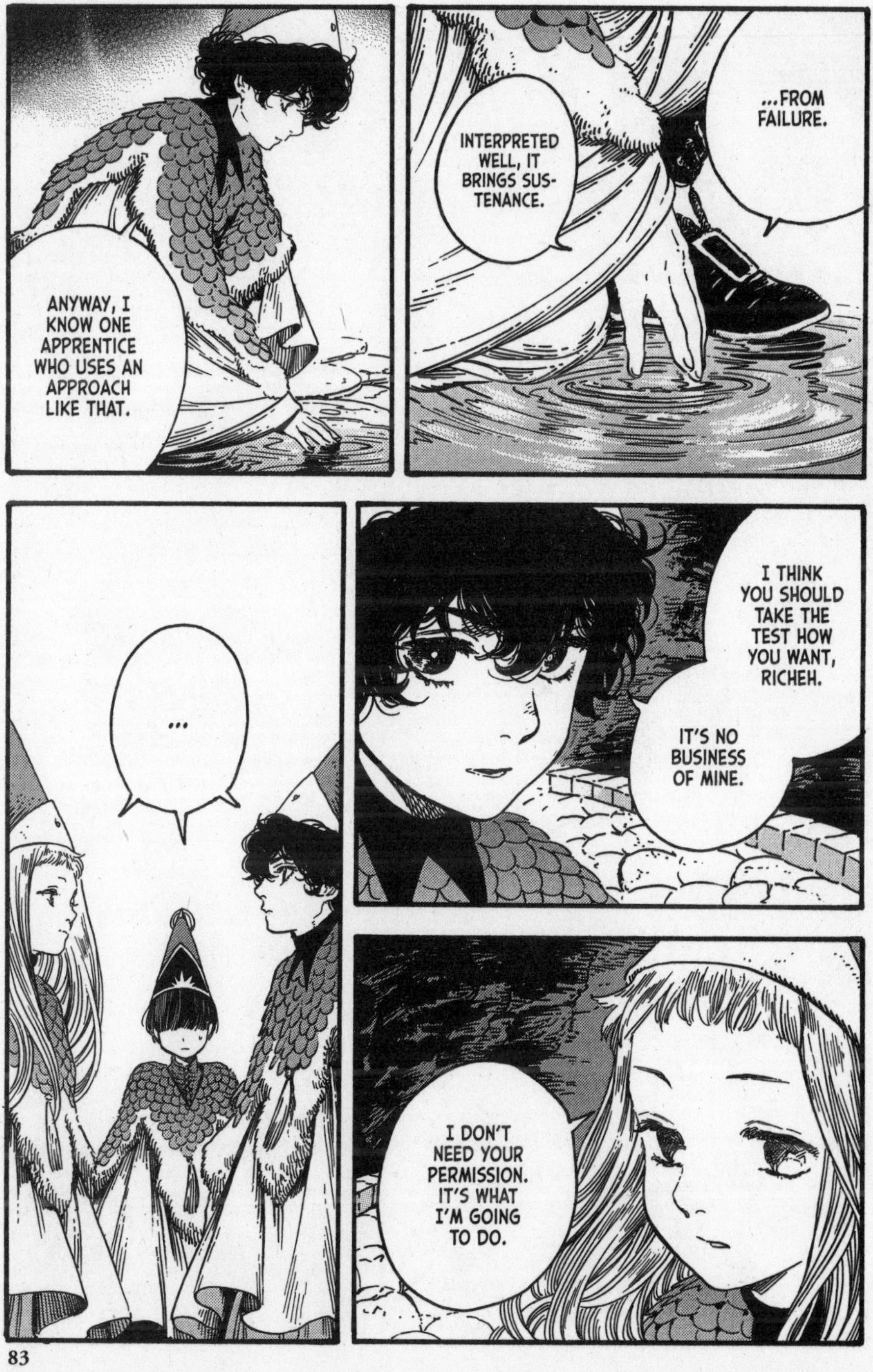
INTERPRETED WELL, IT BRINGS SUS-TENANCE.
...FROM FAILURE.
ANYWAY, I KNOW ONE APPRENTICE WHO USES AN APPROACH LIKE THAT.
I THINK YOU SHOULD TAKE THE TEST HOW YOU WANT, RICHEH.
IT'S NO BUSINESS OF MINE.
I DON'T NEED YOUR PERMISSION. IT'S WHAT I'M GOING TO DO.
...

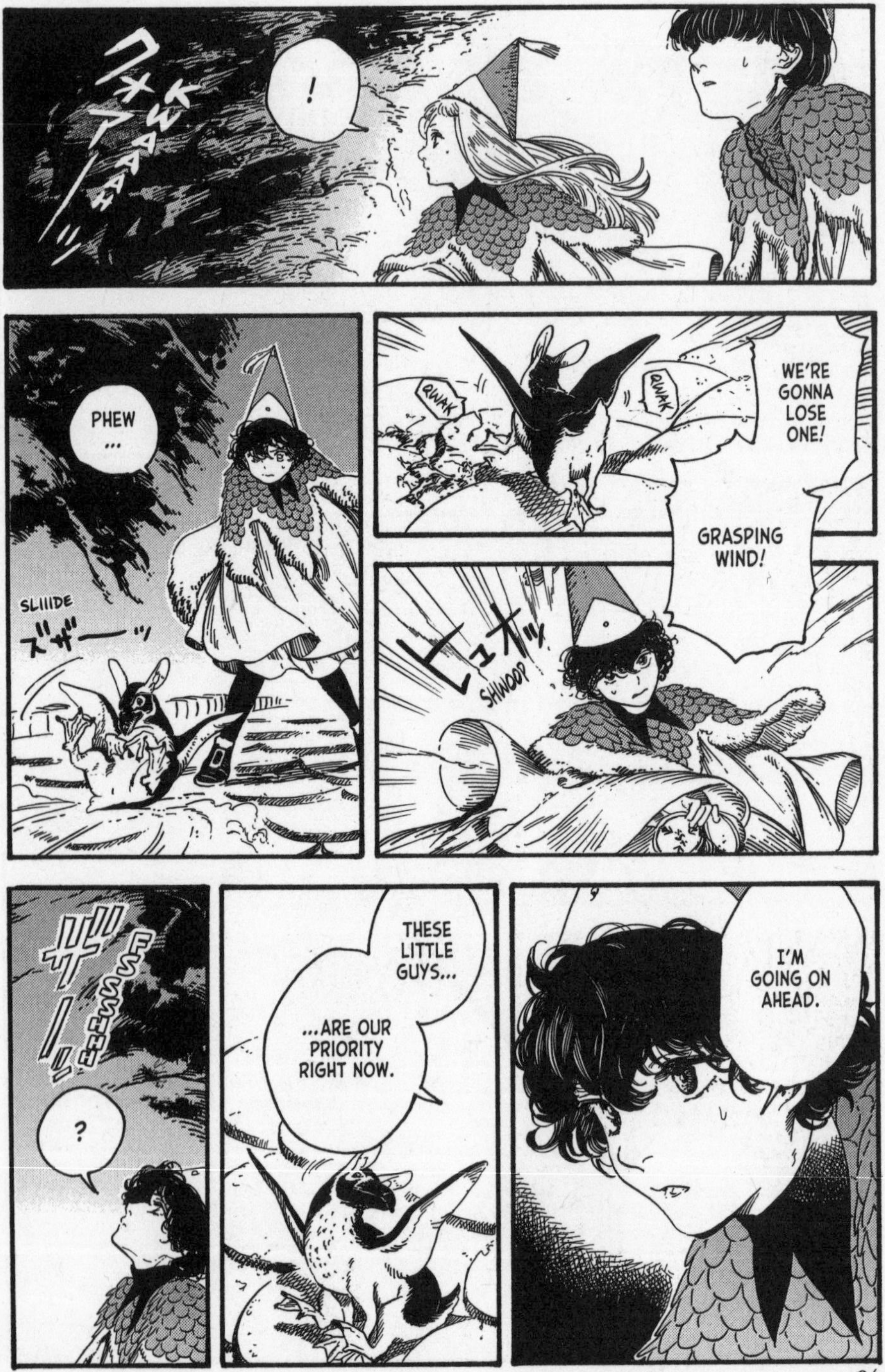
KWAAAAH
!
QWAK
QWAK
WE'RE GONNA LOSE ONE!
GRASPING WIND!
SHWOOP
PHEW ...
SLIIIDE
I'M GOING ON AHEAD.
THESE LITTLE GUYS...
...ARE OUR PRIORITY RIGHT NOW.
FSSSHHH
?

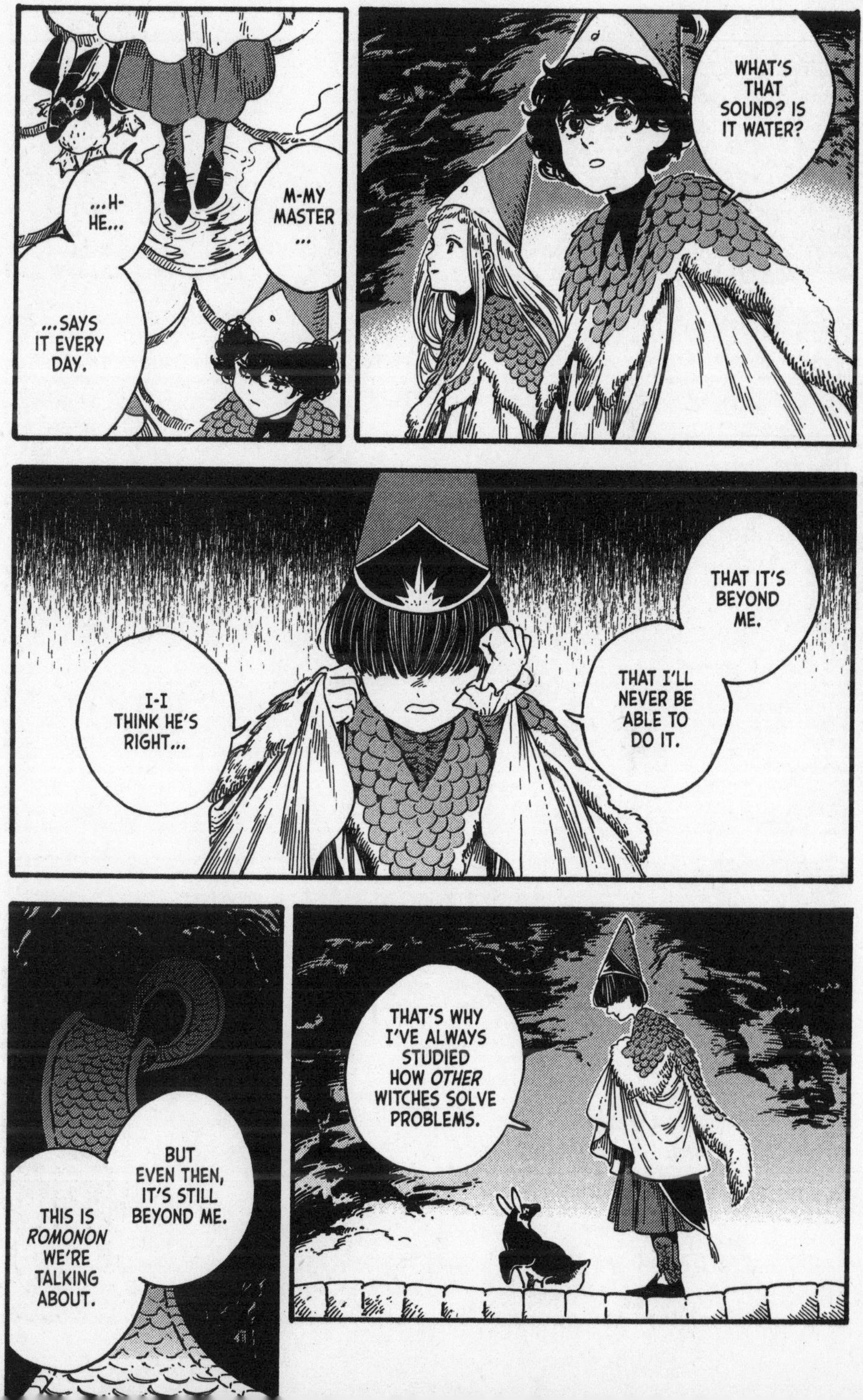
WHAT'S THAT SOUND? IS IT WATER?
M-MY MASTER ...
...H-HE...
...SAYS IT EVERY DAY.
THAT IT'S BEYOND ME.
THAT I'LL NEVER BE ABLE TO DO IT.
I-I THINK HE'S RIGHT...
THAT'S WHY I'VE ALWAYS STUDIED HOW *OTHER* WITCHES SOLVE PROBLEMS.
BUT EVEN THEN, IT'S STILL BEYOND ME.
THIS IS *ROMONON* WE'RE TALKING ABOUT.

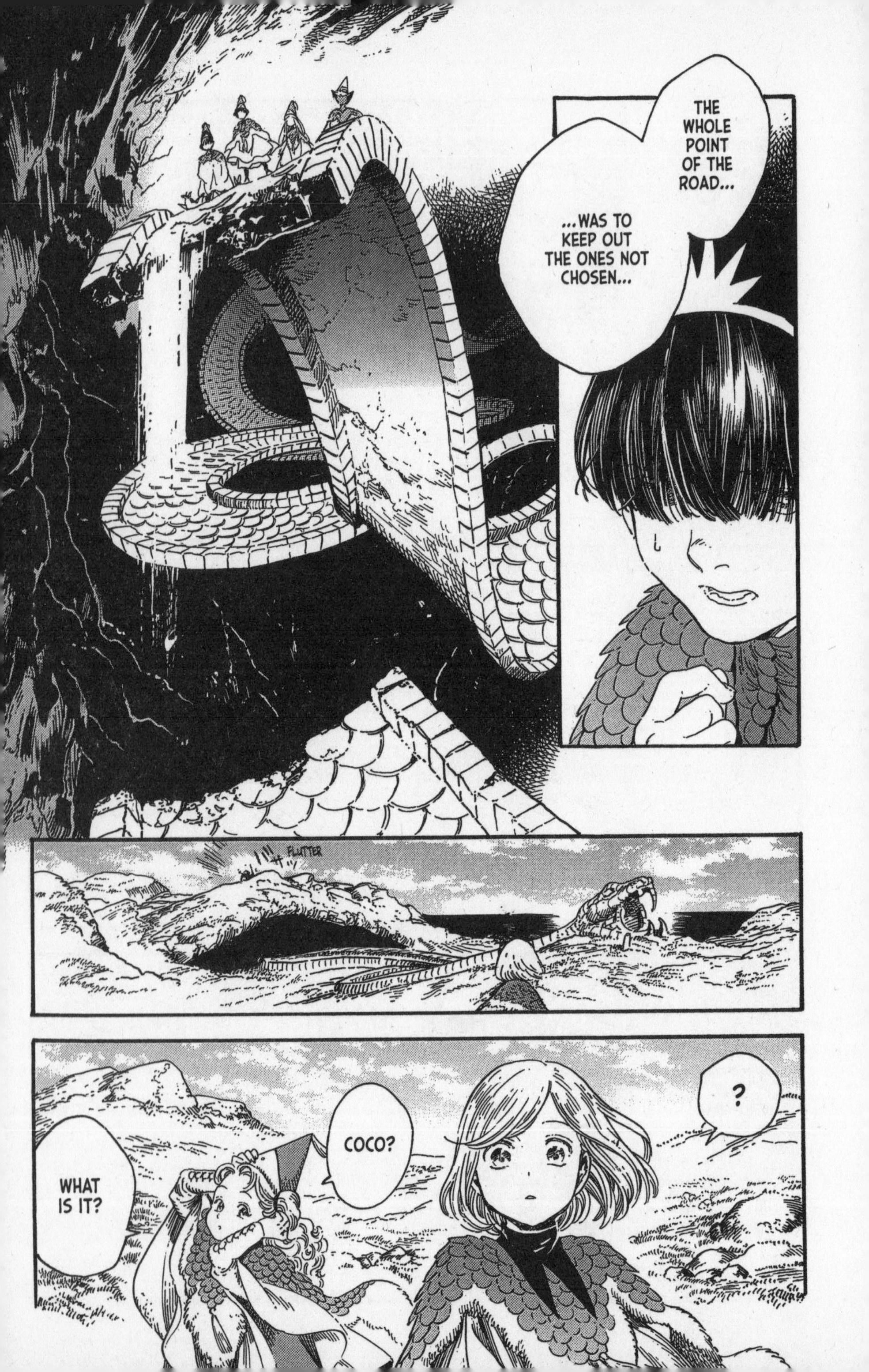
THE WHOLE POINT OF THE ROAD...
...WAS TO KEEP OUT THE ONES NOT CHOSEN...
FLUTTER
?
COCO?
WHAT IS IT?

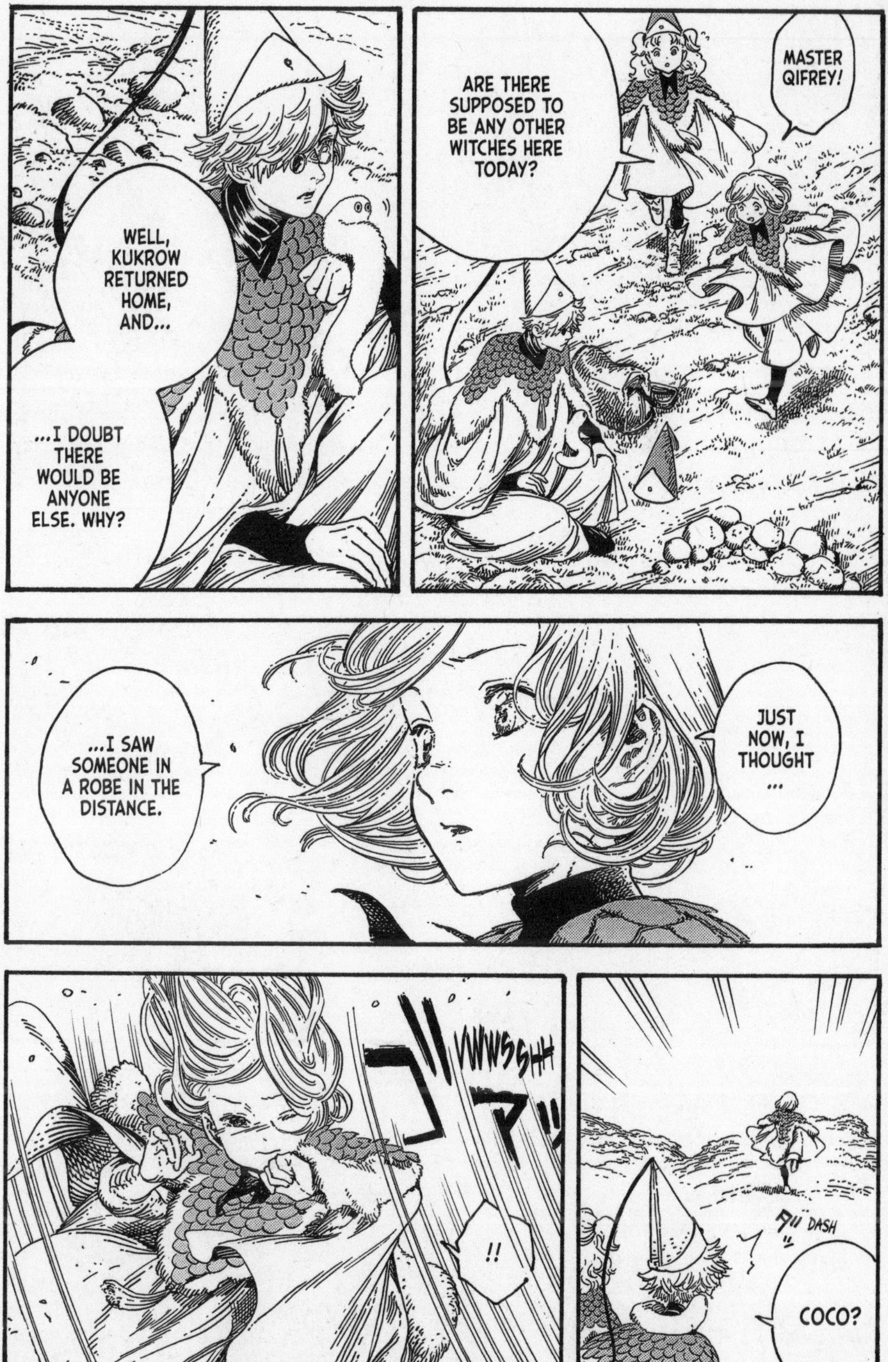
MASTER QIFREY!
ARE THERE SUPPOSED TO BE ANY OTHER WITCHES HERE TODAY?
WELL, KUKROW RETURNED HOME, AND...
...I DOUBT THERE WOULD BE ANYONE ELSE. WHY?
JUST NOW, I THOUGHT ...
...I SAW SOMEONE IN A ROBE IN THE DISTANCE.
DASH
COCO?
VWWSSHH
!!

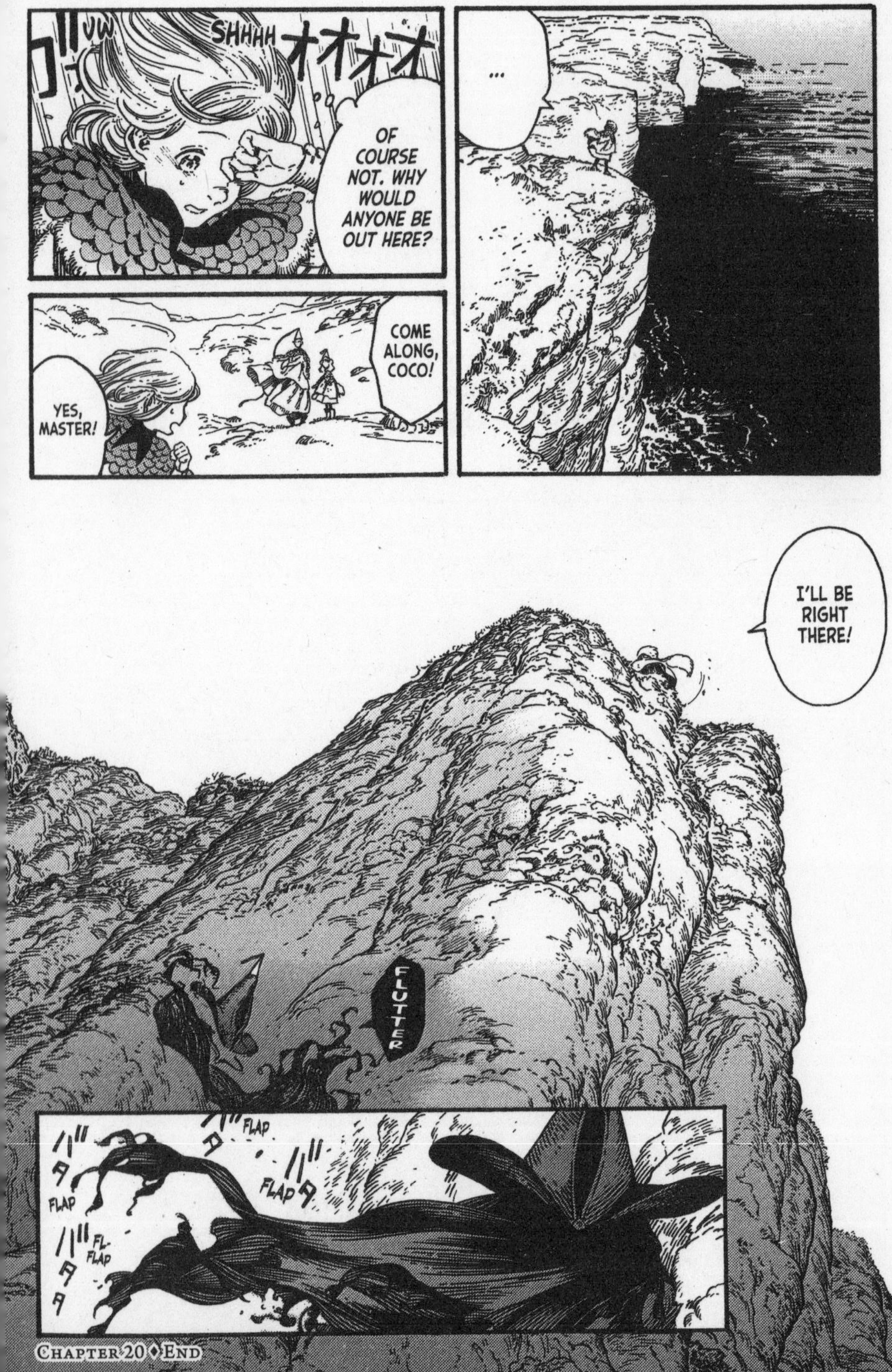
...
SHHHH オオオオ
OF COURSE NOT. WHY WOULD ANYONE BE OUT HERE?
COME ALONG, COCO!
YES, MASTER!
I'LL BE RIGHT THERE!
FLUTTER
FLAP
FLAP
FLAP
FL-FLAP

Chapter 20 ◆ End

Witch Hat
Atelier

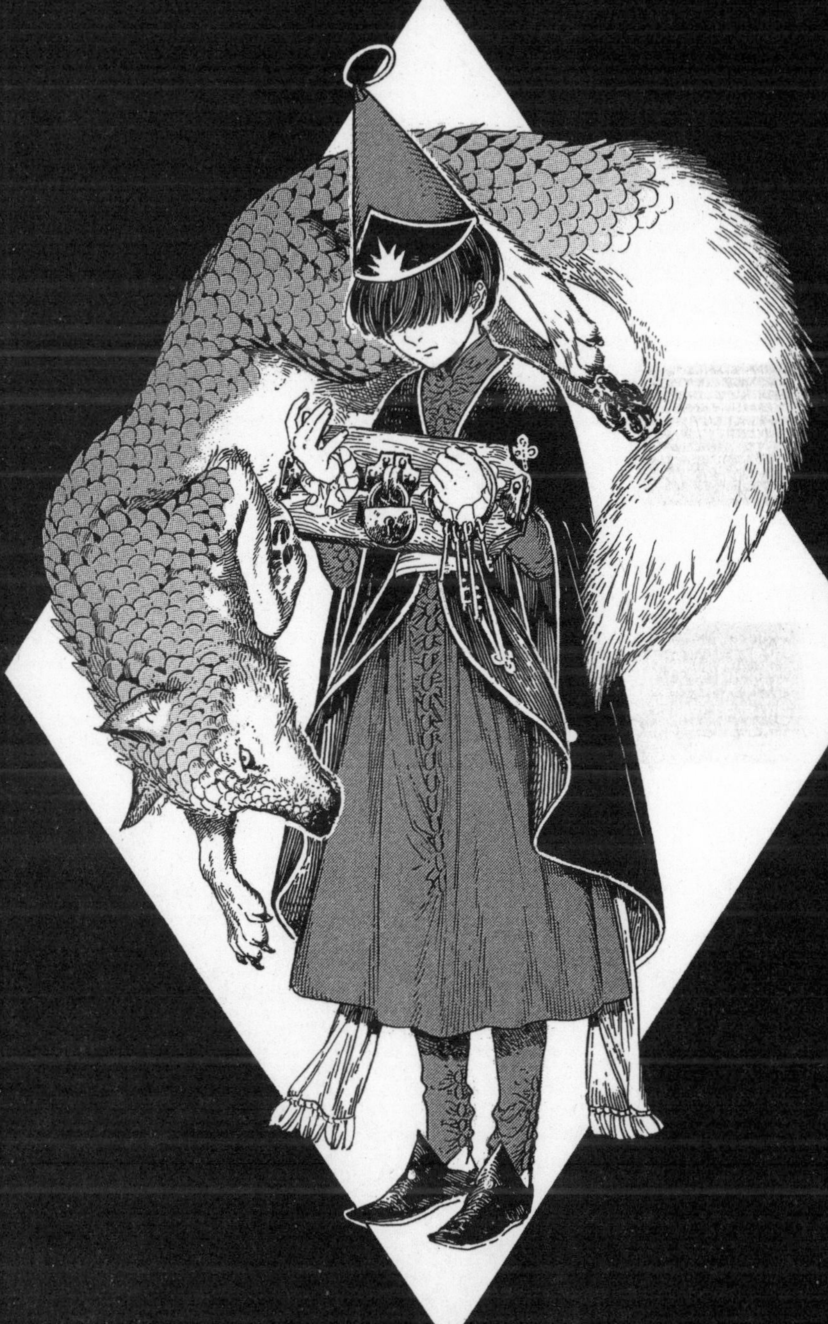

Chapter 21

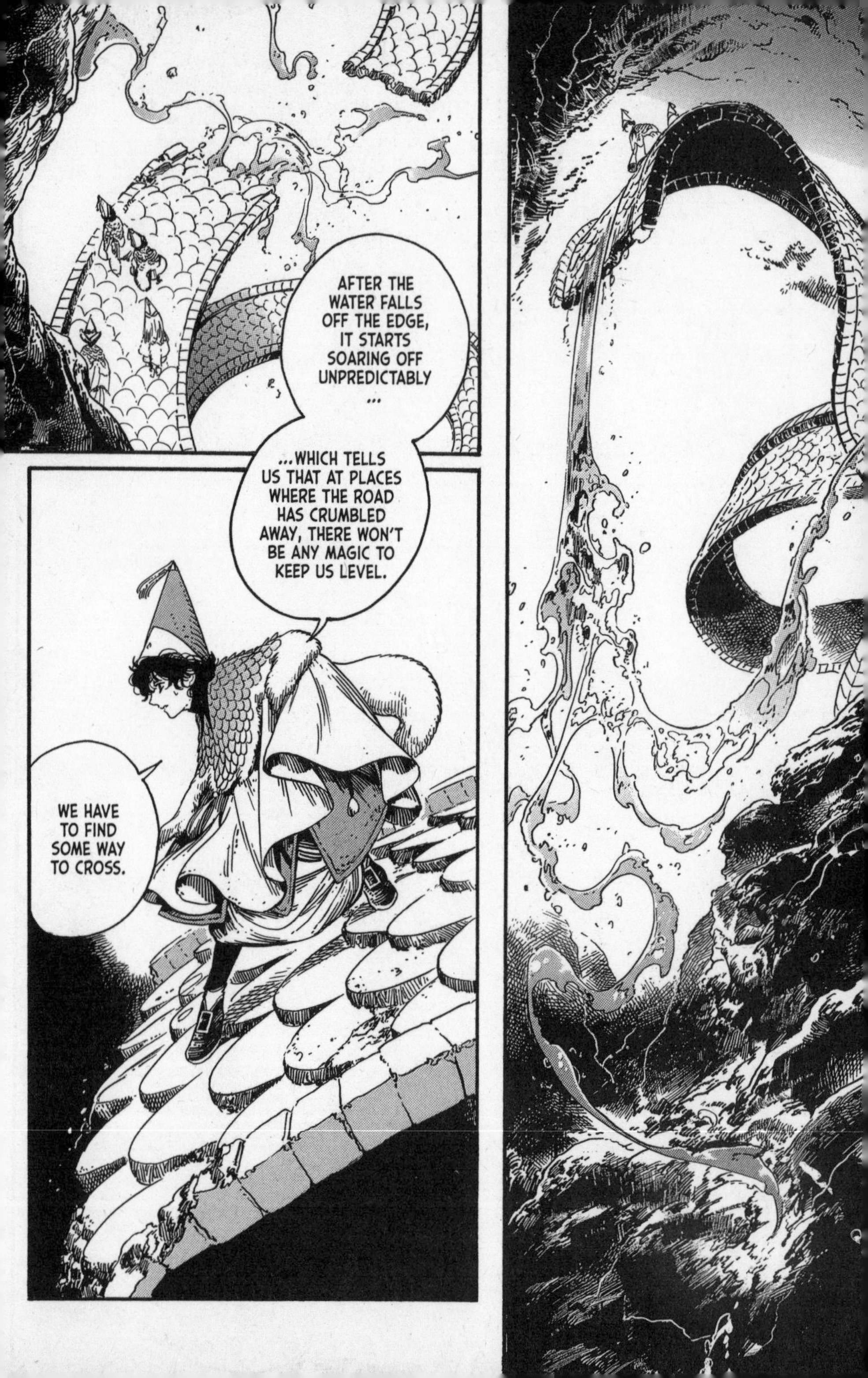
AFTER THE WATER FALLS OFF THE EDGE, IT STARTS SOARING OFF UNPREDICTABLY ...
...WHICH TELLS US THAT AT PLACES WHERE THE ROAD HAS CRUMBLED AWAY, THERE WON'T BE ANY MAGIC TO KEEP US LEVEL.
WE HAVE TO FIND SOME WAY TO CROSS.

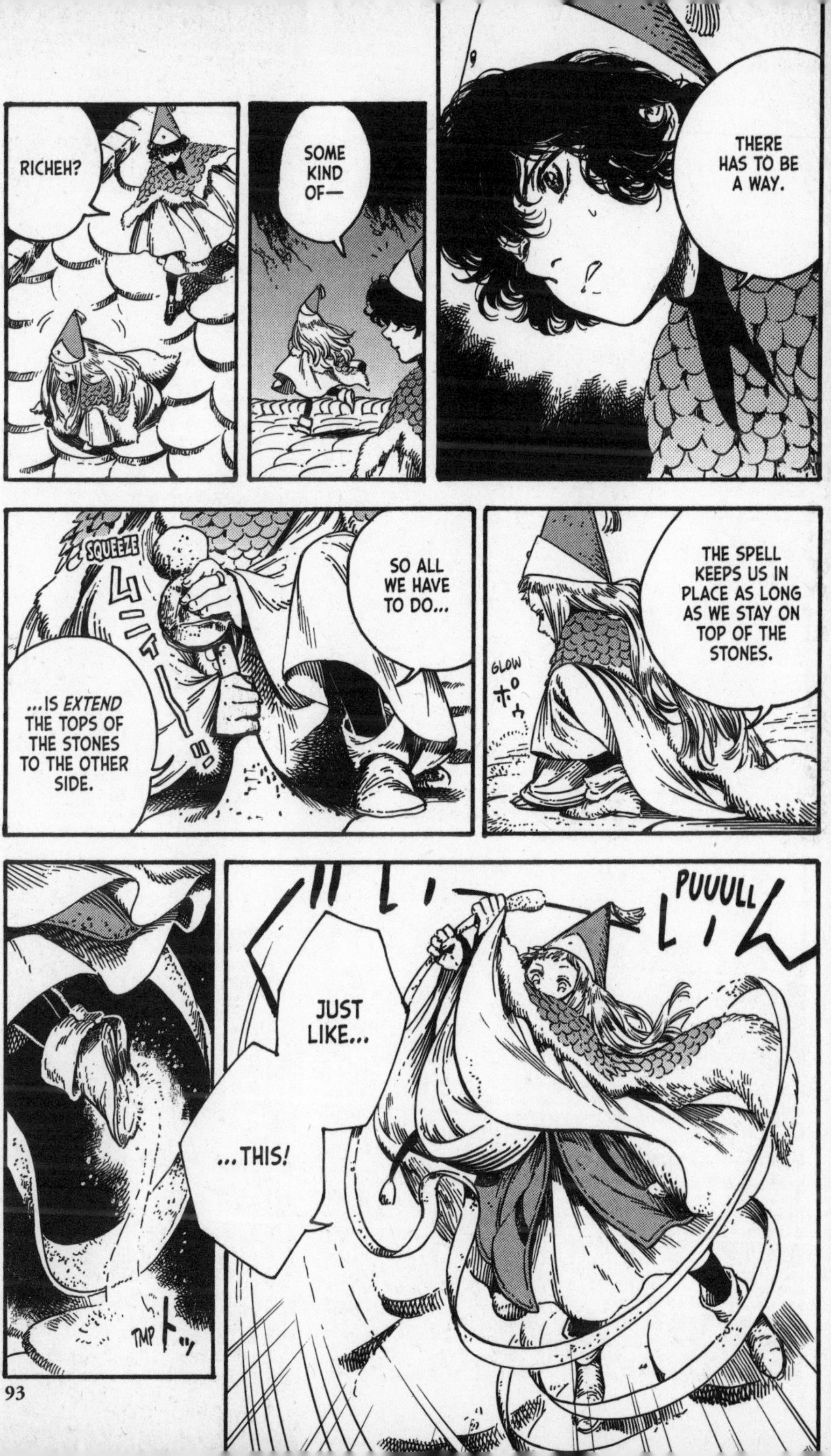
THERE HAS TO BE A WAY.
SOME KIND OF—
RICHEH?
THE SPELL KEEPS US IN PLACE AS LONG AS WE STAY ON TOP OF THE STONES.
GLOW
SO ALL WE HAVE TO DO...
SQUEEZE
...IS *EXTEND* THE TOPS OF THE STONES TO THE OTHER SIDE.
PUUULL
JUST LIKE...
...THIS!
TMP

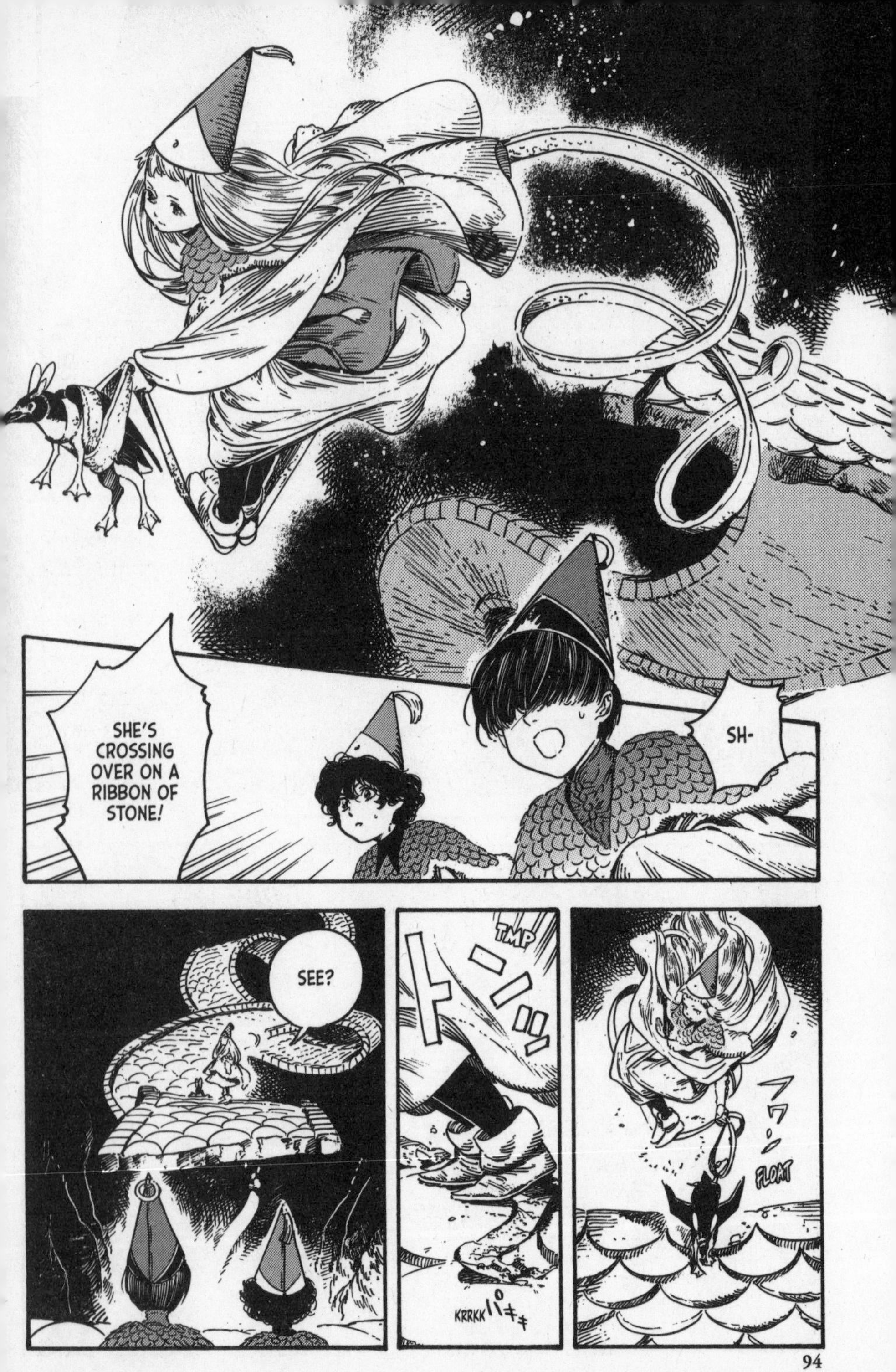

SH-
SHE'S CROSSING OVER ON A RIBBON OF STONE!
フワ
FLOAT
トーン
TMP
パキ
KRRKK
SEE?

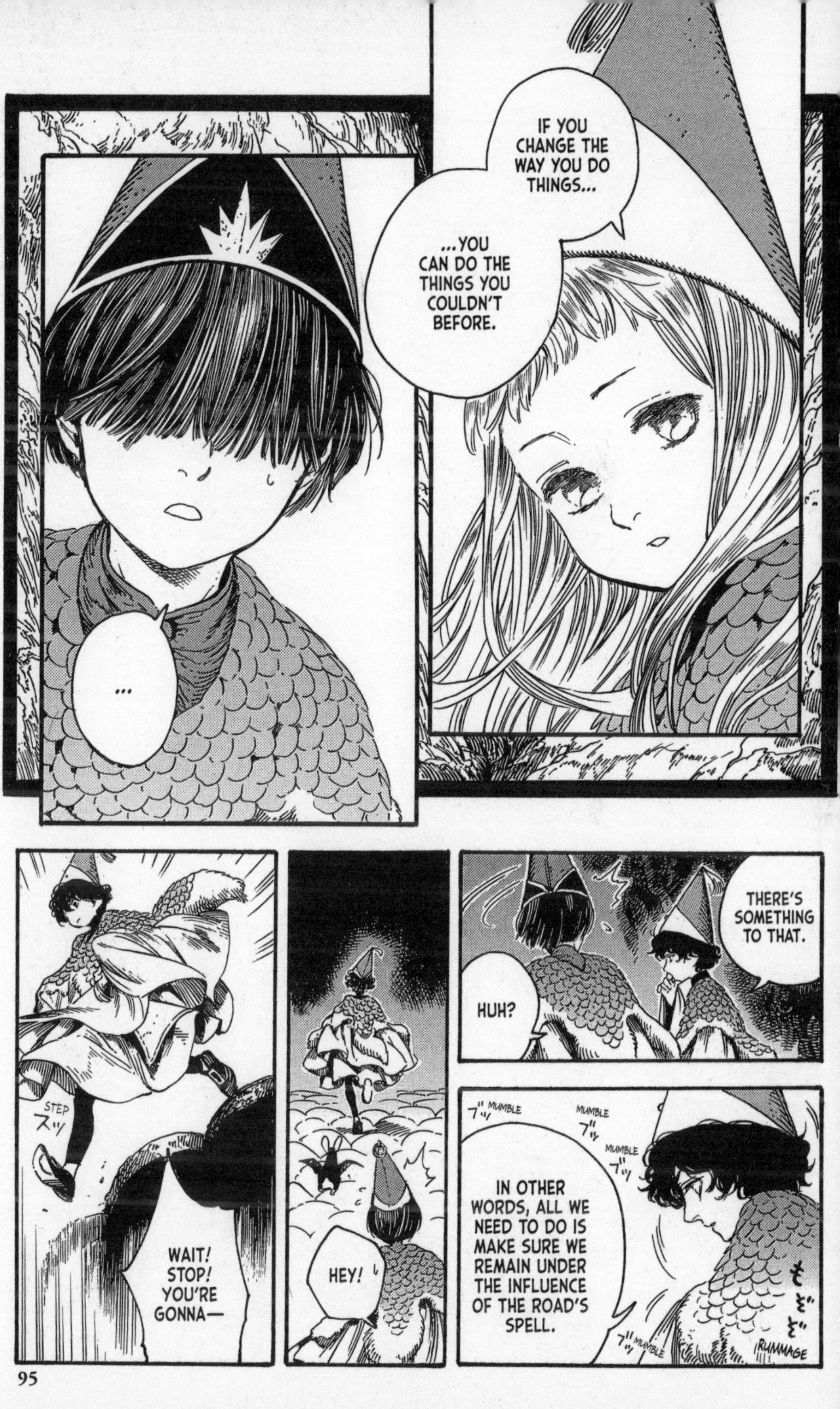
IF YOU CHANGE THE WAY YOU DO THINGS...
...YOU CAN DO THE THINGS YOU COULDN'T BEFORE.
...
THERE'S SOMETHING TO THAT.
HUH?
MUMBLE
MUMBLE
MUMBLE
IN OTHER WORDS, ALL WE NEED TO DO IS MAKE SURE WE REMAIN UNDER THE INFLUENCE OF THE ROAD'S SPELL.
MUMBLE
RUMMAGE
HEY!
STEP
WAIT! STOP! YOU'RE GONNA—

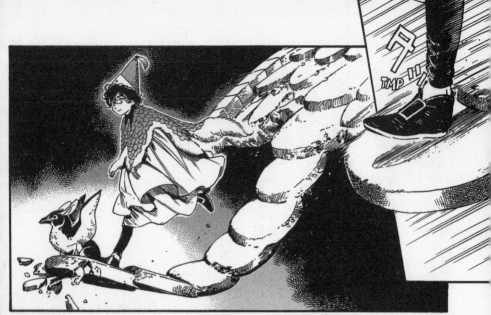

A COMBINATION OF REPLICATION AND REPETITION MAGIC!

THE EFFECT DOESN'T SPREAD VERY WIDE, BUT IT'S ENOUGH!

AHH!!

CRMBLL

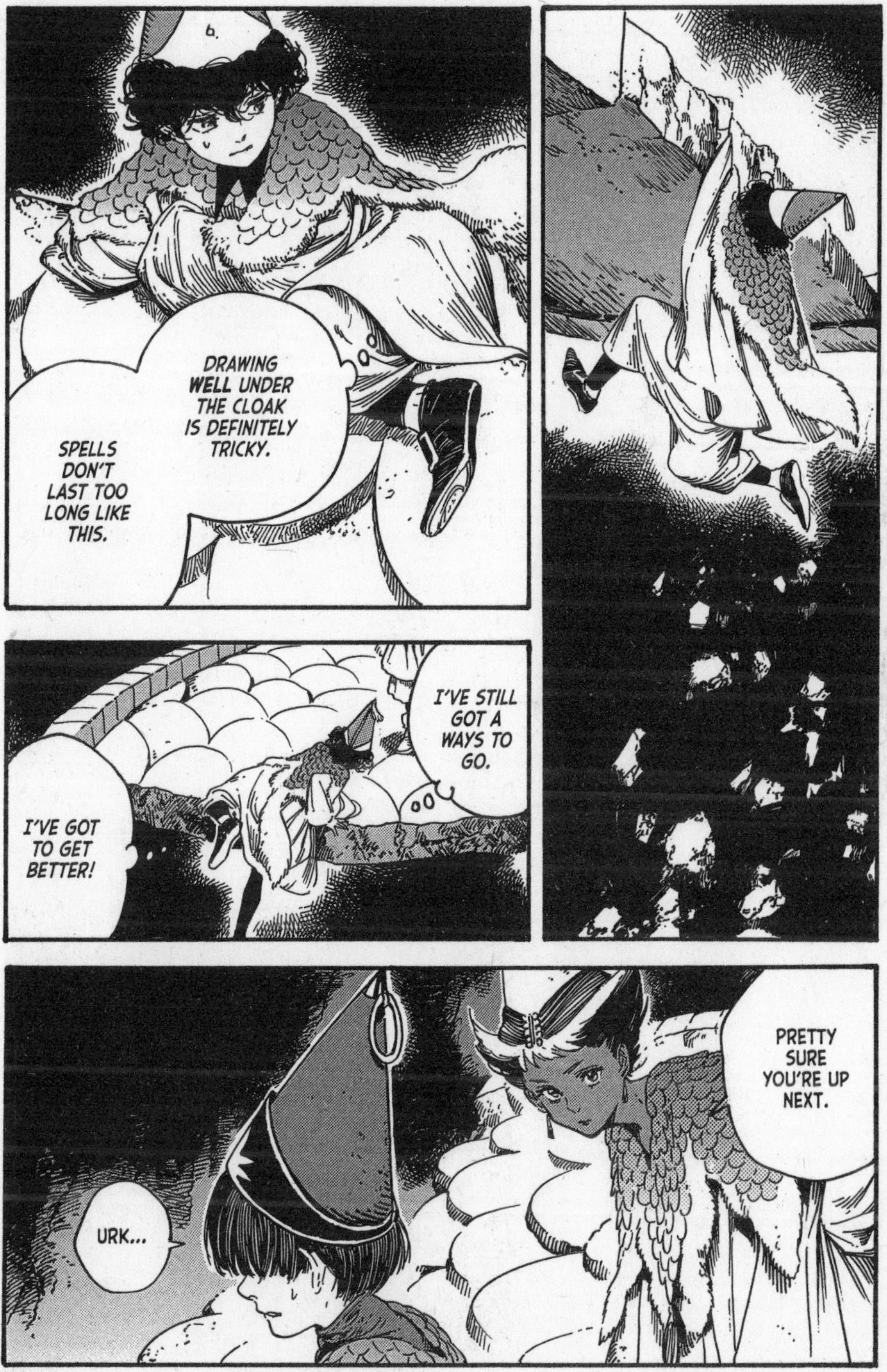
DRAWING WELL UNDER THE CLOAK IS DEFINITELY TRICKY.
SPELLS DON'T LAST TOO LONG LIKE THIS.
I'VE STILL GOT A WAYS TO GO.
I'VE GOT TO GET BETTER!
PRETTY SURE YOU'RE UP NEXT.
URK...

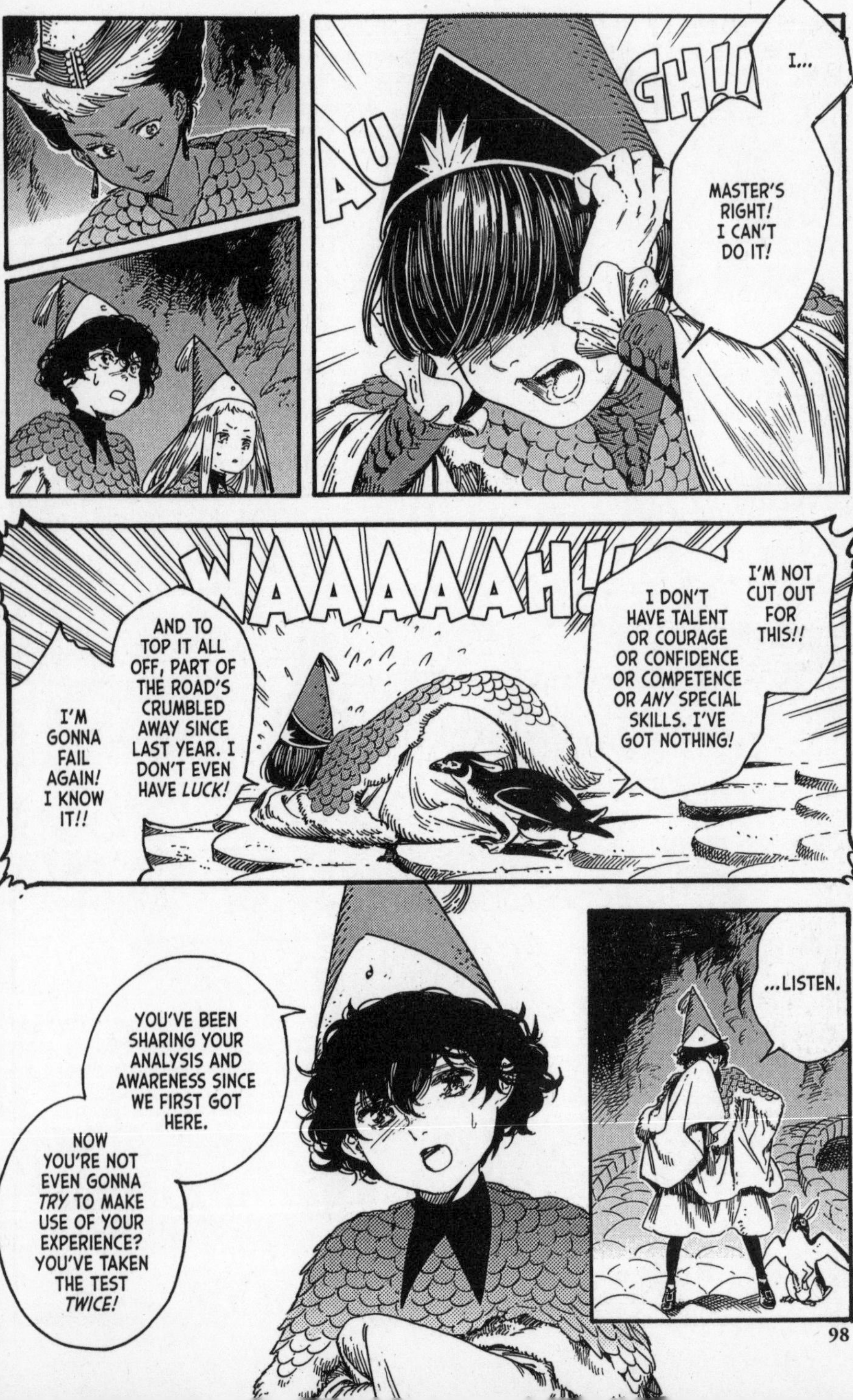
AUGH!!
I...
MASTER'S RIGHT! I CAN'T DO IT!
WAAAAAH!!
I'M NOT CUT OUT FOR THIS!!
I DON'T HAVE TALENT OR COURAGE OR CONFIDENCE OR COMPETENCE OR *ANY* SPECIAL SKILLS. I'VE GOT NOTHING!
AND TO TOP IT ALL OFF, PART OF THE ROAD'S CRUMBLED AWAY SINCE LAST YEAR. I DON'T EVEN HAVE *LUCK!*
I'M GONNA FAIL AGAIN! I KNOW IT!!
...LISTEN.
YOU'VE BEEN SHARING YOUR ANALYSIS AND AWARENESS SINCE WE FIRST GOT HERE.
NOW YOU'RE NOT EVEN GONNA *TRY* TO MAKE USE OF YOUR EXPERIENCE? YOU'VE TAKEN THE TEST *TWICE!*

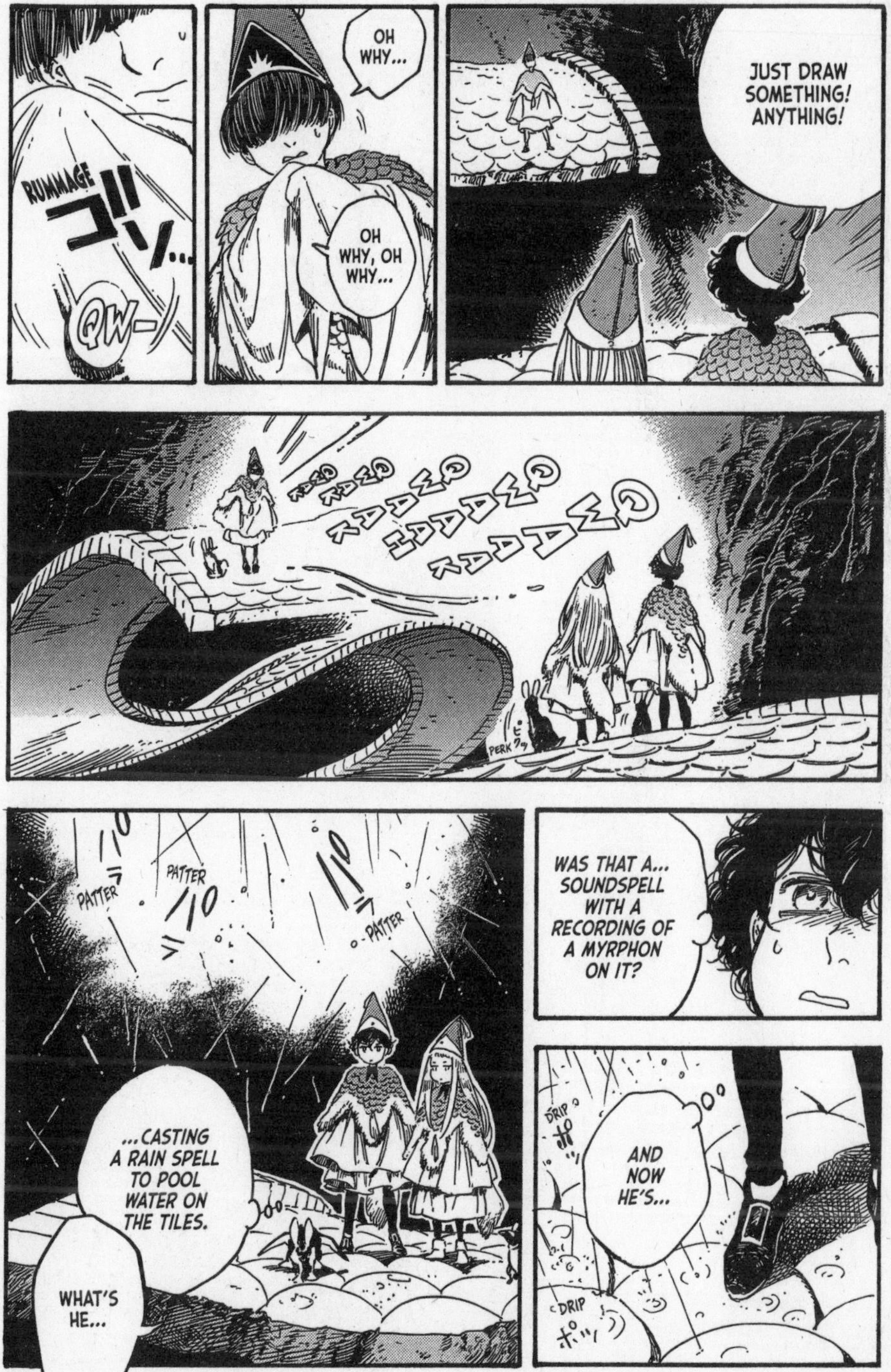
JUST DRAW SOMETHING! ANYTHING!
OH WHY...
OH WHY, OH WHY...
RUMMAGE
ゴソ...
QW–
QWAAAK
QWAAA!
QWAAK
QWAK
QWAK
PERK
ピクッ
WAS THAT A... SOUNDSPELL WITH A RECORDING OF A MYRPHON ON IT?
DRIP
DRIP
ポツ
AND NOW HE'S...
PATTER
PATTER
PATTER
パラ
...CASTING A RAIN SPELL TO POOL WATER ON THE TILES.
WHAT'S HE...

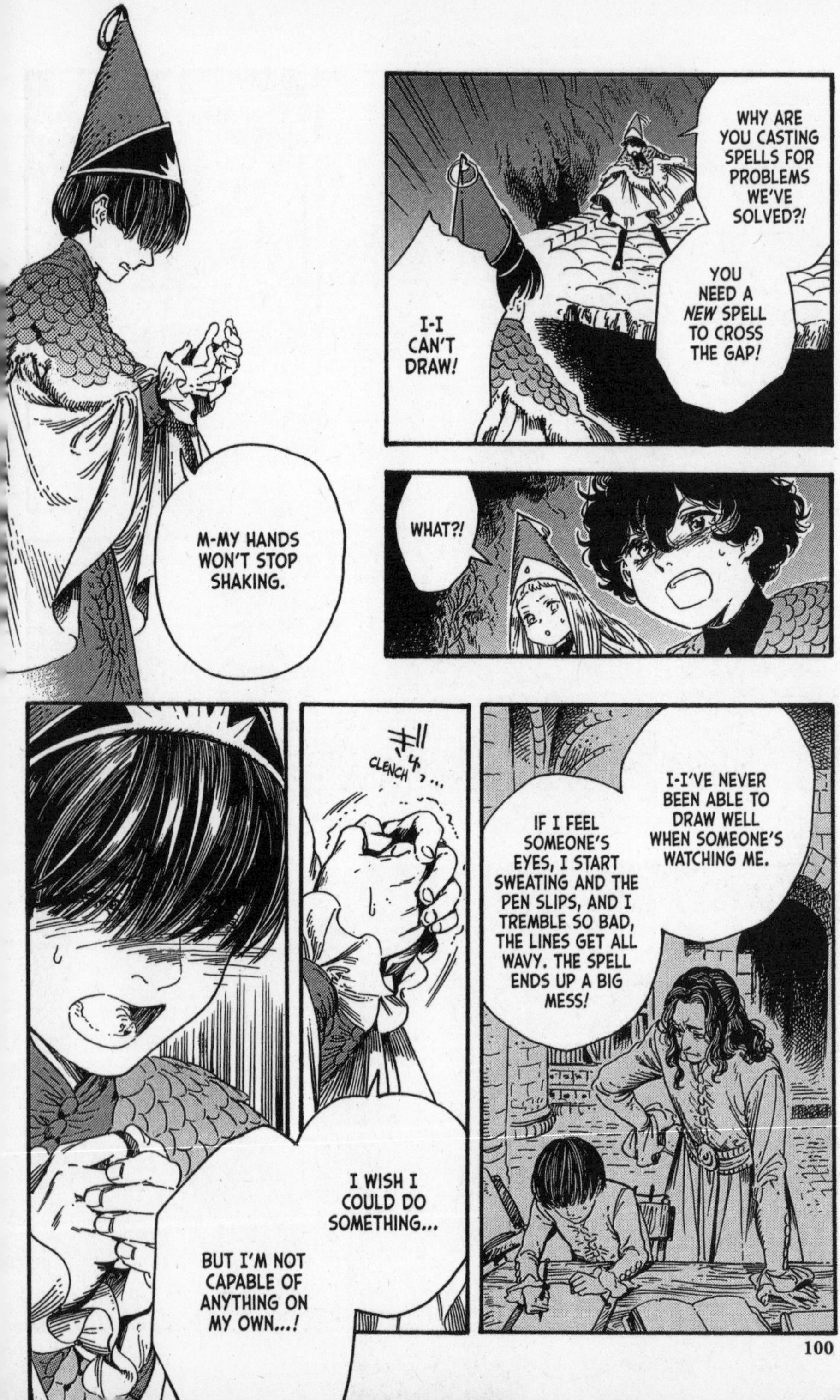
WHY ARE YOU CASTING SPELLS FOR PROBLEMS WE'VE SOLVED?!
YOU NEED A *NEW* SPELL TO CROSS THE GAP!
I-I CAN'T DRAW!
WHAT?!
M-MY HANDS WON'T STOP SHAKING.
I-I'VE NEVER BEEN ABLE TO DRAW WELL WHEN SOMEONE'S WATCHING ME.
IF I FEEL SOMEONE'S EYES, I START SWEATING AND THE PEN SLIPS, AND I TREMBLE SO BAD, THE LINES GET ALL WAVY. THE SPELL ENDS UP A BIG MESS!
CLENCH
I WISH I COULD DO SOMETHING...
BUT I'M NOT CAPABLE OF ANYTHING ON MY OWN...!

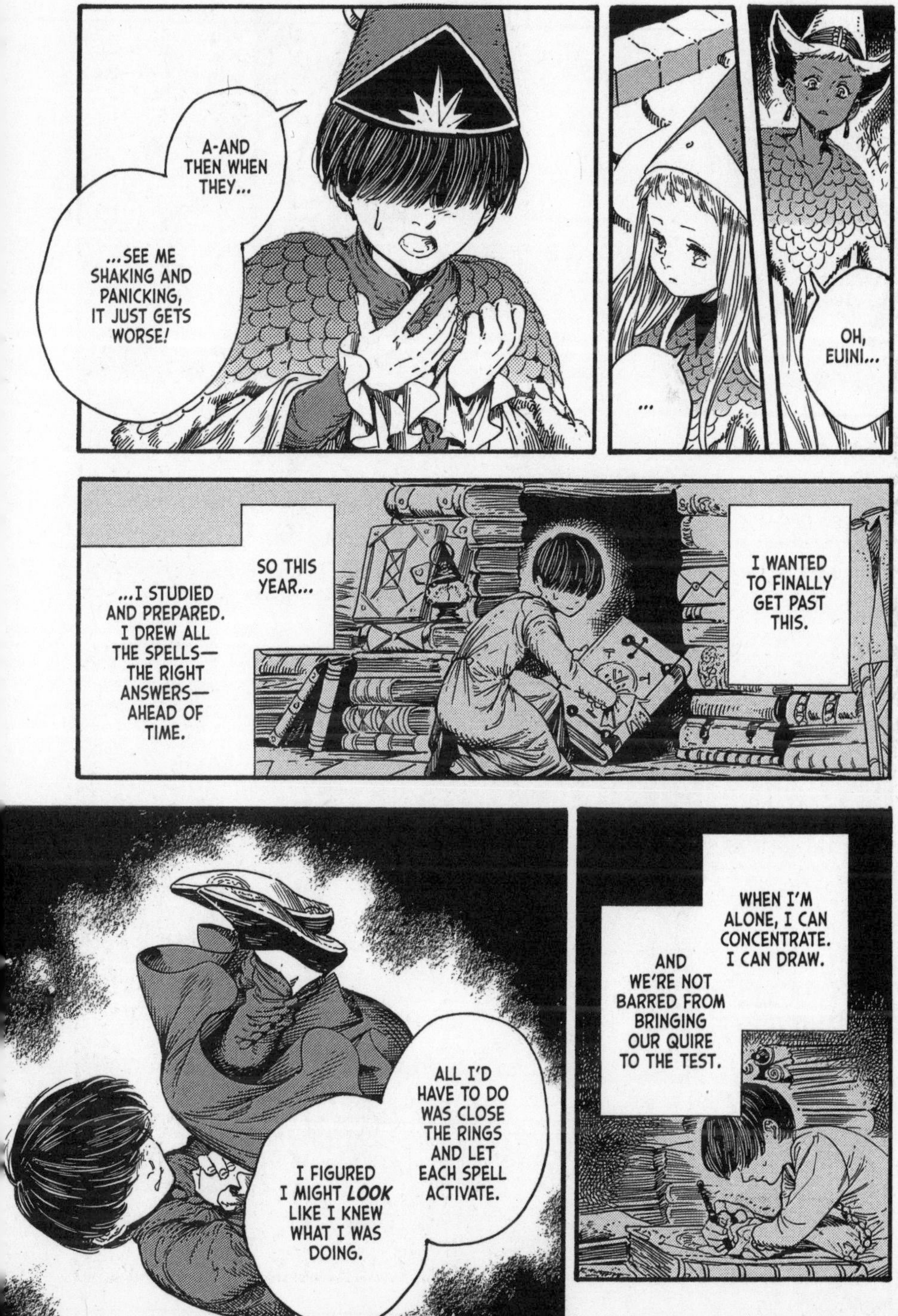
OH, EUINI...
...
A-AND THEN WHEN THEY...
...SEE ME SHAKING AND PANICKING, IT JUST GETS WORSE!
I WANTED TO FINALLY GET PAST THIS.
SO THIS YEAR...
...I STUDIED AND PREPARED. I DREW ALL THE SPELLS—THE RIGHT ANSWERS—AHEAD OF TIME.
WHEN I'M ALONE, I CAN CONCENTRATE. I CAN DRAW.
AND WE'RE NOT BARRED FROM BRINGING OUR QUIRE TO THE TEST.
ALL I'D HAVE TO DO WAS CLOSE THE RINGS AND LET EACH SPELL ACTIVATE.
I FIGURED I MIGHT *LOOK* LIKE I KNEW WHAT I WAS DOING.

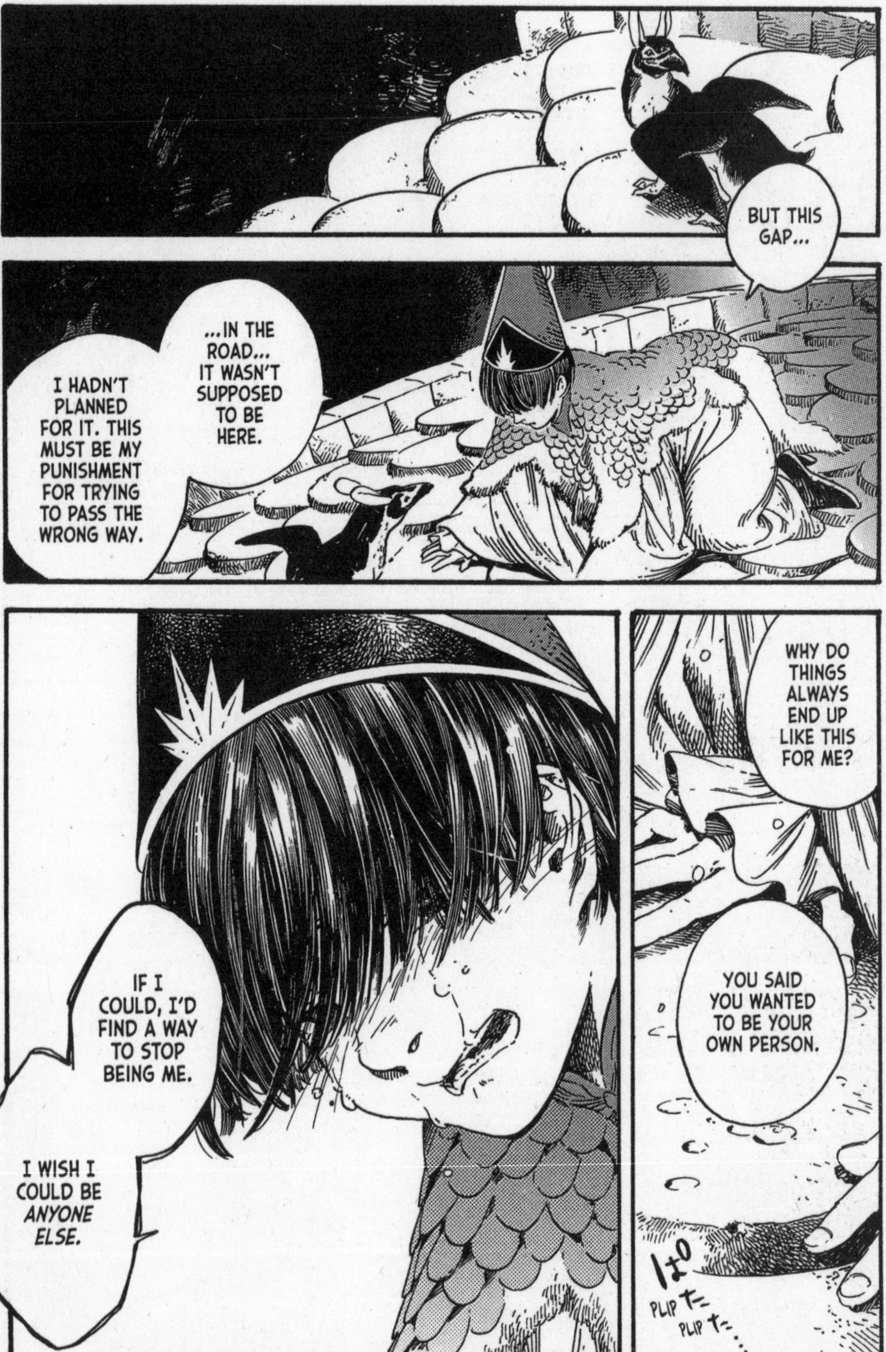
BUT THIS GAP...
...IN THE ROAD... IT WASN'T SUPPOSED TO BE HERE.
I HADN'T PLANNED FOR IT. THIS MUST BE MY PUNISHMENT FOR TRYING TO PASS THE WRONG WAY.
WHY DO THINGS ALWAYS END UP LIKE THIS FOR ME?
YOU SAID YOU WANTED TO BE YOUR OWN PERSON.
PLIP
PLIP
IF I COULD, I'D FIND A WAY TO STOP BEING ME.
I WISH I COULD BE *ANYONE ELSE.*

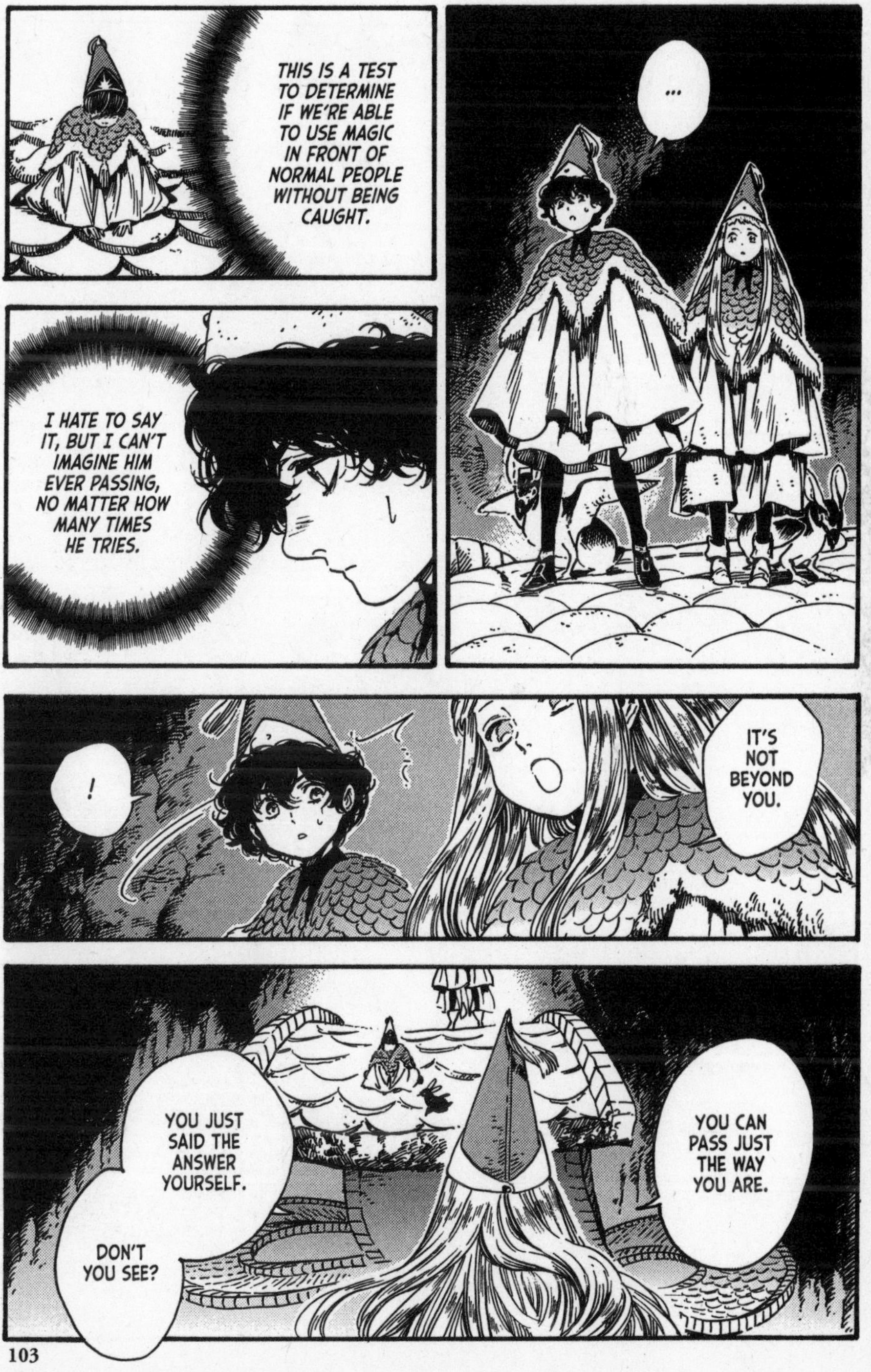
...
THIS IS A TEST TO DETERMINE IF WE'RE ABLE TO USE MAGIC IN FRONT OF NORMAL PEOPLE WITHOUT BEING CAUGHT.
I HATE TO SAY IT, BUT I CAN'T IMAGINE HIM EVER PASSING, NO MATTER HOW MANY TIMES HE TRIES.
IT'S NOT BEYOND YOU.
!
YOU CAN PASS JUST THE WAY YOU ARE.
YOU JUST SAID THE ANSWER YOURSELF.
DON'T YOU SEE?

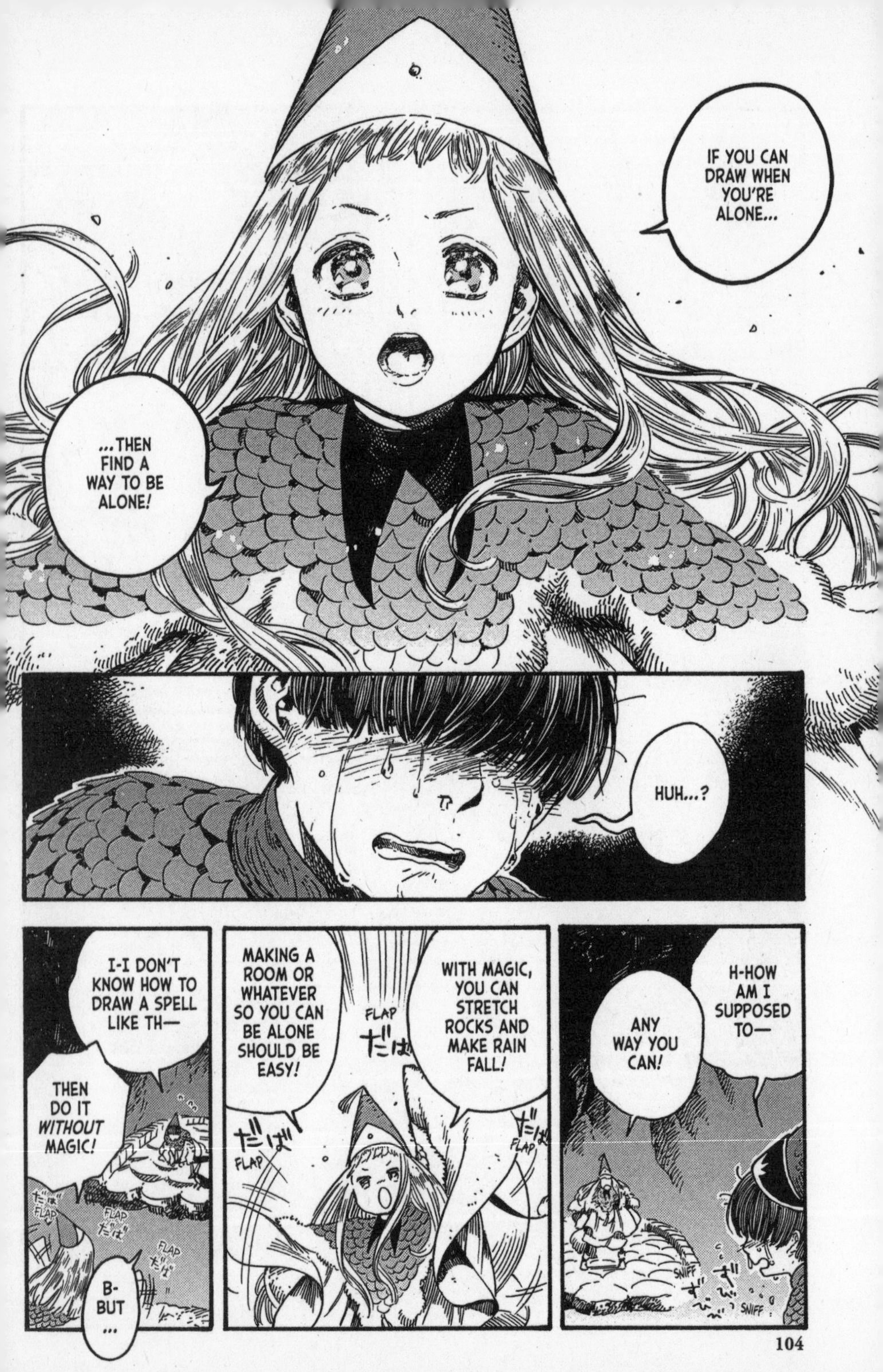
IF YOU CAN DRAW WHEN YOU'RE ALONE...
...THEN FIND A WAY TO BE ALONE!
HUH...?
H-HOW AM I SUPPOSED TO—
ANY WAY YOU CAN!
SNIFF
SNIFF
WITH MAGIC, YOU CAN STRETCH ROCKS AND MAKE RAIN FALL!
FLAP
MAKING A ROOM OR WHATEVER SO YOU CAN BE ALONE SHOULD BE EASY!
FLAP
FLAP
I-I DON'T KNOW HOW TO DRAW A SPELL LIKE TH—
THEN DO IT WITHOUT MAGIC!
FLAP
FLAP
FLAP
B-BUT ...

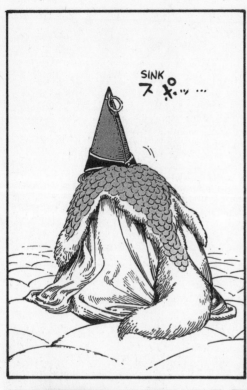

SINK
スポッ…

THAT'S IMPOSSIBLE...

I CAN'T JUST COME UP WITH SOMETHING ON THE SPOT.

I....

I CAN'T...

...

...

...

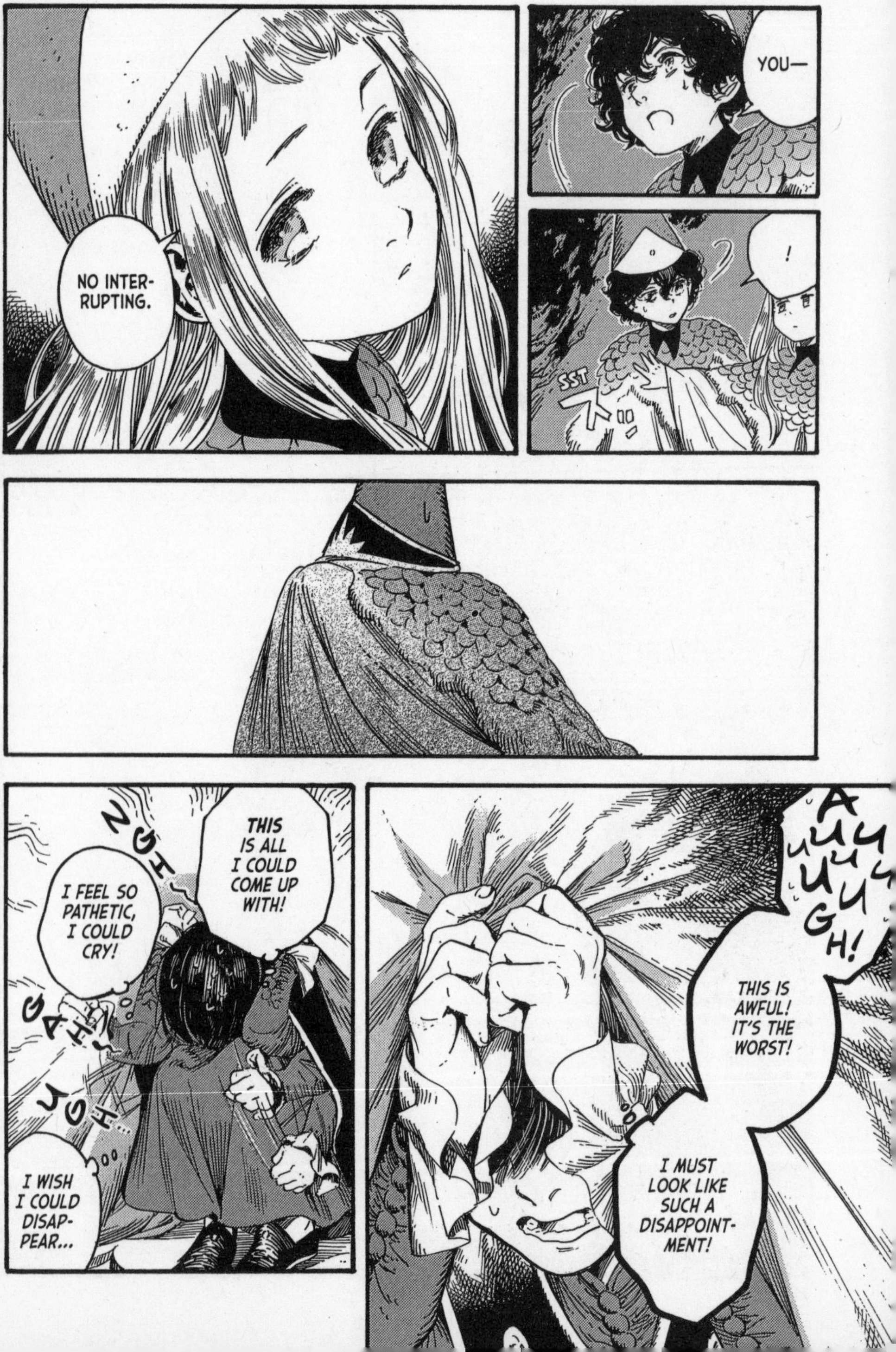
YOU—
!
SST
NO INTER-RUPTING.
AUUUUUUGH!
THIS IS AWFUL! IT'S THE WORST!
I MUST LOOK LIKE SUCH A DISAPPOINT-MENT!
THIS IS ALL I COULD COME UP WITH!
I FEEL SO PATHETIC, I COULD CRY!
GAH~
UGH...
I WISH I COULD DISAP-PEAR...

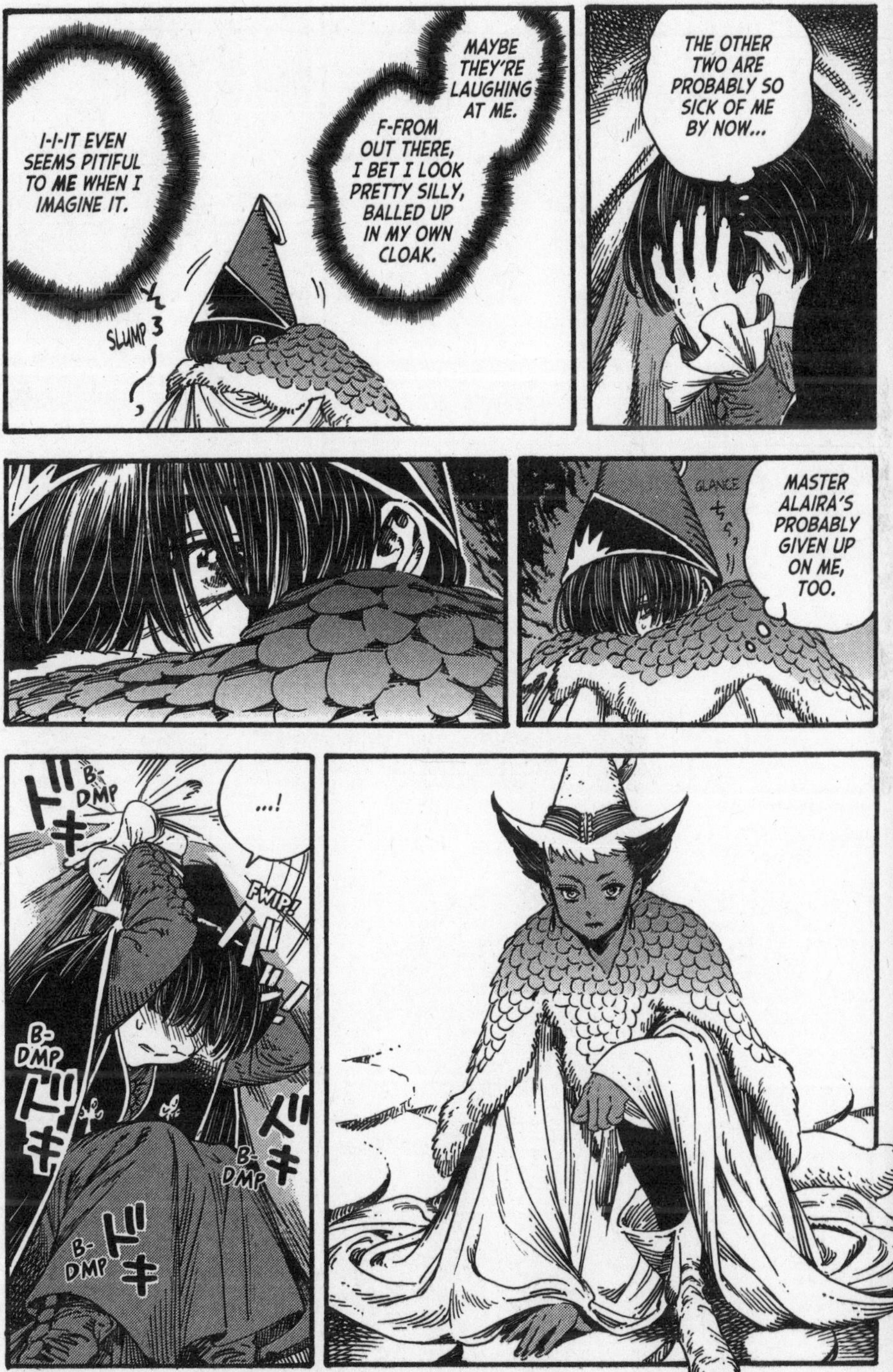
THE OTHER TWO ARE PROBABLY SO SICK OF ME BY NOW...
MAYBE THEY'RE LAUGHING AT ME.
F-FROM OUT THERE, I BET I LOOK PRETTY SILLY, BALLED UP IN MY OWN CLOAK.
I-I-IT EVEN SEEMS PITIFUL TO ME WHEN I IMAGINE IT.
SLUMP
GLANCE
MASTER ALAIRA'S PROBABLY GIVEN UP ON ME, TOO.
...!
B-DMP
FWIP!
B-DMP
B-DMP
B-DMP

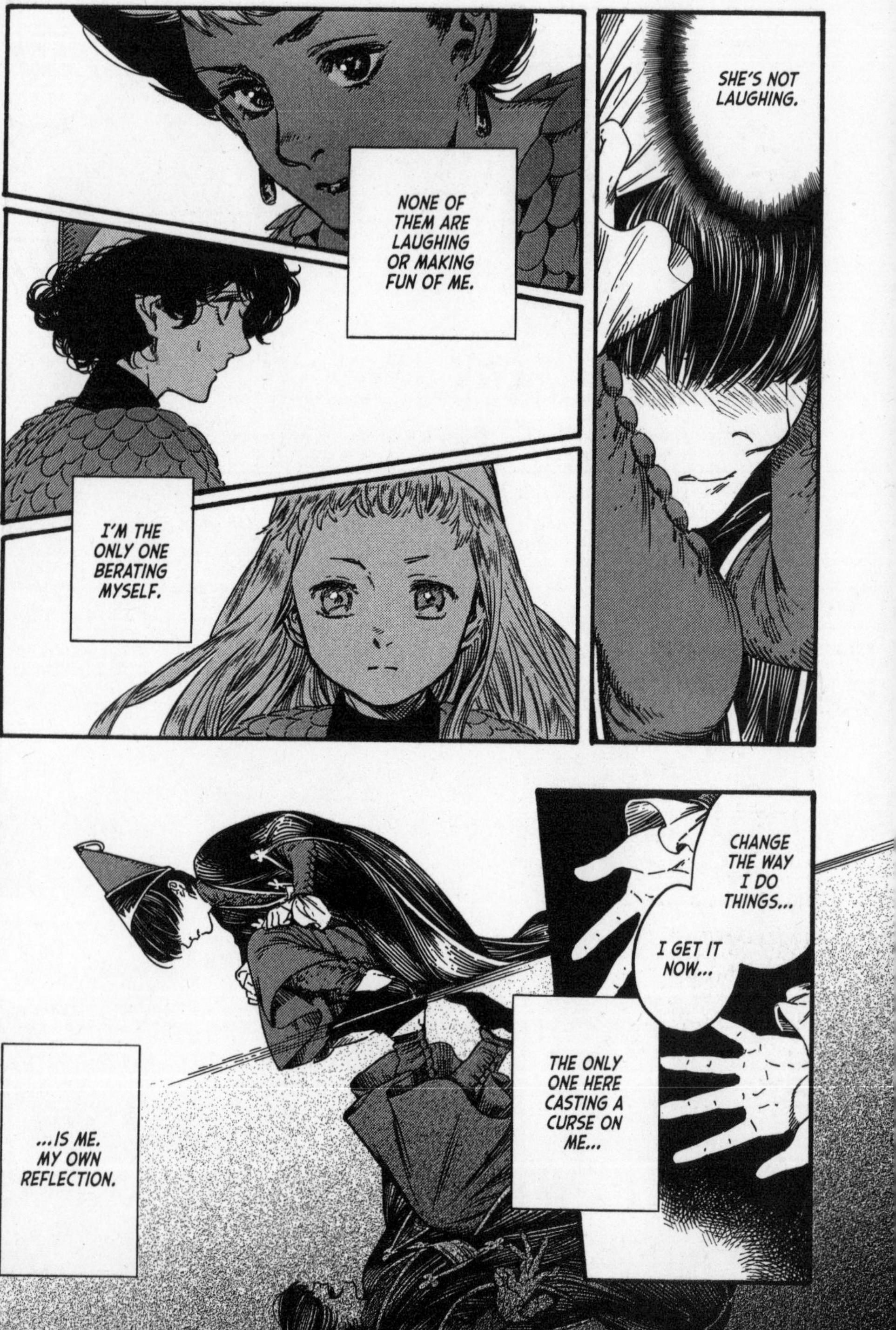
SHE'S NOT LAUGHING.
NONE OF THEM ARE LAUGHING OR MAKING FUN OF ME.
I'M THE ONLY ONE BERATING MYSELF.
CHANGE THE WAY I DO THINGS...
I GET IT NOW...
THE ONLY ONE HERE CASTING A CURSE ON ME...
...IS ME. MY OWN REFLECTION.

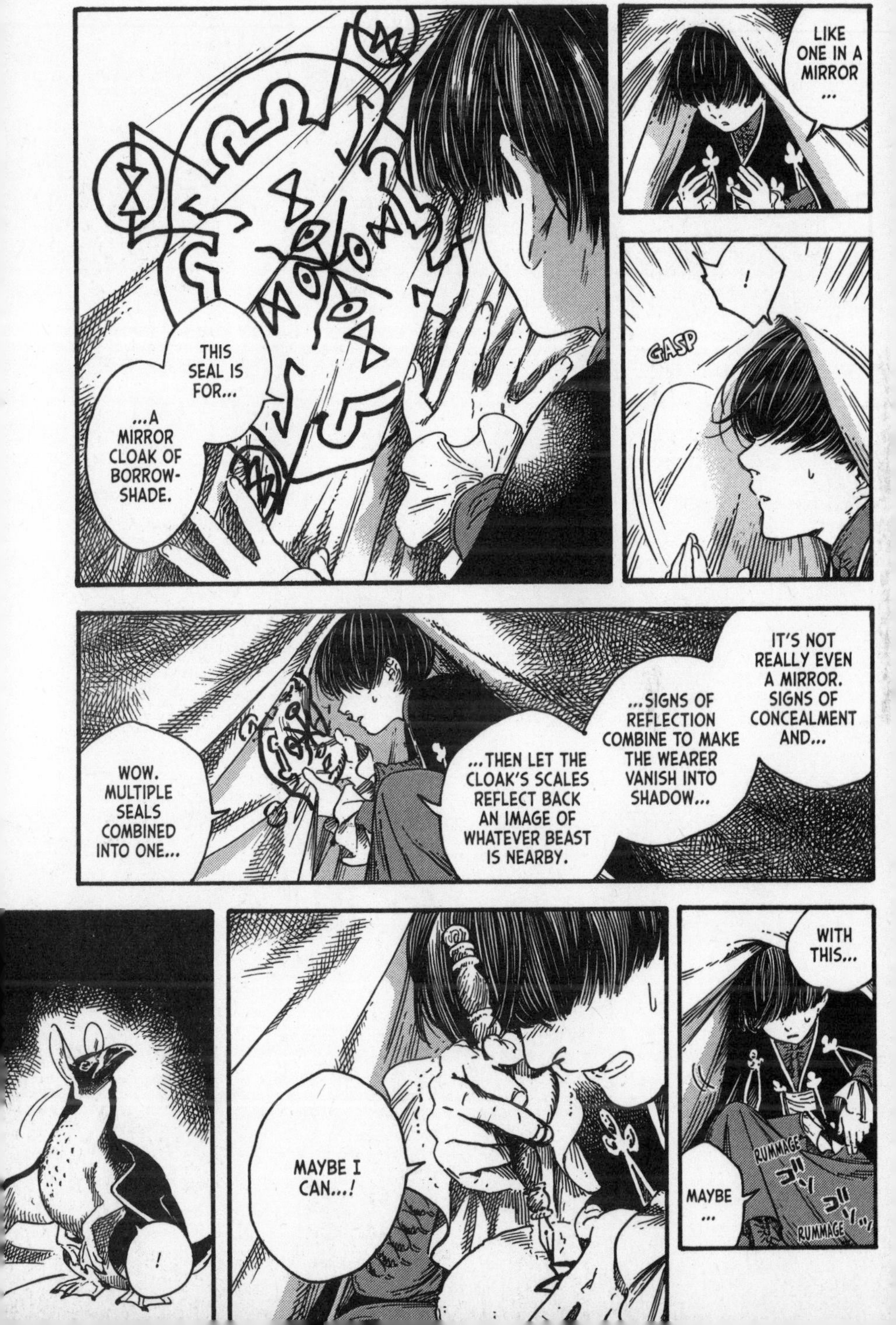
LIKE ONE IN A MIRROR ...
!
GASP
THIS SEAL IS FOR...
...A MIRROR CLOAK OF BORROW-SHADE.
IT'S NOT REALLY EVEN A MIRROR. SIGNS OF CONCEALMENT AND...
...SIGNS OF REFLECTION COMBINE TO MAKE THE WEARER VANISH INTO SHADOW...
...THEN LET THE CLOAK'S SCALES REFLECT BACK AN IMAGE OF WHATEVER BEAST IS NEARBY.
WOW. MULTIPLE SEALS COMBINED INTO ONE...
WITH THIS...
RUMMAGE
ゴソ
ゴソッ
RUMMAGE
MAYBE ...
MAYBE I CAN...!
!

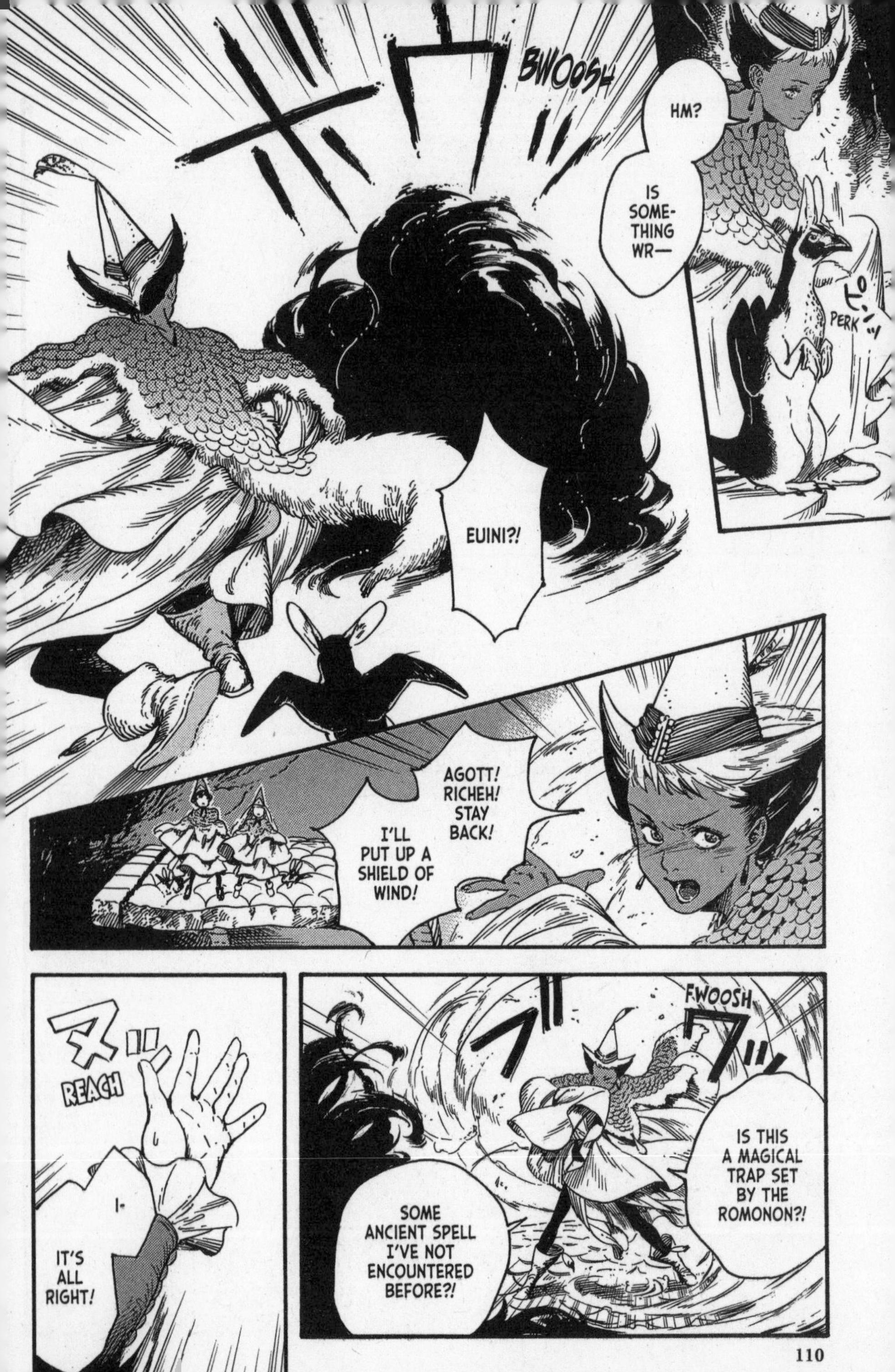
HM?
IS SOMETHING WR—
PERK
BWOOSH
EUINI?!
AGOTT! RICHEH! STAY BACK!
I'LL PUT UP A SHIELD OF WIND!
FWOOSH
IS THIS A MAGICAL TRAP SET BY THE ROMONON?!
SOME ANCIENT SPELL I'VE NOT ENCOUNTERED BEFORE?!
REACH
I-
IT'S ALL RIGHT!

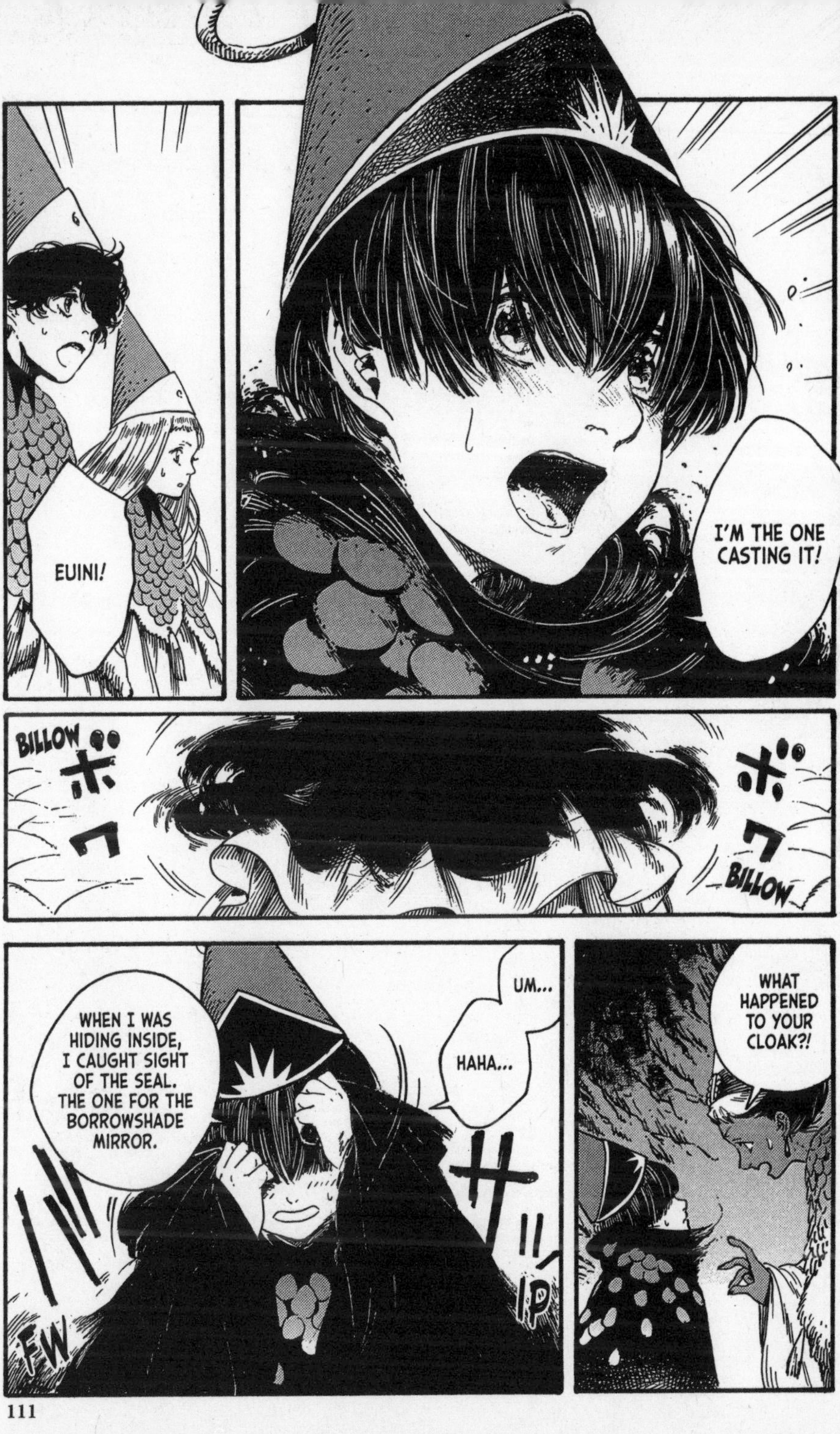
I'M THE ONE CASTING IT!
EUINI!
ボワ
BILLOW
ボワ
BILLOW
WHAT HAPPENED TO YOUR CLOAK?!
UM...
HAHA...
サッ
IP
WHEN I WAS HIDING INSIDE, I CAUGHT SIGHT OF THE SEAL. THE ONE FOR THE BORROWSHADE MIRROR.
FW

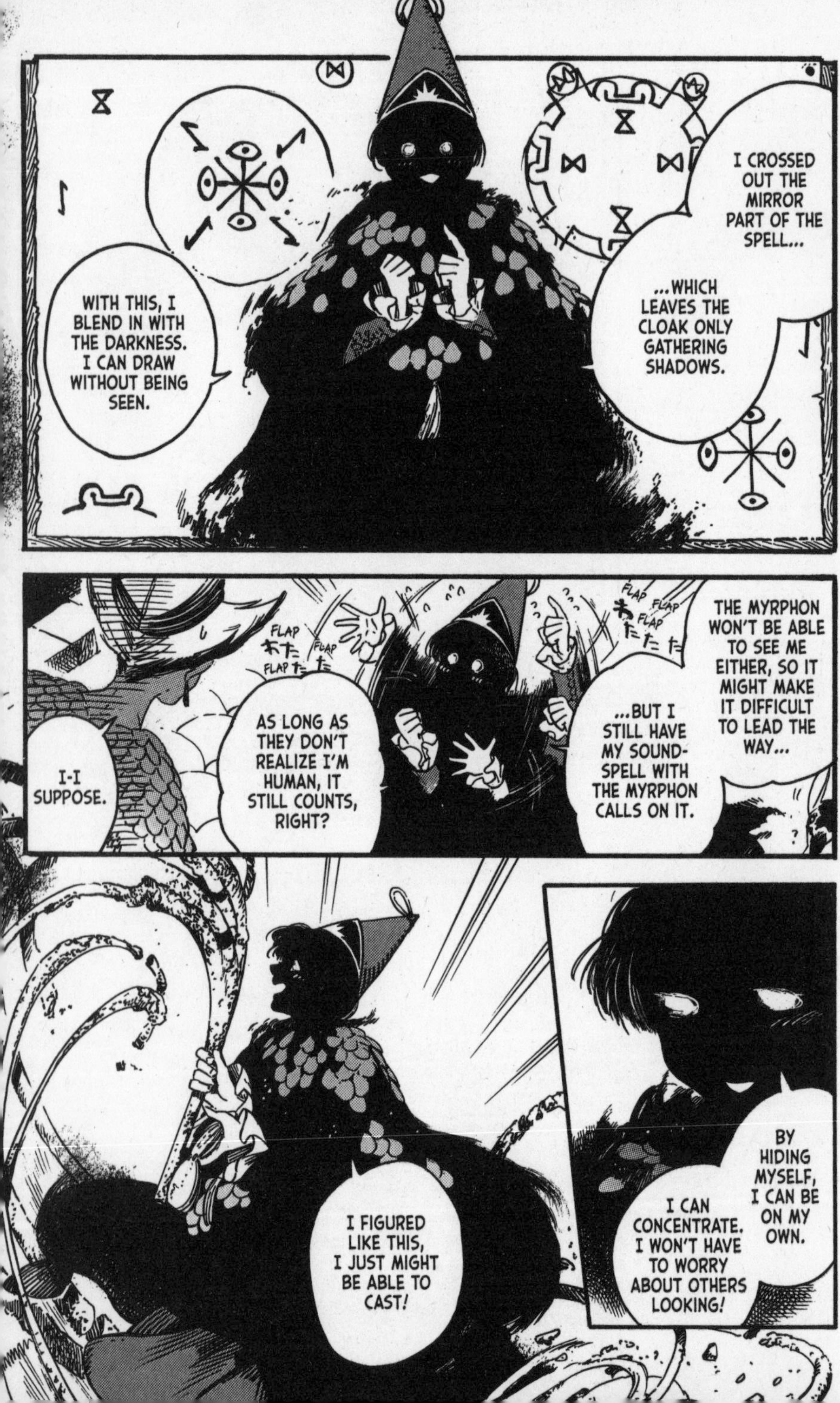
I CROSSED OUT THE MIRROR PART OF THE SPELL...
...WHICH LEAVES THE CLOAK ONLY GATHERING SHADOWS.
WITH THIS, I BLEND IN WITH THE DARKNESS. I CAN DRAW WITHOUT BEING SEEN.
THE MYRPHON WON'T BE ABLE TO SEE ME EITHER, SO IT MIGHT MAKE IT DIFFICULT TO LEAD THE WAY...
FLAP FLAP FLAP
...BUT I STILL HAVE MY SOUND-SPELL WITH THE MYRPHON CALLS ON IT.
FLAP FLAP FLAP
AS LONG AS THEY DON'T REALIZE I'M HUMAN, IT STILL COUNTS, RIGHT?
I-I SUPPOSE.
BY HIDING MYSELF, I CAN BE ON MY OWN.
I CAN CONCENTRATE. I WON'T HAVE TO WORRY ABOUT OTHERS LOOKING!
I FIGURED LIKE THIS, I JUST MIGHT BE ABLE TO CAST!

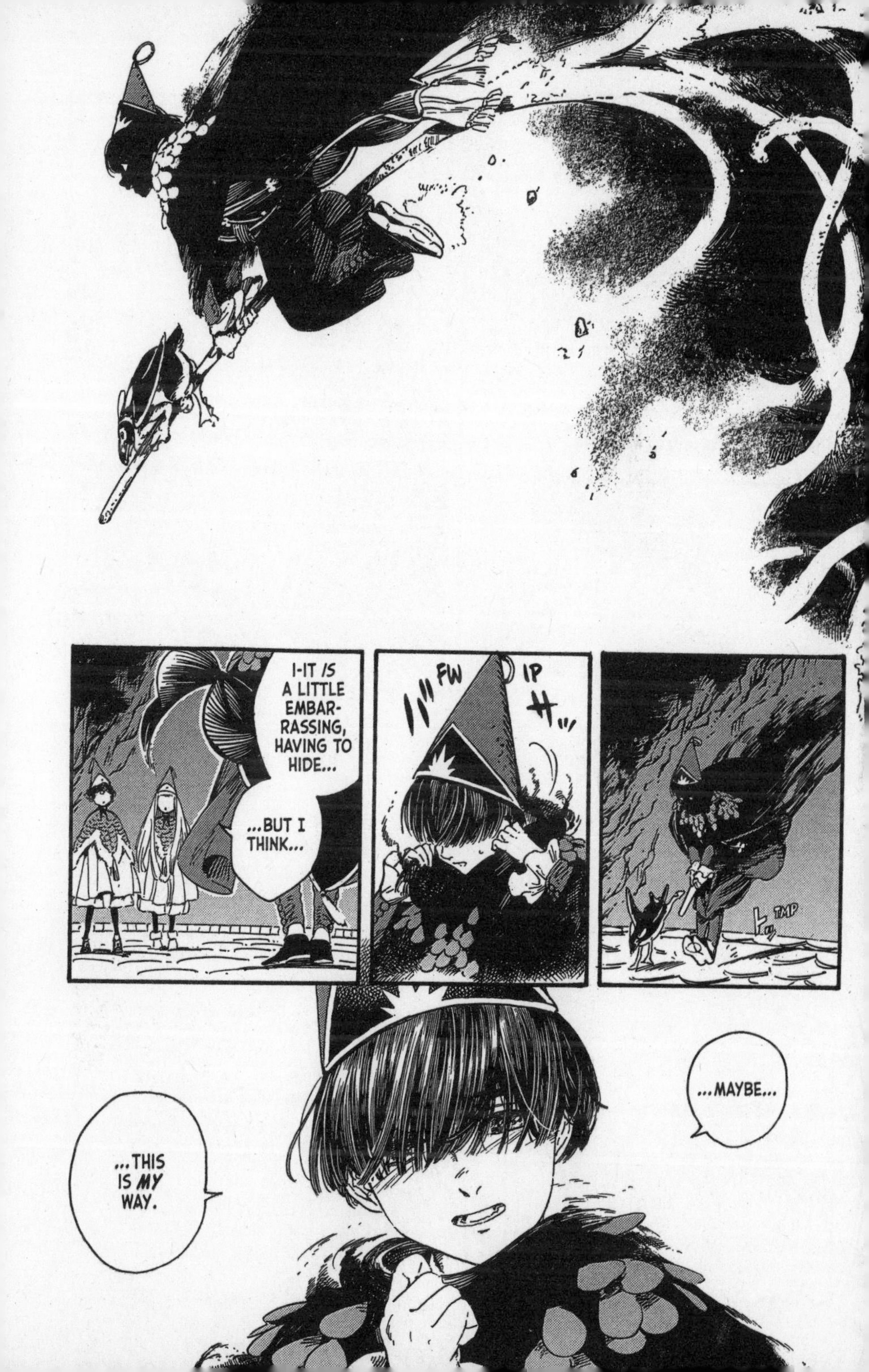
TMP
FWIP
I-IT *IS* A LITTLE EMBARRASSING, HAVING TO HIDE...
...BUT I THINK...
...MAYBE...
...THIS IS *MY* WAY.

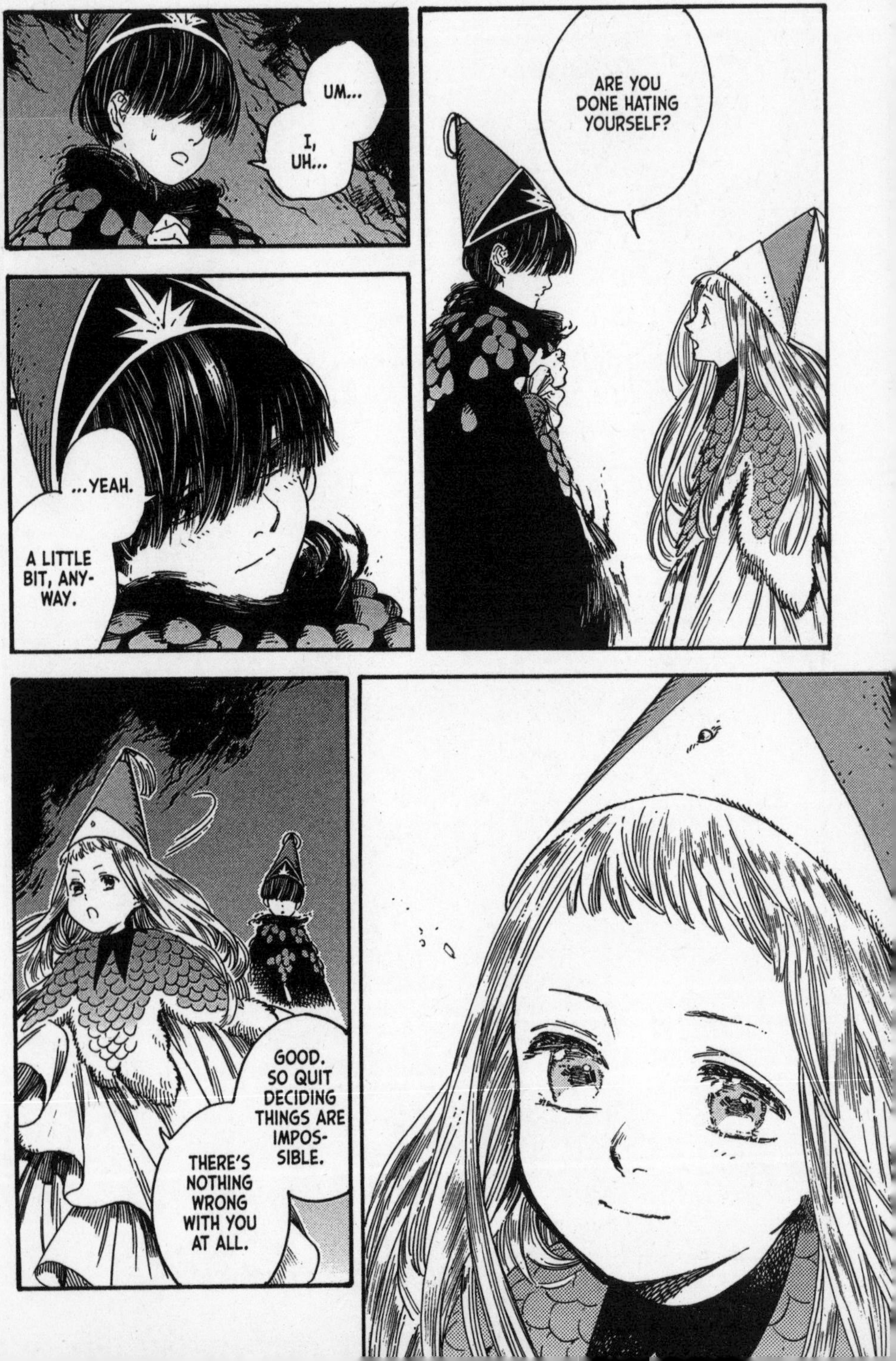
ARE YOU DONE HATING YOURSELF?
UM...
I, UH...
...YEAH.
A LITTLE BIT, ANY-WAY.
GOOD. SO QUIT DECIDING THINGS ARE IMPOS-SIBLE.
THERE'S NOTHING WRONG WITH YOU AT ALL.

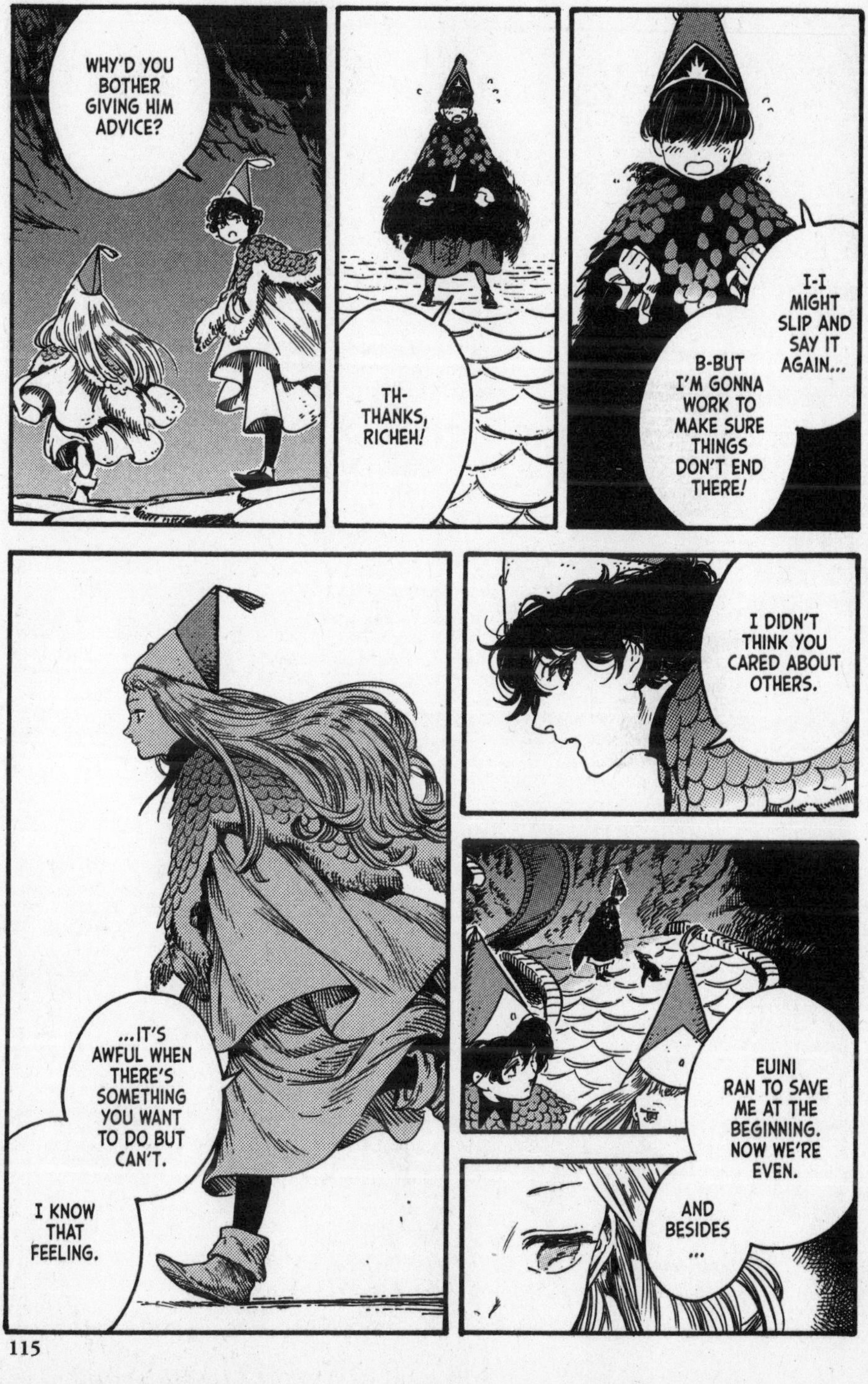
I-I MIGHT SLIP AND SAY IT AGAIN...
B-BUT I'M GONNA WORK TO MAKE SURE THINGS DON'T END THERE!
TH-THANKS, RICHEH!
WHY'D YOU BOTHER GIVING HIM ADVICE?
I DIDN'T THINK YOU CARED ABOUT OTHERS.
EUINI RAN TO SAVE ME AT THE BEGINNING. NOW WE'RE EVEN.
AND BESIDES ...
...IT'S AWFUL WHEN THERE'S SOMETHING YOU WANT TO DO BUT CAN'T.
I KNOW THAT FEELING.

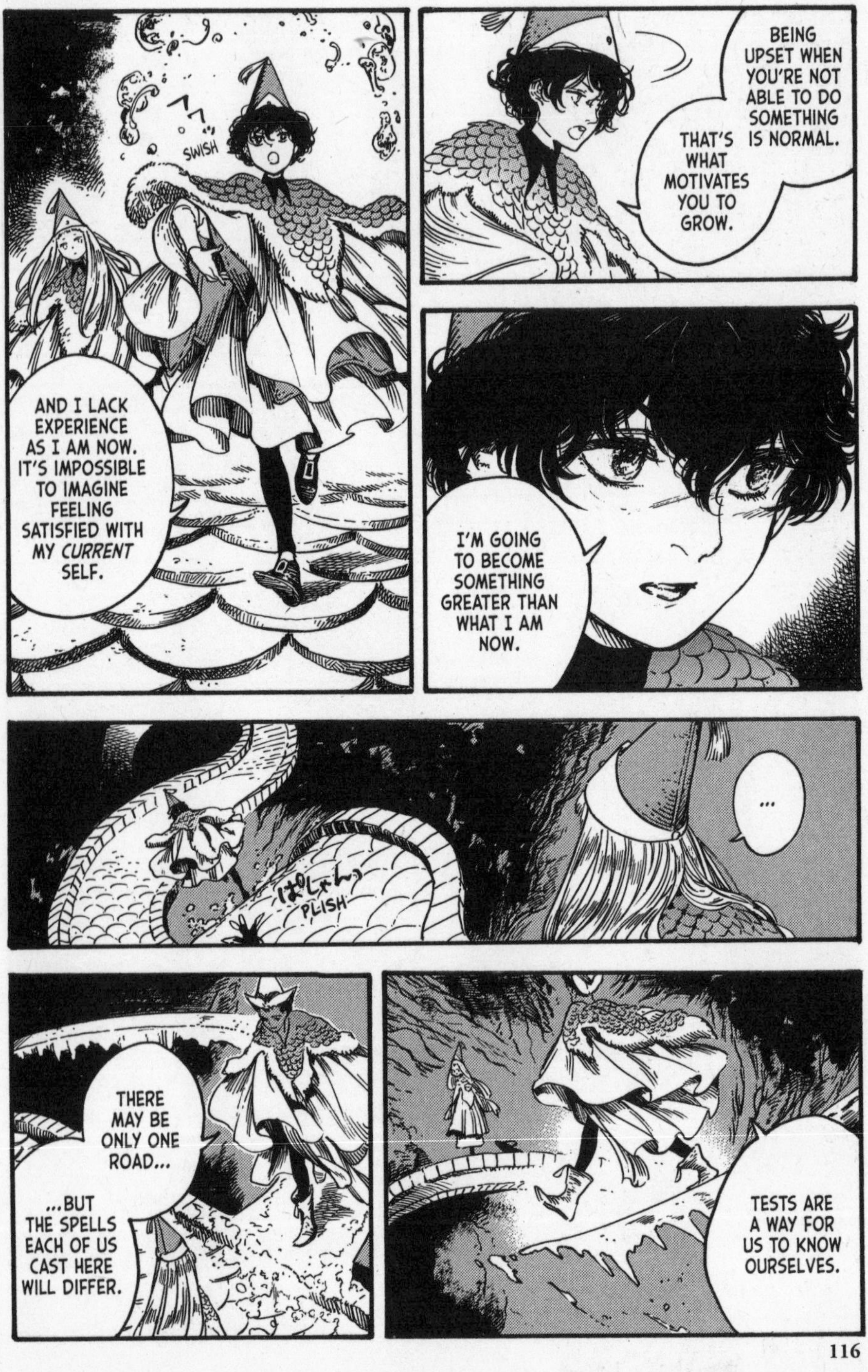
BEING UPSET WHEN YOU'RE NOT ABLE TO DO SOMETHING IS NORMAL.
THAT'S WHAT MOTIVATES YOU TO GROW.
I'M GOING TO BECOME SOMETHING GREATER THAN WHAT I AM NOW.
SWISH
AND I LACK EXPERIENCE AS I AM NOW. IT'S IMPOSSIBLE TO IMAGINE FEELING SATISFIED WITH MY *CURRENT* SELF.
...
ぱしゃんっ
PLISH
TESTS ARE A WAY FOR US TO KNOW OURSELVES.
THERE MAY BE ONLY ONE ROAD...
...BUT THE SPELLS EACH OF US CAST HERE WILL DIFFER.

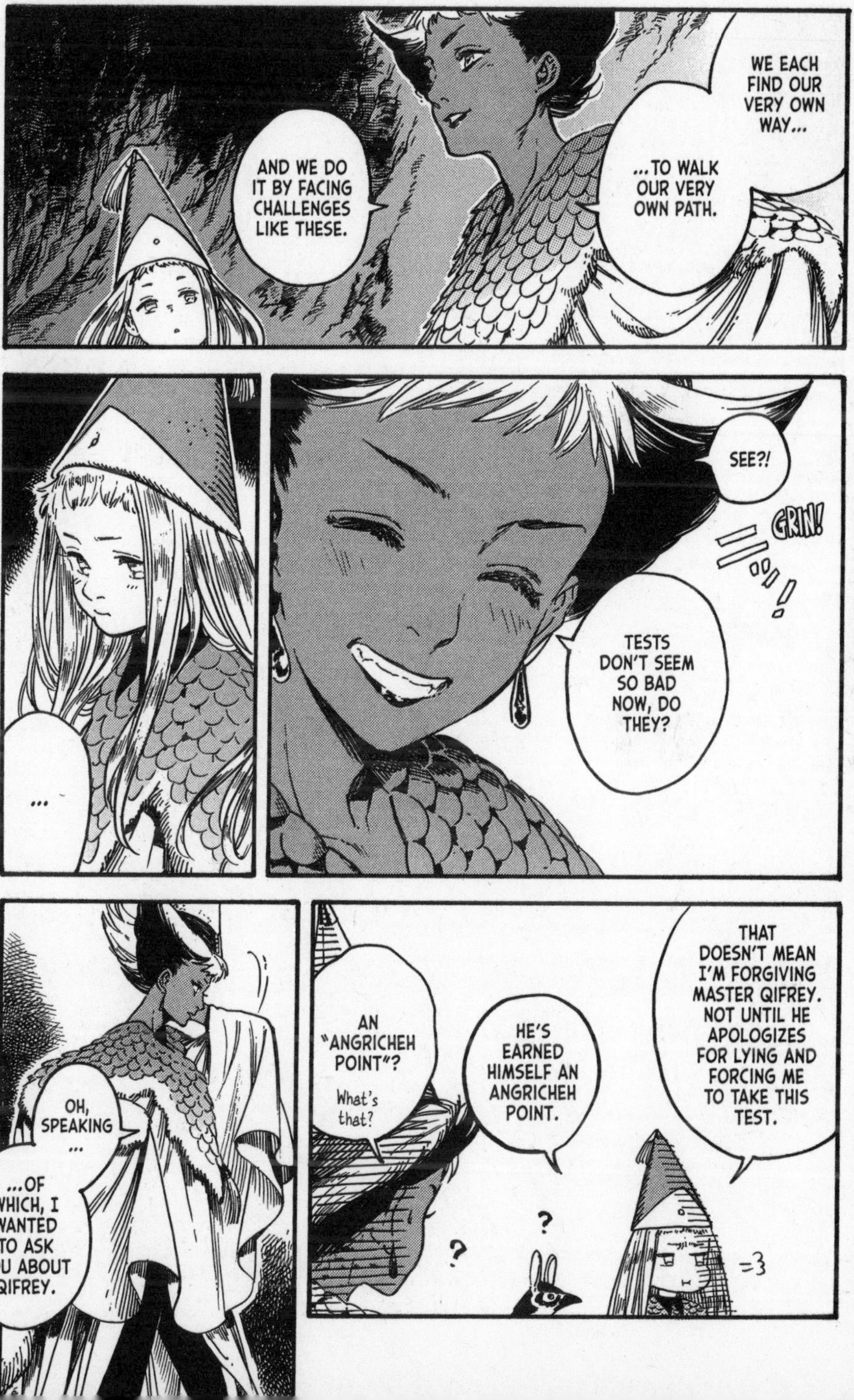
WE EACH FIND OUR VERY OWN WAY...
...TO WALK OUR VERY OWN PATH.
AND WE DO IT BY FACING CHALLENGES LIKE THESE.
SEE?!
GRIN!
TESTS DON'T SEEM SO BAD NOW, DO THEY?
...
THAT DOESN'T MEAN I'M FORGIVING MASTER QIFREY. NOT UNTIL HE APOLOGIZES FOR LYING AND FORCING ME TO TAKE THIS TEST.
HE'S EARNED HIMSELF AN ANGRICHEH POINT.
AN "ANGRICHEH POINT"?
What's that?
?
?
OH, SPEAKING...
...OF WHICH, I WANTED TO ASK YOU ABOUT QIFREY.

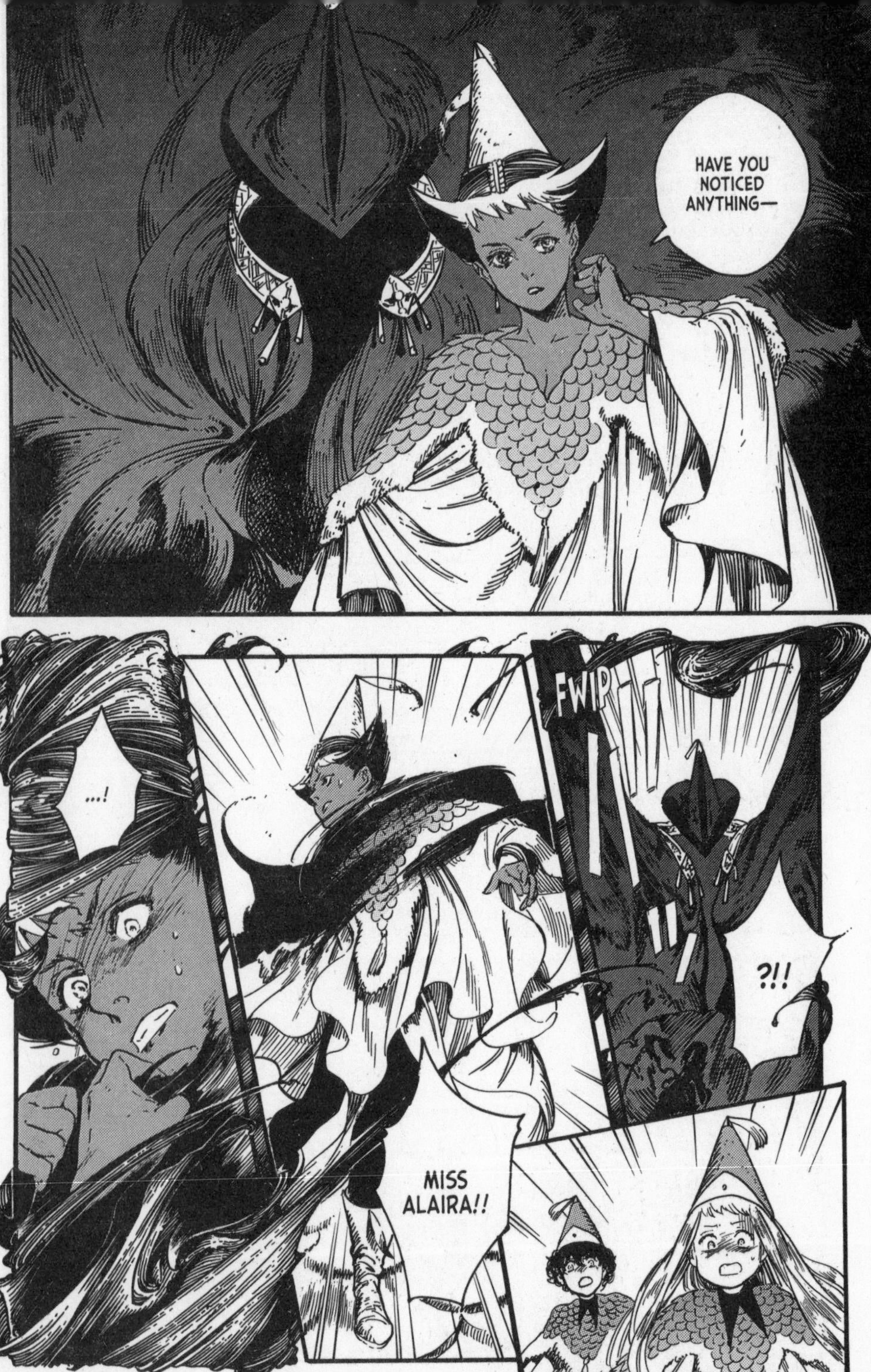

HAVE YOU NOTICED ANYTHING—
FWIP
?!!
MISS ALAIRA!!
...!

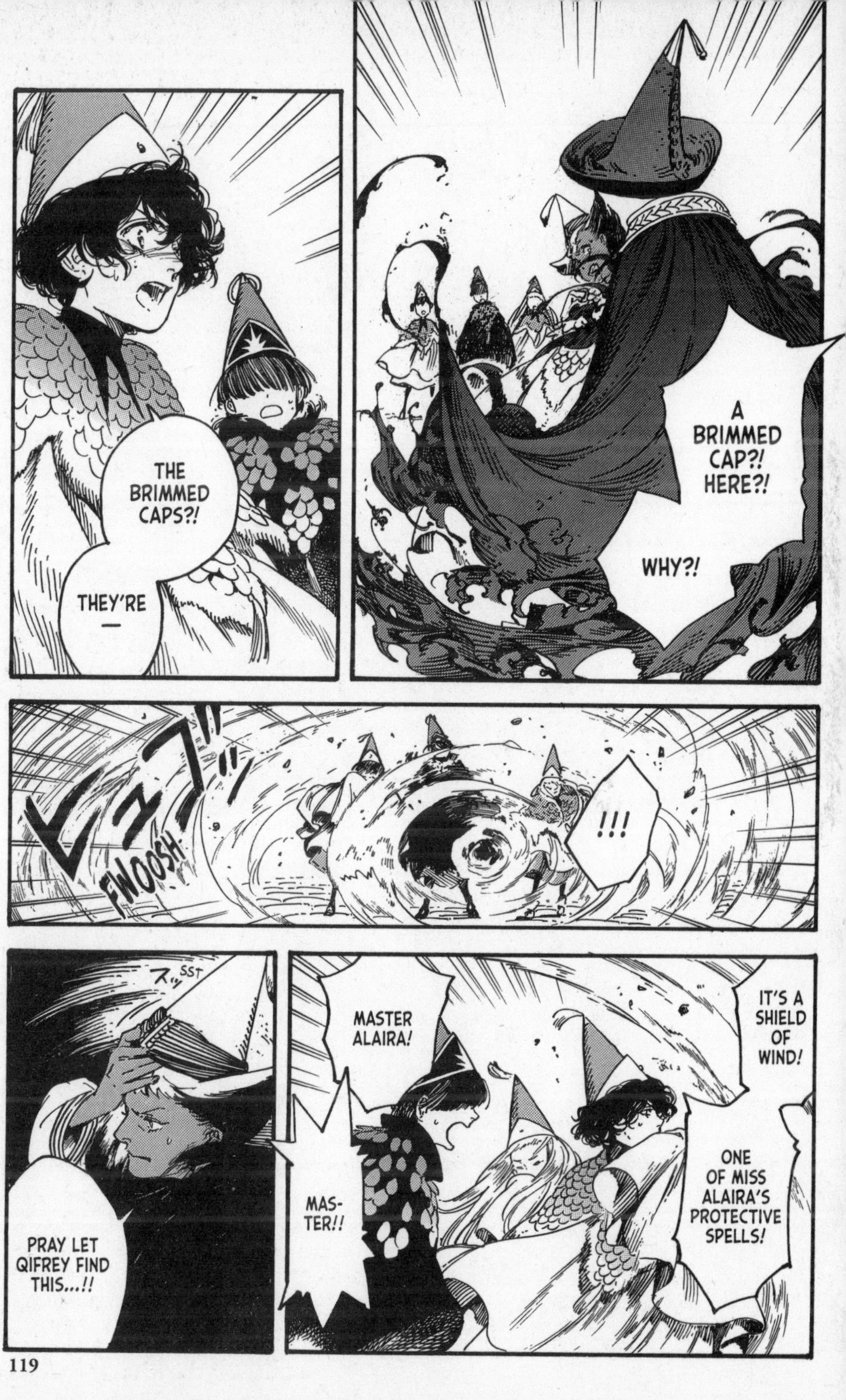
A BRIMMED CAP?! HERE?!
WHY?!
THE BRIMMED CAPS?!
THEY'RE —
!!!
FWOOSH
IT'S A SHIELD OF WIND!
MASTER ALAIRA!
ONE OF MISS ALAIRA'S PROTECTIVE SPELLS!
MASTER!!
SST
PRAY LET QIFREY FIND THIS...!!

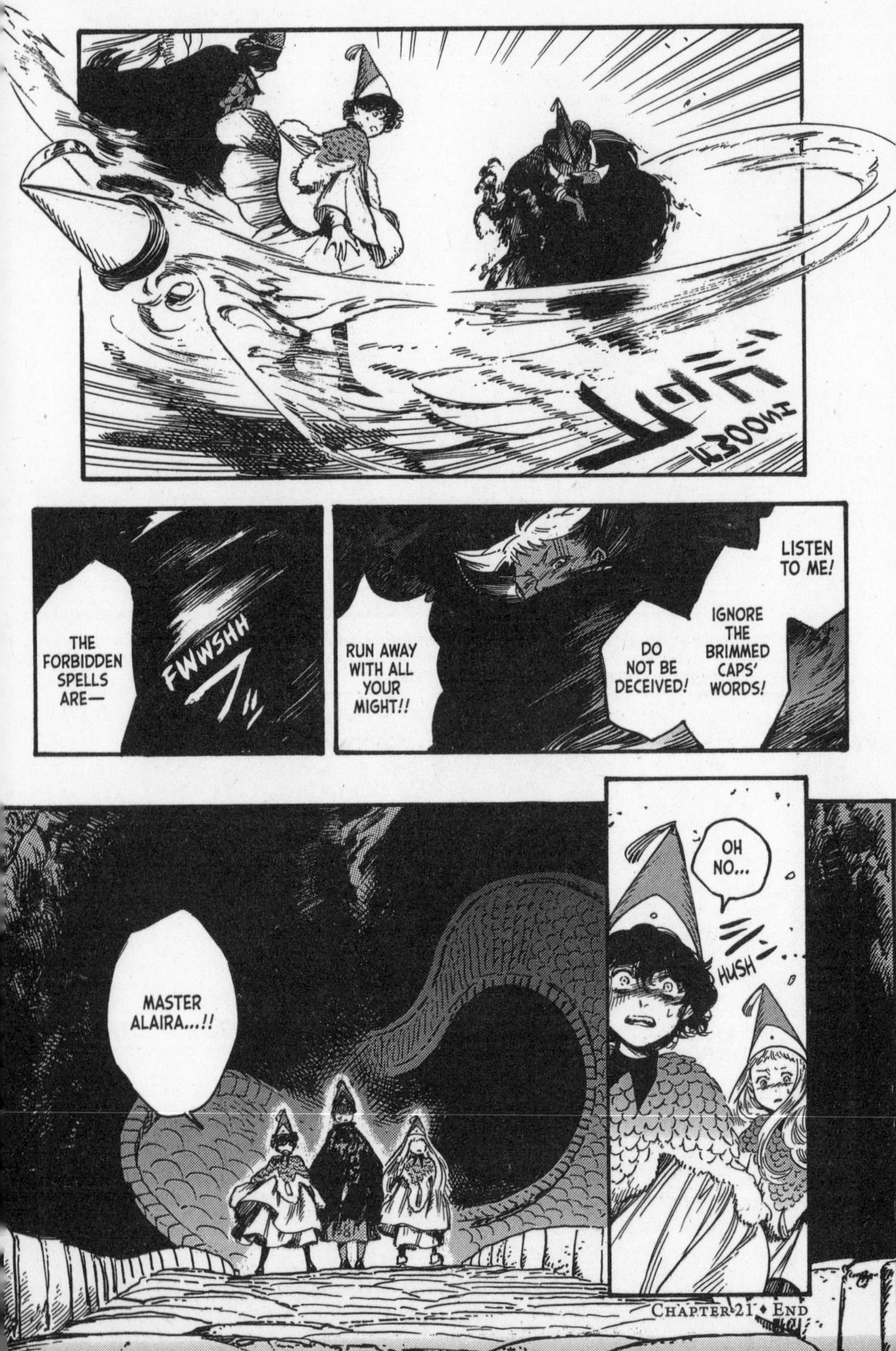
WOOSH
LISTEN TO ME!
IGNORE THE BRIMMED CAPS' WORDS!
DO NOT BE DECEIVED!
RUN AWAY WITH ALL YOUR MIGHT!!
FWWSHH
THE FORBIDDEN SPELLS ARE—
OH NO...
HUSH
MASTER ALAIRA...!!

Chapter 21 ◆ End

Witch Hat Atelier

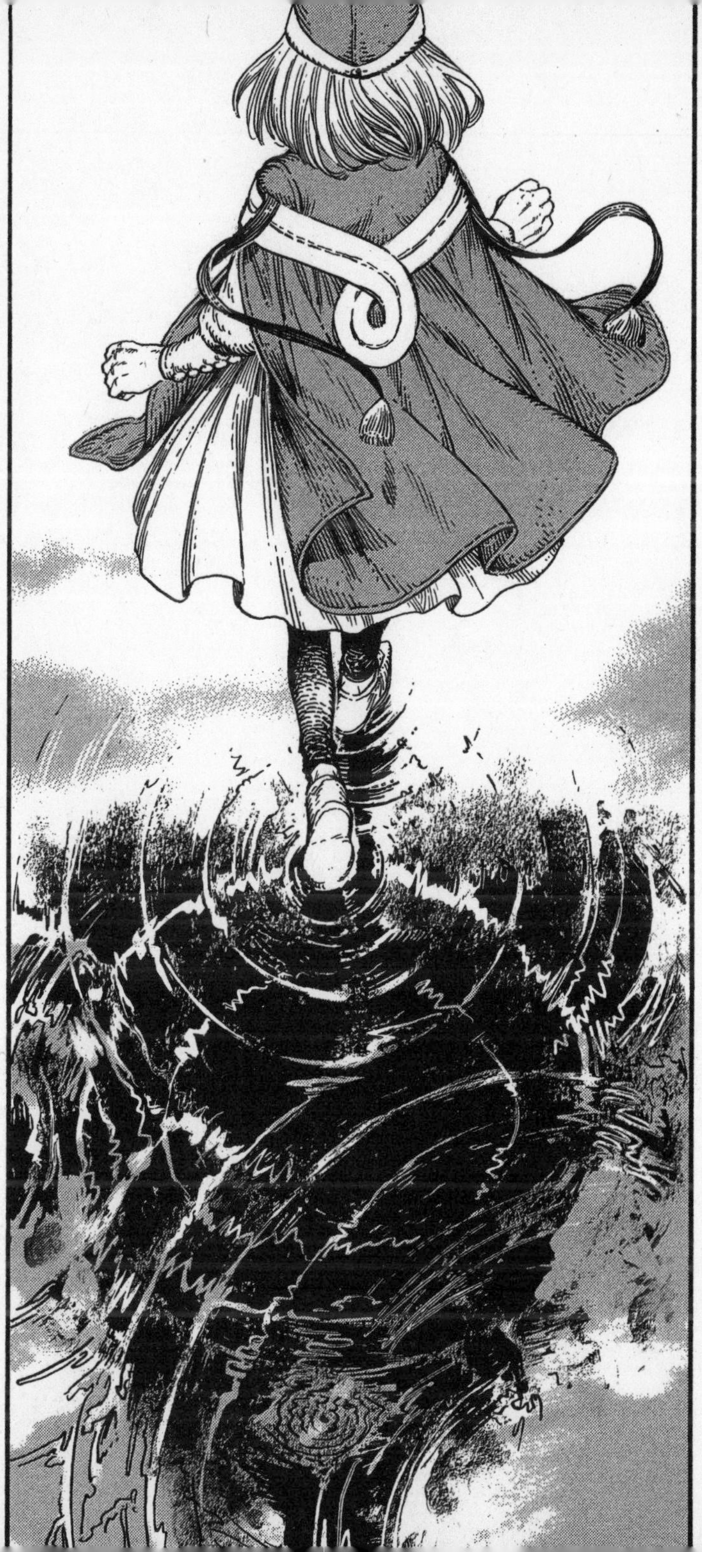

Chapter 22

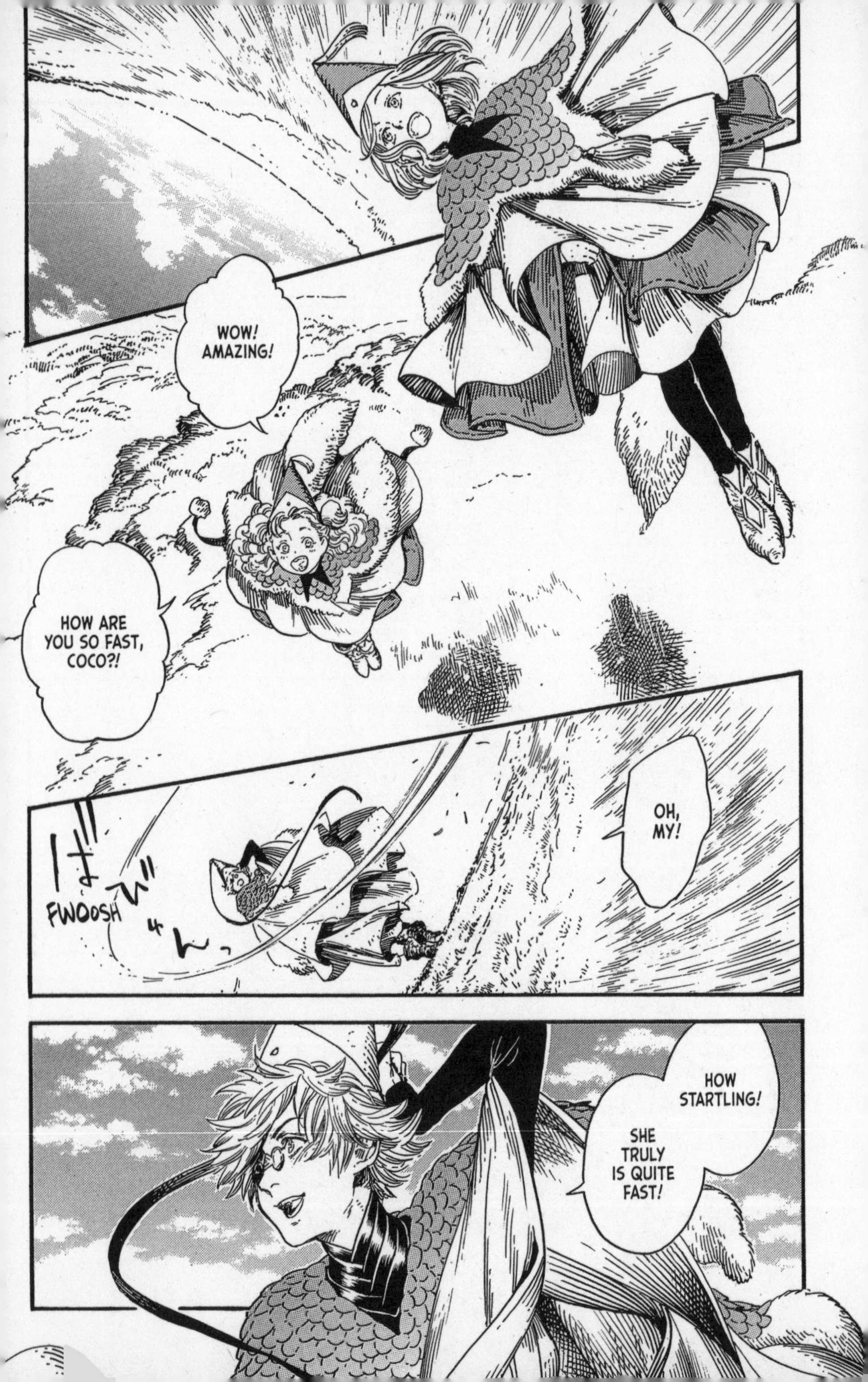
WOW! AMAZING!
HOW ARE YOU SO FAST, COCO?!
OH, MY!
FWOOSH
HOW STARTLING!
SHE TRULY IS QUITE FAST!

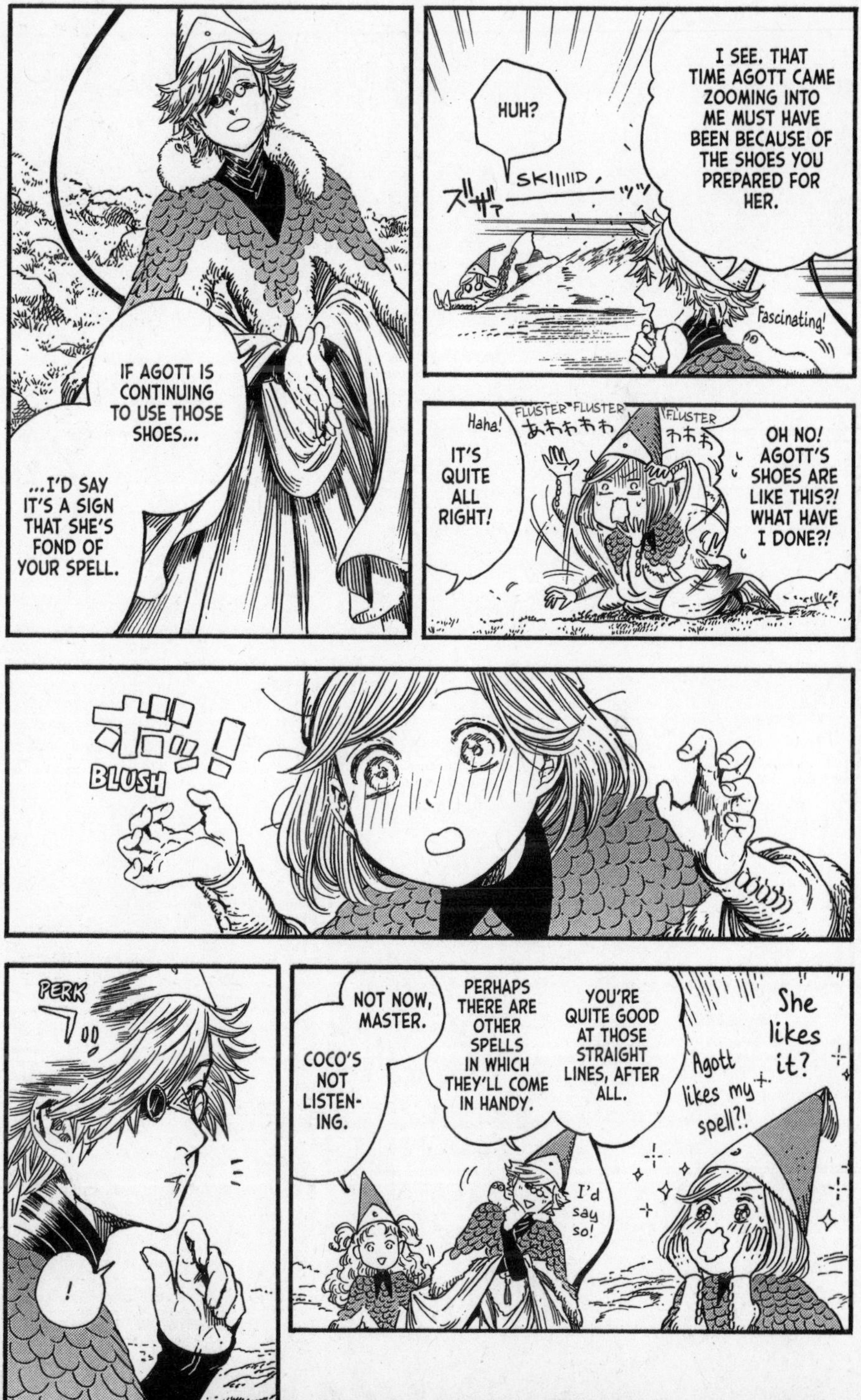

I SEE. THAT TIME AGOTT CAME ZOOMING INTO ME MUST HAVE BEEN BECAUSE OF THE SHOES YOU PREPARED FOR HER.
Fascinating!
HUH?
ズザァーッ
SKIIIID
OH NO! AGOTT'S SHOES ARE LIKE THIS?! WHAT HAVE I DONE?!
FLUSTER
わわわ
FLUSTER FLUSTER
あわわわわ
IT'S QUITE ALL RIGHT!
Haha!
IF AGOTT IS CONTINUING TO USE THOSE SHOES...
...I'D SAY IT'S A SIGN THAT SHE'S FOND OF YOUR SPELL.
ボッ!
BLUSH
She likes it?
Agott likes my spell?!
YOU'RE QUITE GOOD AT THOSE STRAIGHT LINES, AFTER ALL.
PERHAPS THERE ARE OTHER SPELLS IN WHICH THEY'LL COME IN HANDY.
I'd say so!
NOT NOW, MASTER.
COCO'S NOT LISTEN-ING.
PERK
!

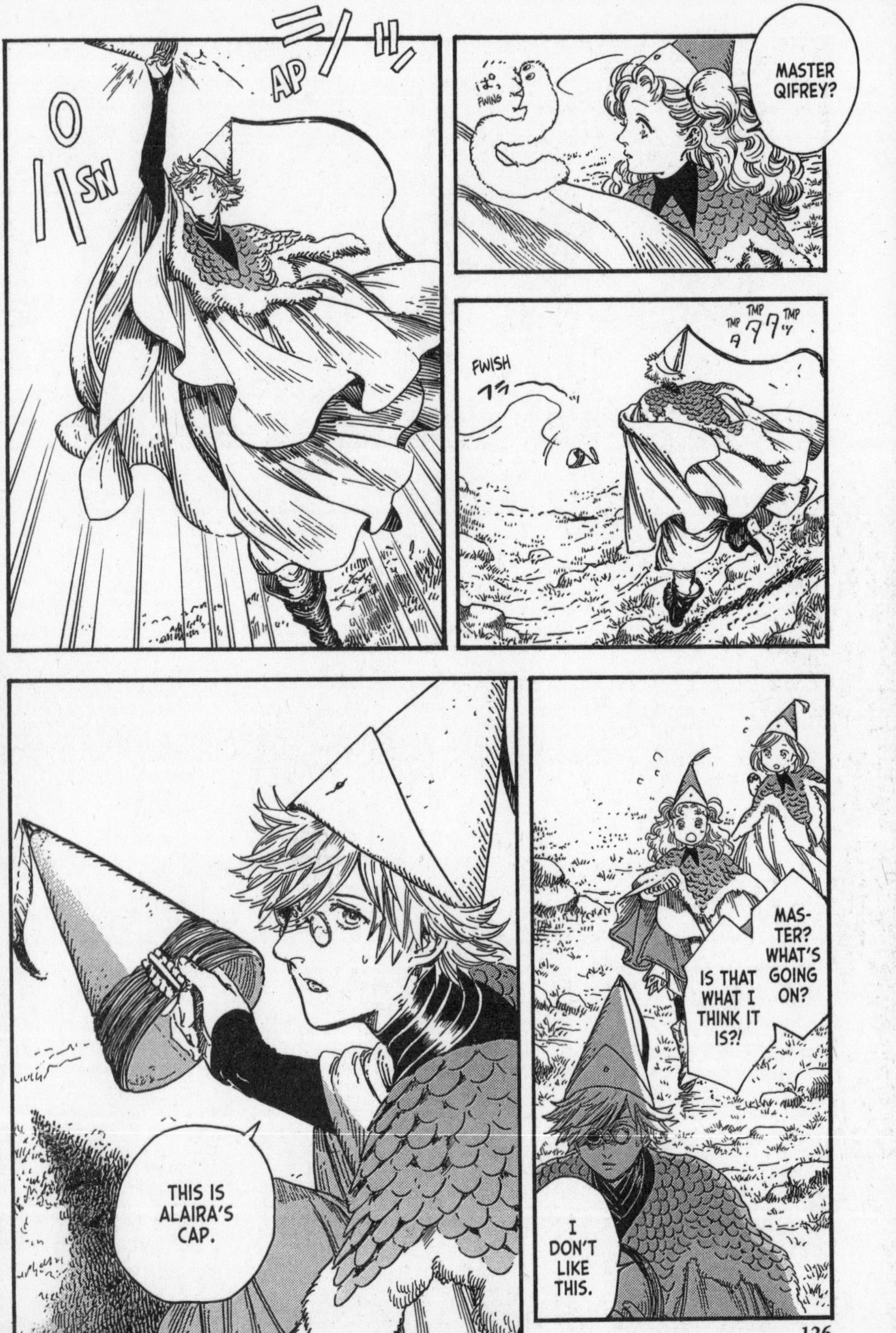

ぱっ
FWING
MASTER QIFREY?
TMP TMP TMP
タタタッ
FWISH
フラ
SNAP
MASTER? WHAT'S GOING ON?
IS THAT WHAT I THINK IT IS?!
I DON'T LIKE THIS.
THIS IS ALAIRA'S CAP.

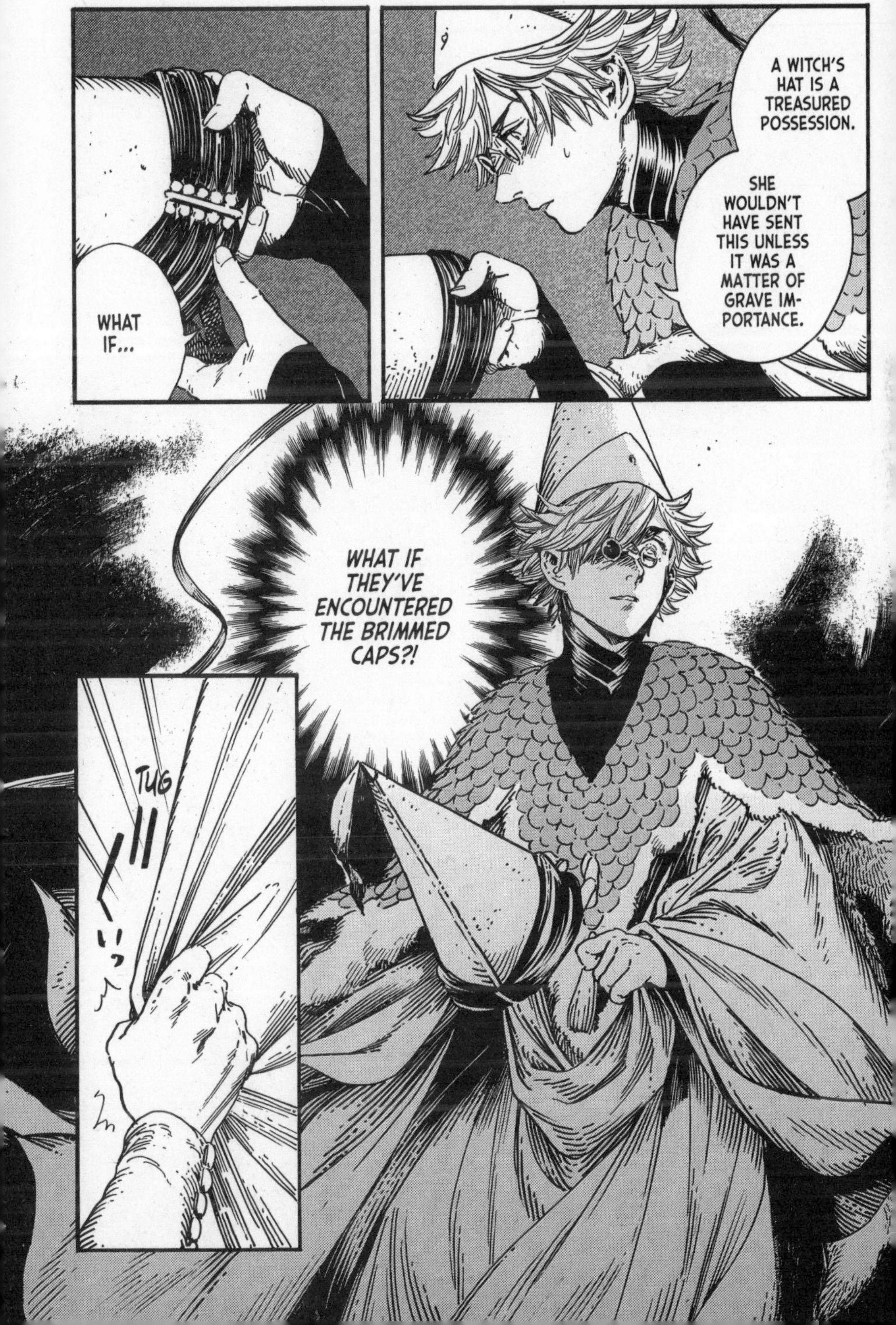
A WITCH'S HAT IS A TREASURED POSSESSION.
SHE WOULDN'T HAVE SENT THIS UNLESS IT WAS A MATTER OF GRAVE IMPORTANCE.
WHAT IF...
WHAT IF THEY'VE ENCOUNTERED THE BRIMMED CAPS?!
TUG
ぐいっ

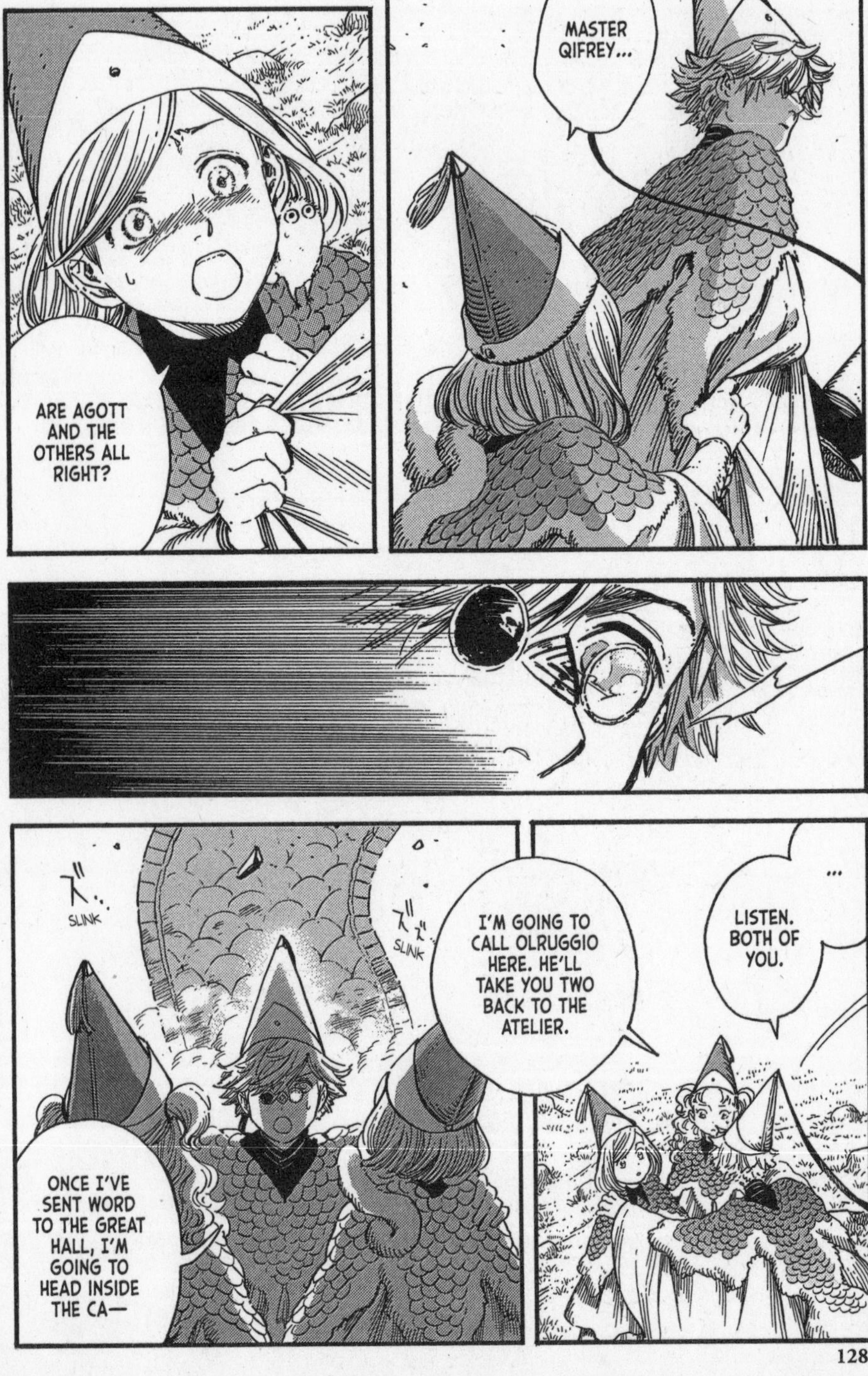
MASTER QIFREY...
ARE AGOTT AND THE OTHERS ALL RIGHT?
...
LISTEN. BOTH OF YOU.
I'M GOING TO CALL OLRUGGIO HERE. HE'LL TAKE YOU TWO BACK TO THE ATELIER.
ズズ... SLINK
ズ... SLINK
ONCE I'VE SENT WORD TO THE GREAT HALL, I'M GOING TO HEAD INSIDE THE CA—

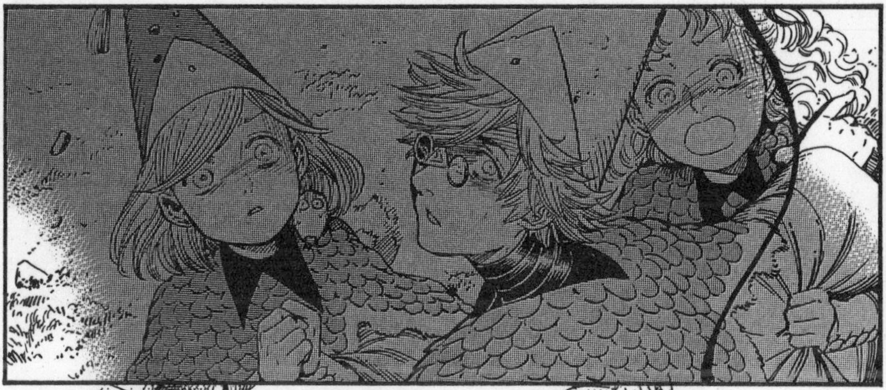

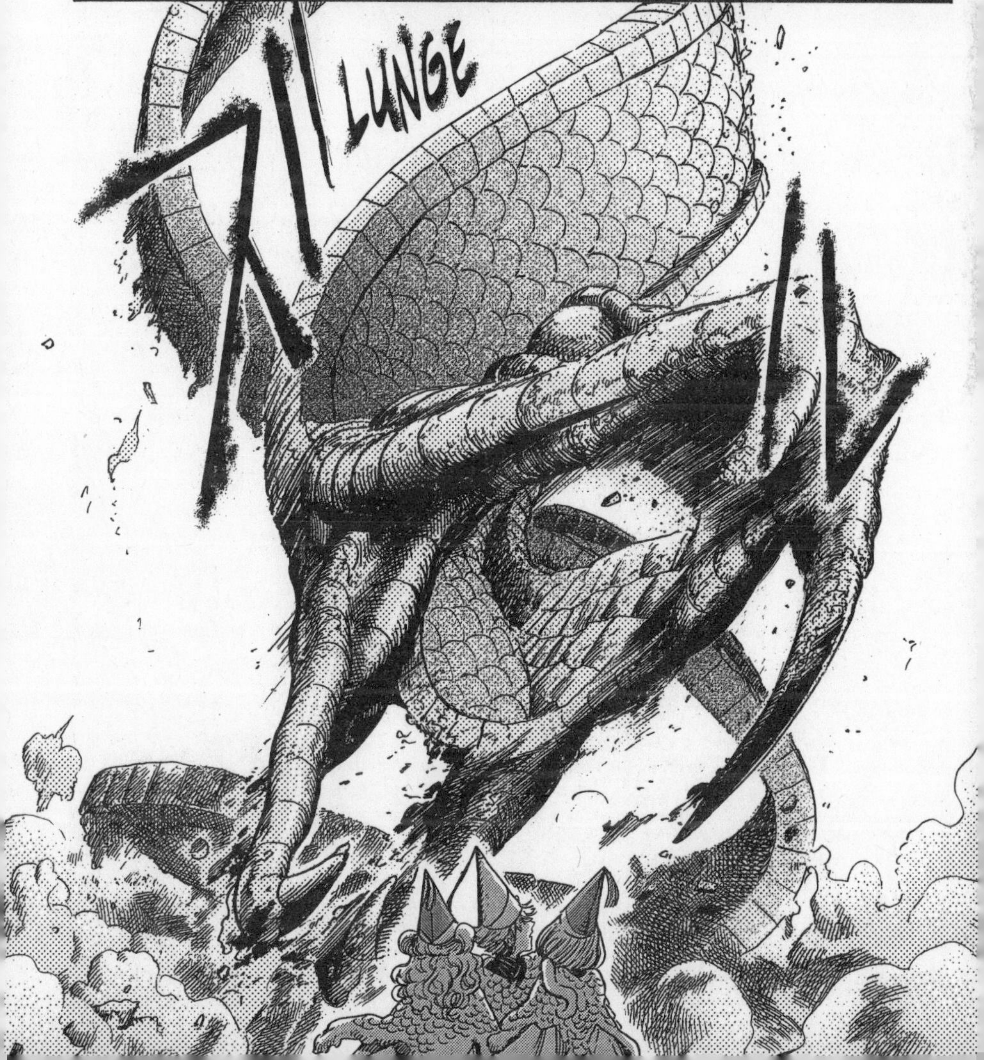
LUNGE

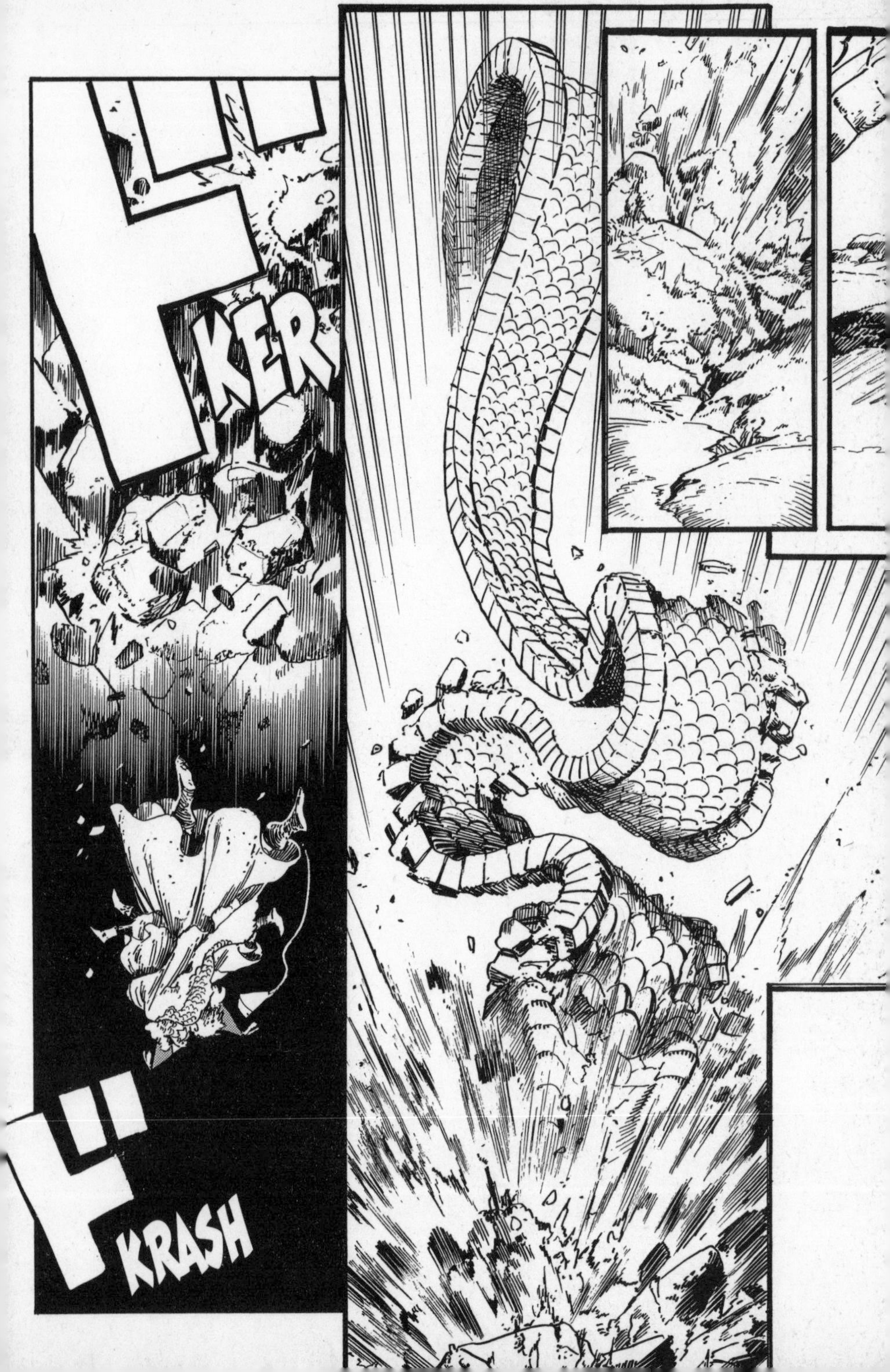

KER
KRASH

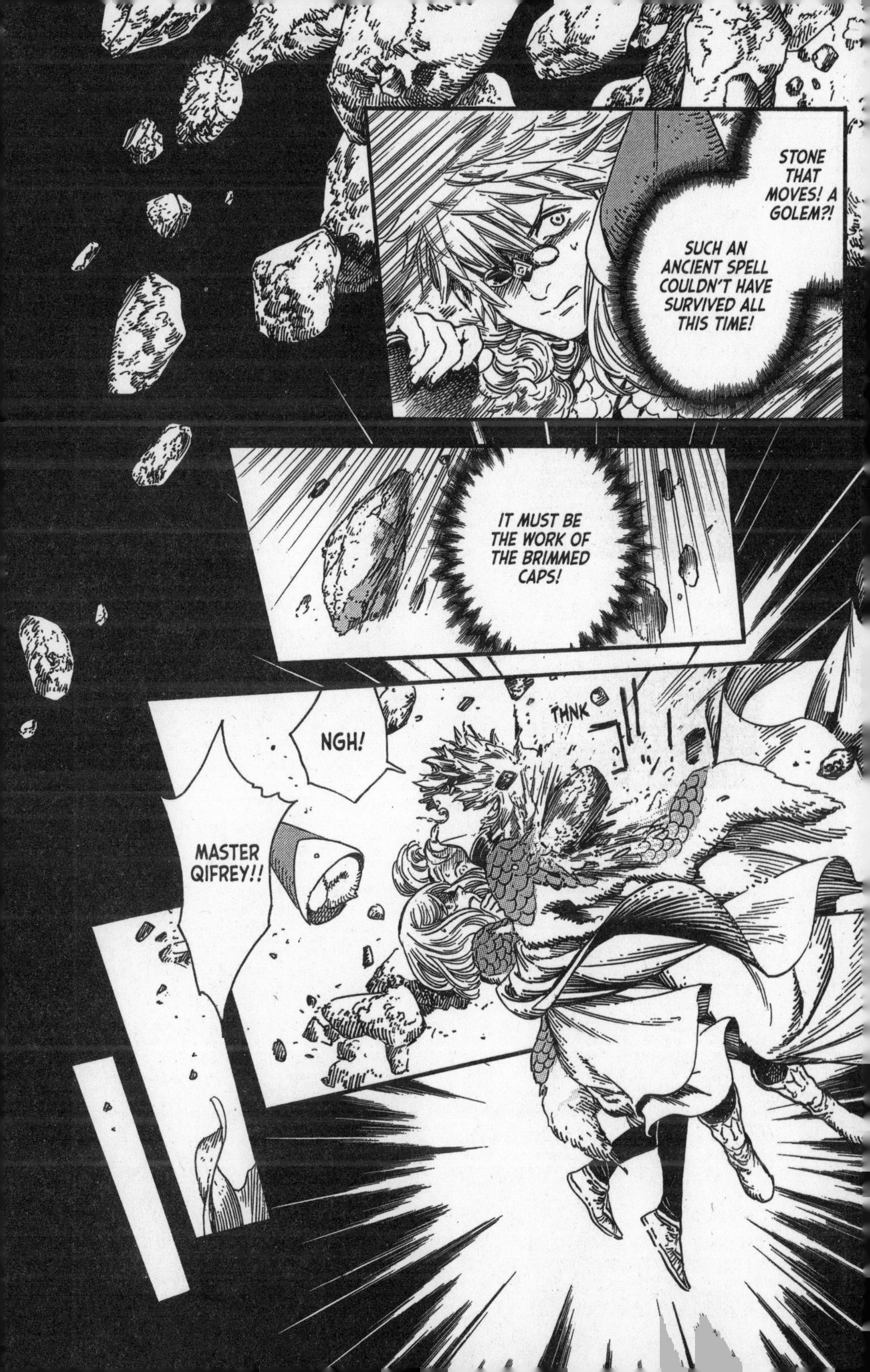
STONE THAT MOVES! A GOLEM?!
SUCH AN ANCIENT SPELL COULDN'T HAVE SURVIVED ALL THIS TIME!
IT MUST BE THE WORK OF THE BRIMMED CAPS!
THNK
NGH!
MASTER QIFREY!!

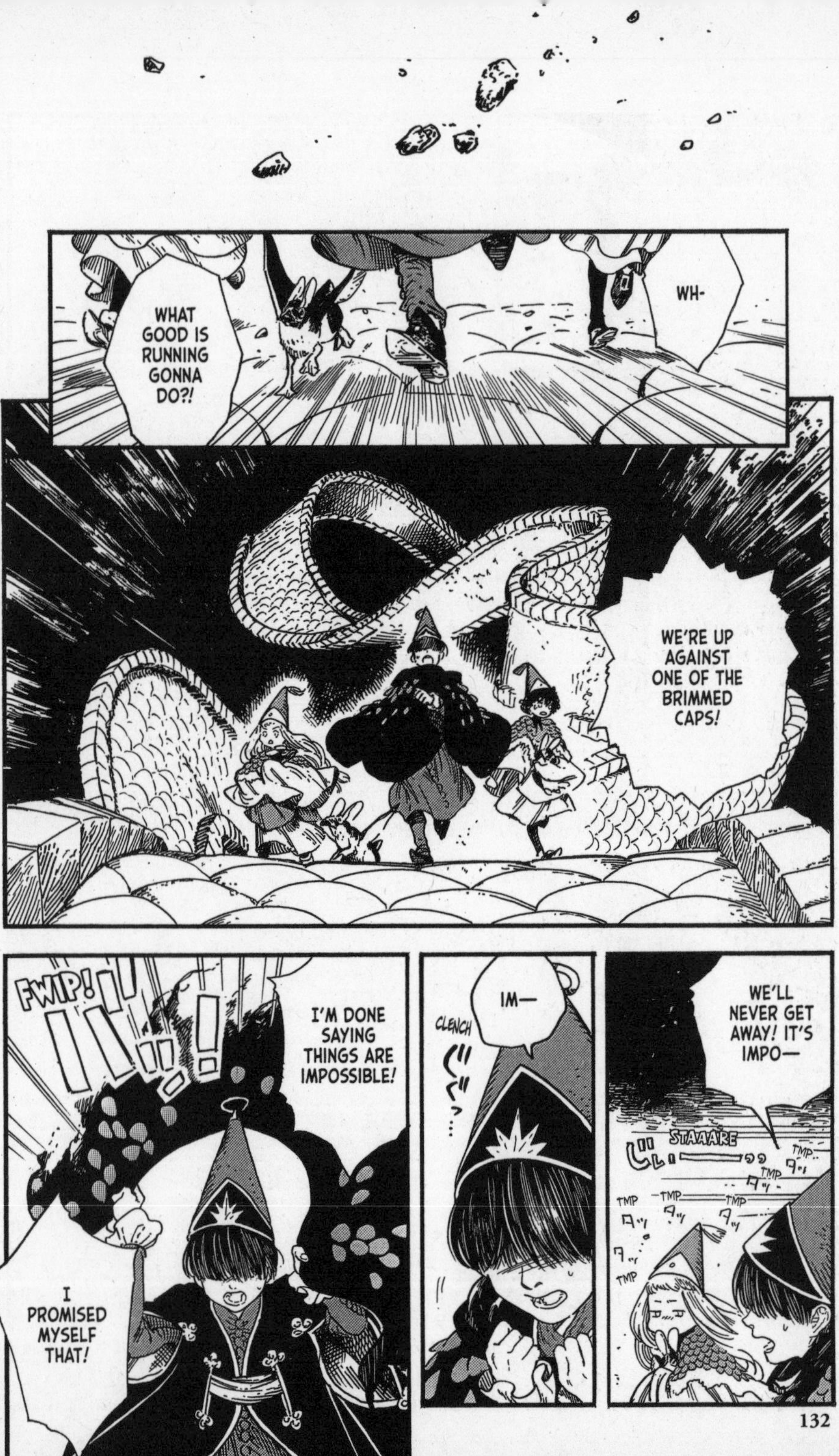
WH-
WHAT GOOD IS RUNNING GONNA DO?!
WE'RE UP AGAINST ONE OF THE BRIMMED CAPS!
WE'LL NEVER GET AWAY! IT'S IMPO—
STAAARE
TMP
TMP
TMP
TMP
TMP
TMP
IM—
CLENCH
FWIP!
I'M DONE SAYING THINGS ARE IMPOSSIBLE!
I PROMISED MYSELF THAT!

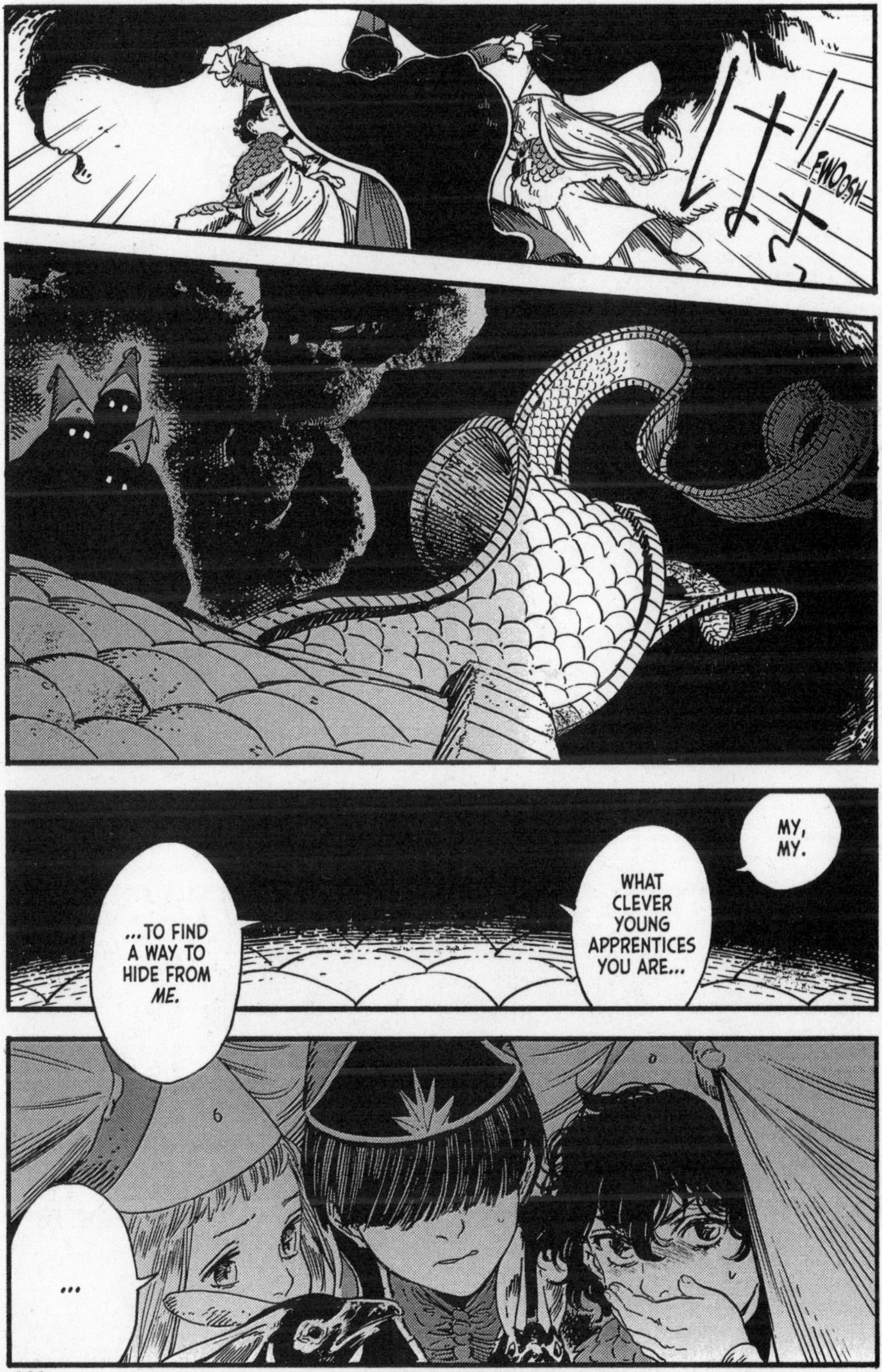
FWOOSH
MY, MY.
WHAT CLEVER YOUNG APPRENTICES YOU ARE...
...TO FIND A WAY TO HIDE FROM *ME.*
...

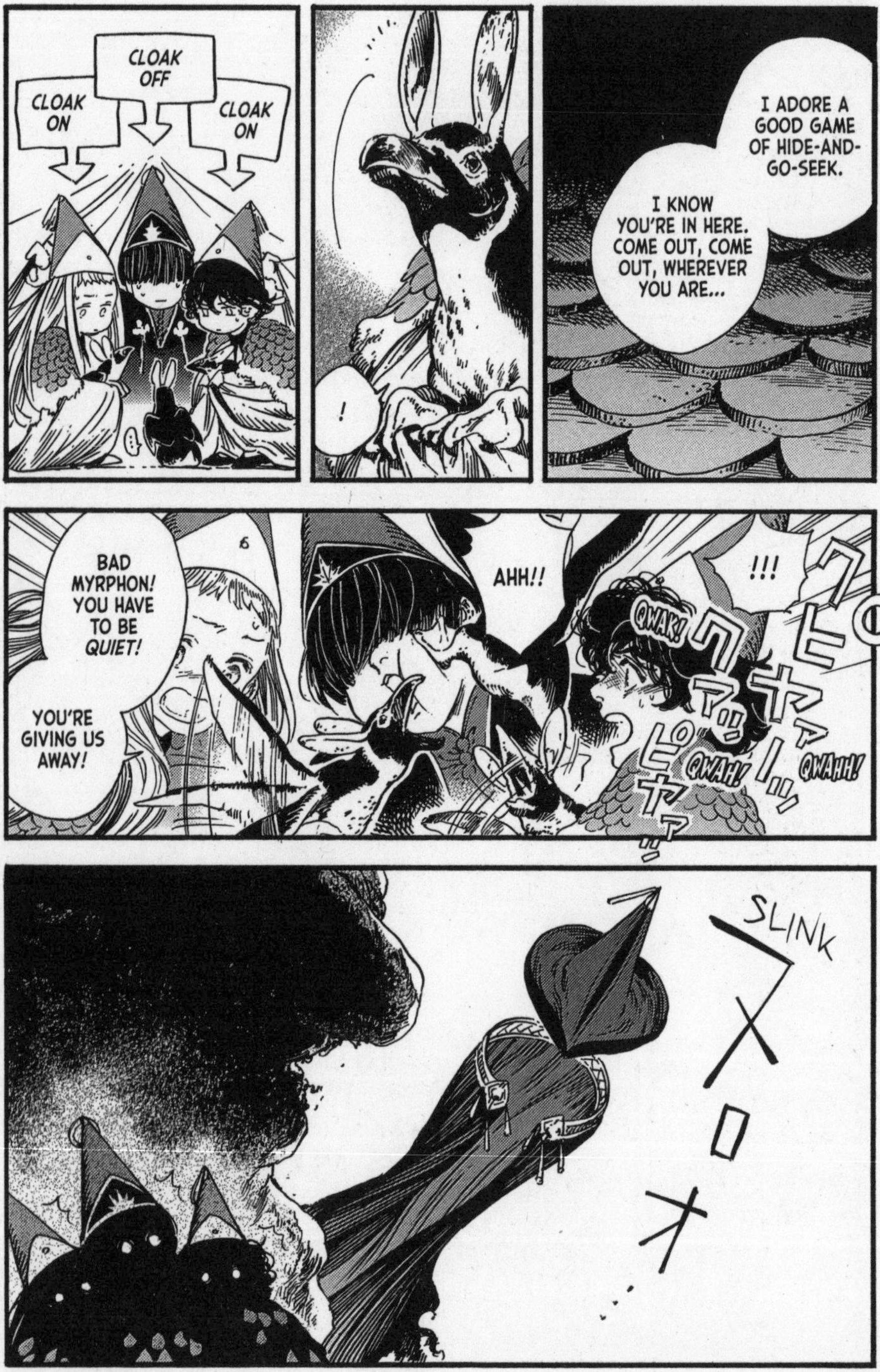
I ADORE A GOOD GAME OF HIDE-AND-GO-SEEK.
I KNOW YOU'RE IN HERE. COME OUT, COME OUT, WHEREVER YOU ARE...
!
CLOAK ON
CLOAK OFF
CLOAK ON
...
QWAHH!
!!!
QWAK!
QWAH!
AHH!!
BAD MYRPHON! YOU HAVE TO BE *QUIET!*
YOU'RE GIVING US AWAY!
SLINK

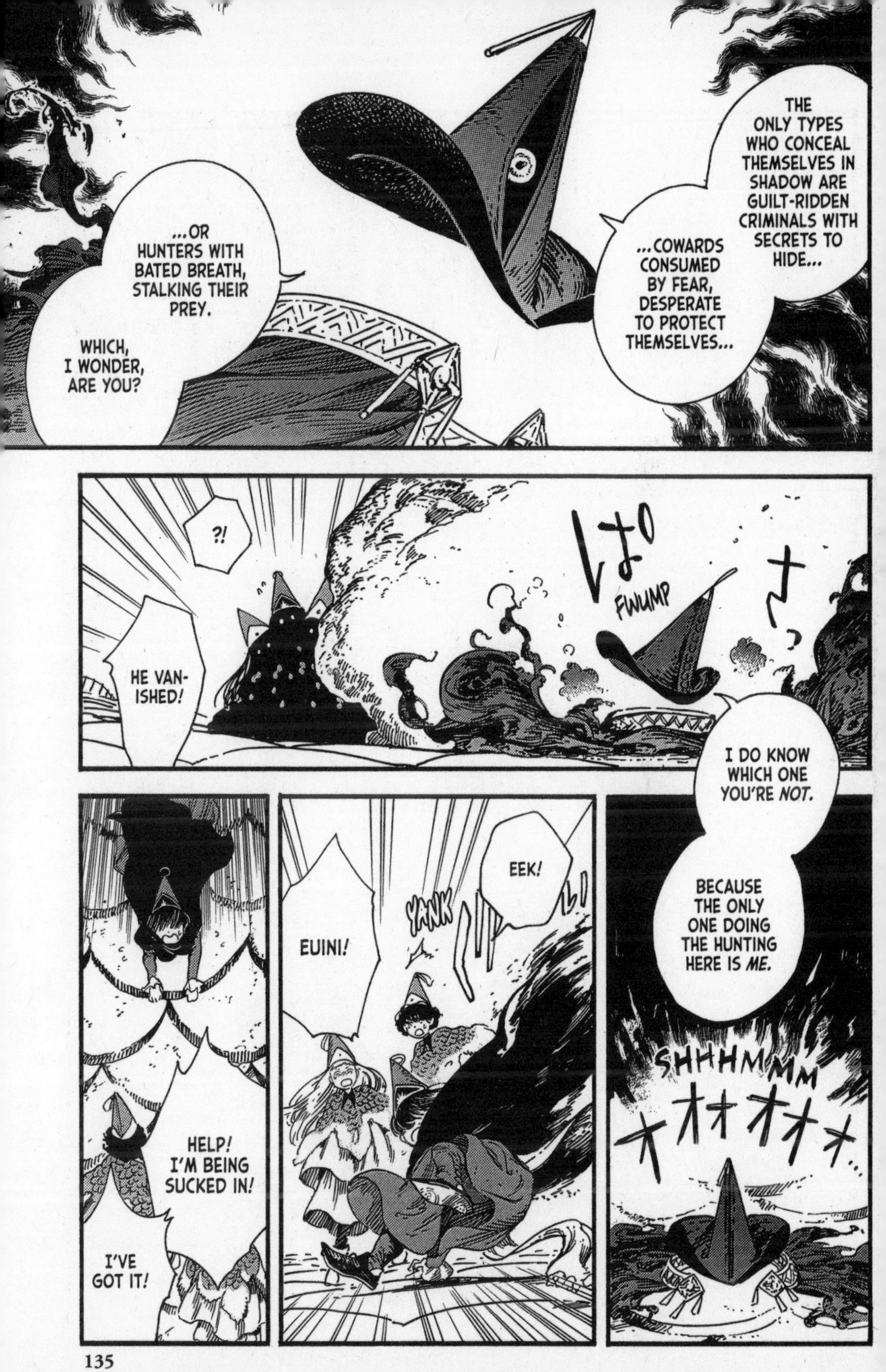
THE ONLY TYPES WHO CONCEAL THEMSELVES IN SHADOW ARE GUILT-RIDDEN CRIMINALS WITH SECRETS TO HIDE...
...COWARDS CONSUMED BY FEAR, DESPERATE TO PROTECT THEMSELVES...
...OR HUNTERS WITH BATED BREATH, STALKING THEIR PREY.
WHICH, I WONDER, ARE YOU?
FWUMP
?!
HE VAN-SHED!
I DO KNOW WHICH ONE YOU'RE *NOT*.
BECAUSE THE ONLY ONE DOING THE HUNTING HERE IS *ME*.
SHHHMMM
EEK!
YANK
EUINI!
HELP! I'M BEING SUCKED IN!
I'VE GOT IT!

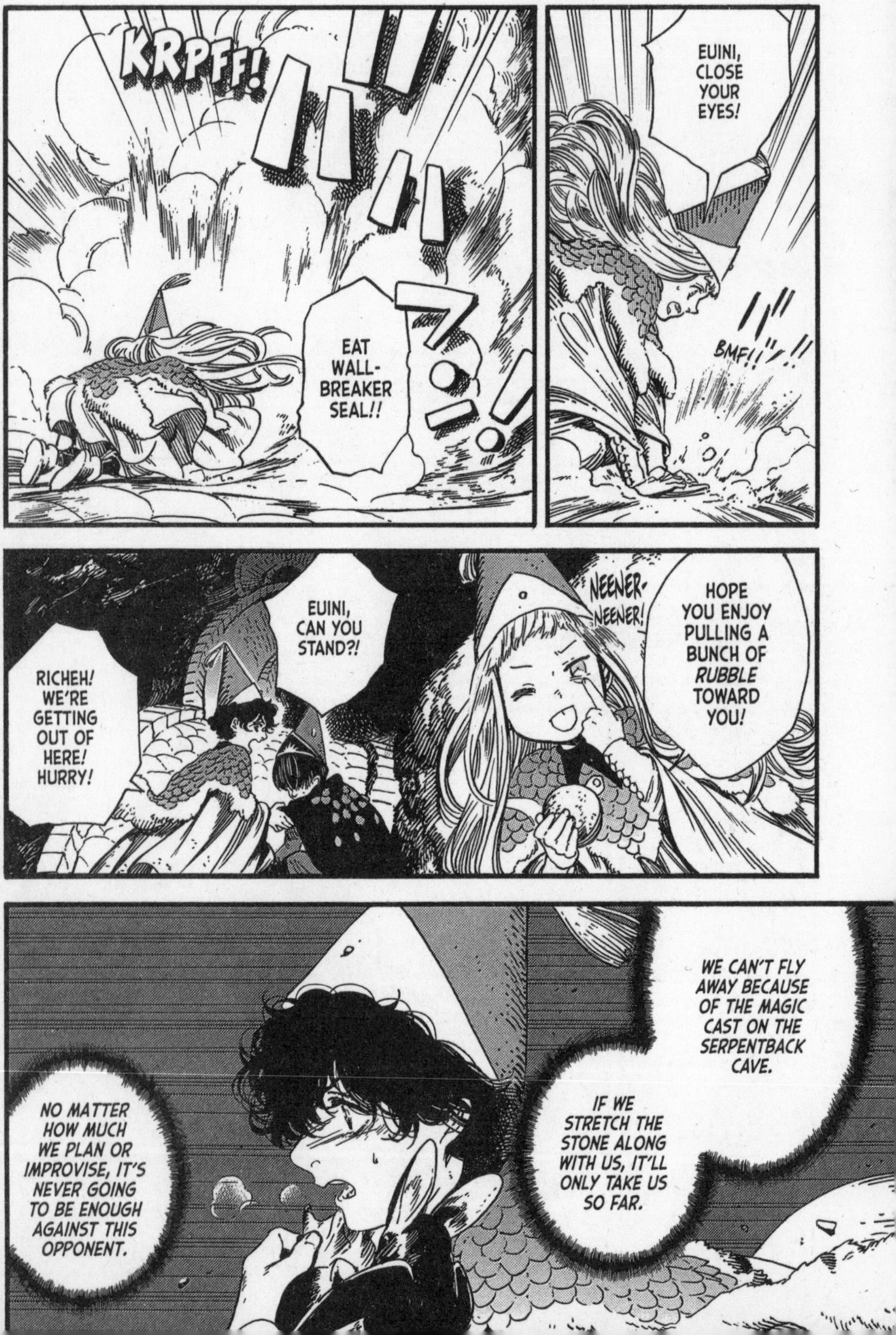
EUINI, CLOSE YOUR EYES!
BMF!!
KRPFFF!
EAT WALL-BREAKER SEAL!!
HOPE YOU ENJOY PULLING A BUNCH OF *RUBBLE* TOWARD YOU!
NEENER-NEENER!
EUINI, CAN YOU STAND?!
RICHEH! WE'RE GETTING OUT OF HERE! HURRY!
WE CAN'T FLY AWAY BECAUSE OF THE MAGIC CAST ON THE SERPENTBACK CAVE.
IF WE STRETCH THE STONE ALONG WITH US, IT'LL ONLY TAKE US SO FAR.
NO MATTER HOW MUCH WE PLAN OR IMPROVISE, IT'S NEVER GOING TO BE ENOUGH AGAINST THIS OPPONENT.

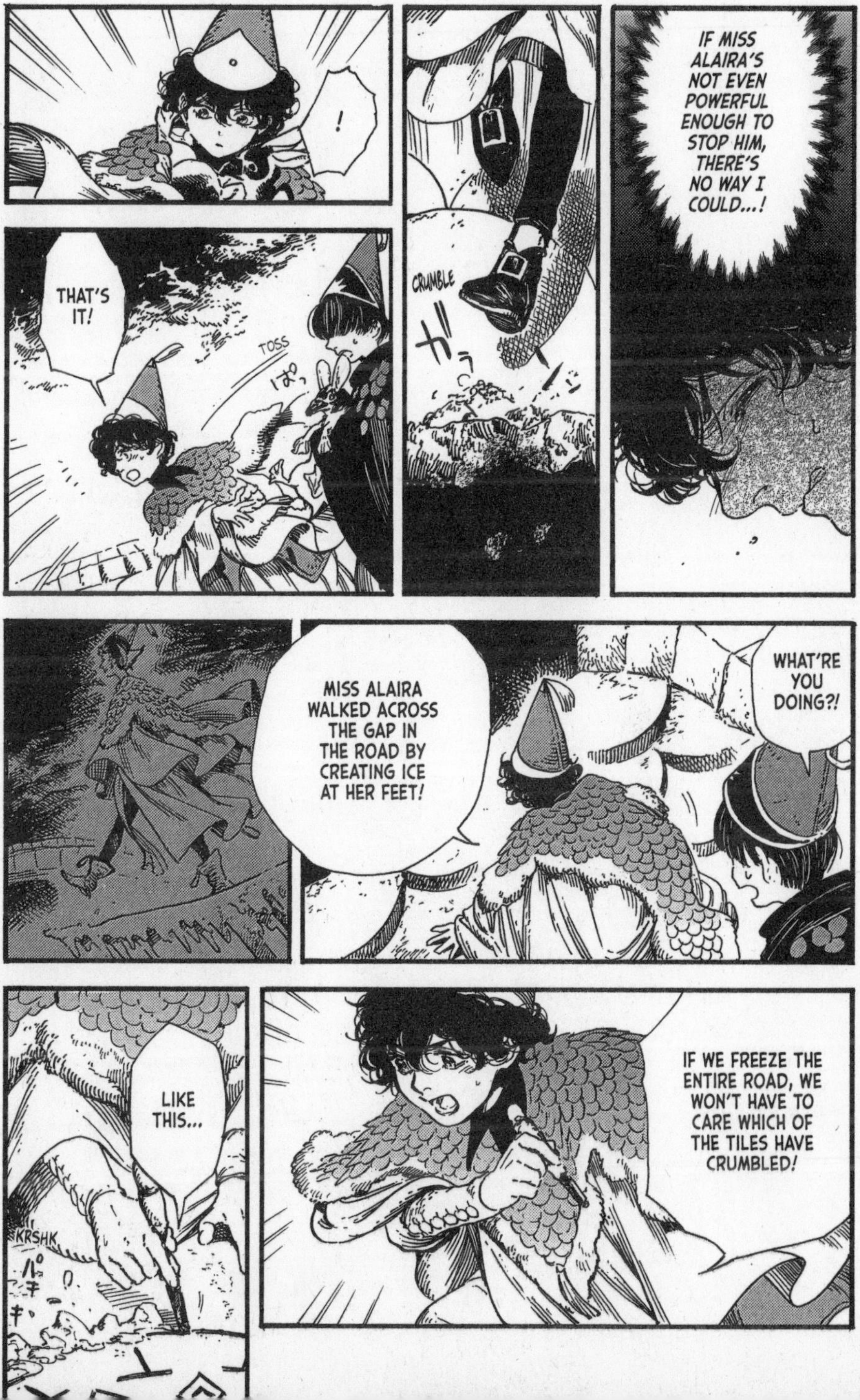
IF MISS ALAIRA'S NOT EVEN POWERFUL ENOUGH TO STOP HIM, THERE'S NO WAY I COULD...!
CRUMBLE
!
THAT'S IT!
TOSS
ぱっ
WHAT'RE YOU DOING?!
MISS ALAIRA WALKED ACROSS THE GAP IN THE ROAD BY CREATING ICE AT HER FEET!
IF WE FREEZE THE ENTIRE ROAD, WE WON'T HAVE TO CARE WHICH OF THE TILES HAVE CRUMBLED!
LIKE THIS...
KRSHK
パキ

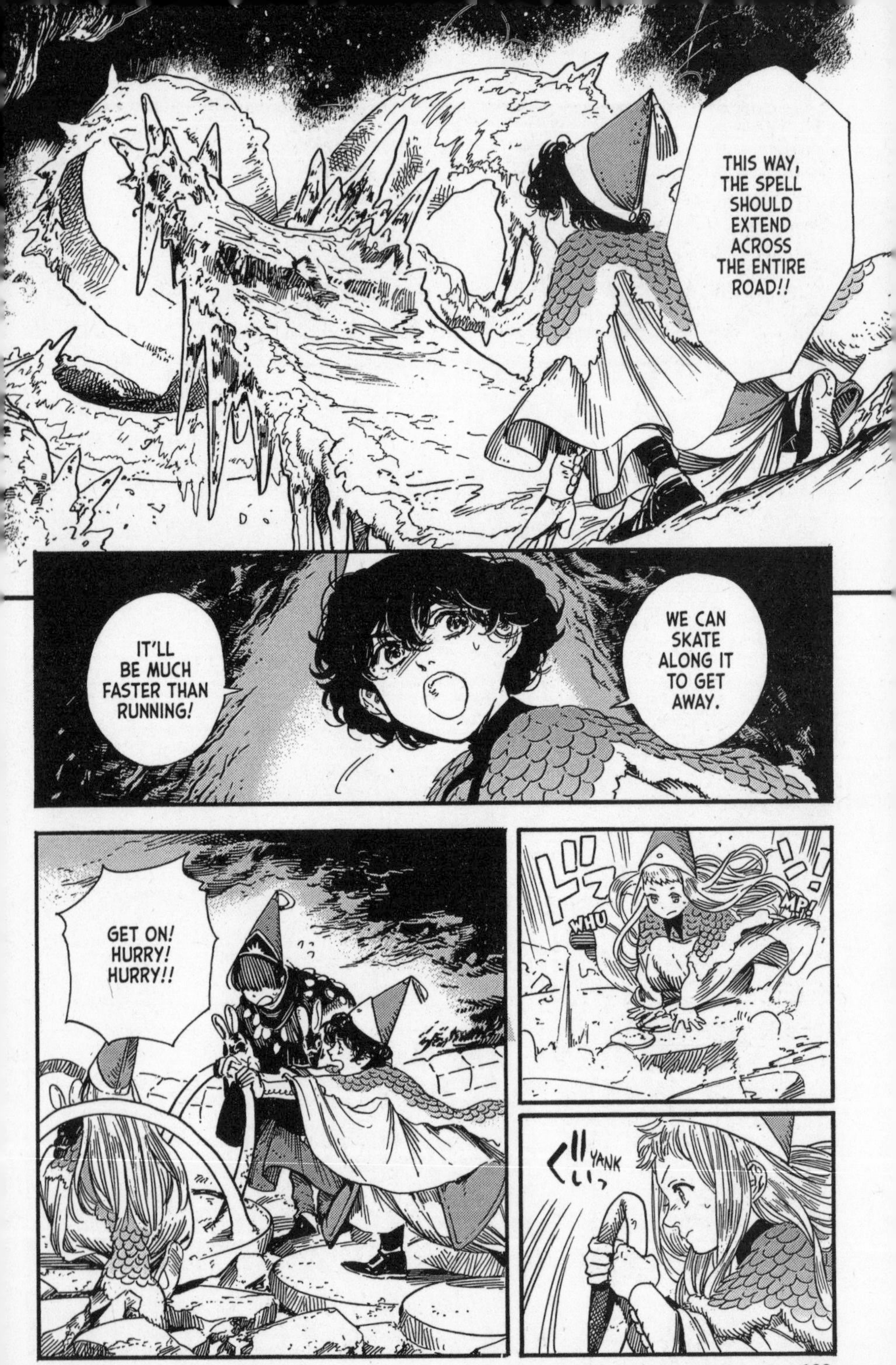
THIS WAY, THE SPELL SHOULD EXTEND ACROSS THE ENTIRE ROAD!!
WE CAN SKATE ALONG IT TO GET AWAY.
IT'LL BE MUCH FASTER THAN RUNNING!
WHUMP!
YANK
GET ON! HURRY! HURRY!!

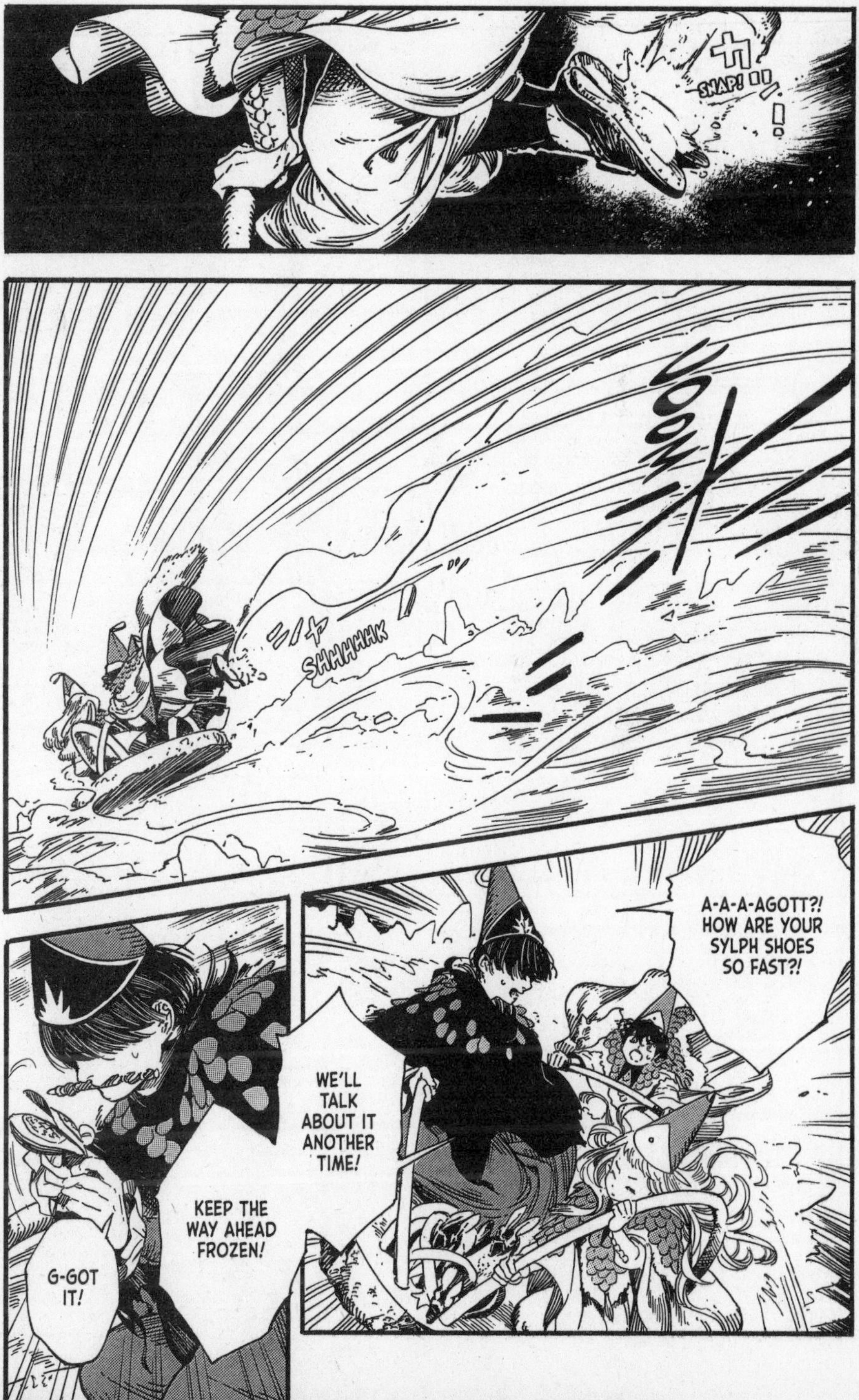
SNAP!
SHHHHHK
A-A-A-AGOTT?! HOW ARE YOUR SYLPH SHOES SO FAST?!
WE'LL TALK ABOUT IT ANOTHER TIME!
KEEP THE WAY AHEAD FROZEN!
G-GOT IT!

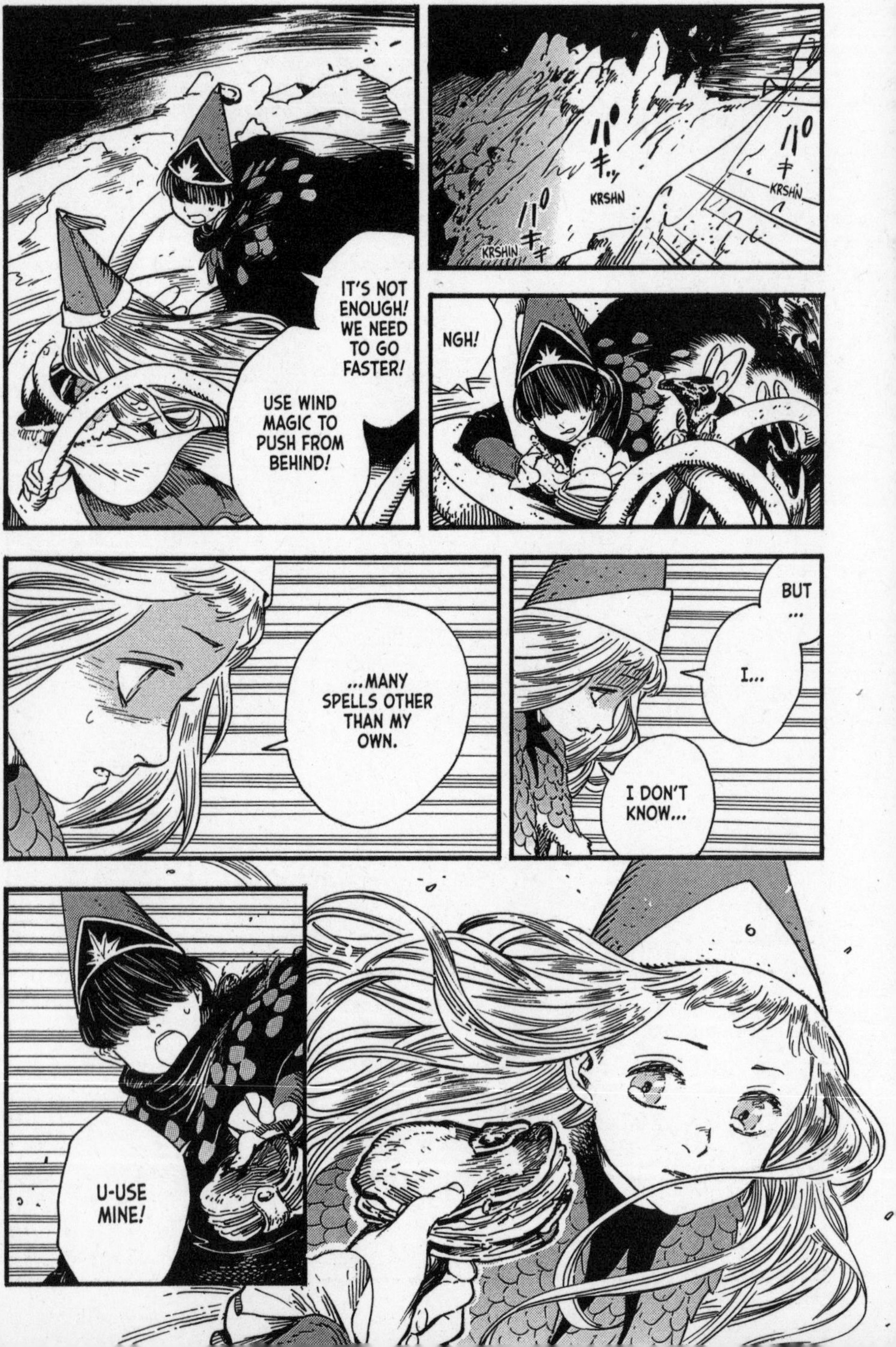
パキ
KRSHN
パキッ
KRSHN
パキ
KRSHIN
NGH!
IT'S NOT ENOUGH! WE NEED TO GO FASTER!
USE WIND MAGIC TO PUSH FROM BEHIND!
BUT...
I...
I DON'T KNOW...
...MANY SPELLS OTHER THAN MY OWN.
U-USE MINE!

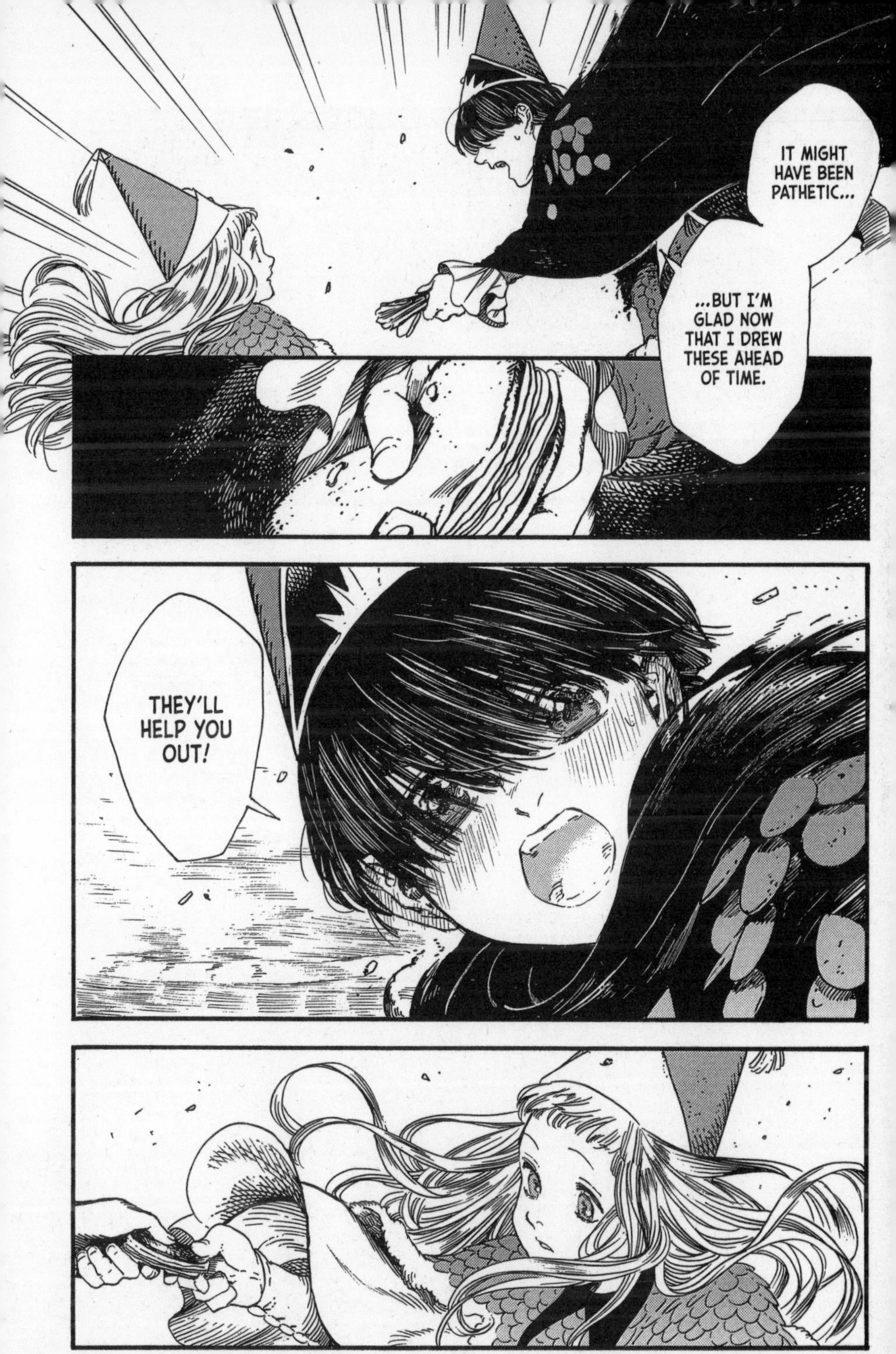
IT MIGHT HAVE BEEN PATHETIC...
...BUT I'M GLAD NOW THAT I DREW THESE AHEAD OF TIME.
THEY'LL HELP YOU OUT!

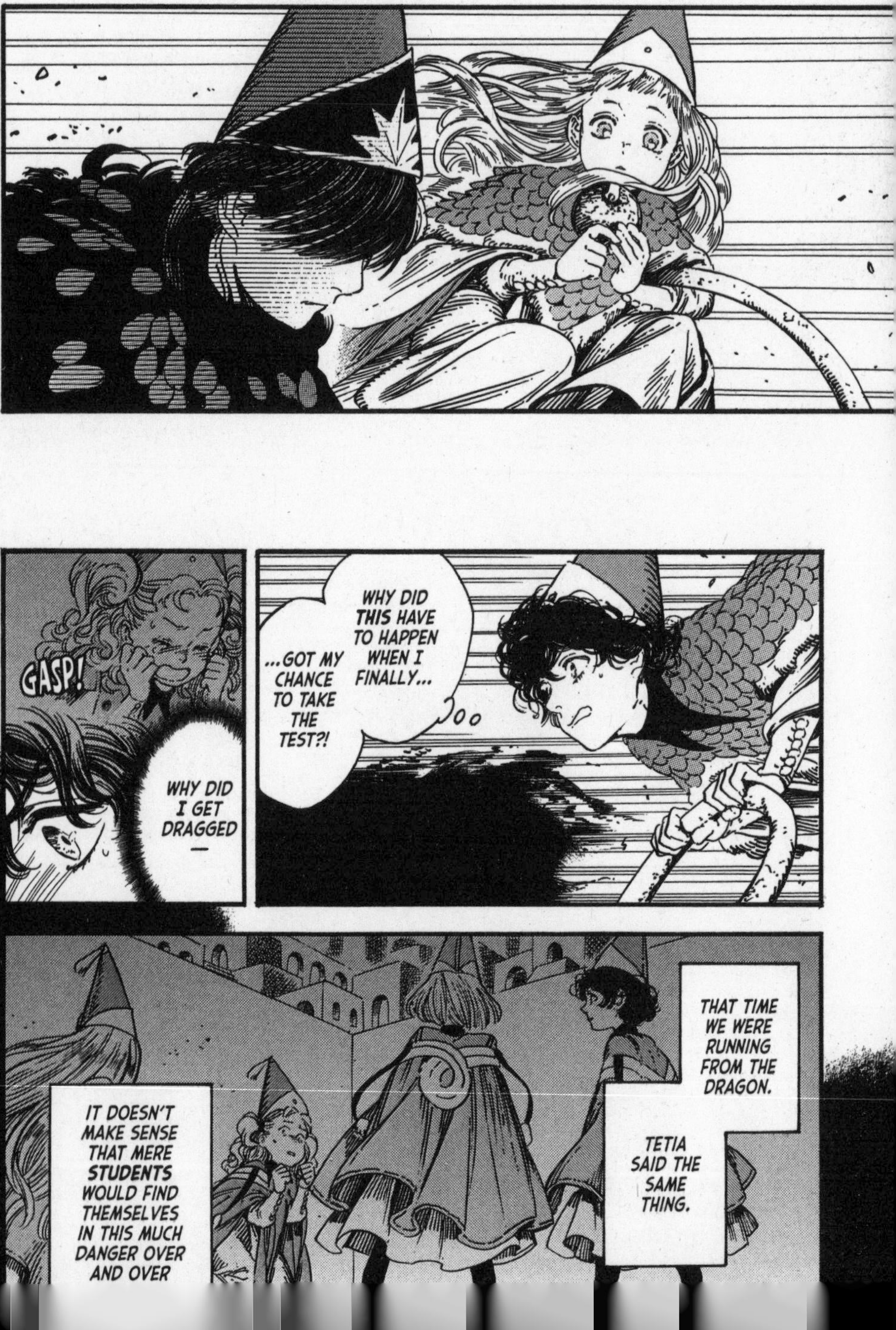
WHY DID THIS HAVE TO HAPPEN WHEN I FINALLY...
...GOT MY CHANCE TO TAKE THE TEST?!
GASP!
WHY DID I GET DRAGGED —
THAT TIME WE WERE RUNNING FROM THE DRAGON.
TETIA SAID THE SAME THING.
IT DOESN'T MAKE SENSE THAT MERE STUDENTS WOULD FIND THEMSELVES IN THIS MUCH DANGER OVER AND OVER

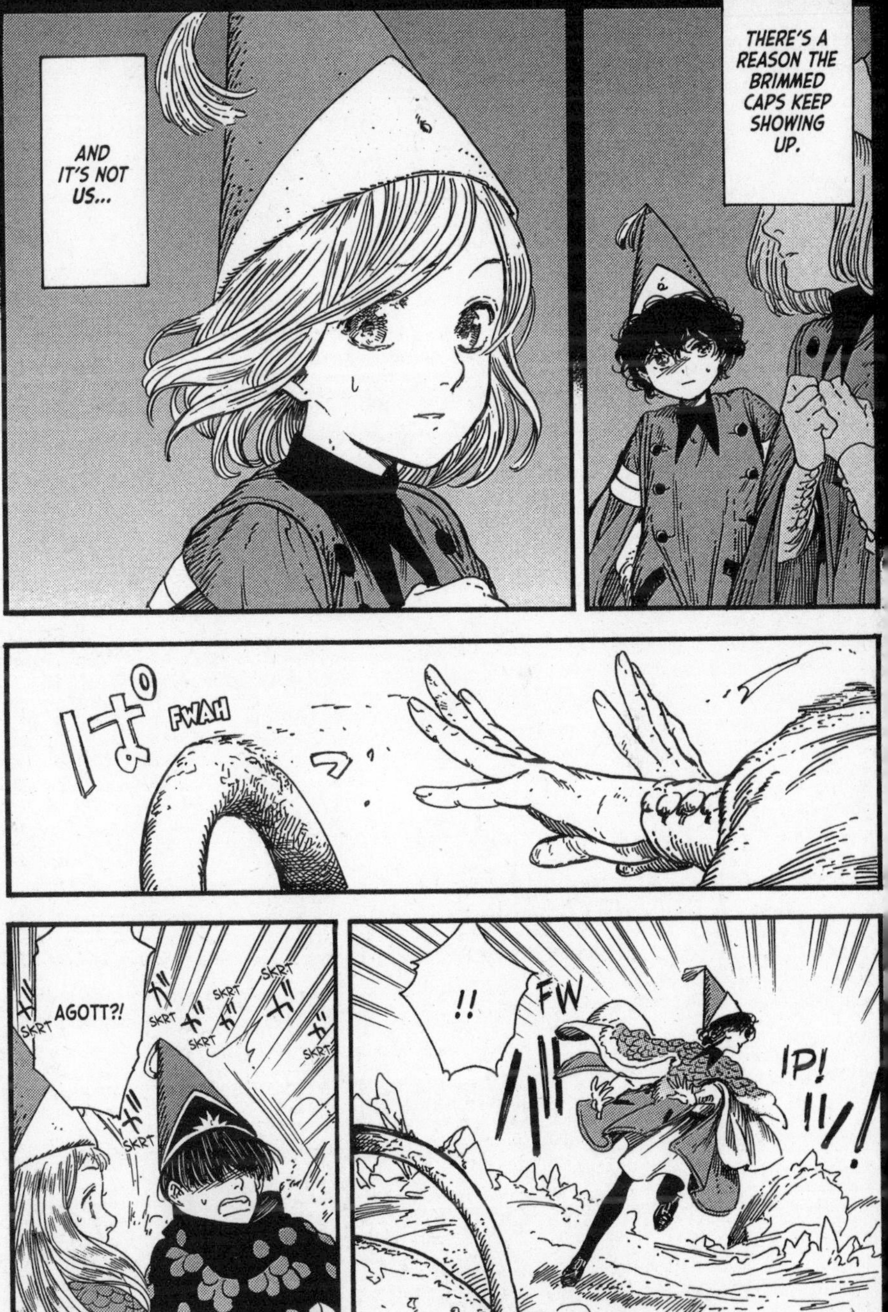
THERE'S A REASON THE BRIMMED CAPS KEEP SHOWING UP.
AND IT'S NOT US...
ぱっ
FWAH
!!
FW
IP!
AGOTT?!
SKRT
SKRT
SKRT
SKRT
SKRT
SKRT
SKRT

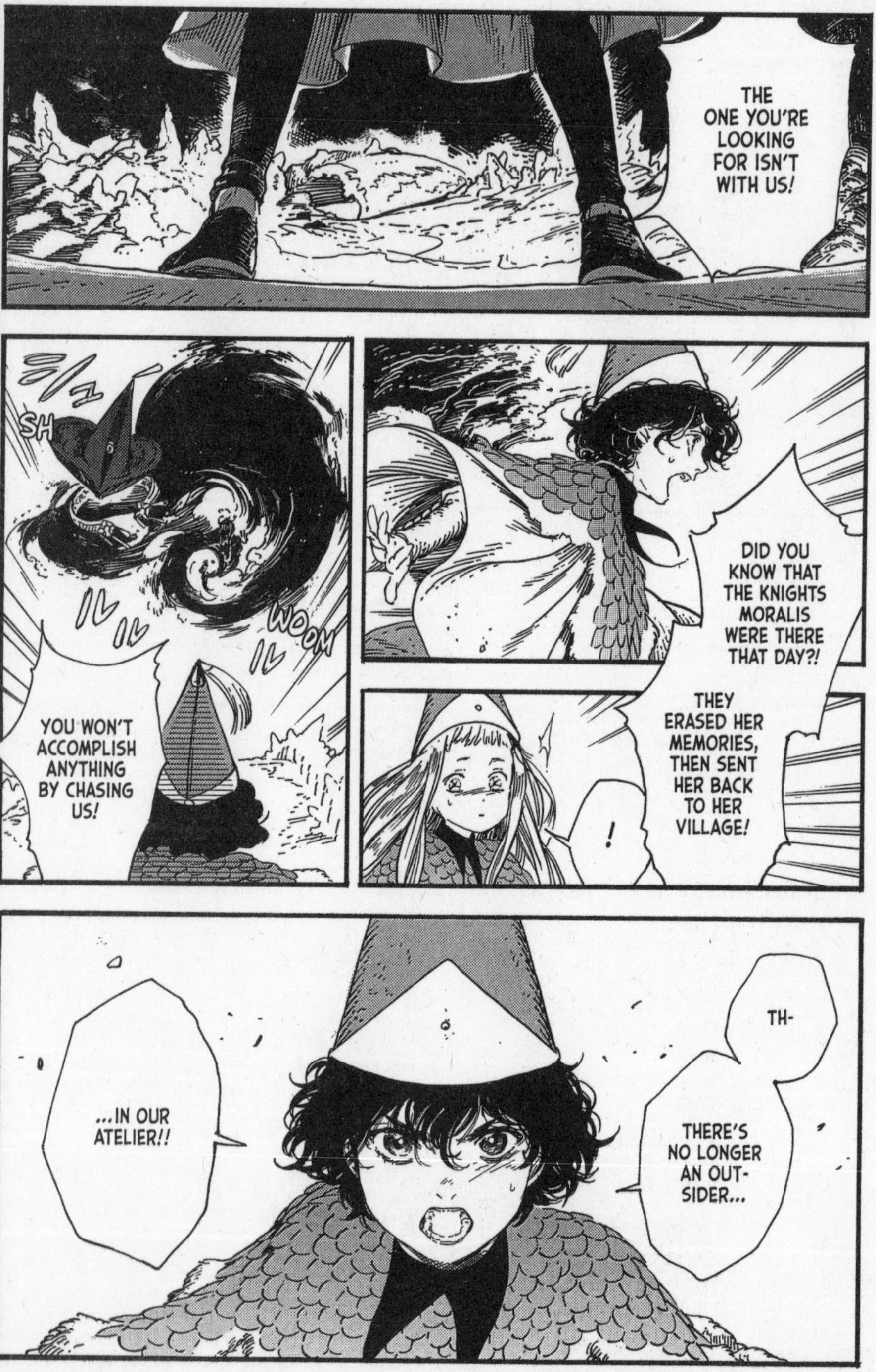
THE ONE YOU'RE LOOKING FOR ISN'T WITH US!
DID YOU KNOW THAT THE KNIGHTS MORALIS WERE THERE THAT DAY?!
THEY ERASED HER MEMORIES, THEN SENT HER BACK TO HER VILLAGE!
!
SH
WOOM
YOU WON'T ACCOMPLISH ANYTHING BY CHASING US!
TH-
THERE'S NO LONGER AN OUT-SIDER...
...IN OUR ATELIER!!

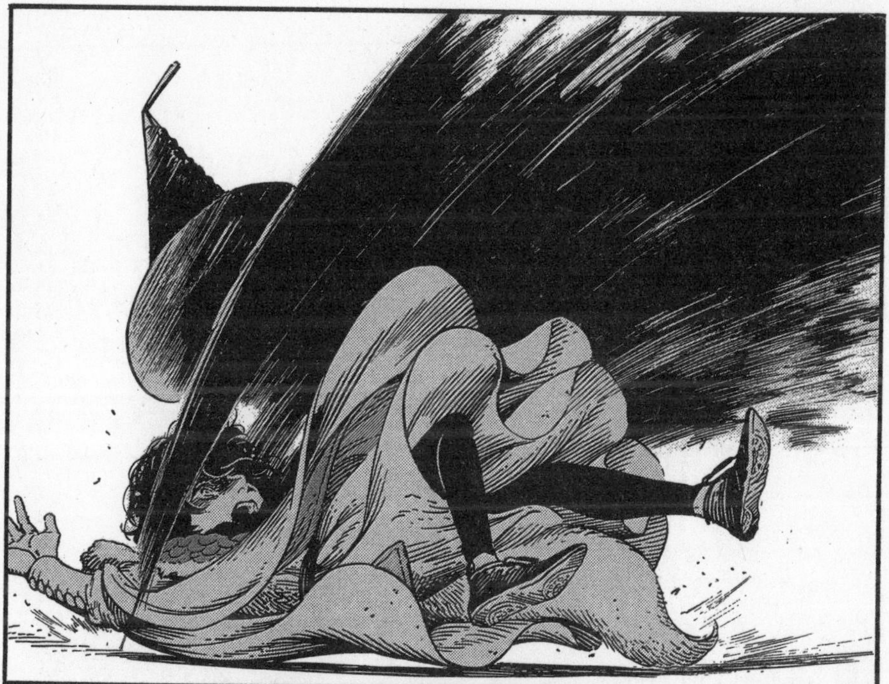

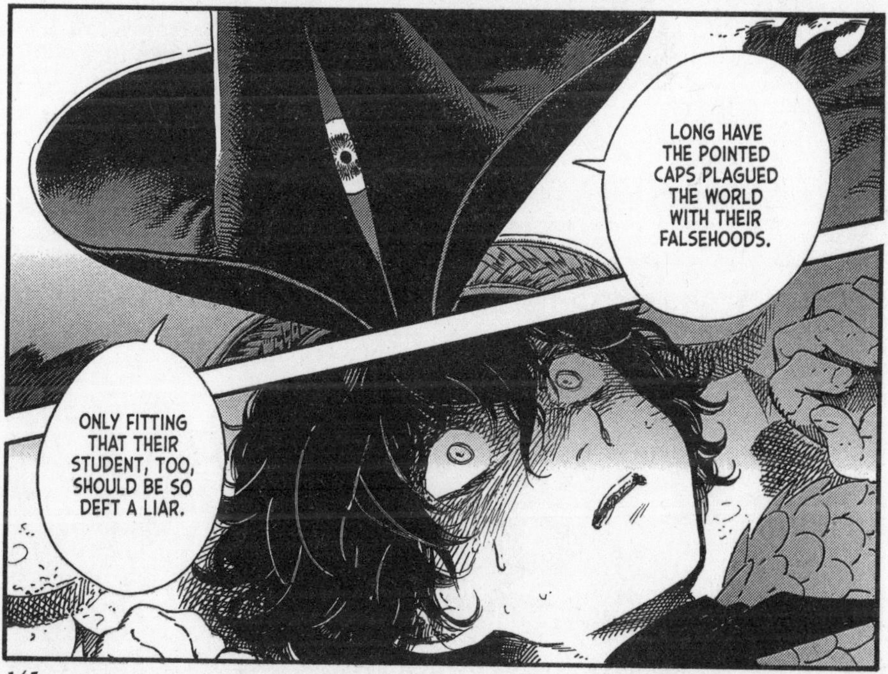
LONG HAVE THE POINTED CAPS PLAGUED THE WORLD WITH THEIR FALSEHOODS.
ONLY FITTING THAT THEIR STUDENT, TOO, SHOULD BE SO DEFT A LIAR.

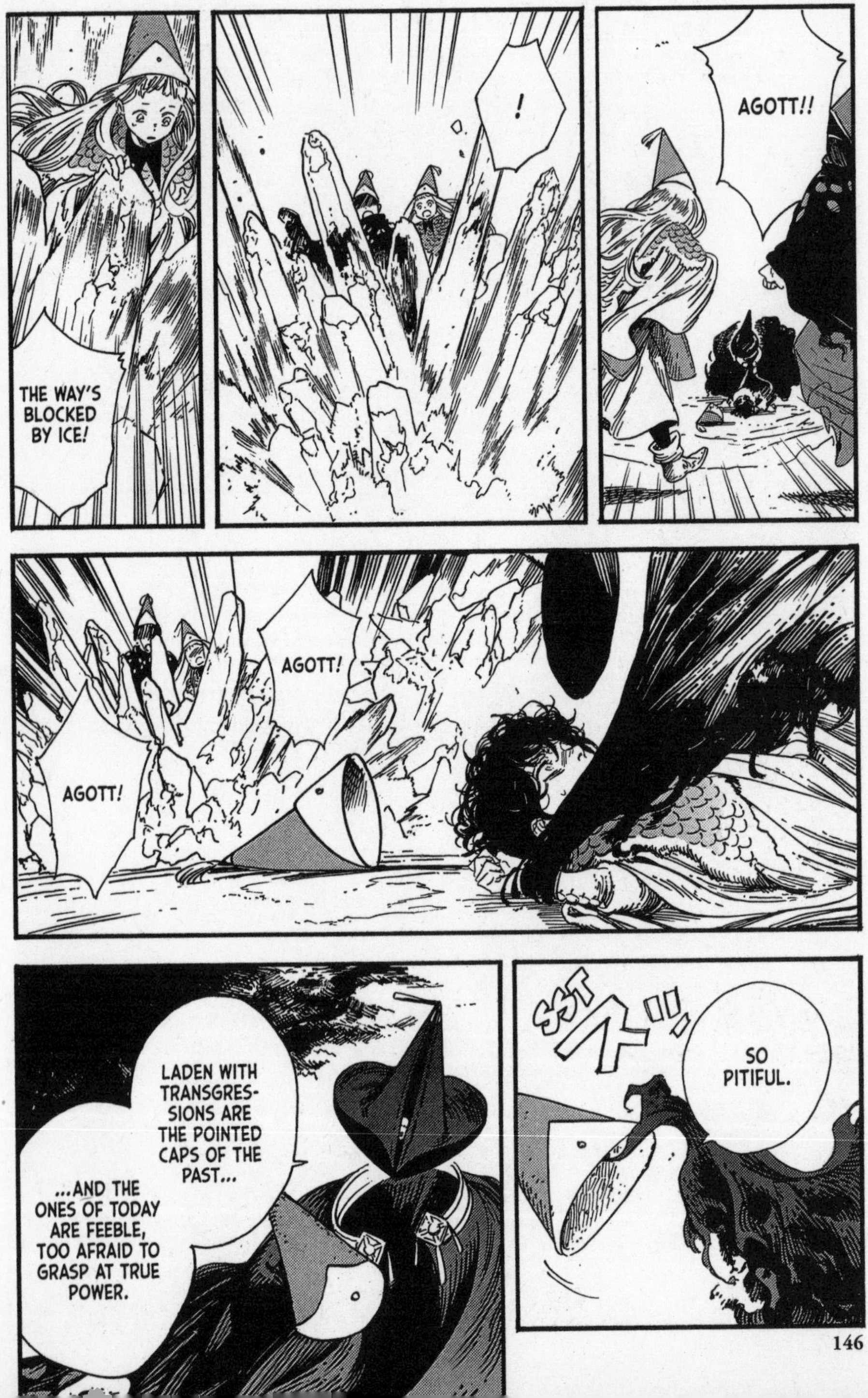
AGOTT!!
!
THE WAY'S BLOCKED BY ICE!
AGOTT!
AGOTT!
SST
SO PITIFUL.
LADEN WITH TRANSGRES-SIONS ARE THE POINTED CAPS OF THE PAST...
...AND THE ONES OF TODAY ARE FEEBLE, TOO AFRAID TO GRASP AT TRUE POWER.

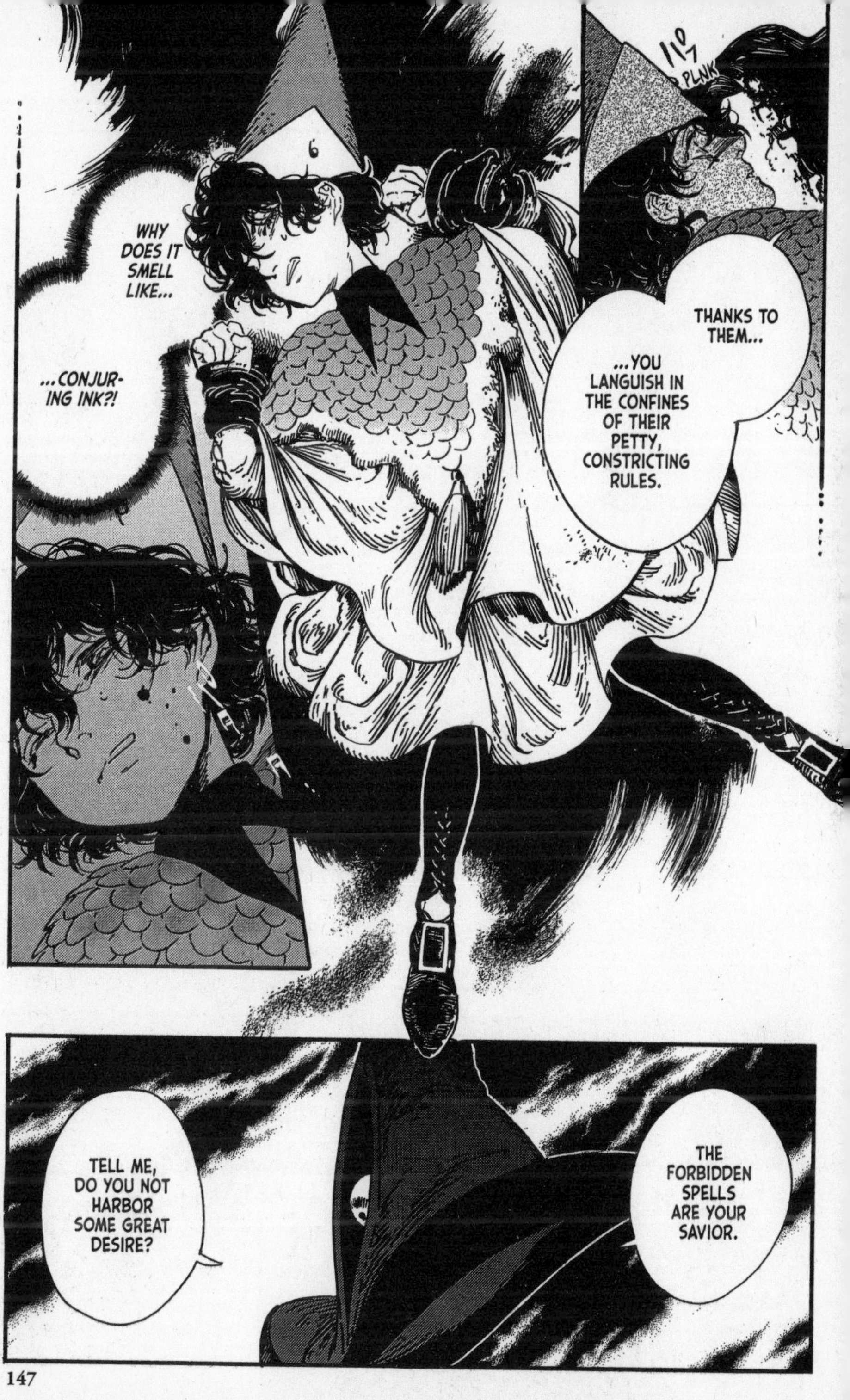
PLNK
THANKS TO THEM...
...YOU LANGUISH IN THE CONFINES OF THEIR PETTY, CONSTRICTING RULES.
WHY DOES IT SMELL LIKE...
...CONJUR-ING INK?!
THE FORBIDDEN SPELLS ARE YOUR SAVIOR.
TELL ME, DO YOU NOT HARBOR SOME GREAT DESIRE?

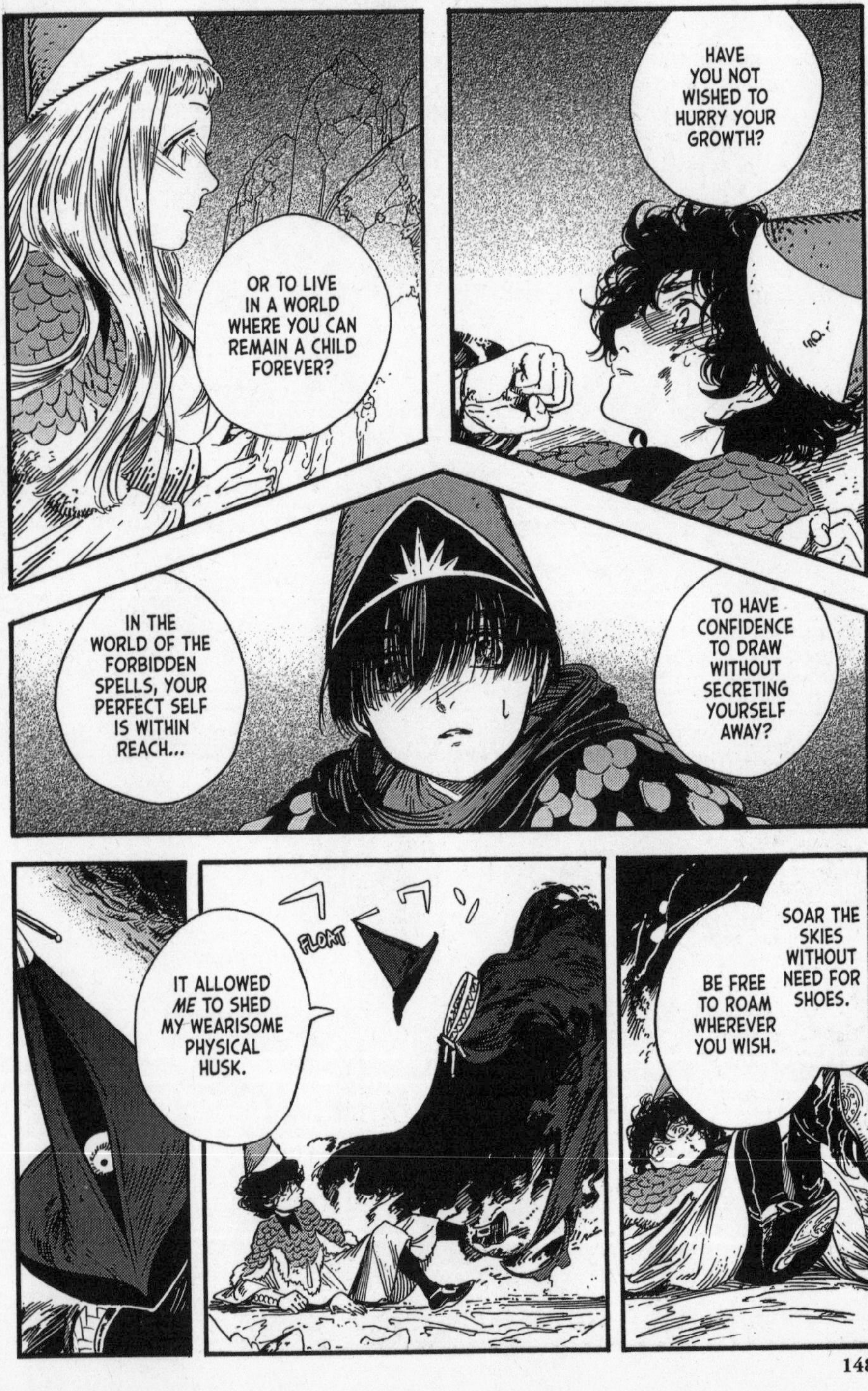
HAVE YOU NOT WISHED TO HURRY YOUR GROWTH?
OR TO LIVE IN A WORLD WHERE YOU CAN REMAIN A CHILD FOREVER?
TO HAVE CONFIDENCE TO DRAW WITHOUT SECRETING YOURSELF AWAY?
IN THE WORLD OF THE FORBIDDEN SPELLS, YOUR PERFECT SELF IS WITHIN REACH...
SOAR THE SKIES WITHOUT NEED FOR SHOES.
BE FREE TO ROAM WHEREVER YOU WISH.
FLOAT
IT ALLOWED *ME* TO SHED MY WEARISOME PHYSICAL HUSK.

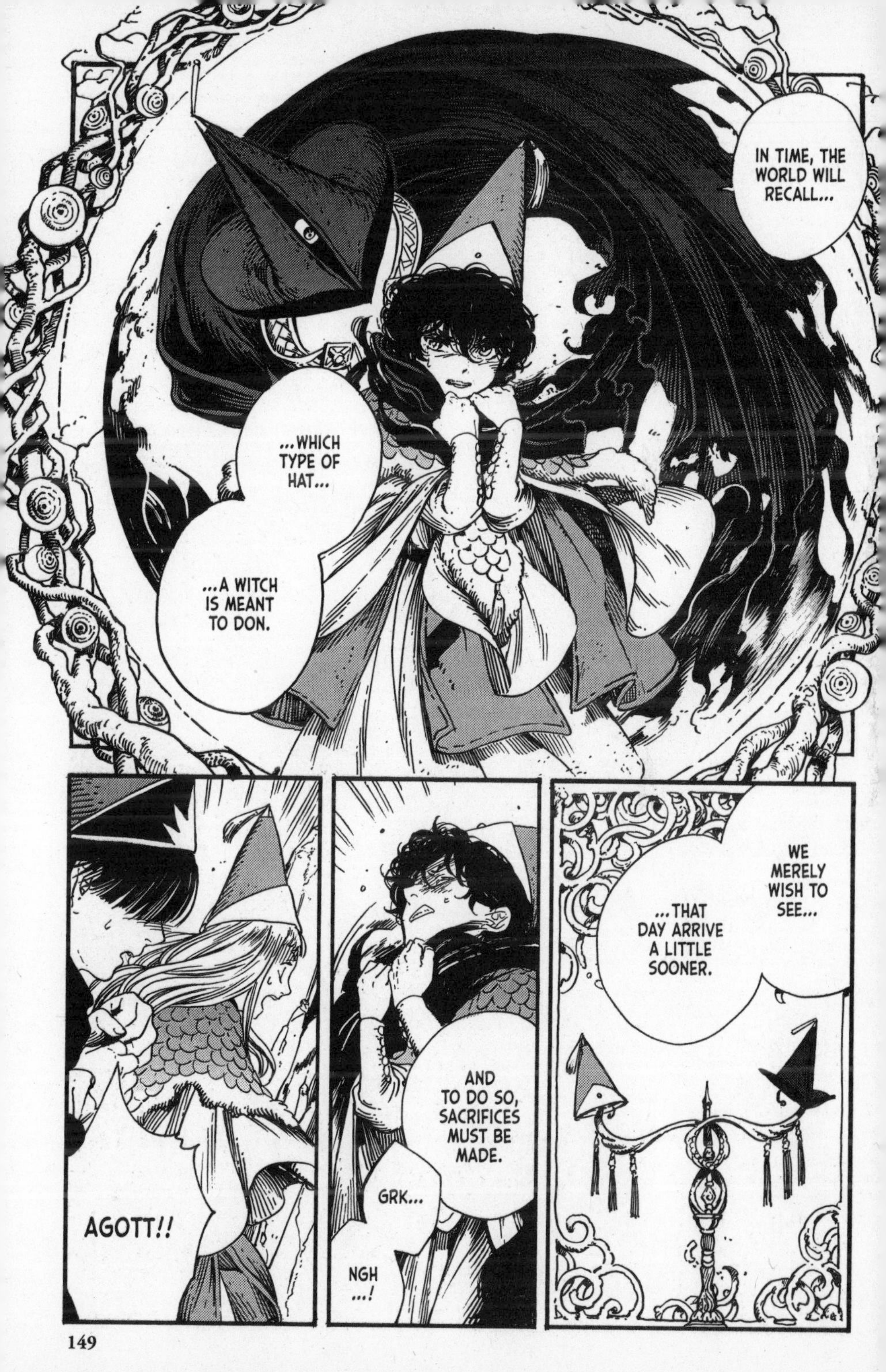
IN TIME, THE WORLD WILL RECALL...
...WHICH TYPE OF HAT...
...A WITCH IS MEANT TO DON.
WE MERELY WISH TO SEE...
...THAT DAY ARRIVE A LITTLE SOONER.
AND TO DO SO, SACRIFICES MUST BE MADE.
GRK...
NGH ...!
AGOTT!!

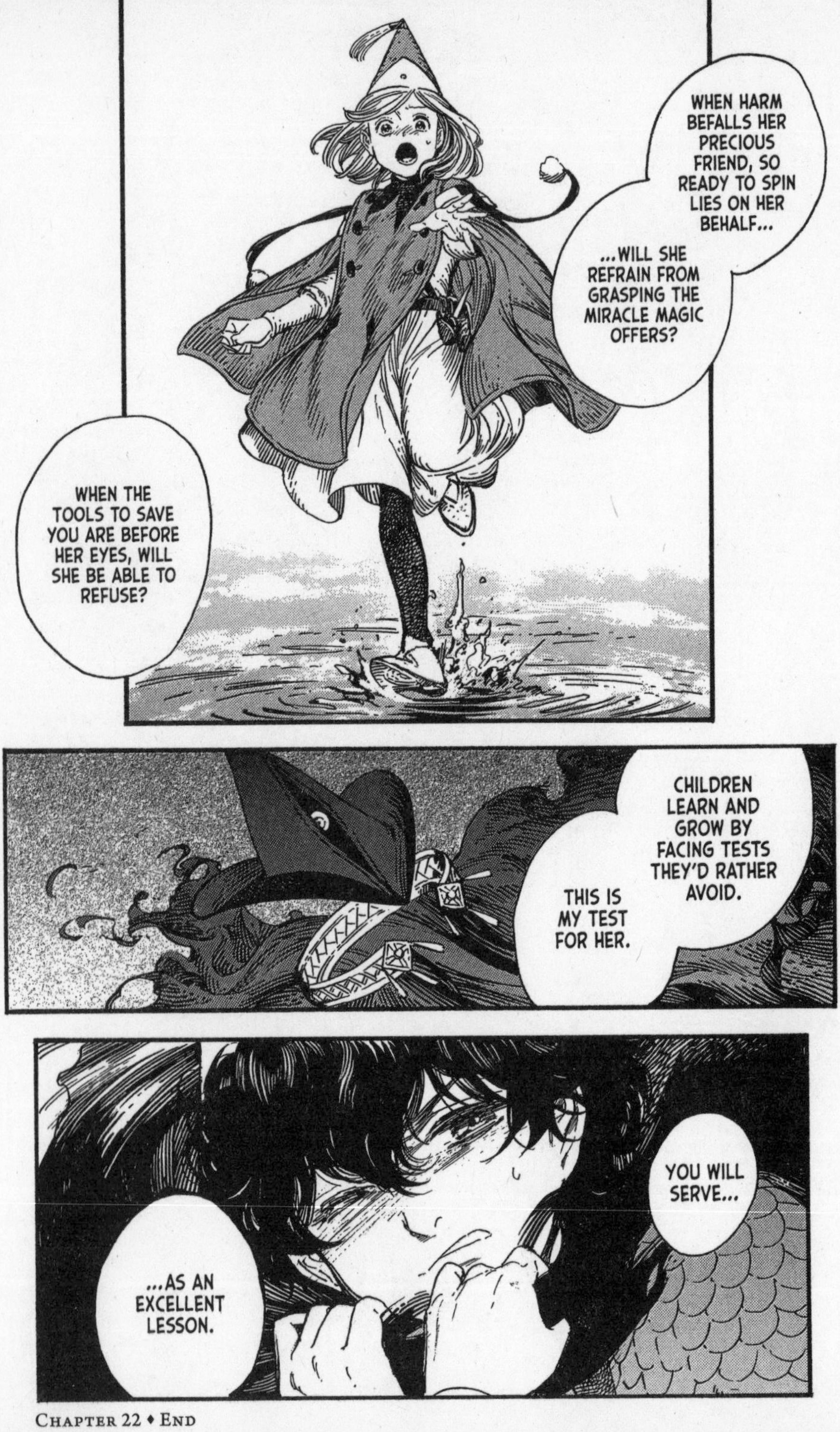
WHEN HARM BEFALLS HER PRECIOUS FRIEND, SO READY TO SPIN LIES ON HER BEHALF...
...WILL SHE REFRAIN FROM GRASPING THE MIRACLE MAGIC OFFERS?
WHEN THE TOOLS TO SAVE YOU ARE BEFORE HER EYES, WILL SHE BE ABLE TO REFUSE?
CHILDREN LEARN AND GROW BY FACING TESTS THEY'D RATHER AVOID.
THIS IS MY TEST FOR HER.
YOU WILL SERVE...
...AS AN EXCELLENT LESSON.

CHAPTER 22 ♦ END

Witch Hat Atelier

Chapter 23

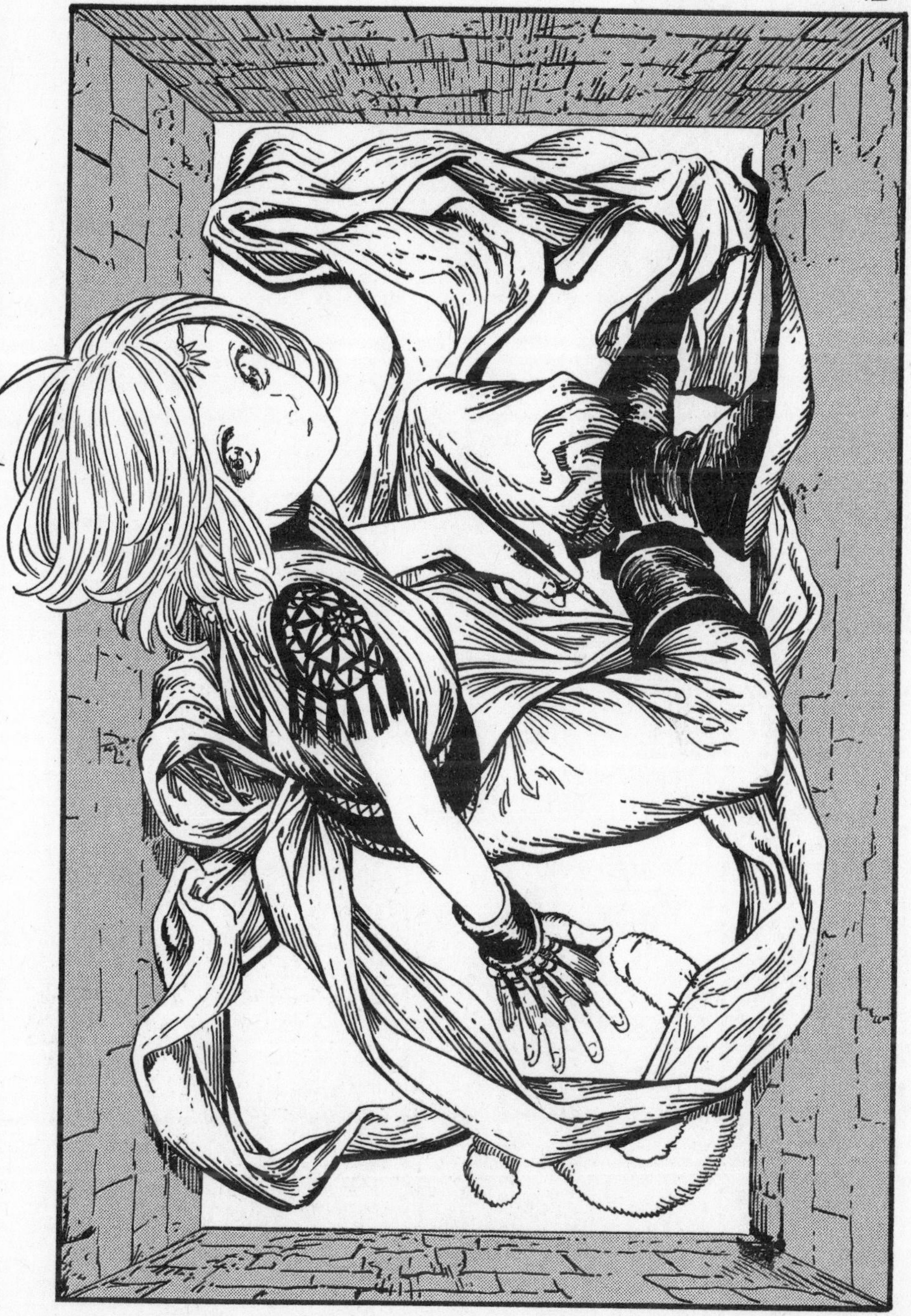

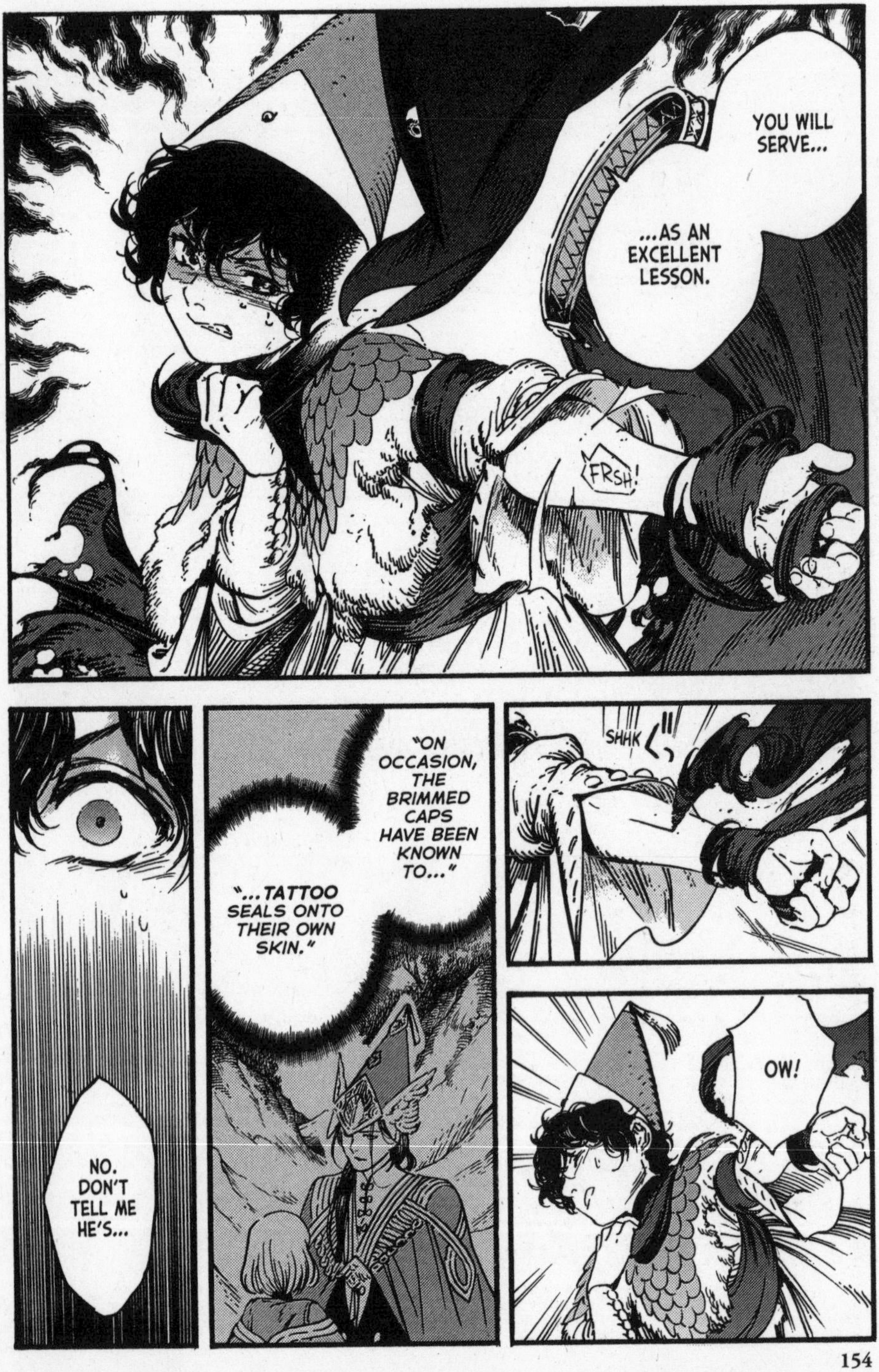
YOU WILL SERVE...
...AS AN EXCELLENT LESSON.
FRSH!
SHHK
OW!
"ON OCCASION, THE BRIMMED CAPS HAVE BEEN KNOWN TO..."
"...TATTOO SEALS ONTO THEIR OWN SKIN."
NO. DON'T TELL ME HE'S...

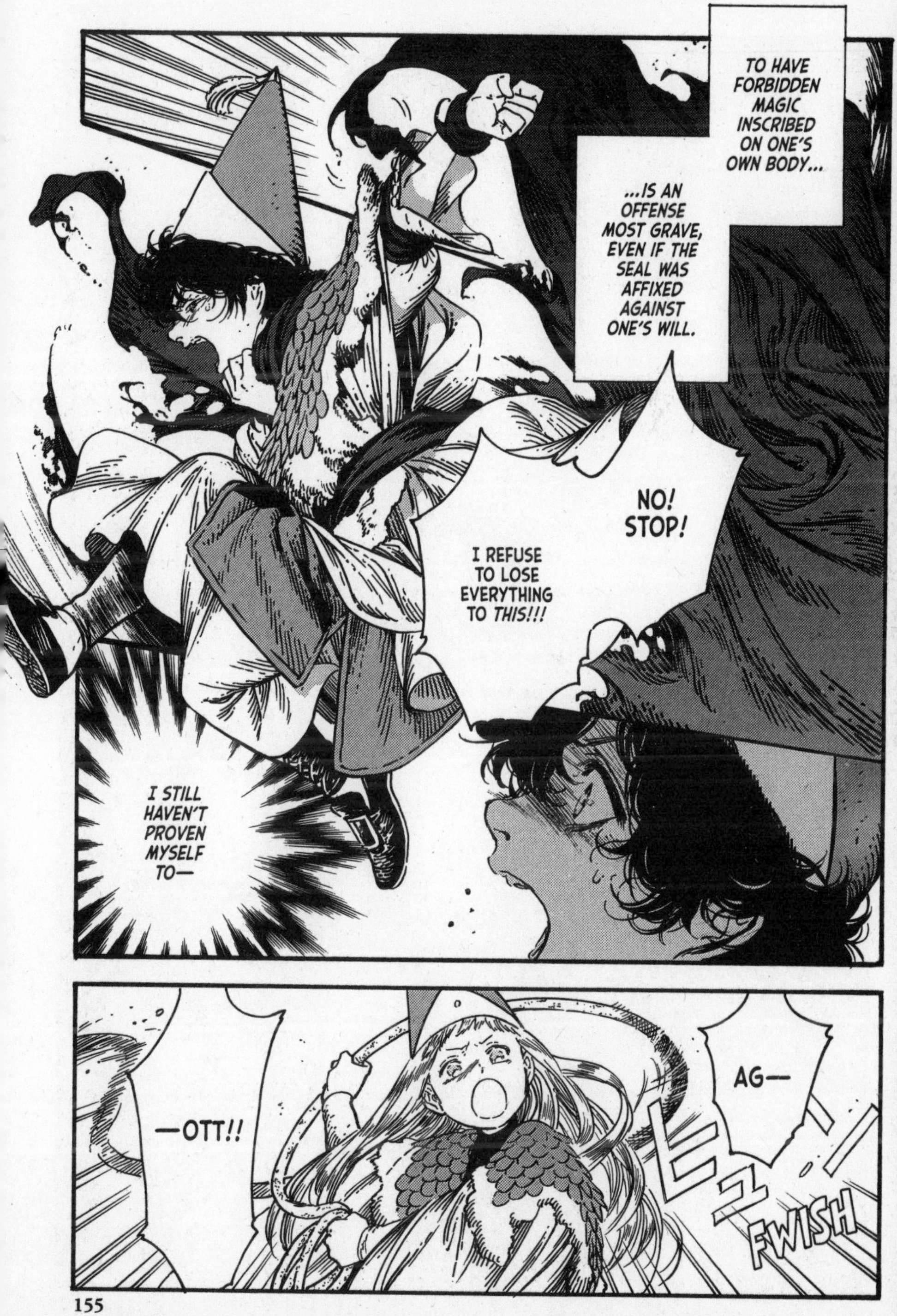
TO HAVE FORBIDDEN MAGIC INSCRIBED ON ONE'S OWN BODY...
...IS AN OFFENSE MOST GRAVE, EVEN IF THE SEAL WAS AFFIXED AGAINST ONE'S WILL.
NO! STOP!
I REFUSE TO LOSE EVERYTHING TO *THIS!!!*
I STILL HAVEN'T PROVEN MYSELF TO—
AG—
FWISH
—OTT!!

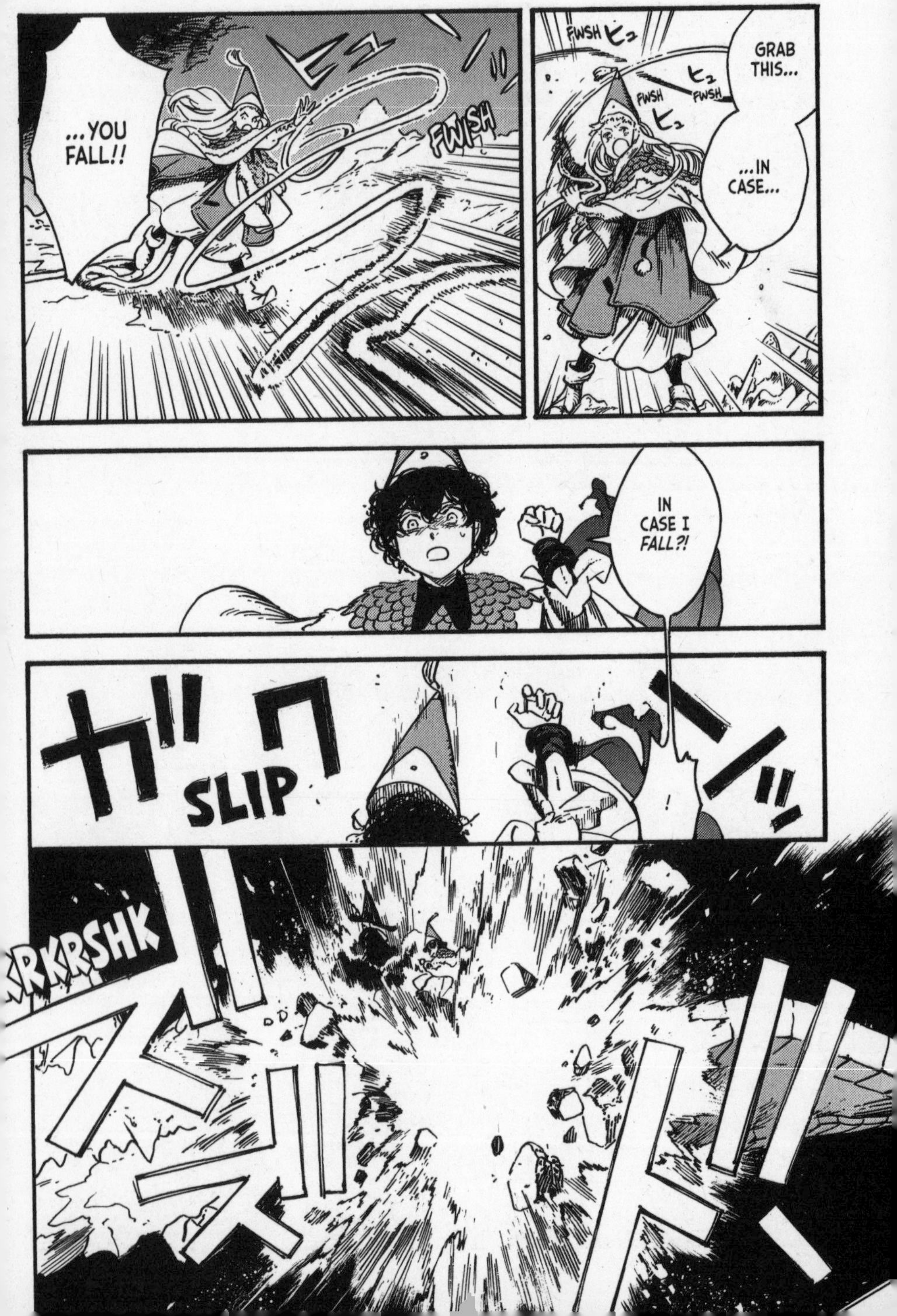
FWSH ヒュ
FWSH ヒュ
FWSH ヒュ
GRAB THIS...
...IN CASE...
ヒュ
FWISH
...YOU FALL!!
IN CASE I FALL?!
ガク
SLIP
!
KRKRSHK

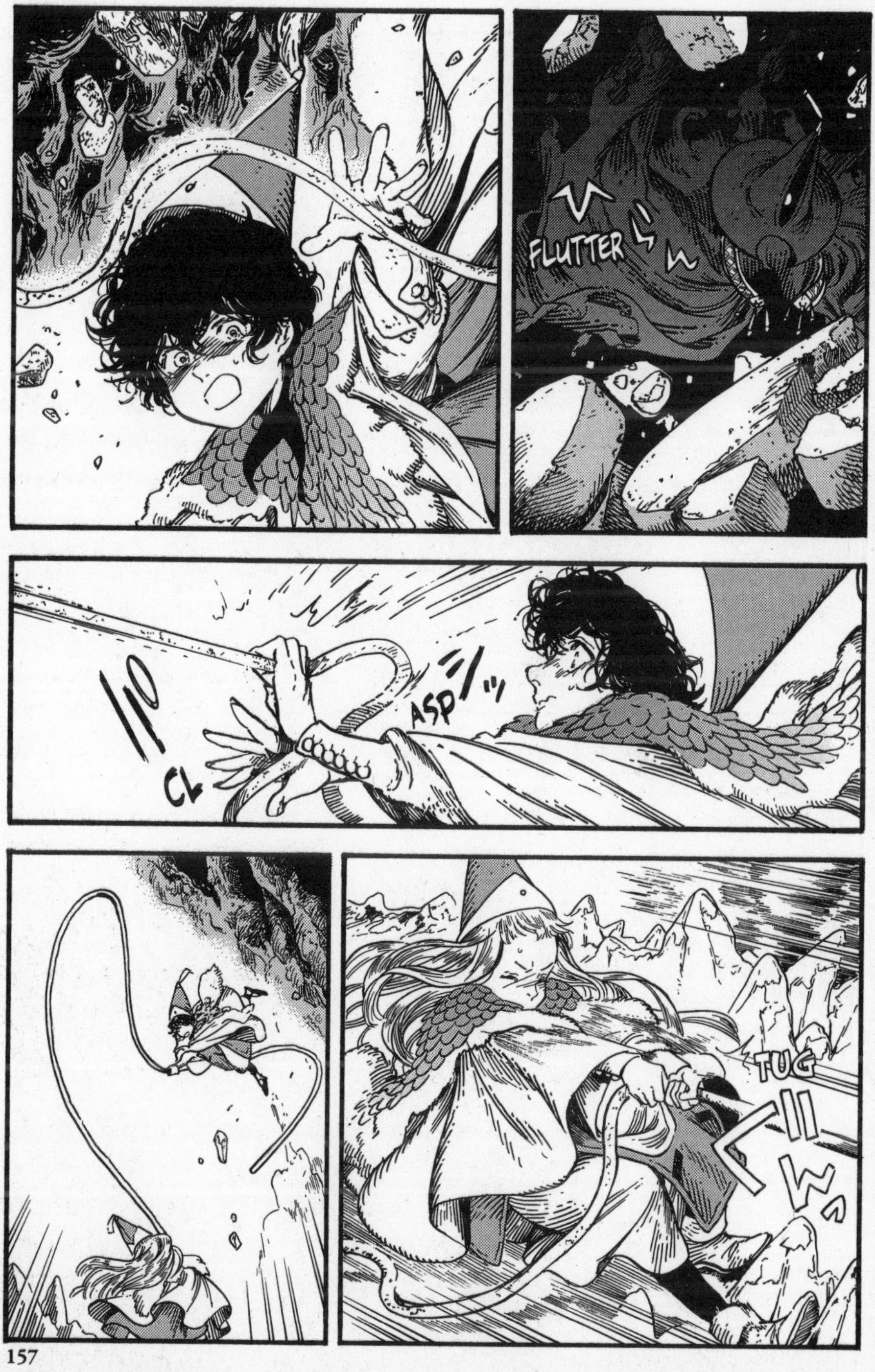
FLUTTER
ASP
CL
TUG

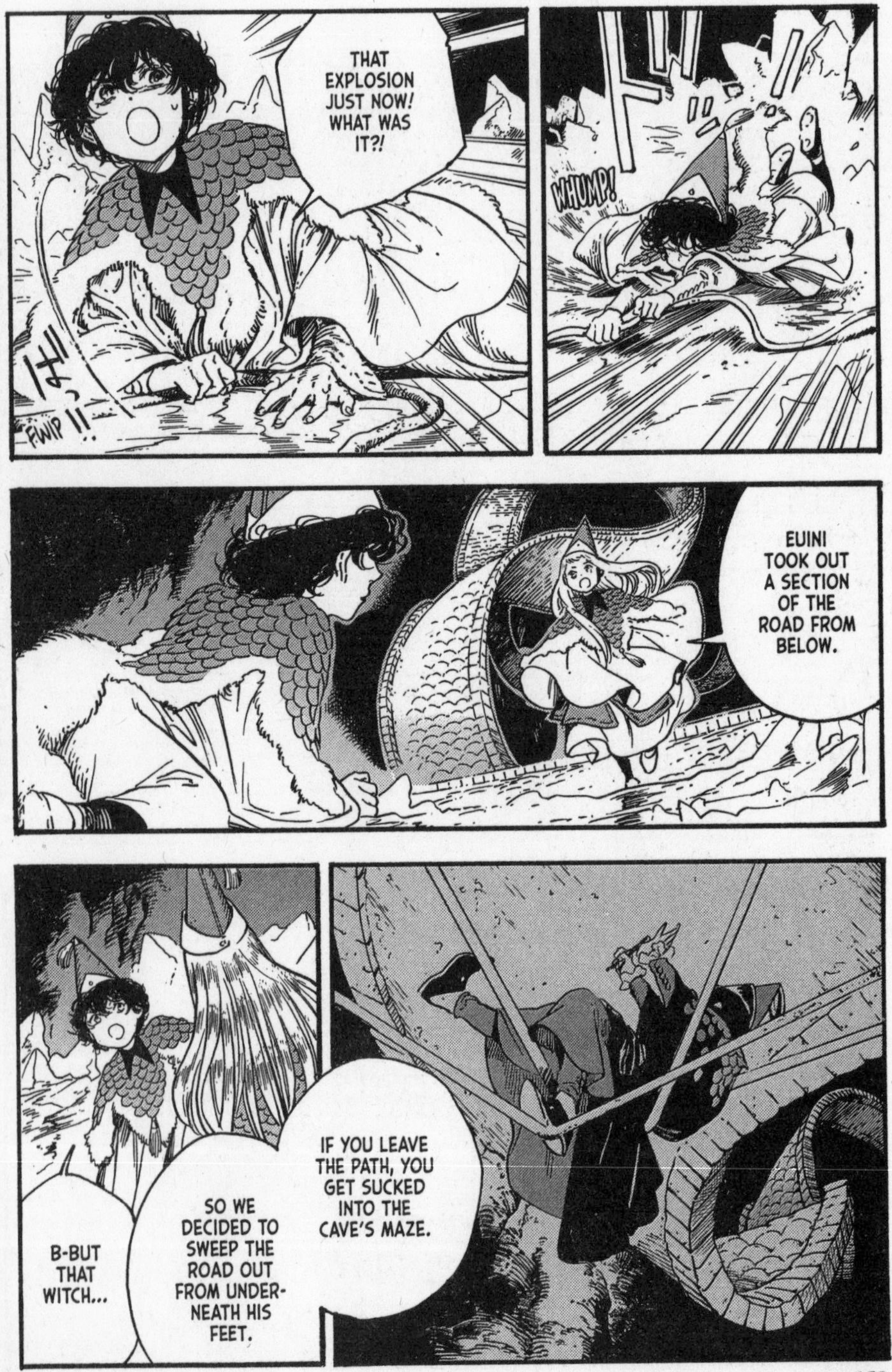
WHUMP!
THAT EXPLOSION JUST NOW! WHAT WAS IT?!
FWIP!!
EUINI TOOK OUT A SECTION OF THE ROAD FROM BELOW.
IF YOU LEAVE THE PATH, YOU GET SUCKED INTO THE CAVE'S MAZE.
SO WE DECIDED TO SWEEP THE ROAD OUT FROM UNDER-NEATH HIS FEET.
B-BUT THAT WITCH...

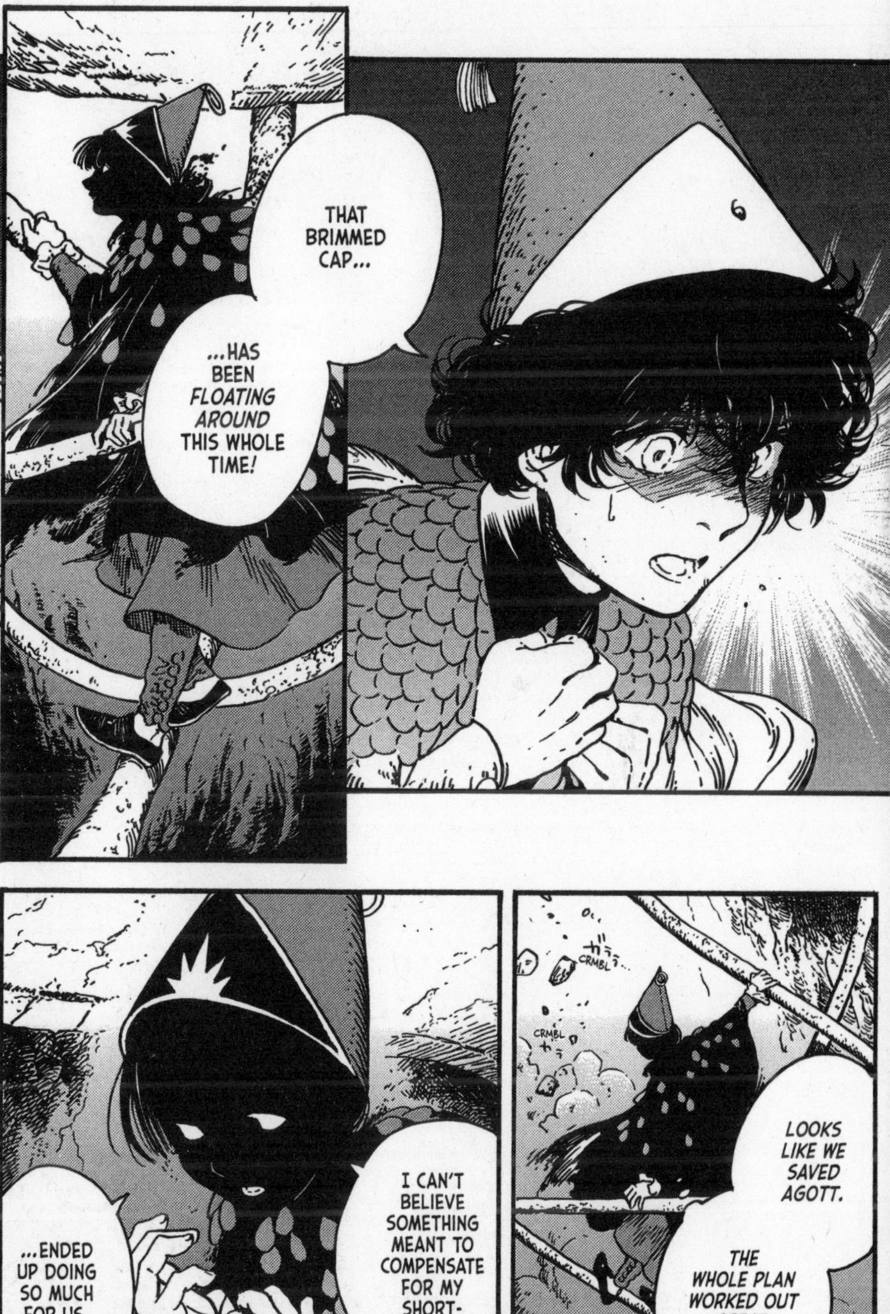
THAT BRIMMED CAP...
...HAS BEEN FLOATING AROUND THIS WHOLE TIME!
CRMBL
CRMBL
LOOKS LIKE WE SAVED AGOTT.
THE WHOLE PLAN WORKED OUT GREAT.
I CAN'T BELIEVE SOMETHING MEANT TO COMPENSATE FOR MY SHORT-COMINGS...
...ENDED UP DOING SO MUCH FOR US.

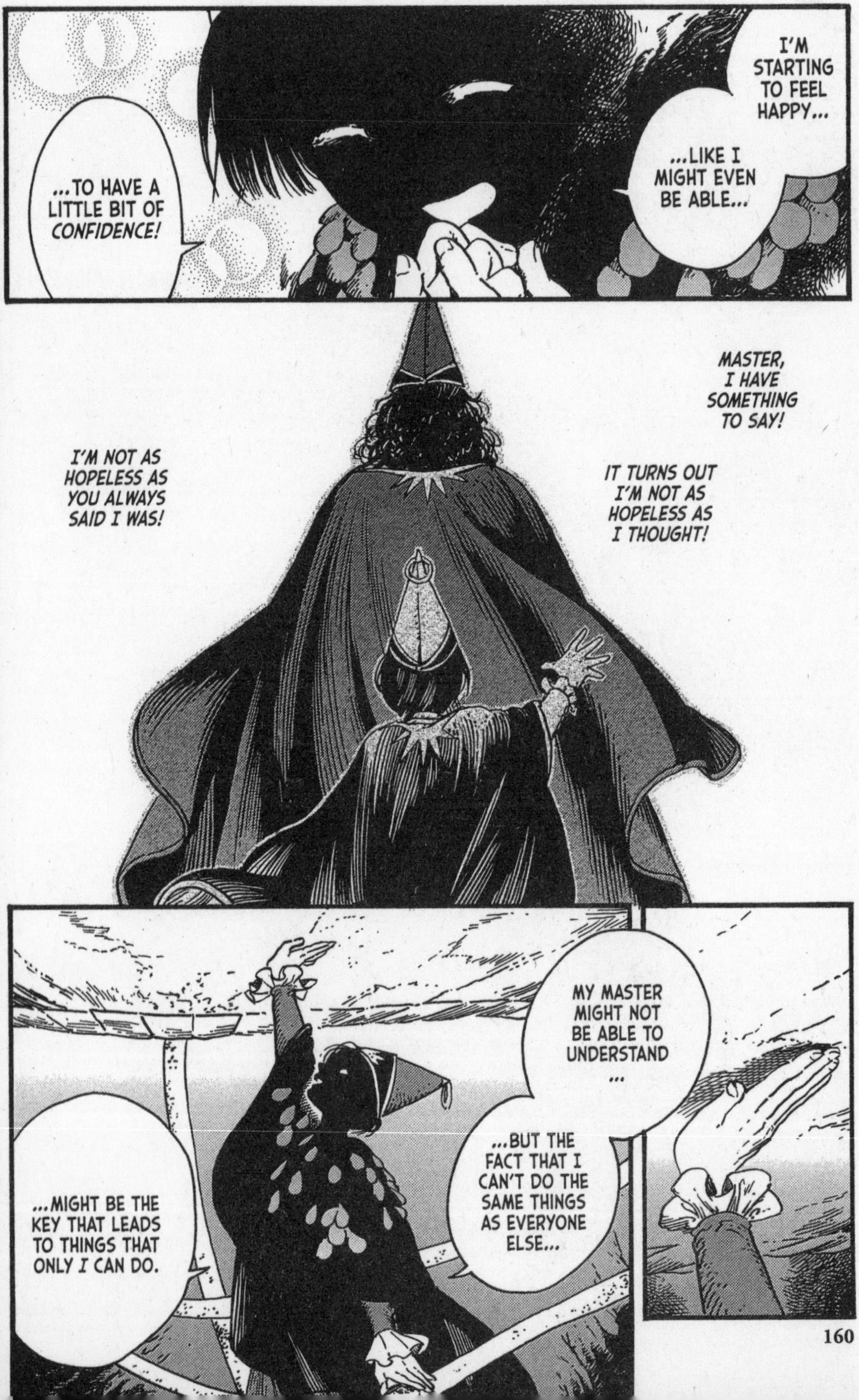
I'M STARTING TO FEEL HAPPY...
...LIKE I MIGHT EVEN BE ABLE...
...TO HAVE A LITTLE BIT OF *CONFIDENCE!*
MASTER, I HAVE SOMETHING TO SAY!
IT TURNS OUT I'M NOT AS HOPELESS AS I THOUGHT!
I'M NOT AS HOPELESS AS YOU ALWAYS SAID I WAS!
MY MASTER MIGHT NOT BE ABLE TO UNDERSTAND ...
...BUT THE FACT THAT I CAN'T DO THE SAME THINGS AS EVERYONE ELSE...
...MIGHT BE THE KEY THAT LEADS TO THINGS THAT ONLY *I* CAN DO.

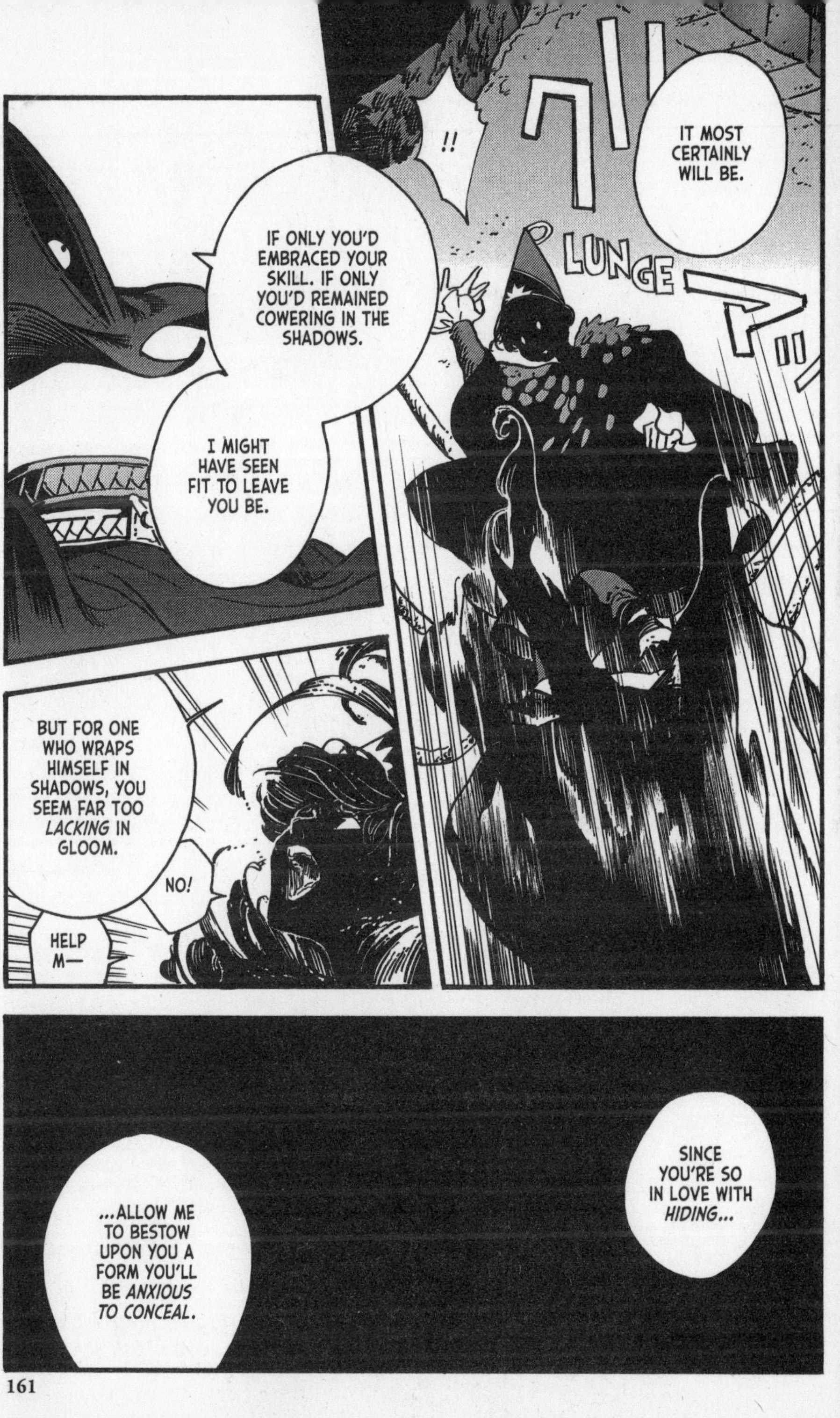
!!
IT MOST CERTAINLY WILL BE.
LUNGE
IF ONLY YOU'D EMBRACED YOUR SKILL. IF ONLY YOU'D REMAINED COWERING IN THE SHADOWS.
I MIGHT HAVE SEEN FIT TO LEAVE YOU BE.
BUT FOR ONE WHO WRAPS HIMSELF IN SHADOWS, YOU SEEM FAR TOO *LACKING* IN GLOOM.
NO!
HELP M—
SINCE YOU'RE SO IN LOVE WITH *HIDING*...
...ALLOW ME TO BESTOW UPON YOU A FORM YOU'LL BE *ANXIOUS TO CONCEAL*.

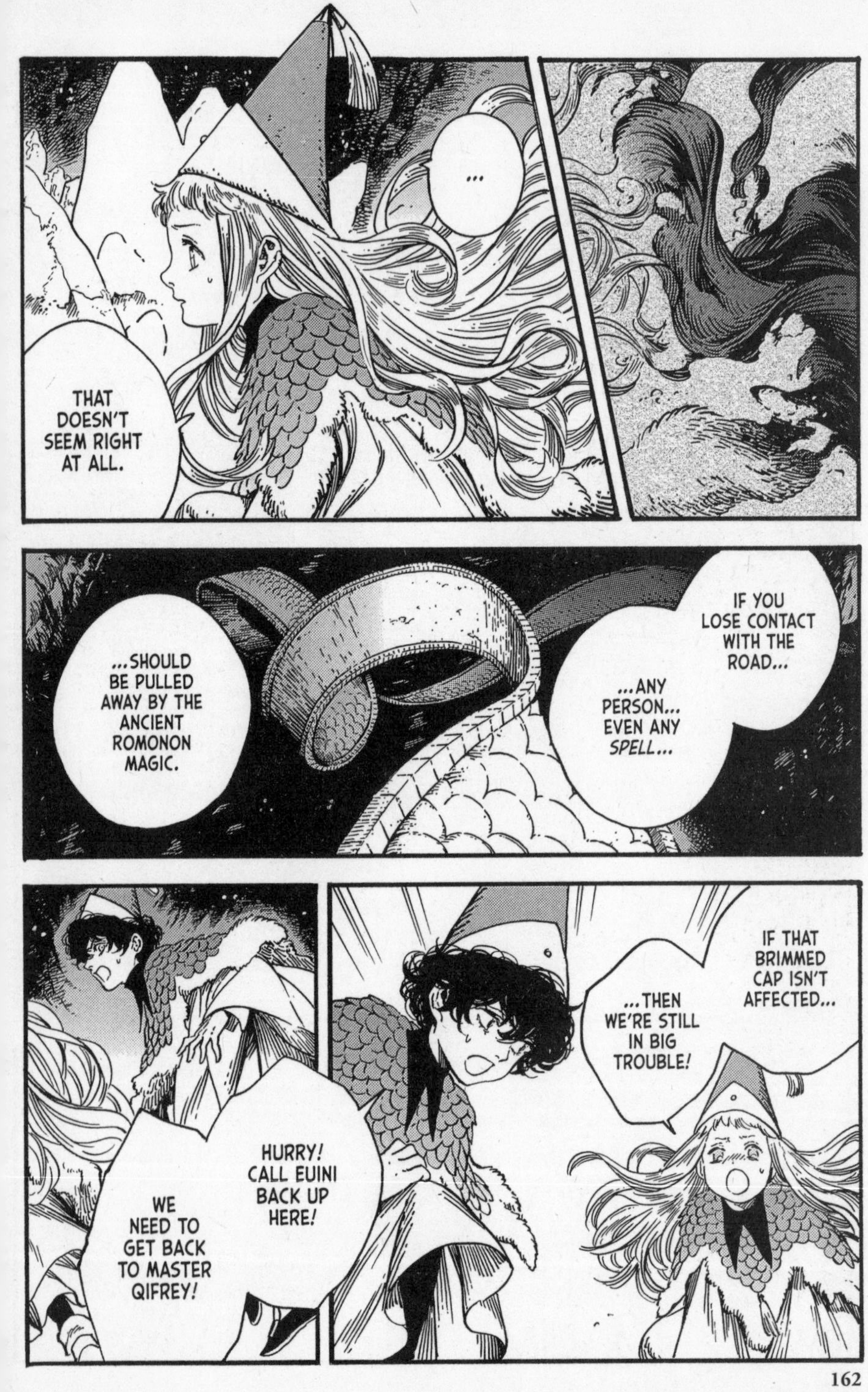
...
THAT DOESN'T SEEM RIGHT AT ALL.
IF YOU LOSE CONTACT WITH THE ROAD...
...ANY PERSON... EVEN ANY *SPELL*...
...SHOULD BE PULLED AWAY BY THE ANCIENT ROMONON MAGIC.
IF THAT BRIMMED CAP ISN'T AFFECTED...
...THEN WE'RE STILL IN BIG TROUBLE!
HURRY! CALL EUINI BACK UP HERE!
WE NEED TO GET BACK TO MASTER QIFREY!

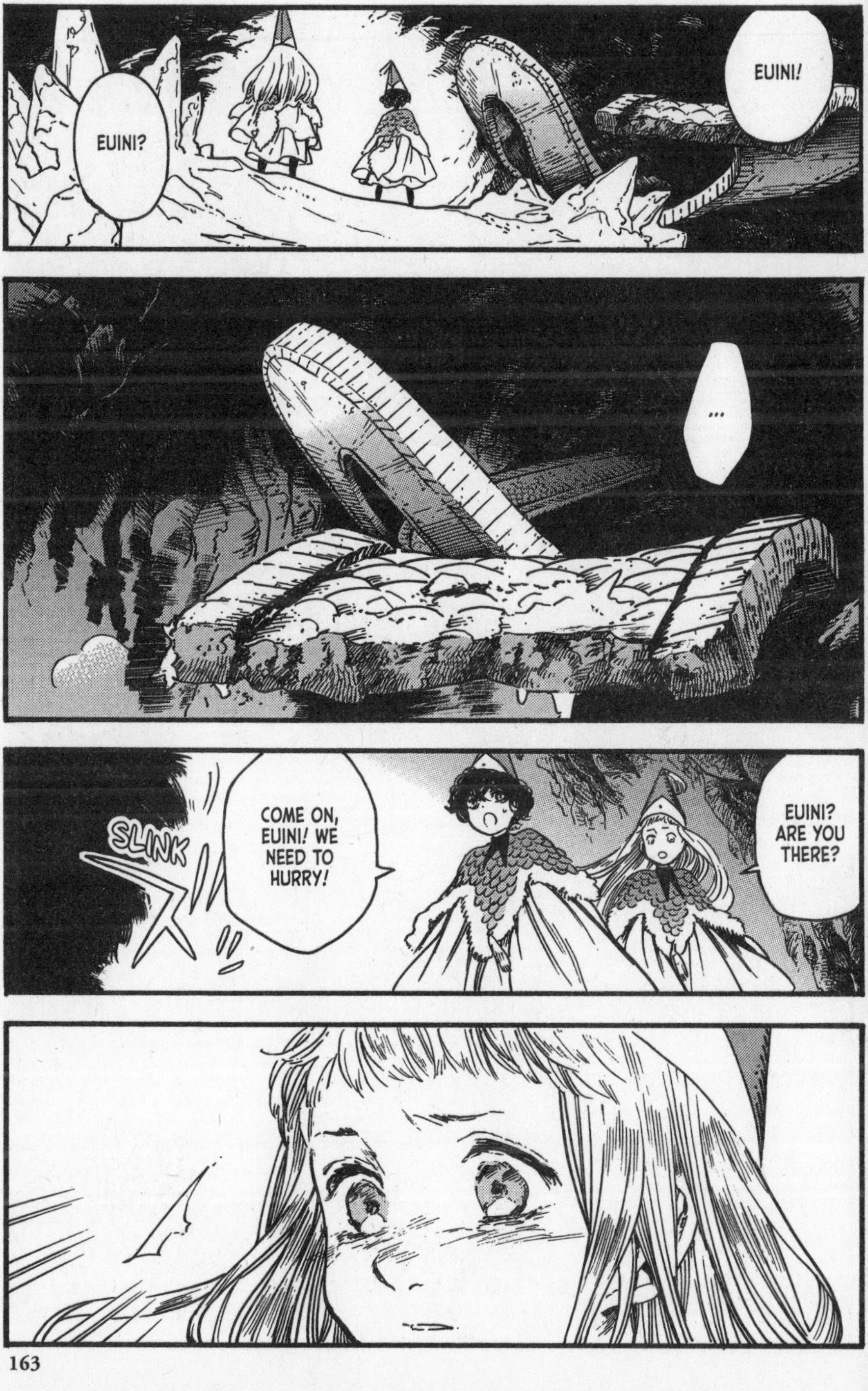
EUINI!
EUINI?
...
EUINI? ARE YOU THERE?
COME ON, EUINI! WE NEED TO HURRY!
SLINK

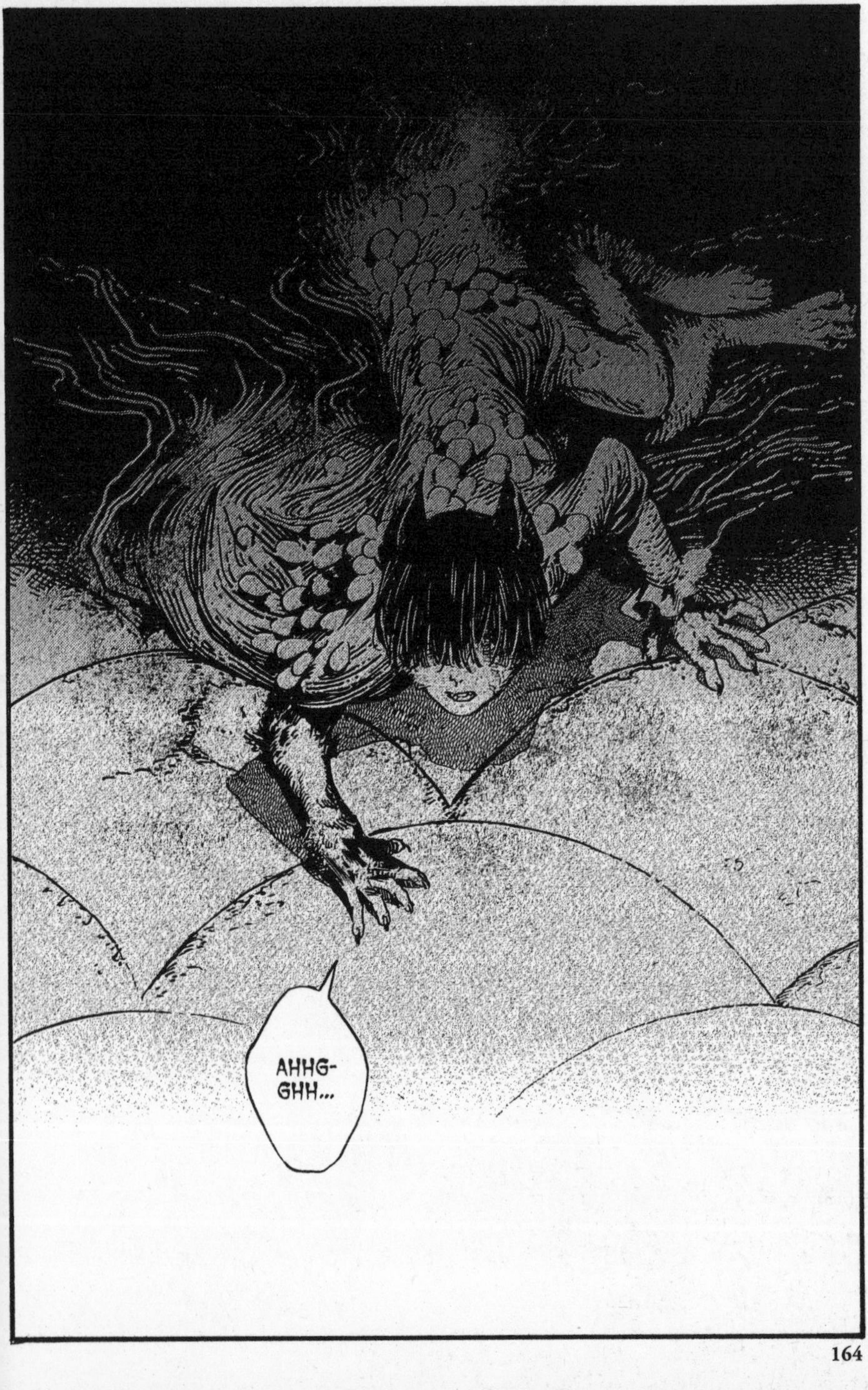
AHHG-
GHH...

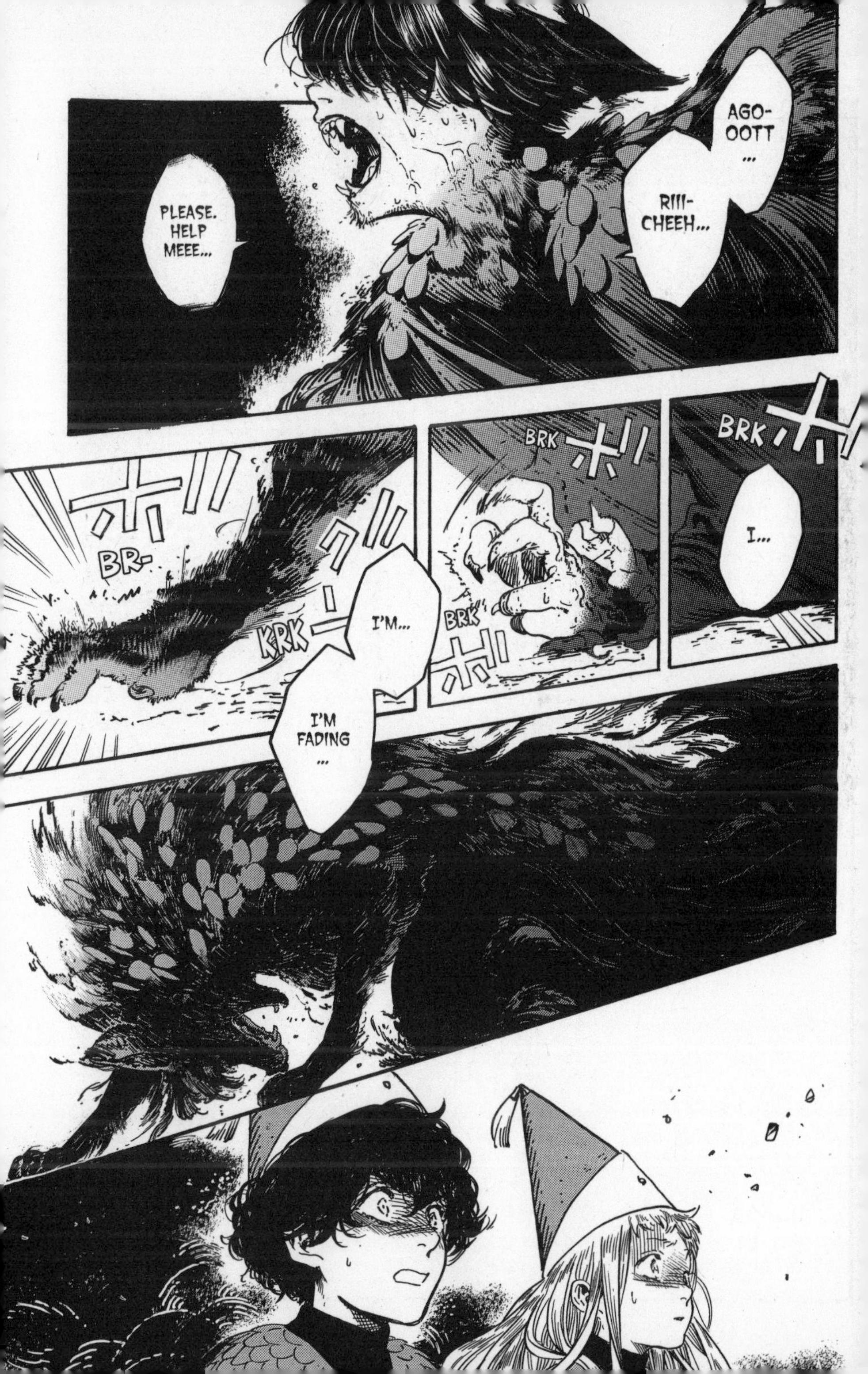
AGO-OOTT...
RIII-CHEEH...
PLEASE. HELP MEEE...
BRK
I...
BRK
BRK
BR-
KRK
I'M...
I'M FADING...

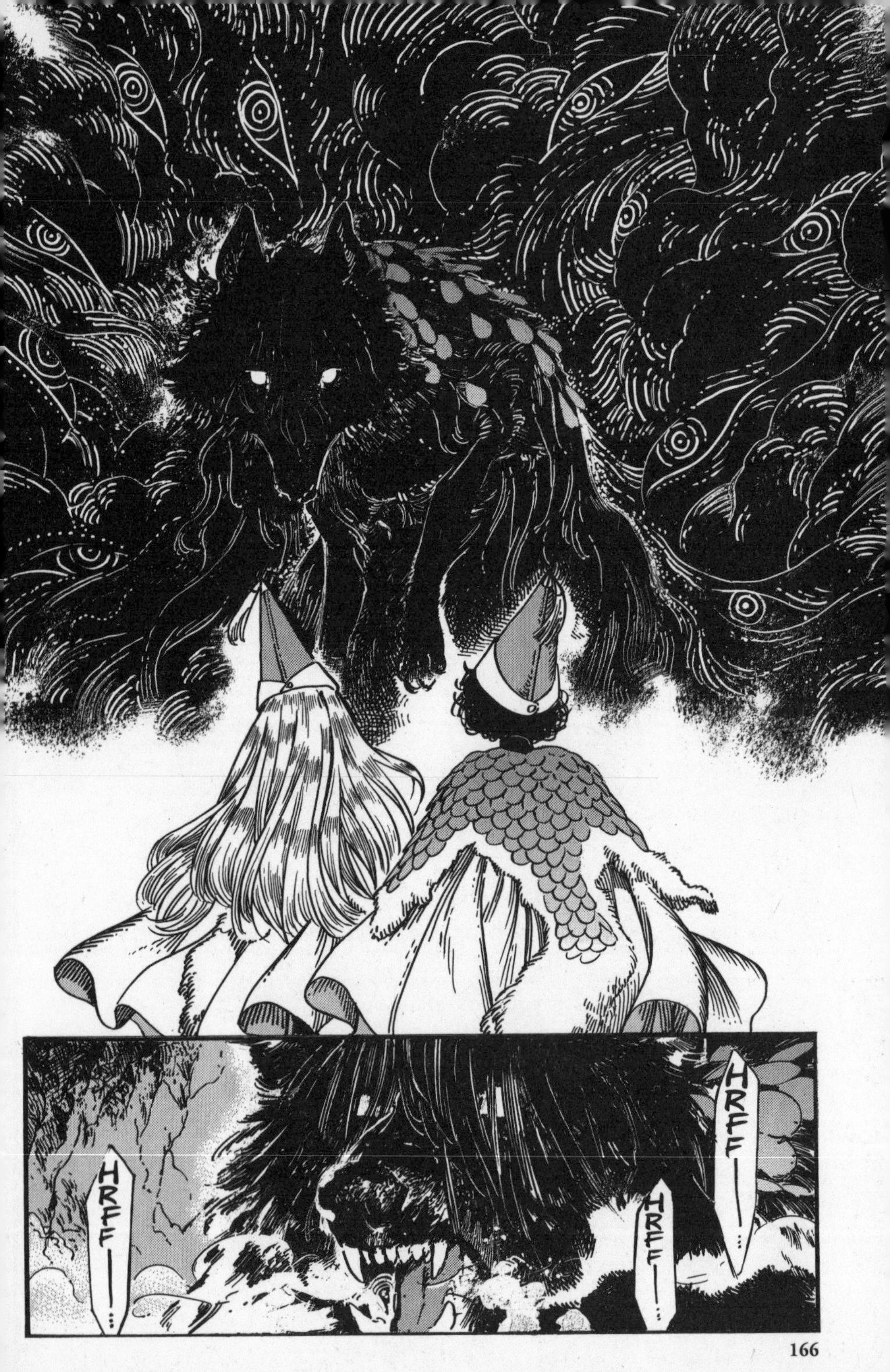
HRFF......
HRFF......
HRFF......

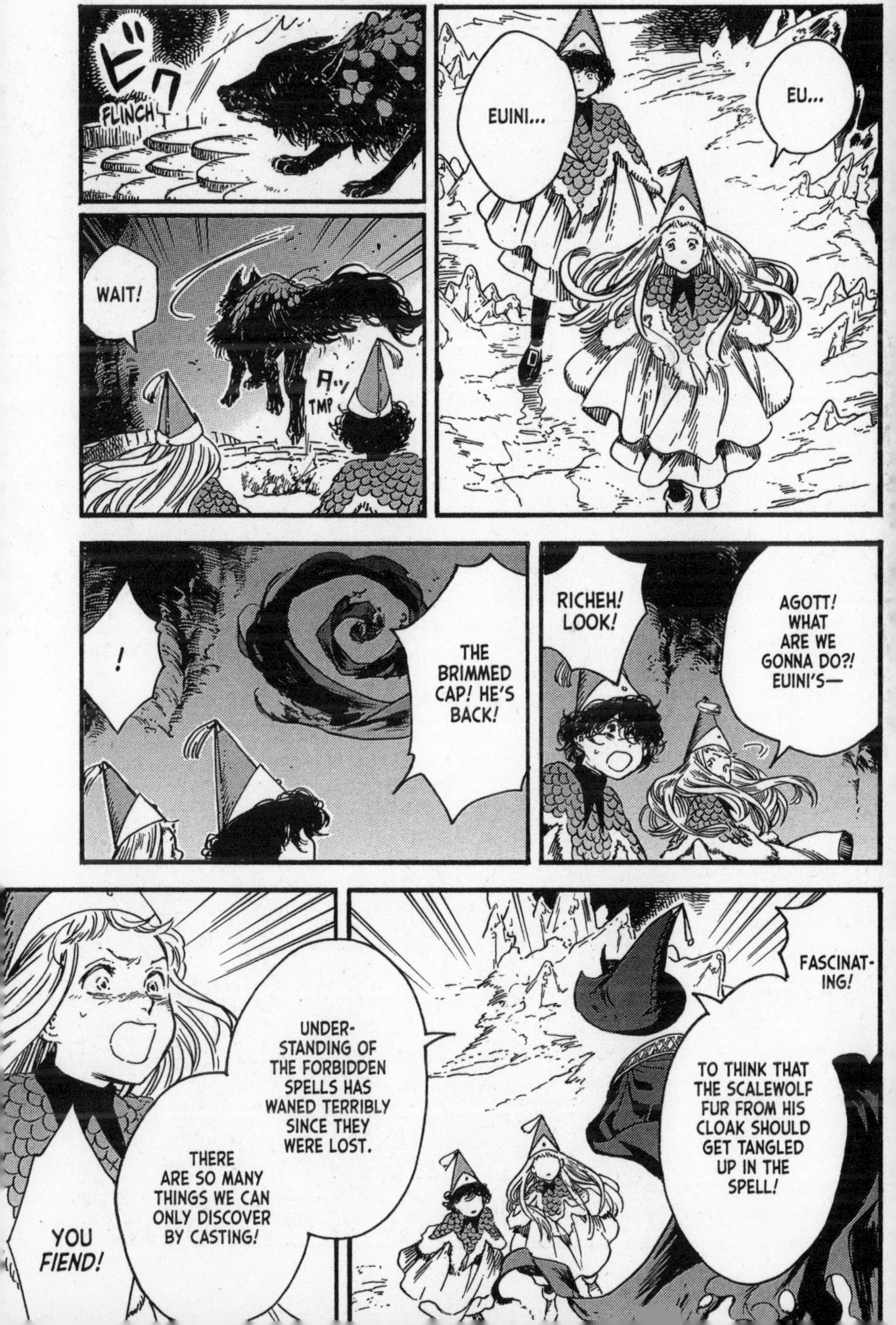
EU...
EUINI...
ビク
FLINCH
WAIT!
タッ
TMP
AGOTT! WHAT ARE WE GONNA DO?! EUINI'S—
RICHEH! LOOK!
THE BRIMMED CAP! HE'S BACK!
!
FASCINATING!
TO THINK THAT THE SCALEWOLF FUR FROM HIS CLOAK SHOULD GET TANGLED UP IN THE SPELL!
UNDER-STANDING OF THE FORBIDDEN SPELLS HAS WANED TERRIBLY SINCE THEY WERE LOST.
THERE ARE SO MANY THINGS WE CAN ONLY DISCOVER BY CASTING!
YOU FIEND!

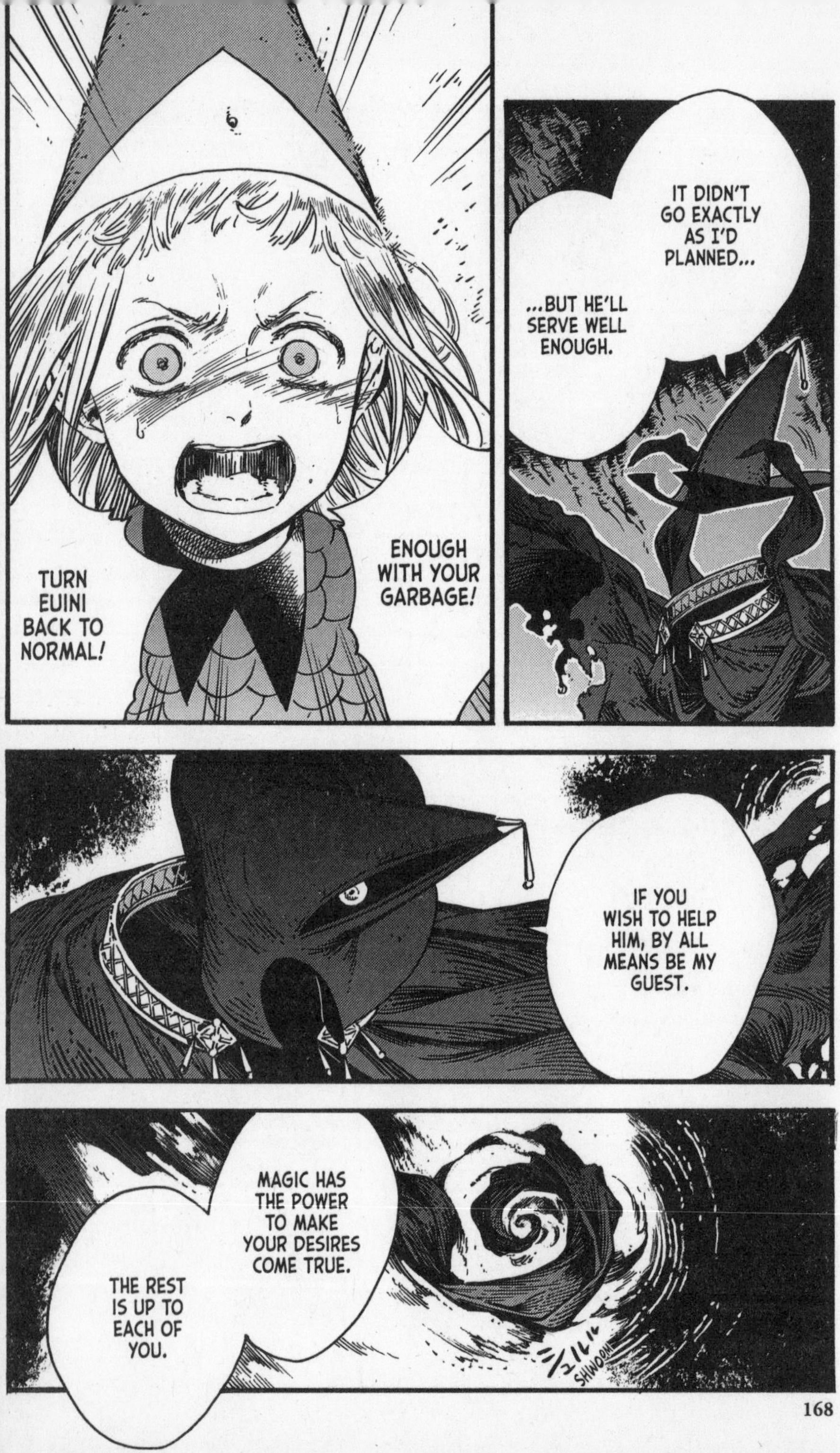
IT DIDN'T GO EXACTLY AS I'D PLANNED...
...BUT HE'LL SERVE WELL ENOUGH.
ENOUGH WITH YOUR GARBAGE!
TURN EUINI BACK TO NORMAL!
IF YOU WISH TO HELP HIM, BY ALL MEANS BE MY GUEST.
MAGIC HAS THE POWER TO MAKE YOUR DESIRES COME TRUE.
THE REST IS UP TO EACH OF YOU.
SHWOOM

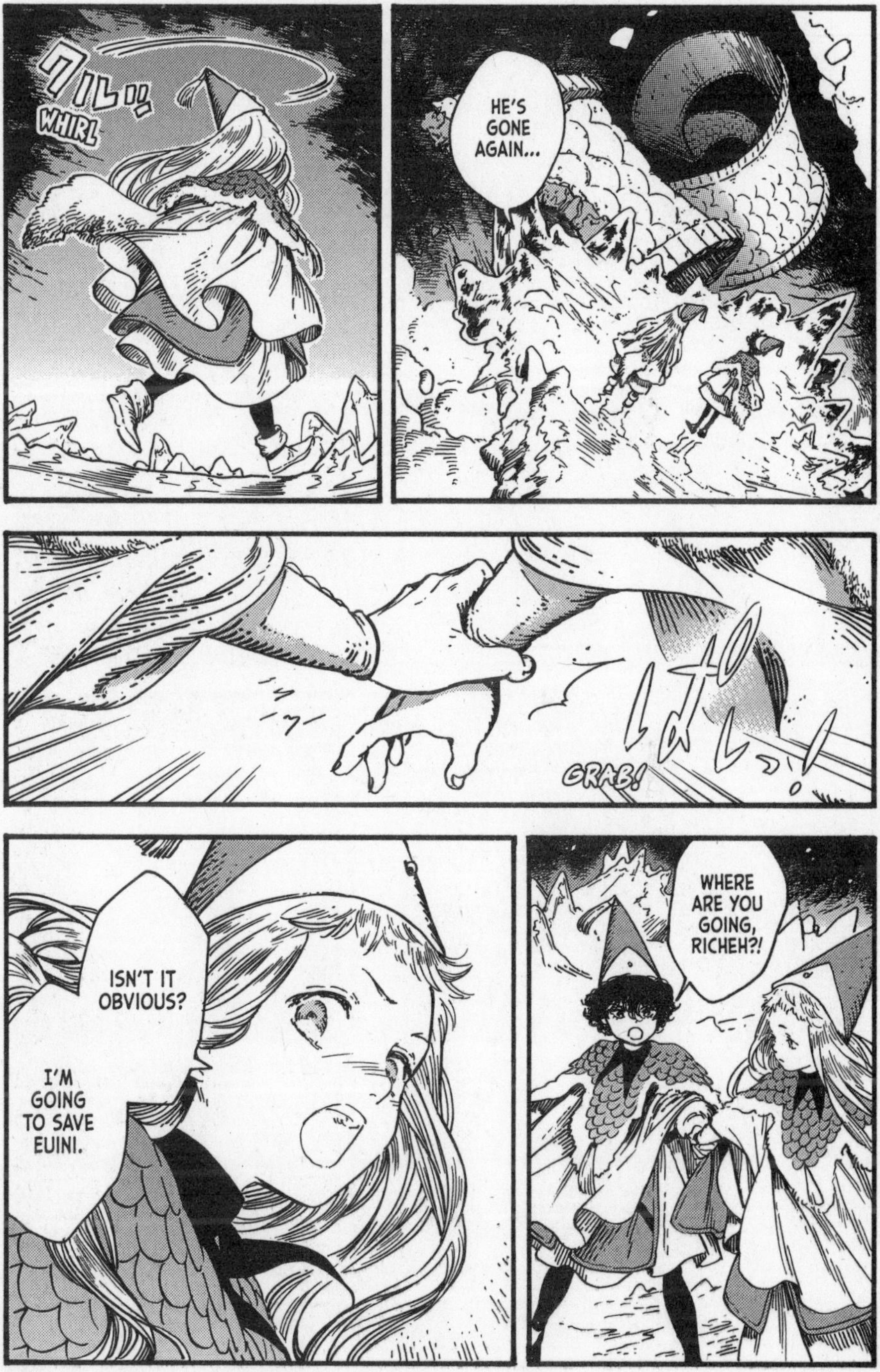
HE'S GONE AGAIN...
WHIRL
GRAB!
WHERE ARE YOU GOING, RICHEH?!
ISN'T IT OBVIOUS?
I'M GOING TO SAVE EUINI.

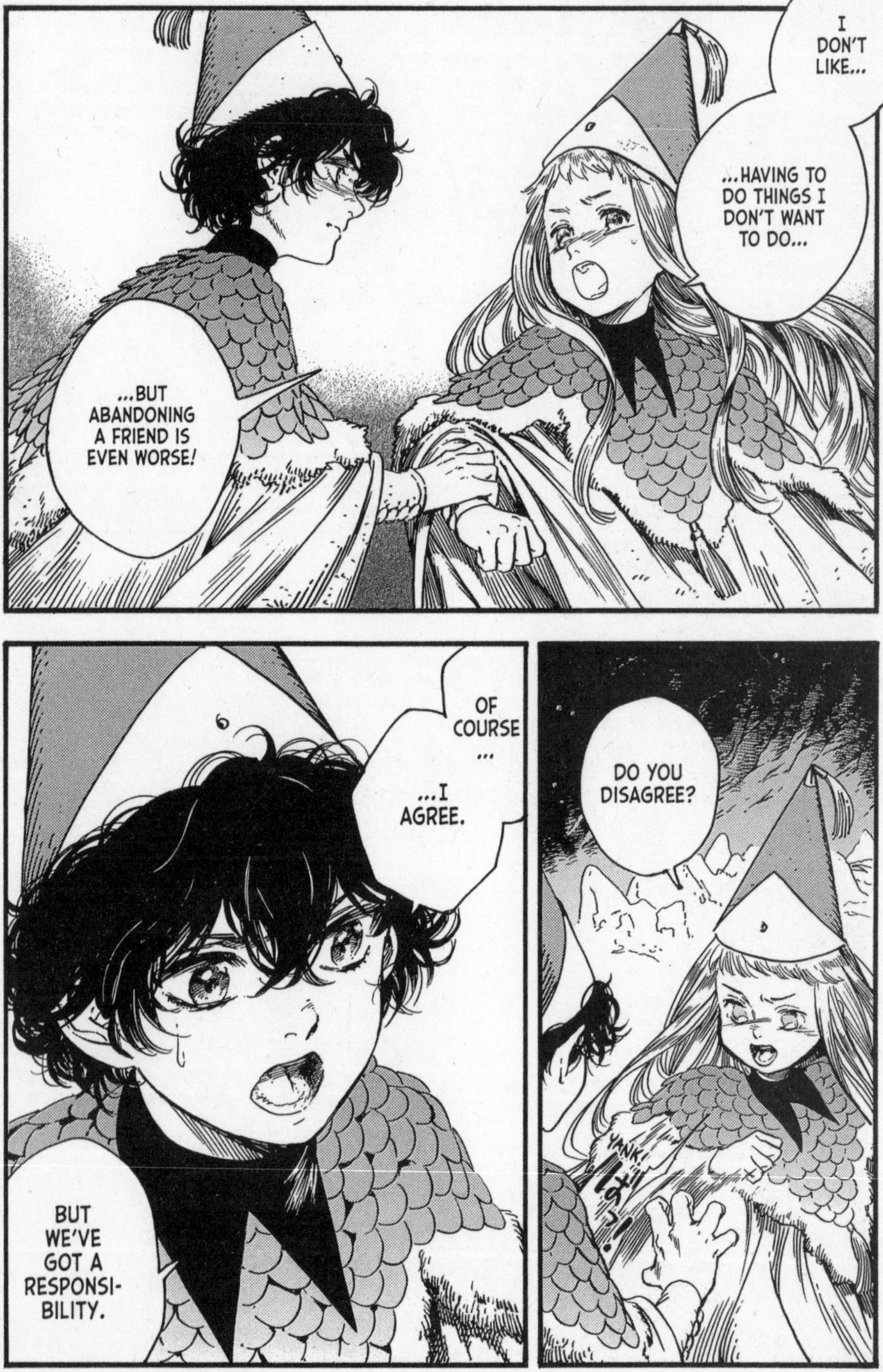
I DON'T LIKE...
...HAVING TO DO THINGS I DON'T WANT TO DO...
...BUT ABANDONING A FRIEND IS EVEN WORSE!
DO YOU DISAGREE?
YANK!
OF COURSE ...
...I AGREE.
BUT WE'VE GOT A RESPONSI-BILITY.

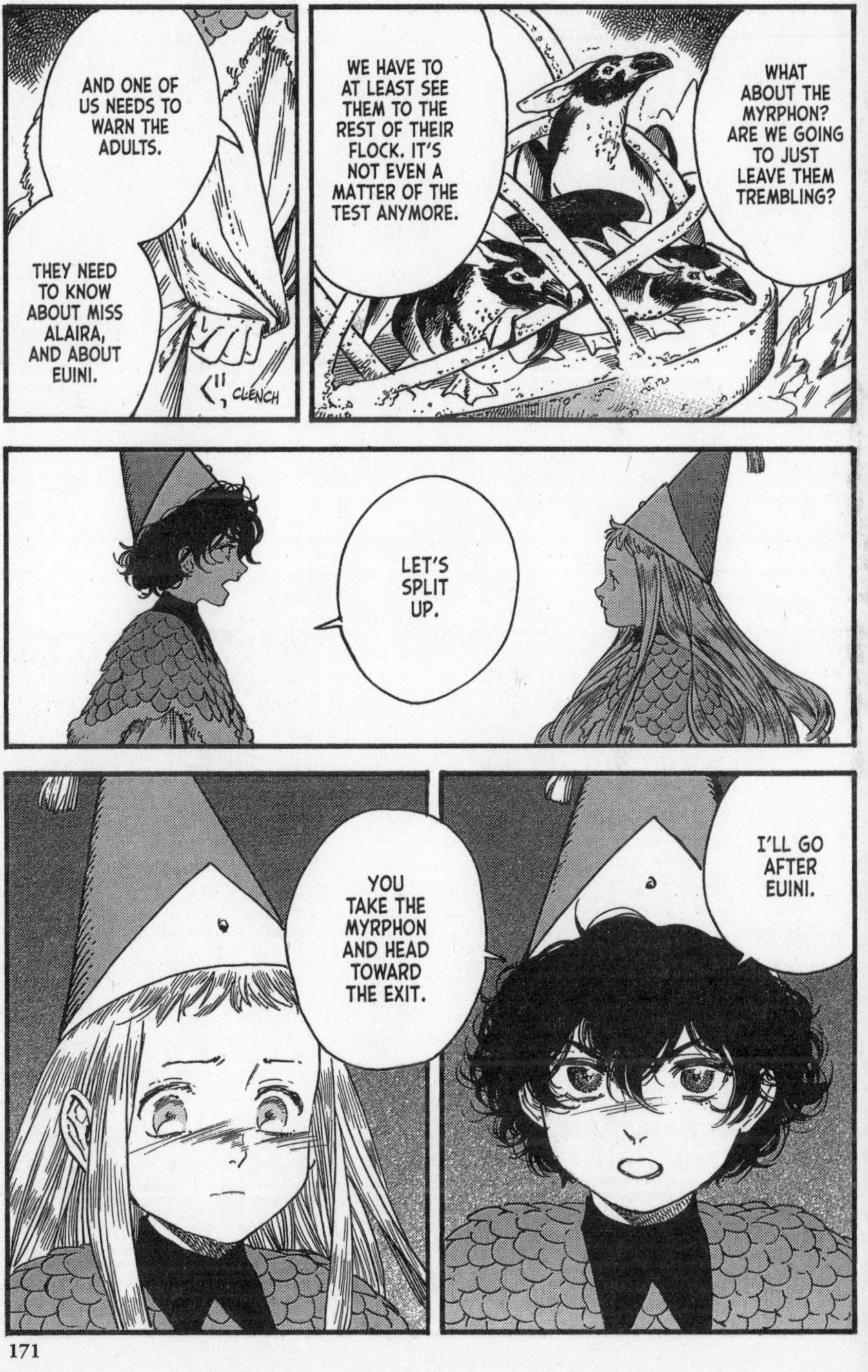
WHAT ABOUT THE MYRPHON? ARE WE GOING TO JUST LEAVE THEM TREMBLING?
WE HAVE TO AT LEAST SEE THEM TO THE REST OF THEIR FLOCK. IT'S NOT EVEN A MATTER OF THE TEST ANYMORE.
AND ONE OF US NEEDS TO WARN THE ADULTS.
THEY NEED TO KNOW ABOUT MISS ALAIRA, AND ABOUT EUINI.
CLENCH
LET'S SPLIT UP.
I'LL GO AFTER EUINI.
YOU TAKE THE MYRPHON AND HEAD TOWARD THE EXIT.

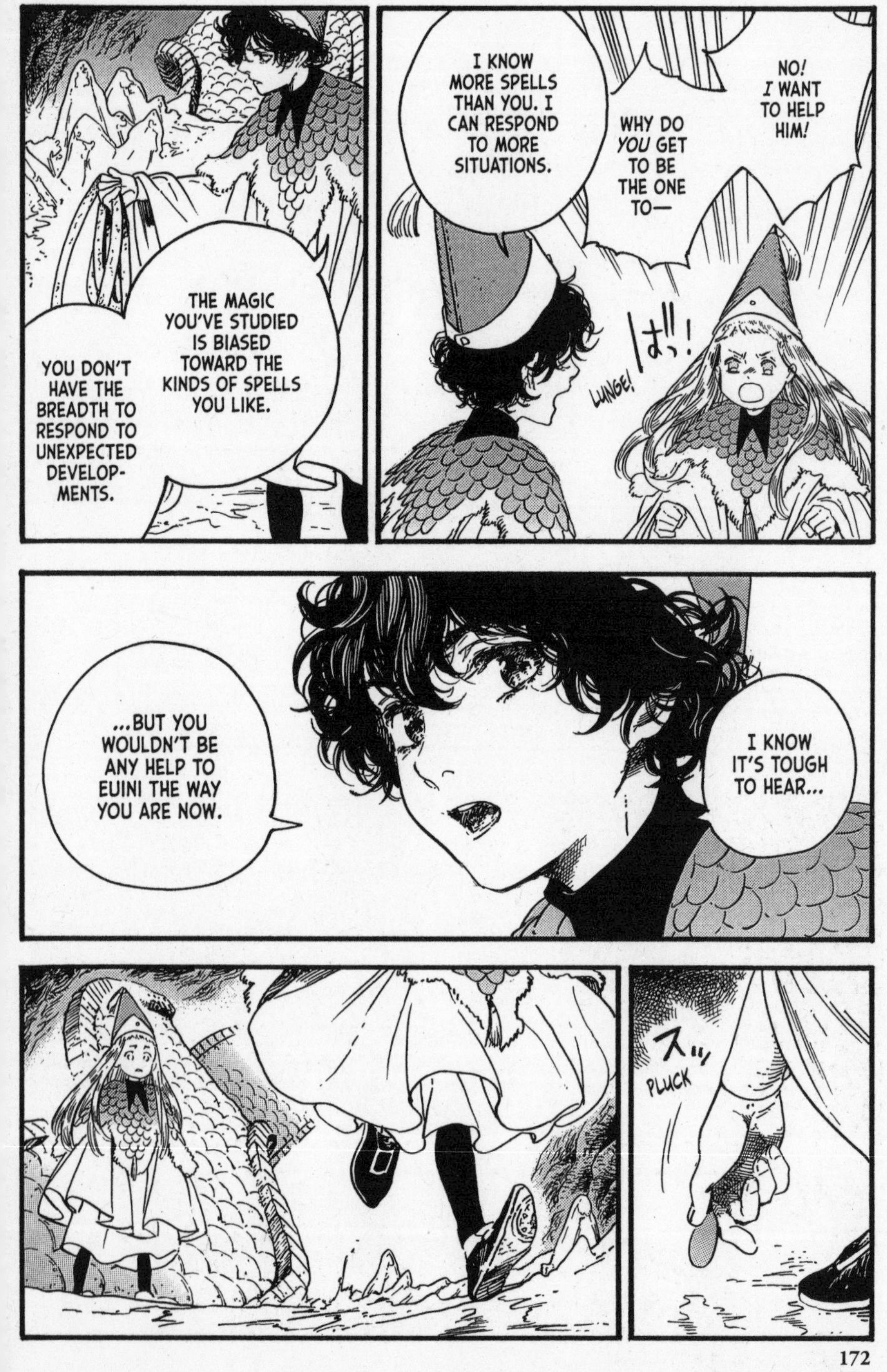
NO! I WANT TO HELP HIM!
WHY DO YOU GET TO BE THE ONE TO—
I KNOW MORE SPELLS THAN YOU. I CAN RESPOND TO MORE SITUATIONS.
ばっ!
LUNGE!
THE MAGIC YOU'VE STUDIED IS BIASED TOWARD THE KINDS OF SPELLS YOU LIKE.
YOU DON'T HAVE THE BREADTH TO RESPOND TO UNEXPECTED DEVELOPMENTS.
I KNOW IT'S TOUGH TO HEAR...
...BUT YOU WOULDN'T BE ANY HELP TO EUINI THE WAY YOU ARE NOW.
スッ
PLUCK

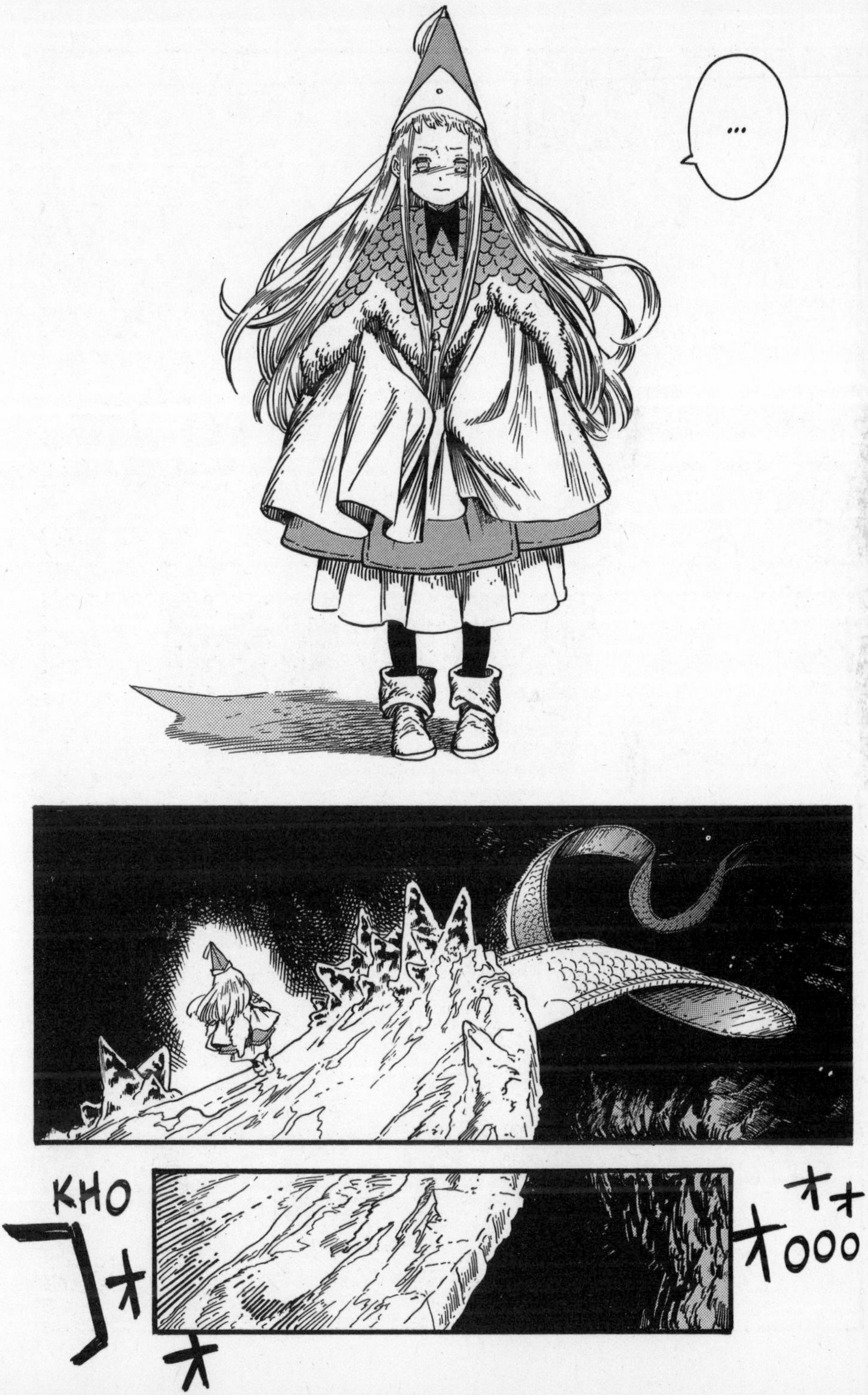
...
KHO
OOO

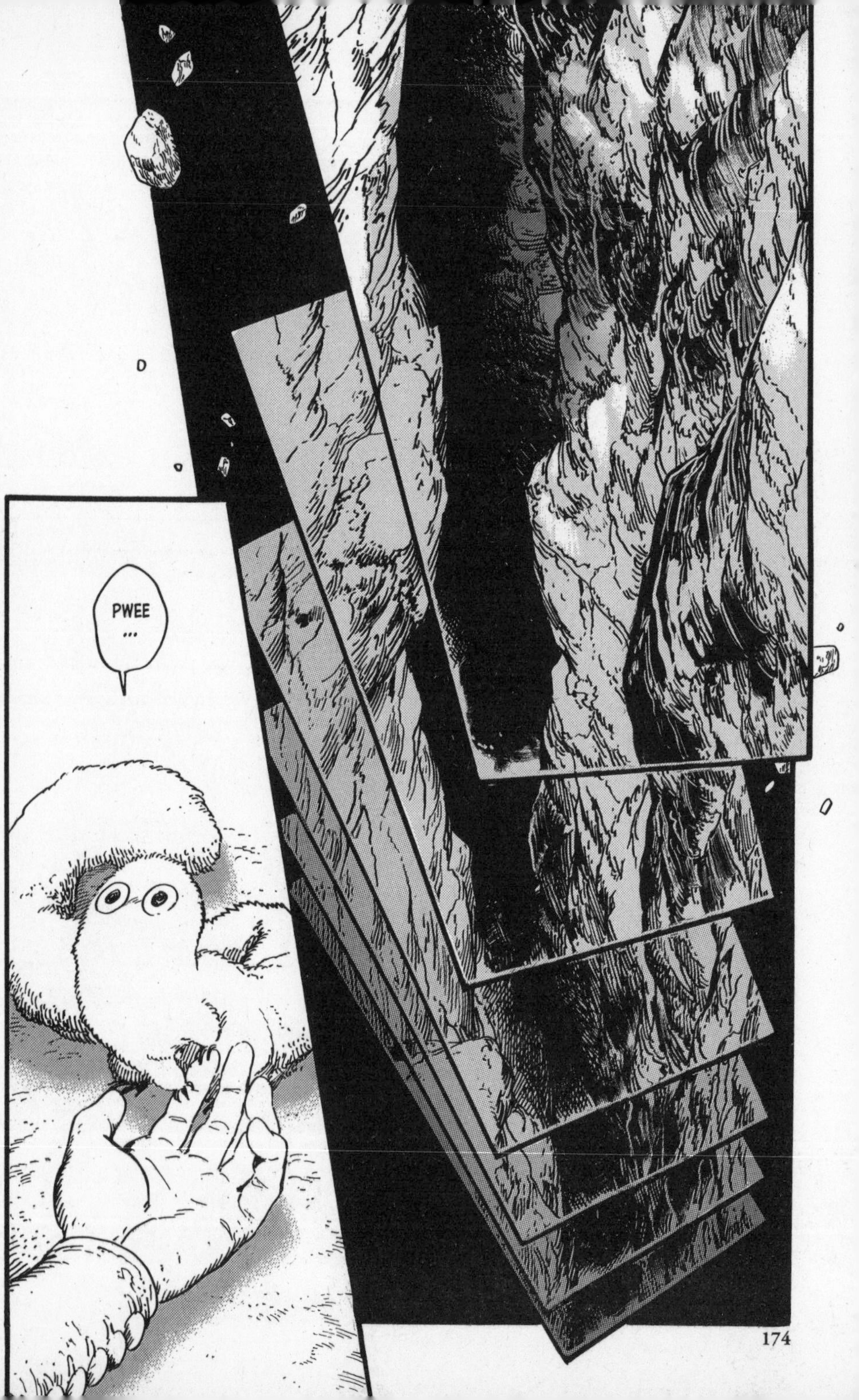
PWEE
...

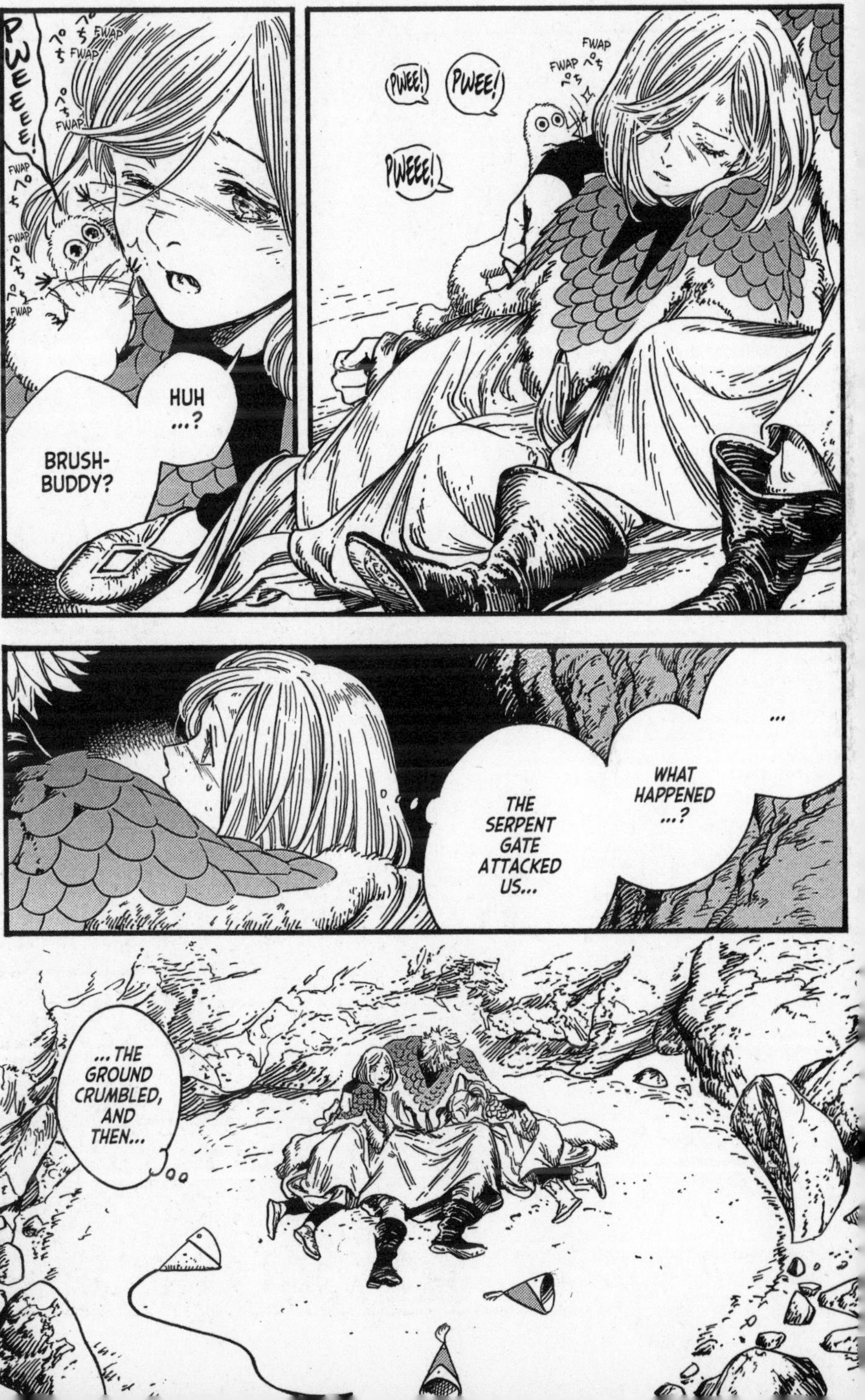
FWAP ぺち
FWAP ぺち
PWEE!
PWEE!
PWEEE!
PWEEEEE!
ぺち FWAP
ぺち FWAP
ぺち FWAP
FWAP ぺち
FWAP ぺち
ぺち FWAP
HUH ...?
BRUSH-BUDDY?
...
WHAT HAPPENED ...?
THE SERPENT GATE ATTACKED US...
...THE GROUND CRUMBLED, AND THEN...

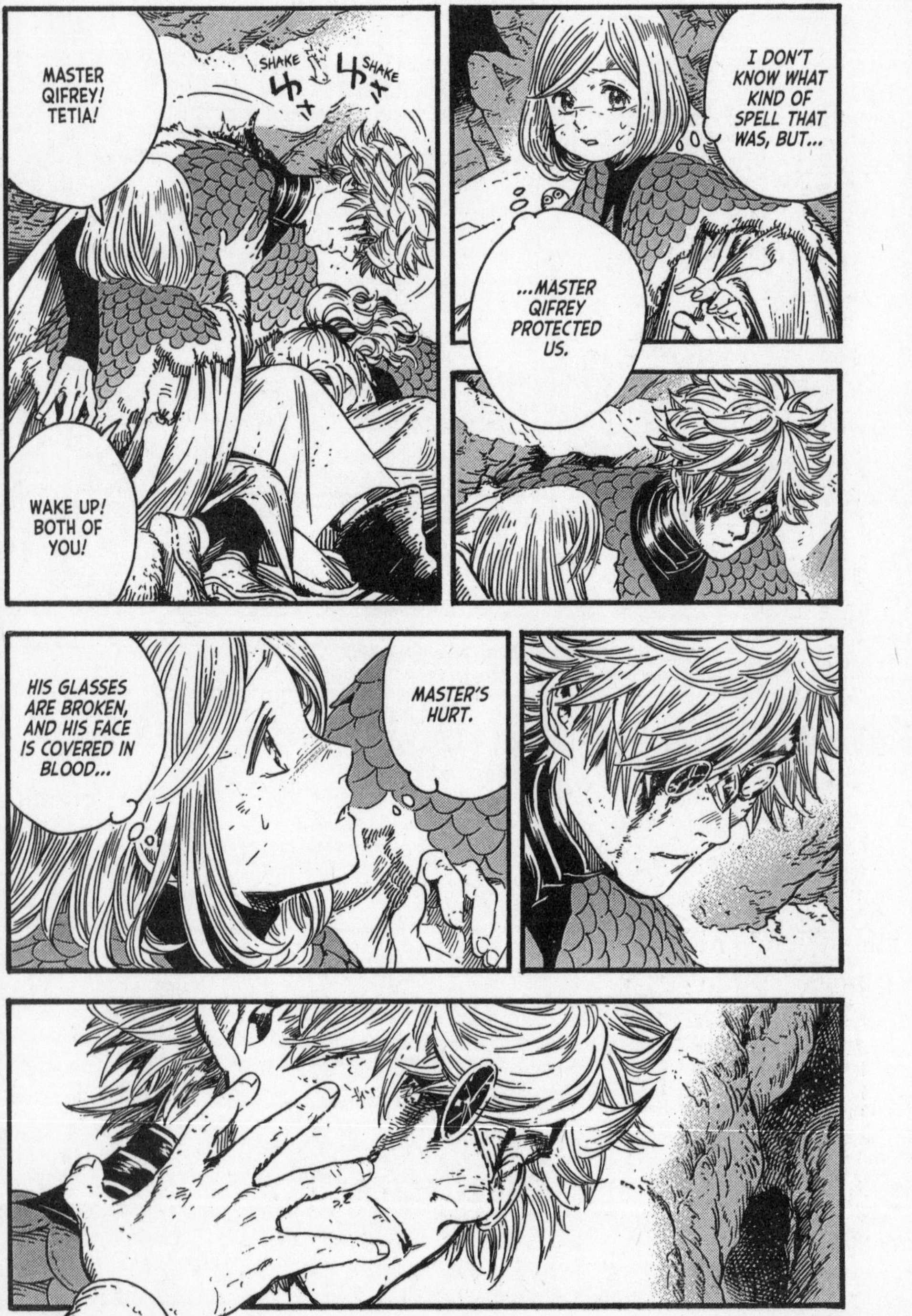
I DON'T KNOW WHAT KIND OF SPELL THAT WAS, BUT...
...MASTER QIFREY PROTECTED US.
MASTER QIFREY! TETIA!
SHAKE ゆさ
SHAKE ゆさ
WAKE UP! BOTH OF YOU!
MASTER'S HURT.
HIS GLASSES ARE BROKEN, AND HIS FACE IS COVERED IN BLOOD...

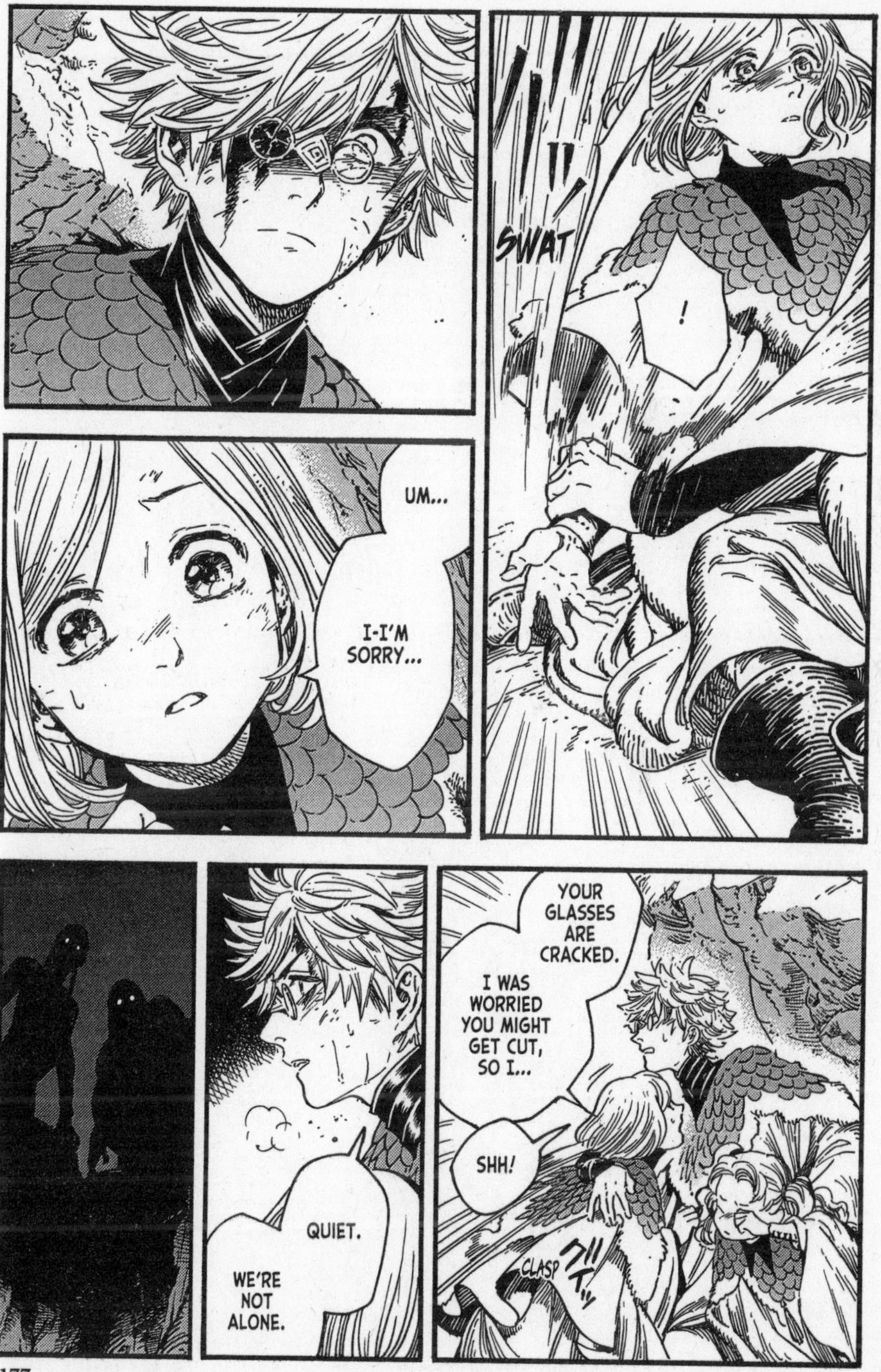
SWAT
!
UM...
I-I'M SORRY...
YOUR GLASSES ARE CRACKED.
I WAS WORRIED YOU MIGHT GET CUT, SO I...
SHH!
CLASP
QUIET.
WE'RE NOT ALONE.

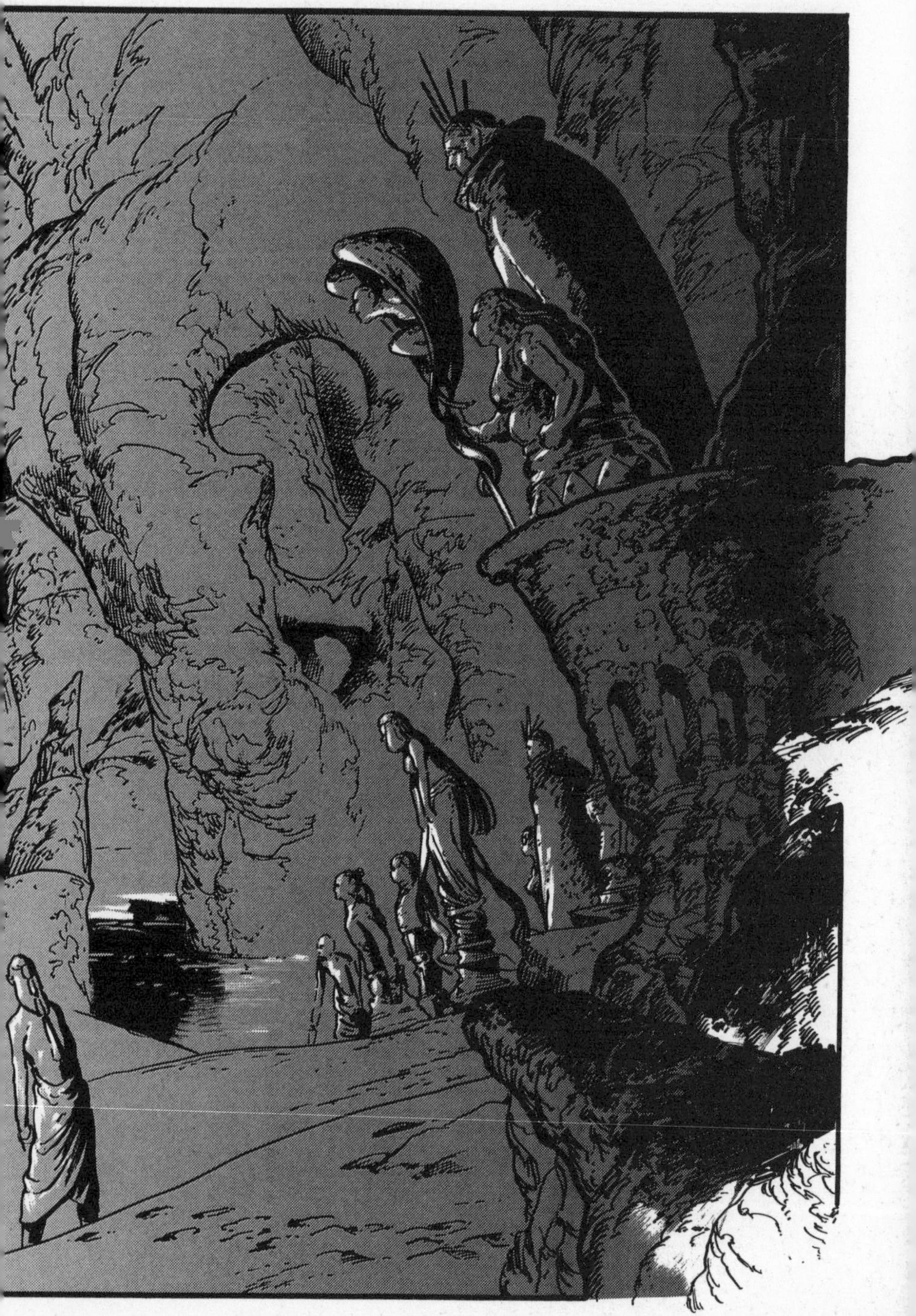

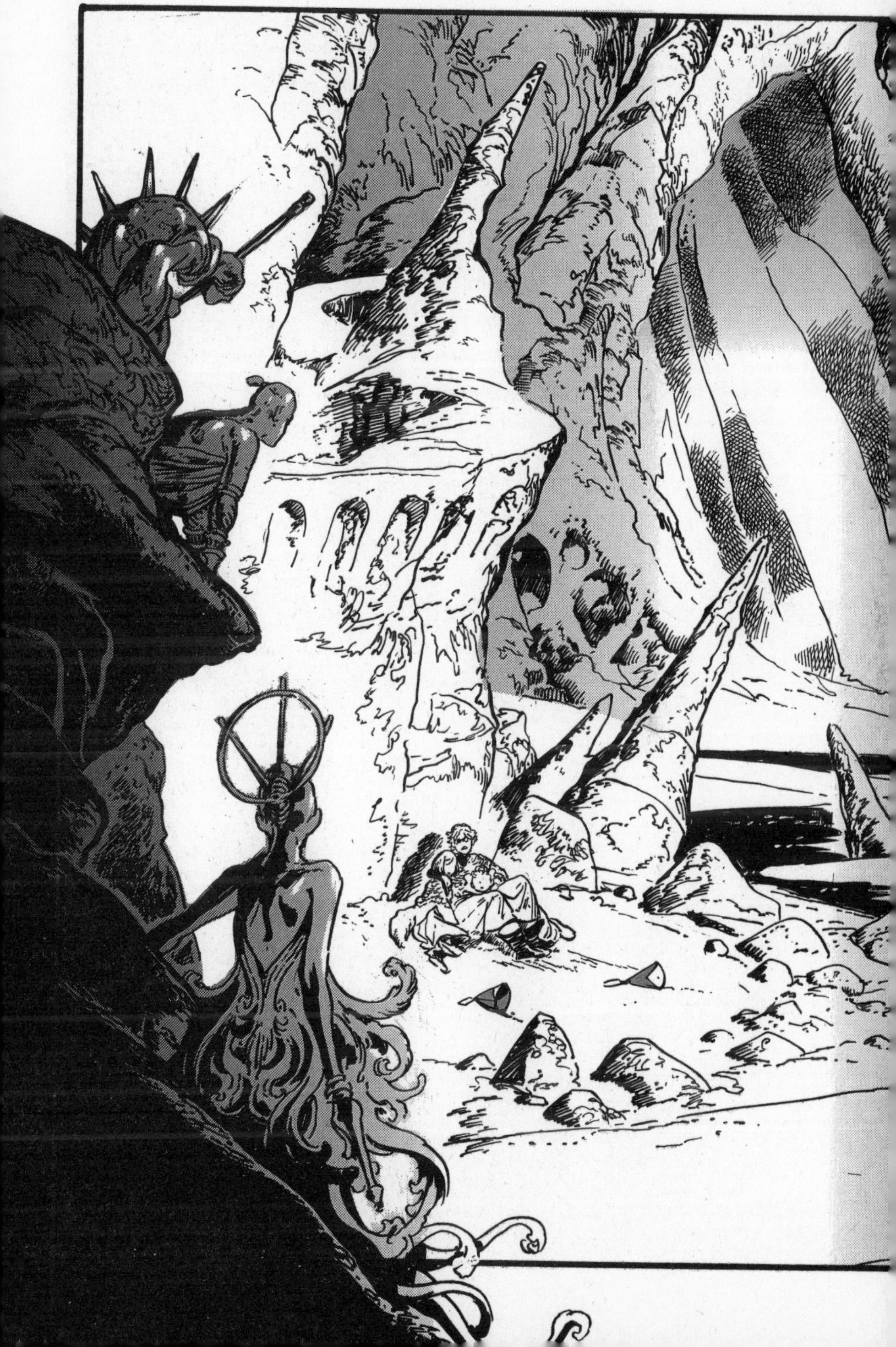

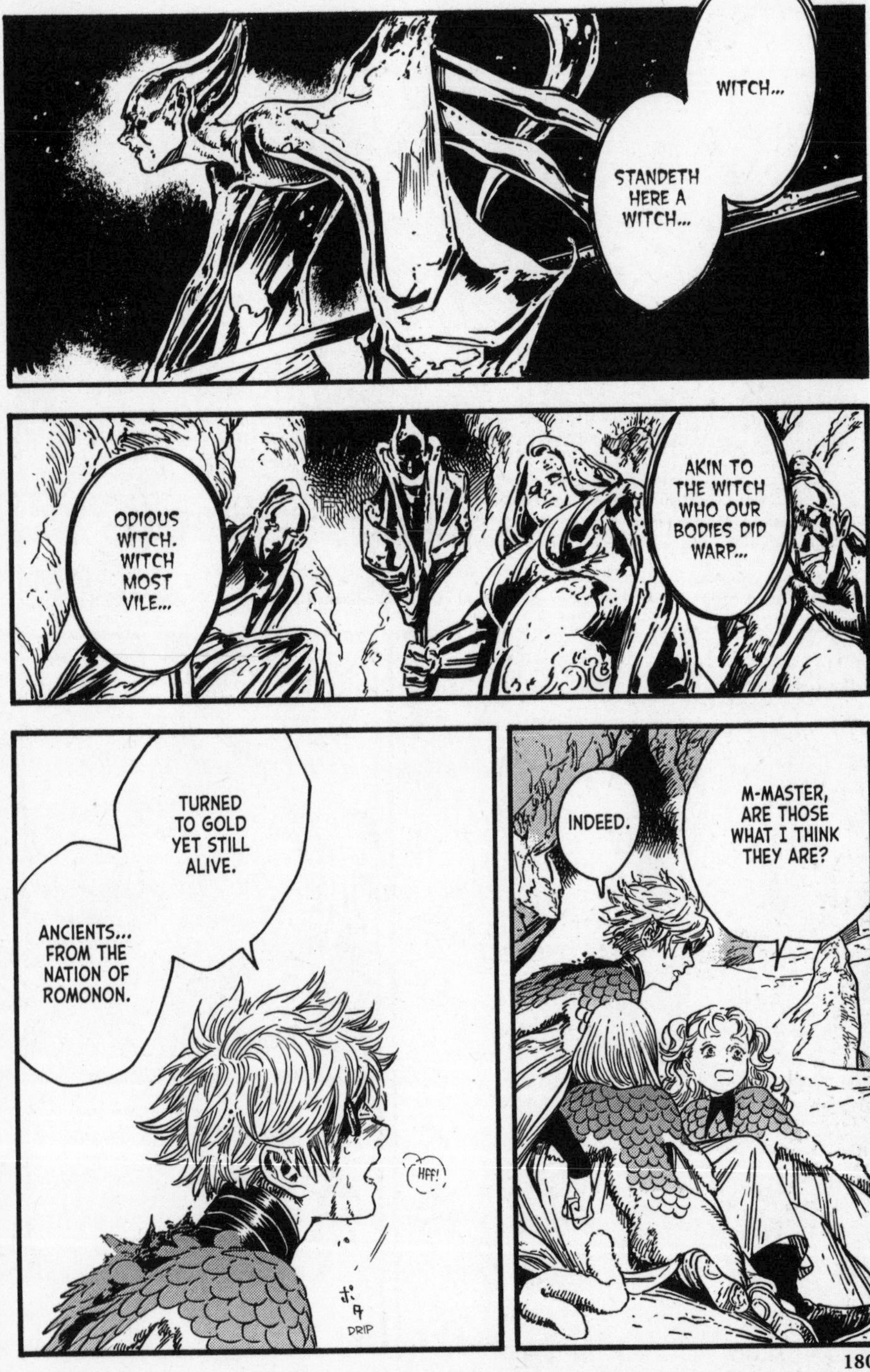

WITCH...
STANDETH HERE A WITCH...
AKIN TO THE WITCH WHO OUR BODIES DID WARP...
ODIOUS WITCH. WITCH MOST VILE...
M-MASTER, ARE THOSE WHAT I THINK THEY ARE?
INDEED.
TURNED TO GOLD YET STILL ALIVE.
ANCIENTS... FROM THE NATION OF ROMONON.
HFF!
DRIP

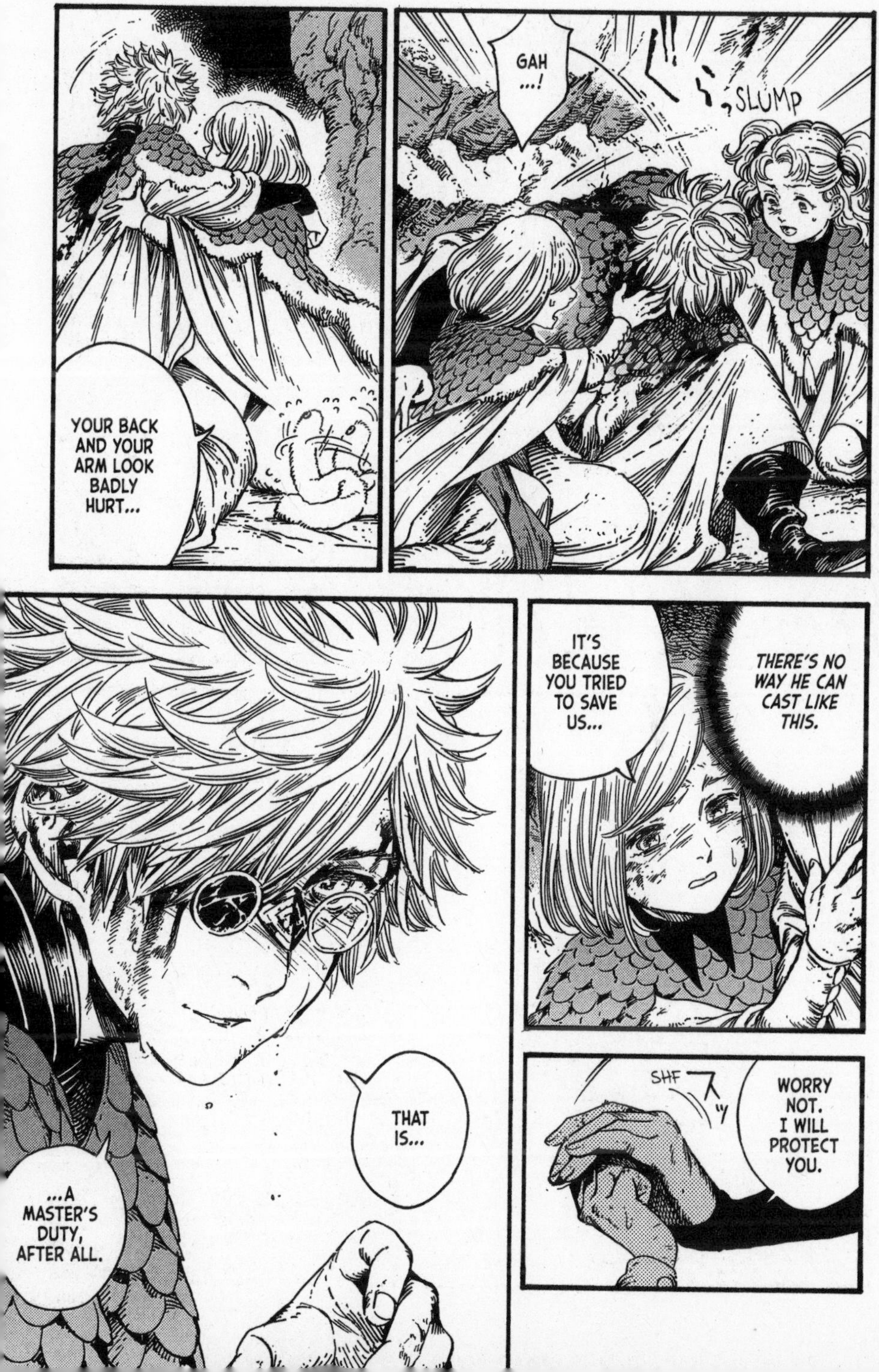

GAH ...!
SLUMP
YOUR BACK AND YOUR ARM LOOK BADLY HURT...
THERE'S NO WAY HE CAN CAST LIKE THIS.
IT'S BECAUSE YOU TRIED TO SAVE US...
WORRY NOT. I WILL PROTECT YOU.
SHF
THAT IS...
...A MASTER'S DUTY, AFTER ALL.

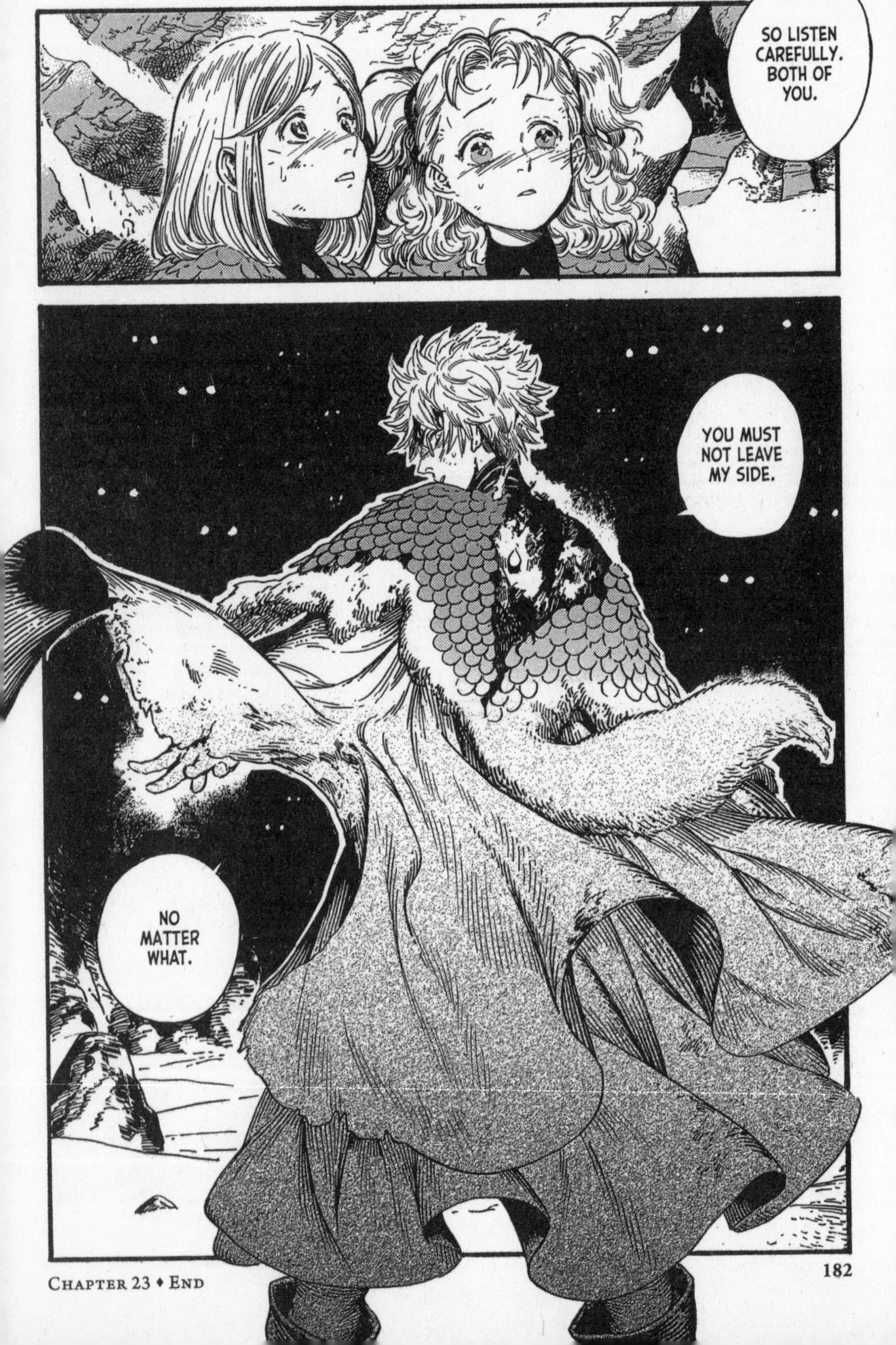
SO LISTEN CAREFULLY. BOTH OF YOU.
YOU MUST NOT LEAVE MY SIDE.
NO MATTER WHAT.

Witch Hat Atelier

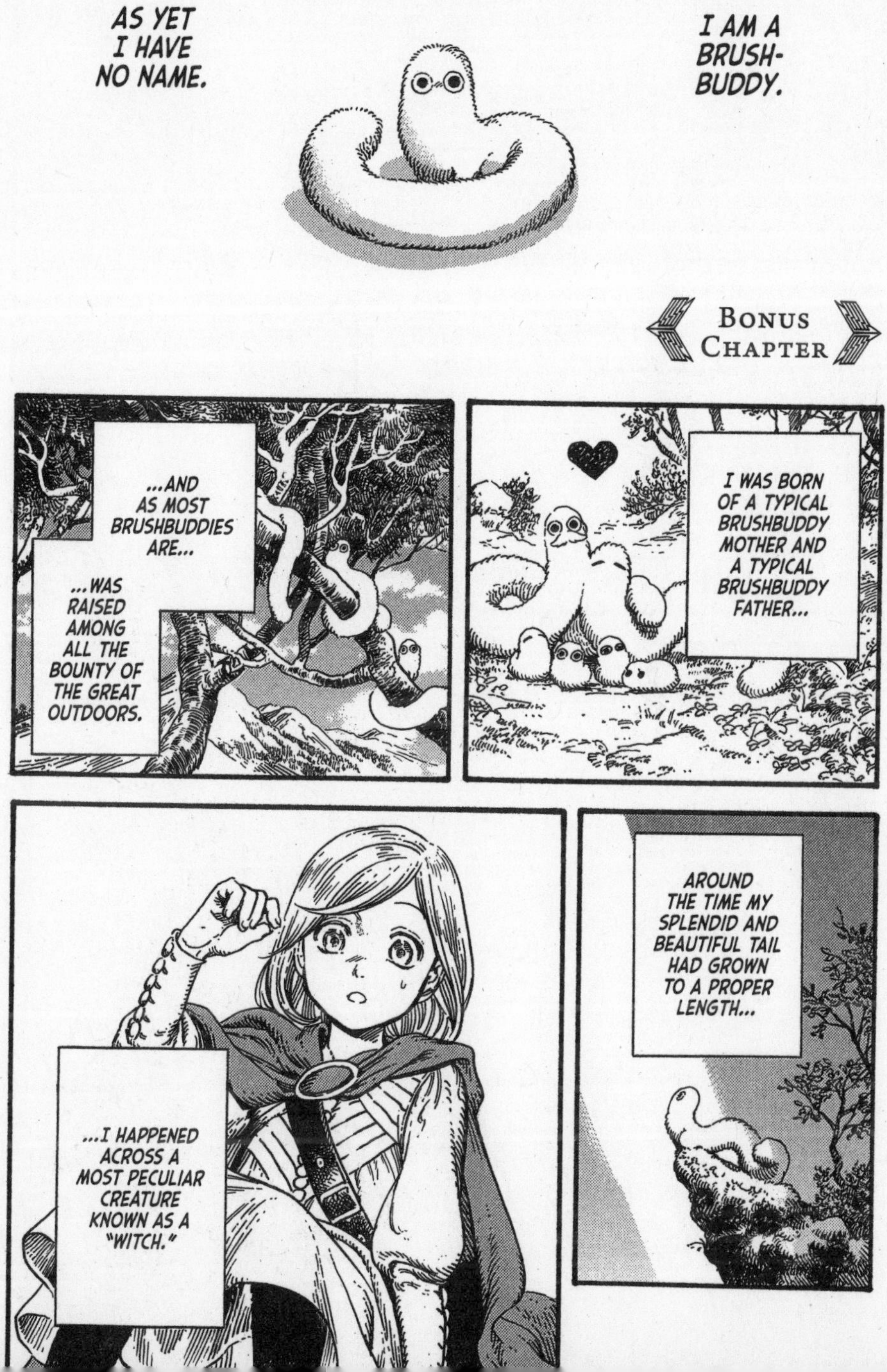
I AM A BRUSH-BUDDY.
AS YET I HAVE NO NAME.
BONUS CHAPTER
I WAS BORN OF A TYPICAL BRUSHBUDDY MOTHER AND A TYPICAL BRUSHBUDDY FATHER...
...AND AS MOST BRUSHBUDDIES ARE...
...WAS RAISED AMONG ALL THE BOUNTY OF THE GREAT OUTDOORS.
AROUND THE TIME MY SPLENDID AND BEAUTIFUL TAIL HAD GROWN TO A PROPER LENGTH...
...I HAPPENED ACROSS A MOST PECULIAR CREATURE KNOWN AS A "WITCH."

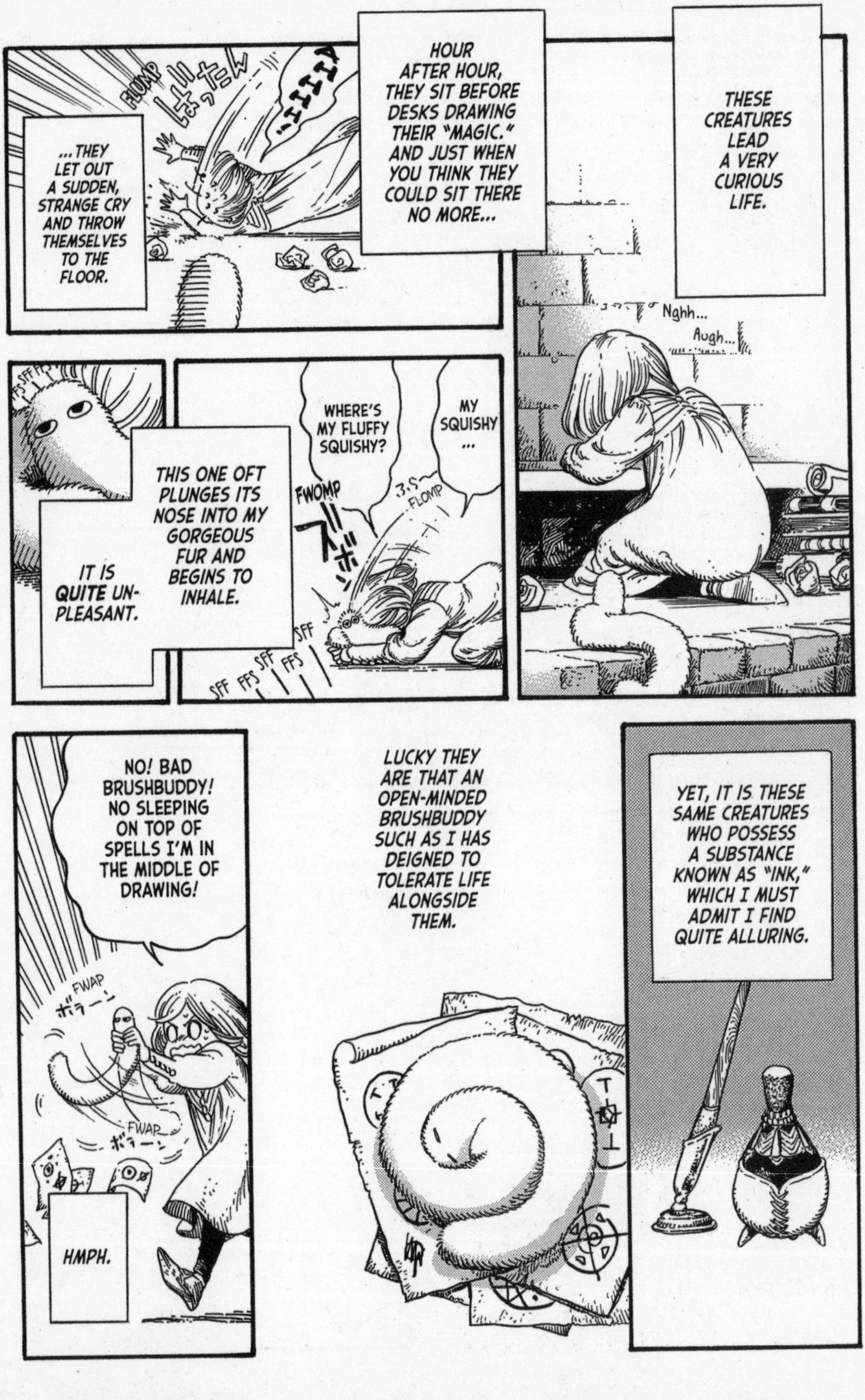
THESE CREATURES LEAD A VERY CURIOUS LIFE.
Nghh...
Augh...
HOUR AFTER HOUR, THEY SIT BEFORE DESKS DRAWING THEIR "MAGIC." AND JUST WHEN YOU THINK THEY COULD SIT THERE NO MORE...
AIIIII!
FLUMP
ばったん
...THEY LET OUT A SUDDEN, STRANGE CRY AND THROW THEMSELVES TO THE FLOOR.
MY SQUISHY ...
WHERE'S MY FLUFFY SQUISHY?
FLOMP
FWOMP
ズボッ
SFF FFS SFF FFS SFF
THIS ONE OFT PLUNGES ITS NOSE INTO MY GORGEOUS FUR AND BEGINS TO INHALE.
IT IS QUITE UN-PLEASANT.
YET, IT IS THESE SAME CREATURES WHO POSSESS A SUBSTANCE KNOWN AS "INK," WHICH I MUST ADMIT I FIND QUITE ALLURING.
LUCKY THEY ARE THAT AN OPEN-MINDED BRUSHBUDDY SUCH AS I HAS DEIGNED TO TOLERATE LIFE ALONGSIDE THEM.
NO! BAD BRUSHBUDDY! NO SLEEPING ON TOP OF SPELLS I'M IN THE MIDDLE OF DRAWING!
FWAP
FWAP
HMPH.

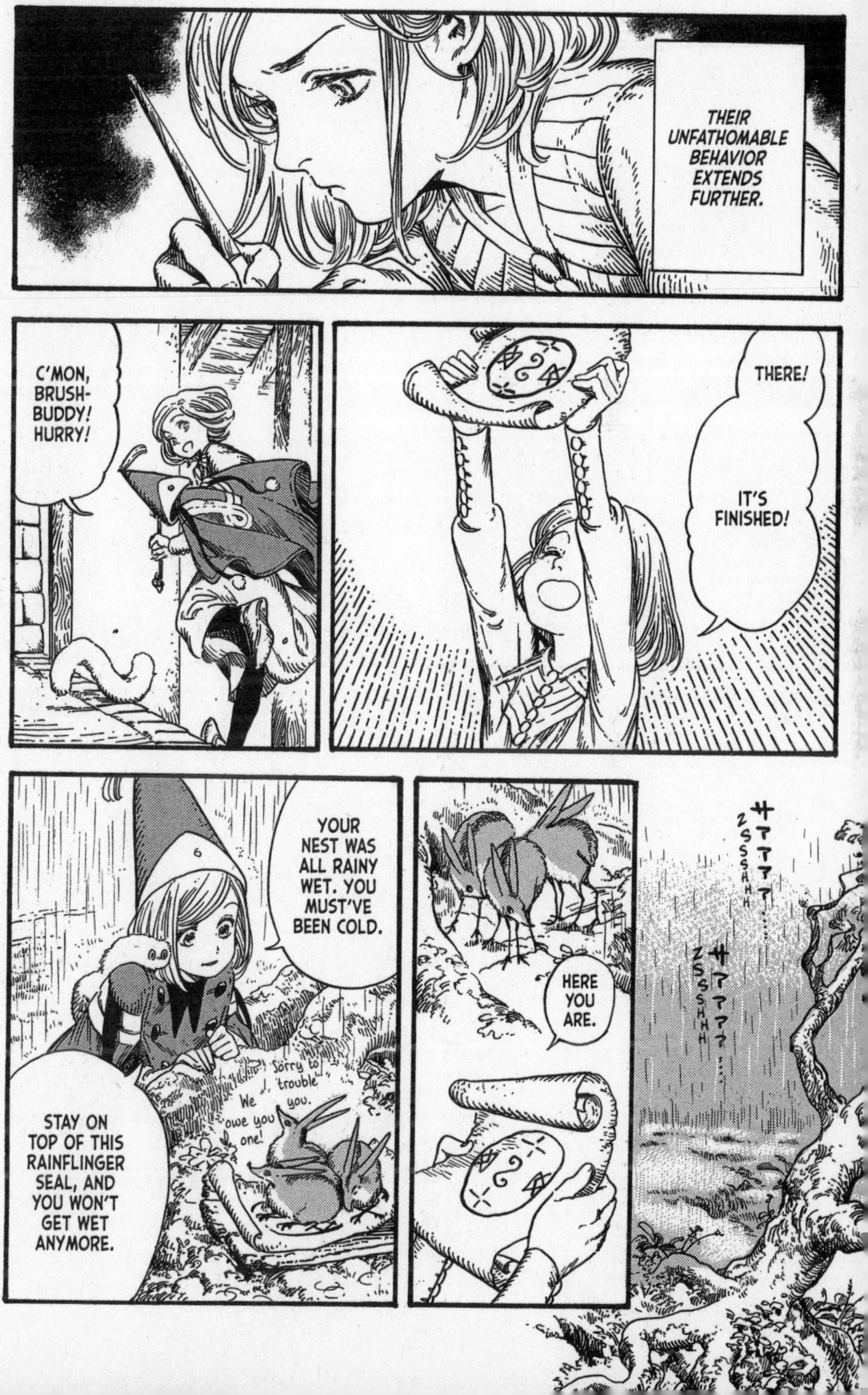
THEIR UNFATHOMABLE BEHAVIOR EXTENDS FURTHER.
THERE!
IT'S FINISHED!
C'MON, BRUSH-BUDDY! HURRY!
ZSSSHH...
ZSSSHH...
HERE YOU ARE.
YOUR NEST WAS ALL RAINY WET. YOU MUST'VE BEEN COLD.
Sorry to trouble you.
We owe you one!
STAY ON TOP OF THIS RAINFLINGER SEAL, AND YOU WON'T GET WET ANYMORE.

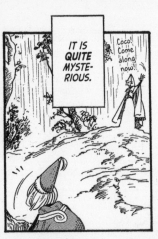

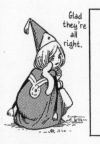

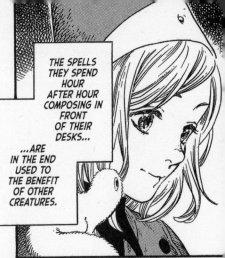

THE SPELLS THEY SPEND HOUR AFTER HOUR COMPOSING IN FRONT OF THEIR DESKS...
...ARE IN THE END USED TO THE BENEFIT OF OTHER CREATURES.
Glad they're all right.
IT IS **QUITE** MYSTERIOUS.
Coco! Come along now!!
YET, IT IS THE MYSTERIES OF LIFE THAT BRING THE GREATEST FASCINATION.
PERHAPS IT WOULD BE PRUDENT TO COMPOSE A DETAILED RECORD...
...FOR FUTURE GENERATIONS OF THESE PECULIAR CREATURES KNOWN AS "WITCHES."
AS FOR THE TITLE, I THINK I SHALL CALL IT...
ACK! MY HAT! MY WITCH HAT!
SMEEEAR
Brush-buddy!!

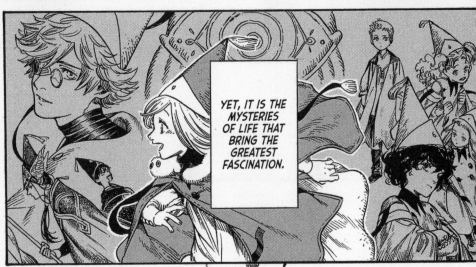

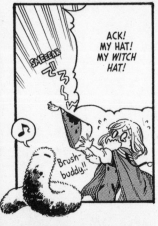

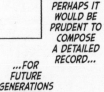

Witch Hat Atelier,

Witch Hat Atelier

THE PLANTS OF WITCH HAT

DIADEM HERB
FIRST APPEARS IN CHAPTER 3

FOUND ONLY ON THE DADAH RANGE, A GROUP OF MOUNTAINS THAT NOW FLOAT IN THE SKY DUE TO AN ANCIENT, FORBIDDEN SPELL. THE PLANT'S NAME COMES FROM ITS CROWN-LIKE APPEARANCE. THOSE WHO WISH TO BECOME APPRENTICES ARE REQUIRED TO HARVEST THIS HERB, AN ACT SYMBOLIC OF THE PUNISHMENT METED OUT TO THE KING OF DADAH, WHO RAISED THE MOUNTAINS INTO THE SKY MERELY TO SEE HIS CROWN STAND ABOVE ALL OTHERS.

SILVERWOOD TREE
FIRST APPEARS IN CHAPTER 5

NECESSARY IN THE PRODUCTION OF CONJURING INK, THE SUBSTANCE USED TO DRAW CASTING SEALS. ITS BRANCHES POSSESS A SILVER SHEEN WHILE ALIVE, BUT UPON WITHERING, THEY TURN PITCH BLACK. FROM THESE DEAD BRANCHES, A SOLUTION KNOWN AS WOODCRUOR IS EXTRACTED, WHICH IS IN TURN REFINED INTO INK. ACCORDING TO LEGEND, A SILVERWOOD ONCE FELL IN LOVE WITH A WITCH AND OFFERED UP ITS BLOOD AS INK AND BRANCHES AS WANDS.

CARAPACE YAM
FIRST APPEARS IN CHAPTER 8

A TYPE OF TUBER COVERED BY AN UNUSUALLY TOUGH OUTER LAYER. COOKED SLOWLY OVER AN APPROPRIATELY-SIZED FLAME, IT YIELDS A DELICIOUS, PIPING-HOT TREAT.

HONEYTREE
APPEARS IN THE *MORNING TWO* 10TH ANNIVERSARY ANTHOLOGY, "EATING"

SNAPPING OPEN THE SWELLING BULGES OF THIS TREE'S BRANCHES WILL REVEAL LARGE QUANTITIES OF A SWEET, HONEY-LIKE SUBSTANCE PACKED INSIDE. USED AS AN INGREDIENT IN SWEETS AND LIQUEURS.

MOUNTAIN APPLE
FIRST APPEARS IN CHAPTER 14

A LOW, SHRUB-LIKE TREE ABLE TO TAKE ROOT IN THE SMALL GAPS OF EVEN THE ROCKIEST AND MOST RUGGED TERRAIN. THE FRUIT IT BEARS IS TART LIKE AN APPLE YET SOFT LIKE A PEAR. AS IT RIPENS, ITS COLOR TYPICALLY TURNS FROM GREEN TO YELLOW. RED FRUIT MAY BE ENCOUNTERED ON OCCASION, BUT SHOULD BE AVOIDED, AS IT IS POISONOUS.

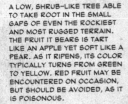

TRANQUILEAF
FIRST APPEARS IN CHAPTER 16

THIS HERB'S LEAVES FUNCTION AS A DISINFECTANT WHEN DIRECTLY APPLIED TO WOUNDS, AND WHEN DRIED AND GROUND TO POWDER, THEY ALSO SERVE AS MEDICATION TO REDUCE FEVER AND SUPPRESS COUGHING. THIS WAS THE SAME HERB CHEWED BY QIFREY IN CHAPTER 15 WHEN ASCERTAINING THAT THE NUMBNESS IN HIS LIMB HAD SUBSIDED. BASED ON HIS EXPRESSION IN THAT SCENE, IT MAY BE SURMISED THAT TRANQUILEAF HAS A PARTICULARLY BITTER TASTE.

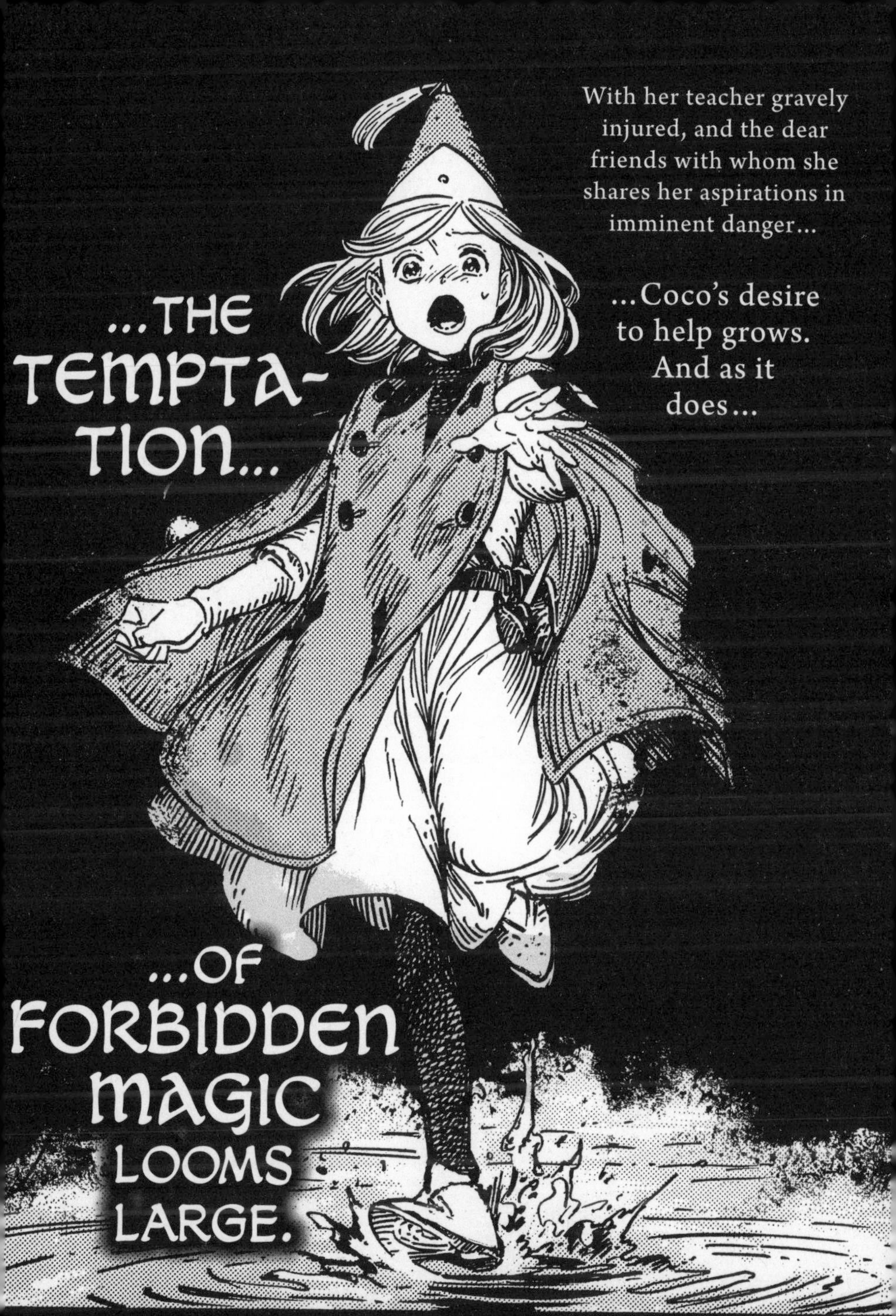
With her teacher gravely injured, and the dear friends with whom she shares her aspirations in imminent danger...
...Coco's desire to help grows. And as it does...
...THE TEMPTA-TION...
...OF FORBIDDEN MAGIC LOOMS LARGE.

VOLUME 5: SCHEDULED FOR SALE IN SPRING 2020!

1/20

Witch Hat Atelier volume 4 is a work of fiction. Names, characters, places, and incidents are the products of the author's imagination or are used fictitiously. Any resemblance to actual events, locales, or persons, living or dead, is entirely coincidental.

A Kodansha Comics Trade Paperback Original.

Witch Hat Atelier volume 4 copyright © 2018 Kamome Shirahama
English translation copyright © 2019 Kamome Shirahama

All rights reserved.

Published in the United States by Kodansha Comics,
an imprint of Kodansha USA Publishing, LLC, New York.

Publication rights for this English edition arranged through Kodansha Ltd.,
Tokyo.

First published in Japan in 2018 by Kodansha Ltd., Tokyo, as *Tongari Bōshi no Atorie* volume 4.

ISBN 978-1-63236-860-7

Printed in the United States of America.

www.kodanshacomics.com

9 8 7 6 5 4 3 2 1

Translation: Stephen Kohler
Lettering: Lys Blakeslee
Editing: Ajani Oloye
Kodansha Comics edition cover design: Phil Balsman